SO-ADK-839

PAKISTAN

ISOBEL SHAW

Saeed Book Bank
Importers & Distributors, Booksellers & Publishers
F-7, Jinnah Super Market, Islamabad-Pakistan.
Tel : 92-51-2651656-9, Fax : 92-51-2651660
E-mail : sales@saeedbookbank.com
Arbab Road, Peshawar Cantt. Pakistan.
Tel : 92-91-273761, 285724
Fax : 92-91-275801, 274081
E-mail : sbb@pes.comsats.net.pk.
Web : www.saeedbookbank.com

Colour

06.100.00.0491
9 789628 711062
12.95 UK.P

Dedicated to my husband Robert

Revised edition 1999

Copyright © Local Colour Limited, 1999, 1996,1991, 1989, 1988
e-mail: ppro@netivator.com

The moral right of the author has been asserted

All rights reserved. No part of this publication may be translated, reproduced, or transmitted in any form or by any means, including photocopying, or by any information storage and retrieval system, without the written permission of the publisher, except brief extracts by a reviewer for inclusion in critical articles or reviews.

Although the Publisher and the Author of this book have made every effort to ensure the information was correct at the time of going to press, the Publisher and the Author do not assume and hereby disclaim any liability to any party for any loss or damage caused by errors, omissions, misleading information, or any potential travel disruption due to labour or financial difficulty, whether such errors or omissions result from negligence, accident, or any other cause.

Every effort is being made to contact the copyright-holders of excerpted material.

Distributed in the United Kingdom, Ireland, and Europe by Hi Marketing Ltd,
38 Carver Road, London SE24 9LT, UK
Fax: (0171) 274-9160

Distribution in the United States by Seven Hills Book Dirstributors
1531 Tremont Street, Cincinnati, OH 45214
Fax: (513) 471-4311

Editor :Aruna Ghose, Geoff Cloke
Maps : Tom Le Bas, Philip Choi
Design : Geoff Cloke, Philip Choi

British Library Cataloguing in Publication Data has been applied for.

Front and back cover photographs: Photobank
Photography: Alain Evrard 22, Fredrik Arvidsson 4, 5, 27, 30 (both), 45, 48, 54-55, 68-69, 72, 76, 101, 104, 137, 141, 144, 164, 165, 197, 201, Isobel Shaw 65. 91 (all except top right), James Montgomery 91 (top right), Kaiser Khan 49, 186, 190, Peter Fredenburg 9, 178-179 (all) 182, 191, 240, 248-249 (both) 257, Photobank 8, 18-19, 50-51, 63, 86-87, 114-115, 123, 187, 196, 204, 219, .222-223, 228-229, 264-265.

Printed in China

Contents

Literary Excerpts

Special Topics

Maps

LIST OF ABBREVIATIONS AND NAMES

GTS	—	*Government Transport Services*
KKH	—	*The Karakoram Highway*
NATCO	—	*Northern Areas Transport Company*
NWFP	—	*North-West Frontier Province*
PCO	—	*Public Call Office*
PIA	—	*Pakistan International Airlines*
PPP	—	*Pakistan People's Party*
PTDC	—	*Pakistan Tourism Development Corporation*
PYHA	—	*Pakistan Youth Hostel Association*
STDC	—	*Sindh Tourism Development Corporation*
TDCP	—	*Tourism Development Corporation of Punjab*
TIC	—	*Tourist Information Centre*
Charpoy	—	*Local rope bed*
Chowkidar	—	*Watchman*
Chapatti	—	*Flat bread*
Naan	—	*Flat levened bread*
Suzuki	—	*Small pickup trucks seating 8 to 10 people*
Datsun	—	*Larger pickup trucks seating 12 to 14 people*

MAP LEGEND

■	Hotel		Major road
★	Restaurant		Minor road
田	Hospital		Jeep road
†	Church		Footpath
Ψ	Mosque	▬	Railway / railway station
☐ or ᚋᚋ	Fort	▲	Peak (height in metres)
∴	Ruins	········	Pass
⊔	Shrine	═════	Airport ✈
⚓	Stupa	══	Bazaar ☐
⊓	City gate	━·━·━	National border
⌂	Tomb	━·━·━	Provincial border

(above) Painted truck, Peshawar (opposire) Baltit Fort watches over Hunza, with Ultar Mountain in the background

Introduction

Pakistan is the land of the Indus River, which flows through the country for 2,500 kilometres (1,600 miles) from the Himalayan and Karakoram mountain ranges to the Arabian Sea. It is a land of snow-covered peaks and burning deserts, of fertile mountain. calleys and irrigated plains. Created in 1947 as a homeland for the Muslims of the Indian subcontinent, it is inhabited by some 140 million people (1999) belonging to many ethnic groups speaking over 20 different languages and wearing distinctive costumes, but all united by the Islamic faith.

'The Land of the Pure' (as the Urdu name *Pakistan* translates into English) is strategically placed at the crossroads of Asia, where the road from China to the Mediterranean meets the route from India to Central Asia. For thousands of years, this junction has been a melting pot of diverse cultures, attracting traders and adventurers, pilgrims and holy men.

Cut off by political events and ignored until recently by most tourists, Pakistan is once again on the main trade route and tourist path to China and Central Asia. The old silk routes have reopened. The spectacular Karakoram Highway threads its way through the Himalaya, Karakoram and Pamir mountains, and enters China over the 4,733-metre (15,528-foot) Khunjerab Pass, one of the highest metalled border crossings in the world. Pakistan is also a gateway to the new Central Asian republics of Uzbekistan, Kazakhstan, Kyrgyzstan and Tajikistan.

For any visitor, Pakistan has a wealth of attractions: its 4,000-year history is richly illustrated by archaeological sites and imposing monuments scattered the length and breadth of the country. Brick cities from the Indus Civilisation, which flourished around 2000 BC, stand beside Buddhist ruins contemporaneous with the birth of Christianity. Magnificent Muslim tombs from the

12th century vie with the palaces, mosques and forts of the Mughal emperors of the 16th and 17th centuries.

The country's main cities reflect the many influences, both historical and modern, that have made Pakistan what it is today. Lahore, close to the Indian border, is the cultural centre of the country, with an elegant core of Mughal architecture embellished by the flowery exuberance of the British Raj. Peshawar, on the North-West Frontier with Afghanistan, is a city straight out of the Arabian Nights, with tribesmen in turbans nonchalantly carrying rifles through the colourful bazaars. Islamabad, the federal capital, is a modern garden city planned by Greek architects. Finally, bustling Karachi, with its population of 11 million, is a huge international port, industrial and financial centre.

Best of all are Pakistan's mountains, rivers, deserts and national parks — playgrounds for the adventurous and those interested in the great outdoors. In the north of the country, four great mountain ranges meet, offering some of the most challenging and scenic mountaineering, trekking   and jeep safaris in the world. Five huge rivers flow south to the sea, forming   the flight-paths for migrating birds and providing exciting white-water rafting and boating. The camel, ship of the desert, is the best means of transport for remote safaris and nature watching far from modern civilisation in the ever-changing desert.

What is more, Pakistan is unspoilt. Tourism is in its infancy, yet the four principal cities offer first-class hotels, with simpler but adequate accommodation available elsewhere.

To the spirit hungry for exploration and adventure, Pakistan beckons.

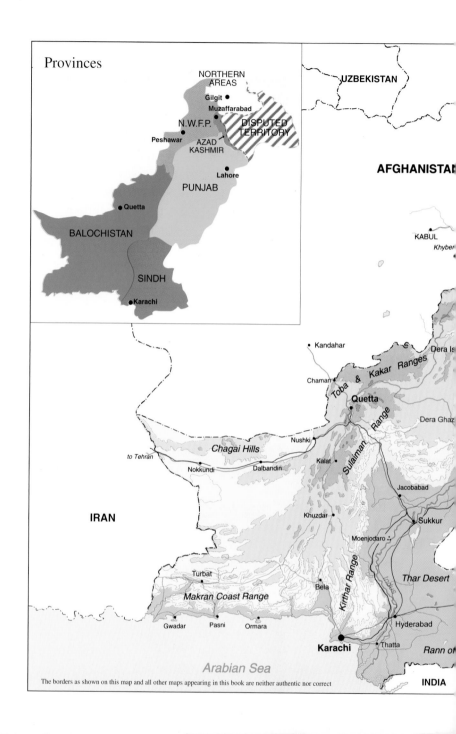

Provinces

NORTHERN AREAS

Gilgit ●

Muzaffarabad ●

N.W.F.P.

DISPUTED TERRITORY

Peshawar ●

AZAD KASHMIR

Lahore ●

PUNJAB

● Quetta

BALOCHISTAN

SINDH

● Karachi

UZBEKISTAN

AFGHANISTAN

KABUL

Khyber

Kandahar ●

Dera Is

Toba & Kakar Ranges

Chaman ●

Quetta

Dera Ghaz

Nushki ●

Sulaiman Range

to Tehrān

Chagai Hills

Kalat ●

Nokkundi ●

Dalbandin ●

Jacobabad ●

Khuzdar ●

Sukkur ●

IRAN

Moenjodaro ⋮

Turbat ●

Kirthar Range

Thar Desert

Bela ●

Makran Coast Range

Gwadar ●   Pasni ●   Ormara ●

Hyderabad ●

Karachi ●

● Thatta

Rann of

Arabian Sea

INDIA

The borders as shown on this map and all other maps appearing in this book are neither authentic nor correct

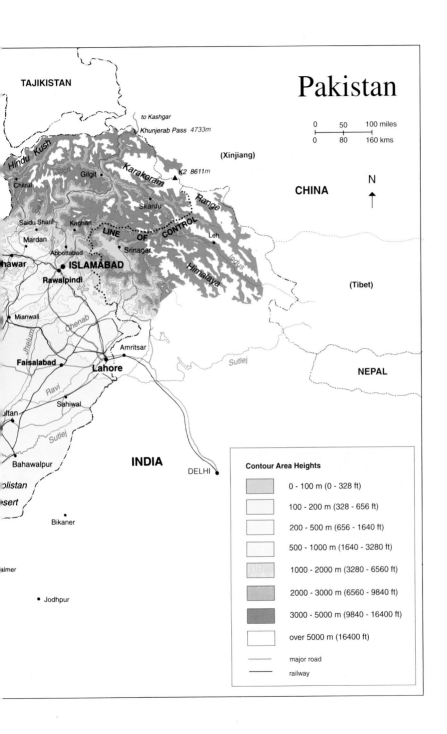

TAJIKISTAN

Pakistan

to Kashgar
Khunjerab Pass 4733m

| 0 | 50 | 100 miles |
| 0 | 80 | 160 kms |

(Xinjiang)

Hindu Kush

Gilgit

Karakoram

K2 8611m

Chitral

Range

CHINA

N

Skardu

Saidu Sharif   Kaghan

LINE   OF   CONTROL

Leh

Mardan

Abbottabad

Srinagar

hawar

ISLAMABAD

Himalaya

Indus

Rawalpindi

(Tibet)

Mianwali

Chenab

Jhelum

Amritsar

Faisalabad

Sutlej

Lahore

NEPAL

Ravi

Sahiwal

ultan

Sutlej

Bahawalpur

INDIA

DELHI

olistan

esert

Bikaner

almer

Jodhpur

Contour Area Heights

	0 - 100 m (0 - 328 ft)
	100 - 200 m (328 - 656 ft)
	200 - 500 m (656 - 1640 ft)
	500 - 1000 m (1640 - 3280 ft)
	1000 - 2000 m (3280 - 6560 ft)
	2000 - 3000 m (6560 - 9840 ft)
	3000 - 5000 m (9840 - 16400 ft)
	over 5000 m (16400 ft)
	major road
	railway

General Information for Travellers

Getting There

By Air

Over 20 international airlines fly to Pakistan from more than 40 countries. Most flights arrive at Karachi, but PIA, British Airways and Saudi fly direct to the twin cities of Islamabad–Rawalpindi, and PIA, Indian Airlines and Saudi fly direct to Lahore.

PIA — Pakistan International Airlines has direct flights from the main Mediterranean and European cities, as well as New York, Toronto and Nairobi. It also runs a Far East network from Tokyo, Beijing, Jakarta, Singapore, Kuala Lumpur and Bangkok and is scheduled to start a new service to Hong Kong towards the end of 1999. There are daily PIA and Air India flights from Delhi and Bombay to Lahore and Karachi, and interesting twice-weekly PIA flights take in the Central Asian republics of Uzbekistan and Kazakhstan.

All Pakistanis have to fly PIA on their first trip each year, so there is little discounting available on scheduled fares. Shop around for discount fares with other airlines in London bucket-shops and check the weekly travel sections in the major newspapers. Most airlines offer reduced fare or Apex tickets, but you can usually find even better deals from companies such as Trailfinders in London or STA worldwide. You should be able to fly London to Karachi return for about £350.

On Arrival

Pakistan's international airports have banks that are always open to change travellers' cheques and foreign currency. It is best to carry only new US dollars or pounds sterling cheques or cash. Karachi's new international terminal is clean and efficient: fixed-price porters are on hand and transport to town readily available. It is easier to pre-pay your taxi fare at the counter inside the terminal: this will save being mobbed outside (or at least find out how much the pre-paid fare is so you know what to bargain for in the free-for-all outside). You should always bargain with the taxi driver and agree on a fare before setting off, or better still try to insist on him using his meter. From the airport to the down-town Karachi hotels should cost about Rs120–180 by taxi. From Islamabad–Rawalpindi airport to Islamabad is about Rs150–180 by taxi; to central Rawalpindi, it is about Rs100. Suzuki vans to Islamabad and Rawalpindi are not allowed into the airport, but wait on the road outside and cost about Rs10–15. From Lahore airport to the town centre is about Rs100–150 by taxi.

Overland
From China The Khunjerab Pass is open (weather permitting) from 1 May to 31 October, for tours, and to 30 November for individual travellers. Customs, immigration and health formalities at Sost, the border post, can be completed daily from 9 am to 11 am for outgoing travellers and up to 4 pm (Pakistani time) for incoming travellers. Travel time from Sost to Tashkurgan, the first Chinese town, is five hours (220 kilometres/137 miles), not counting formalities at the new Chinese border post just before Tashkurgan (moved from Pir Ali). The Chinese border post is open 12 noon to 2 pm (Beijing time) for outgoing travellers and up to 7 pm for incoming travellers. Beijing time is three hours ahead of Pakistani time. Daily PTDC (Pakistan Tourism Development Corporation) and NATCO (Northern Areas Transport Company) buses ply between Tashkurgan, Sost and Gilgit.

From India The only land border open between India and Pakistan is at Wagah, between Amritsar and Lahore, open for foreigners seven days a week: 8.30 am to 2.30 pm in summer (16 April to 15 October) and 9.30 am to 3.30 pm in winter (16 October to 15 April). Minibus number 12 leaves Wagah for Lahore every 15 minutes. Take a bus or taxi from Amritsar to the border, then walk accross no-man's-land and catch a bus or taxi to Lahore. Pakistani and Indian nationals are only allowed to cross the border by train. (see new bus route below) The **Lahore–Delhi train** leaves Lahore on Mondays and Thursdays only at 11 am. Check-in time at Lahore station is three hours before departure. India and Pakistan agreed years ago to open the railway line from Jodhpur in Rajasthan to Hyderabad in Sindh, but as we go to press this has not yet happened. Check with other tourists and the authorities for the latest information.

The first direct bus service between Delhi and Lahore since 1947 was opened in February 1999 by India's Prime Minister Atal Behari Vajpayee in a well publicised Pak–Indian public relations exercise. The journey from Delhi to Lahore takes about 11 and enters Pakistan at Wagah. Ask at PTDC or TDCP if it is running.

From Iran The border is open only at Taftan, from 9 am to 1 pm and 2 pm to 5 pm. Seven buses daily take 18 hours to cover the 634 kilometres (396 miles) from Taftan to Quetta in Balochistan. Five days a week an air-conditioned coach makes the same journey in 16 hours, or you can rent a Datsun wagon to share with other travellers. The road from Taftan to Quetta crosses hot arid desert, so you will need enough food and drinking water for the journey. The first 84 kilometres (52 miles) to Nukkundi is gravel and in poor condition; from there on to Quetta the road is surfaced. Petrol and diesel are available only at Nukkundi, Dalbandin (384 kilometres/240 miles from Quetta) and Nushki.

A safer but slower option is the Sunday **train** from Zahidan in Iran which takes about 27 hours via Taftan to Quetta. The fare from Zahidan to Mirjawa (the Iranian check-post) must be paid in Iranian rials, then you buy a second ticket for the rest of the journey to Quetta. A second train leaves Taftan for Quetta every Thursday.

Note that the road from Taftan to Quetta, and Quetta to Sukkur is the only one in Balochistan open to foreign tourists without a special permit. You can take the train or fly from Quetta to Sindh or Punjab. If you plan to leave Pakistan for Iran, you must obtain your visa from the Iranian embassy in Islamabad as the Iranian consulate in Quetta only issues visas to Pakistanis. All foreigners must obtain their Iranian visas in Islamabad.

From Afghanistan Afghanistan is still closed to foreigners due to the troubles. The two possible entry points, from Kabul via Torkham and the Khyber Pass, and from Kandahar via Chaman and the Khojak Pass, are both closed except to local traffic. Check with other tourists for the latest information.

By Sea

No boats for the general public sail to or from Pakistan. A few pilgrim boats do, however, ply between Karachi and the Gulf States.

When To Go

The climate in Pakistan is so varied that, no matter what time of year you go, the weather will be pleasant somewhere. Winter (November to February) is the best time to visit Sindh and southern Punjab. The rest of the country is at its most colourful in spring (March to May, depending on altitude), when flowers bloom, and autumn (mid-September to mid-November), when the leaves change. For trekking and mountaineering, June to September is the recommended time.

It is best to avoid Ramazan (known as Ramadan in most other Muslim countries), the Muslim month of fasting, when no food, drink, cigarettes or sex are taken from sunrise to sunset. This is a difficult time for everyone, including visitors, as no food or drink is sold during the day except in a handful of Chinese restaurants in the major cities and in the indoor dining rooms of large hotels. Office hours are erratic and everyone is rather dopey. Tourists visiting at this time should be careful not to eat, drink or smoke anywhere in public during daylight hours. The dates of Ramazan vary from year to year: the exact dates being subject to the lunar calendar.

Ramazan Dates

1999/2000	—	8/9	December	to	5/6	January
2000	—	27/28	November	to	25/26	December
2001	—	15/16	November	to	14/15	December
2002	—	3/4	November	to	2/3	December

Visas

Nationals of all countries need a visa to enter Pakistan. It is safer and easier to arrive with a valid tourist visa obtained in your home country. In theory, 72 hour transit visas (landing permits) are supposedly issued free on arrival at every entry point. You then have the hassle of trying to get your tourist visa from the nearest passport office, which is only valid for a maximum of 30 days. If you enter Pakistan by road from China, for example, it will take you three days hard travelling to reach the nearest passport office at Islamabad (which is only open from 9 am to 1 pm Monday to Friday).

Most visas are valid for only six months from the date of issue, though British nationals can sometimes get a two-year multiple entry visa. On an ordinary tourist visa issued in your own country you can stay a maximum of three months, but visa extensions can (in theory) be obtained from any of Pakistan's Regional Passport Offices (see list next page), though you may find you have (in fact) to go to Islamabad or Karachi to get it. The length of the extension is up to the officer in charge.

Allow plenty of time to get your visa from any Pakistani embassy or consulate. Be sure to get a double entry visa if you plan to go to China, India or one of the Central Asian republics and return to Pakistan. In Islamabad you can (with patience) have a single entry visa changed to a double entry if you decide to leave Pakistan at the last minute and plan to return.

When applying for a visa it is best to telephone the Pakistani embassy in your own country and ask for a complete list of all you need. Even so they may 'forget' one or two items and so delay issuing the visa. A likely check-list is: a completed visa application form; two, three or four passport photos; proof of return or onward tickets; proof of adequate money for your stay in Pakistan; if you are not applying for your visa in your own country, you may need a photocopy of visa or permit for the country in which you are

applying; a self-addressed envelope with sufficient stamps to cover returning your passport to you by registered post (though some embassies may not accept applications by post) and a visa fee, the amount of which depends on your nationality. You can get a visa in one day at the Pakistan embassy in London if you show a return ticket and $300 in travellers' cheques.

There are regional passport offices in Pakistan in Abbottabad, Bahawalpur, Dera Ghazi Khan, Dera Ismail Khan, Faisalabad, Gujranwala, Gujrat, Hyderabad, Islamabad tel 260773, 9207290 Karachi-Nazimabad tel 6648571, Karachi-Saddar tel 5681135, 5680360, Kohat, Lahore tel 7325459, Mirpur (AK), Multan tel 520250, Muzaffarabad (AK), Peshawar tel 240178, Quetta tel 71275, Saidu Sharif (Swat), Sargodha, Sialkot and Sukkur.

It is best to find out at the main police station, foreigners' registration office, if you can indeed get visa extensions at your chosen regional passport office, what hours they accept applications and how to get there (the addresses are complicated and not very helpful). Regional offices will forward all applications to Islamabad, so the process will take at least three days. Perhaps it is best to go directly to Islamabad.

Guard your documents carefully and let nothing expire. Getting replacements and renewals involves a frustrating paper chase.

Foreigners Registration

All Indian and Afghan visitors are required to register at the foreigners' registration office which in most large cities is part of the police office. All other nationals planning to live or work in Pakistan must also register. Short-term tourists are occasionally given a Form C: certificate of foreigners' registration, on entry. If so, save it and return it when you leave. Tourists staying longer than 30 days are supposed to register at the nearest foreigners' registration office: it is worth doing this, so that in the unlikely event of your having an accident, your papers will all be in order. To register you need two passport photos and Form C. You will be given a Certificate of Registration and a Residence Permit which must be handed in to the foreigners' registration office at the last town you stay in. You will then be given an Exit Permit to give to emigration on departure. If you are a tourist and are stopped on departure because you have not registered, just explain very quietly and politely that you knew nothing about it and, if necessary, put this in writing. Pakistan is trying to encourage tourism, so the emigration officials are unlikely to make any trouble for a genuine tourist.

(previous page) Autumn at Khaplu in Baltistan

Check-posts At certain sensitive points around the country you will be stopped at police check-posts and asked to sign a register; you will also be required to sign hotel registers. This is for your own protection. In any country anywhere in the world people do occasionally go missing. You will be easier to trace if you leave a record.

Customs

Alcohol is not admitted into Pakistan, and any alcohol found will be impounded. A non-Muslim can easily buy liquor in the large hotels authorised to sell alcohol to hotel guests, and also from government liquor shops in the main cities if he/she has a licence, which is easily obtainable. Ask a tourism official, or in a big hotel, how to get the licence.

Duty free allowances are 200 cigarettes, 1/2 pint of perfume, and one camera, watch, hair-dryer, portable computer, tape recorder and typewriter. But officials are generally not strict with genuine tourists and bags are rarely opened unless you are Indian or a visiting Pakistani, in which case a gift may be necessary before you are cleared.

Departure

Emigration authorities demand three photocopies of the front pages of your passport and Pakistani visa when you leave Pakistan; they may also ask for your Form C (see previous page). There is no limit to the amount of foreign exchange you can take out, nor on the amount of rupees you can change back into foreign currency provided you show foreign exchange certificates to the value you wish to change.

Exports Antiques such as Gandharan statues may not be exported from the country. Only jewellery and precious stones worth less than Rs25,000, and carpets and other purchases worth less than Rs75,000 are allowed out as personal baggage. There is no limit to the value of goods you may export with an export permit which your dealer can arrange for you, or an international moving company such as Freeline Movers, Khalid Plaza, Blue Area, Islamabad, tel 9212471, fax 9211934, who are happy to supply any information you may require on import–export regulations. To get your permit you will need photocopies of your passport, the purchase receipts and a letter of request from you addressed to the Chief Controller of Imports and Exports, your credit card receipts or encashment receipts to the value of

The honour guard of the Tomb of Allama Muhammad Iqbal seen before the gate of Badshahi Mosque in Lahore

the items to be exported. Make sure the receipts are completed in full, showing the amount in foreign currency, the exchange rate and the rupee total, and are officially signed and stamped. All unaccompanied baggage also needs an export permit.

Bags are almost always searched by customs on departure. Females can ask for a female customs officer, but I usually just pack all my underwear in a plastic bag at the bottom of the case so as to deny male officers their kinky delights.

Airport tax is Rs400 for economy class, Rs600 for club and Rs800 for first class on international flights. The tax for all economy class domestic flights is Rs40.

Foreign travel tax If you buy an international airline ticket in Pakistan you have to pay a foreign travel tax as well as the airport tax.

Health

Vaccinations Allow several months to get all your injections, as they can't all be given at once.

Like most of Asia the streets and public transport are crowded in Pakistan, so you will come into close contact with all the normal childhood diseases. If you have not already had these diseases, check that you have been vaccinated against **diphtheria, tetanus, measles, mumps** and **rubella.** I caught both measles and mumps while living in Pakistan, which was no fun at all as an adult. These injections are safe even if you have already had one or more of the diseases.

Be sure that your **polio** and **typhoid** vaccinations are up to date, and I strongly recommend the new vaccines for **hepatitis A, Japanese encephalitis** and **rabies;** all three involve courses of three easy injections given over several months. I was bitten by a dog on my last visit and wish I had been vaccinated against rabies in advance, though good foreign vaccine is readily available in the major cities. **Cholera** vaccine is considered useless: it is only 50 percent effective and may have quite severe side-effects, so it is not recommended. Discuss this with your doctor. If you are coming from infected areas you will need both cholera and yellow fever vaccination certificates dated at least 10 days before your arrival, otherwise you will be kept in quarantine. If you are staying in Pakistan for more than a year you supposedly need a certificate that you are not HIV (human immuno-deficiency virus) positive (but this is not strictly enforced).

Malaria exists year round in the whole of Pakistan below 2,000 metres. Some doctors recommend Chloroquin taken weekly plus Paludrin taken daily for the best coverage, though the World Health Organisation bulletin suggests that you need not take anti-malaria pills in Pakistan, but should instead carry an emergency treatment of Fansidar or Larium in case you catch malaria. Discuss this with your doctor and ask him for the latest information, and how to recognise an attack of malaria. To protect yourself from being bitten by mosquitoes, keep your skin covered and use an insect repellent containing at least 25 mg of diaethyltoluamid (DEET) on your skin and clothes at dusk, and throughout the night. Some doctors suggest that taking vitamin B1 also discourages mosquitoes from biting, but this has never been proven. Researchers are testing a new malaria vaccine, which will hopefully be on the market soon.

AIDS and **Tuberculosis** are everywhere, so avoid the red-light districts and if you find yourself in an enclosed space where people are coughing, it is wise to go outside. But that said, our dear cook who worked for us for three years died the following year of tuberculosis, and no one else in the household caught it. (Though there is so much tuberculosis in Ireland that I had built up my resistance to it before I finished primary school.)

Prevention Water-borne and faecally spread diseases and parasites are your greatest enemy, and some form of upset stomach will be your most likely problem. If your vaccinations are all up-to-date you should be reasonably protected against polio, hepatitis, typhoid, tetanus and cholera, all of which are endemic in Pakistan. But that still leaves the water-born parasites such as giardia lamblia, various amoeba and a selection of intestinal worms to deal with.

The best solution is to be extremely careful about what you eat and drink, and to wash your hands frequently. In Pakistan none of the water is adequately treated. Even in Europe where all water is treated we are advised not to drink tap water in certain areas. In Pakistan you should never drink tap or river water, and you should not even clean your teeth in anything other than boiled, purified or bottled water. Don't imagine that you may have built up some resistance; these diseases and parasites attack everyone, though some people are slower to succumb and may not develop the symptoms so quickly.

Finding safe water to drink is not so easy. There are many brands of bottled water for sale in the cities and towns, though this is not a foolproof solution as the Aga Khan Hospital tests have shown some brands to be contaminated. Imported water from the Arab countries tested purer than the Pakistani brands, so buy Arab water as your first choice, though any bottled water will be safer than tap or river water. Avoid ice everywhere, even in major hotels, as it is usually made with unboiled water. International-class hotels claim that their water is safe because it is filtered, but it is wiser not to risk it: only very expensive filters correctly used are really effective. Soft drinks and fruit jucies in cardboard cartons are reasonably safe and are available in all major towns and many smaller ones, but avoid the straws in restaurants as they are sometimes reused and are unlikely to be clean.

The best solution is to purify all your drinking water yourself. I always carry a light plastic iodine water filter cup called Penta Pure travel cup, made by WTC Industries in Plymouth, Minnesota, USA, which kills almost everything, including giardia, leaves the water tasting pleasant, is small enough to carry in your handbag or pocket, and is good for 600 cups. Using this I can drink any water that is not too cloudy, and I feel no embarrassment about producing my filter in restaurants and even in private houses. The little plastic cup is also handy for soft drinks and tea. You can order it in England from Travelling Light, Freepost, Morland, Penrith, Cambria CA10 3AZ for £25.

The best water purifying tablets are the iodine-based Aquapure or Potable Aqua. Other commonly available water purifying tablets, such as Puritabs and Micropure, do not kill giardia cysts which are now found in most water worldwide, so these must be used in combination with iodine to be effective. Talk to your pharmacist, read all the fine print and follow the instructions to the letter. To disguise the unpleasant taste of chemicals you can add some- thing like Tang, Isostar or Gatorade after you have waited the stipulated time for the purification tablets and iodine to work.

Most foreigners and many Pakistanis purify their water by boiling, but this is not very practical for the traveller.

Read the Food and Drink section, page 37, for further tips.

Cure If you do get diarrhoea, buy yourself some rehydration salts in the pharmacy, follow the instructions carefully, and be sure to take plenty of liquids as dehydration is a serious danger. If you are vomiting, try taking little sips of water every five minutes which should stay down better than a whole glassful taken at once. Eat only plain boiled rice and try to rest.

A broad spectrum antibiotic like ciprofloxacin should be reserved for serious infections such as diarrhoea accompanied by a high fever, but it can also be used to cure any infection caused by bacteria, such as typhoid, salmonella, serious chest infections, serious abscesses, boils and badly infected insect bites.

It is a good idea to have an anti-fungal skin ointment with you, such as Clotrimizole for crotch-rot and athletes foot. But better still, to avoid the fungus wear loose cotton underwear and sandals.

Strep throats can be cured with ordinary penicillin or stabicillin.

Having read all this, don't panic! All that is needed is a little care and you should have no problems whatsoever. However, if you do return home ill, be sure to tell your doctor exactly where you have been and what you were doing.

Bedbugs, fleas and lice (Bedbugs are red mites that leave bites in neat rows that itch for weeks.) Tourists using really cheap doss houses should beware of biting bedfellows. I always carry a bottle of flea powder or bug spray with me to shake or spray around the room, and I lay a plastic sheet beneath my sleeping bag. You can buy plastic by the metre in the bazaars. If you have a choice, always sleep in the top bunk as bugs fall downwards, and spray the ceiling above you.

Hospitals and Doctors The major towns have good doctors, all of whom speak English. The Aga Khan Hospital in Karachi and the PIMS and Shifa International Hospitals in Islamabad have good reputations, though the nursing care tends to be less good than the doctors and general facilities. However, if you suffer a major accident I would recommend having your limbs immobilised in hospital in Pakistan and then fly home for pinning and traction or whatever else is needed. If you need an injection in Pakistan, buy your own needle in the pharmacy first. Never accept a blood transfusion as blood is not screened for hepatitis or AIDS in Pakistan.

Chemists stock a wide range of foreign medicines, vaccines and syringes that are cheap and often obtainable without a prescription. But be sure you know what you are doing if you buy medicines without a prescription. In a pharmacy in Gilgit I was offered penicillamine as a substitute for penicillin.

Insurance

Accidents and theft are always possible so it is wise to take out a good holiday or travel insurance policy.

Money

The unit of currency is the rupee, which is divided into 100 paise. The rupee falls constantly in value. In July 1999 the conversion rates were approximately Rs 52 to one US Dollar, Rs 81 to one pound sterling and Rs 53 to one Euro.

Any amount of foreign currency or travellers' cheques can be taken into and out of Pakistan and you can reconvert unused rupees back into foreign currency. Save all your encashment receipts as you will need to show them, not only for reconverting your rupees, but also if you wish to buy an overseas airline ticket (other than from PIA) using rupees.

It is probably best to take new US dollar or pound sterling travellers' cheques or cash as these can be readily changed at banks, hotels, tourist shops or private authorised dealers. Some shops and international hotels accept credit cards.

You will usually get the best exchange rates in the major cities from private authorised dealers or banks and less favourable rates from hotels, shops or in the Northern Areas. Hotels tend to offer the worst rates.

American Express which has offices in Karachi, Lahore, Islamabad and Rawalpindi will cash personal cheques for AmEx cardholders up the value of US$1,000 every 21 days. You will need your current account cheque-book for the account from which you pay your AmEx bill, passport and AmEx card. If you need money to be sent to you in Pakistan, it is quicker and more reliable to have a bank draft sent by courier or express registered mail to an address you can use, eg your embassy, rather than have it transferred bank to bank which can take over a week.

Travelling in Pakistan

By Air Pakistan is a large country. The most comfortable but boring way to get from A to B is to fly. You save up to 30 percent by buying your domestic tickets in Pakistan, but most flights are usually fully booked, so get your name into the computer as soon as possible, even if you do not actually pay until the last minute.

In January 1999 there were only four domestic airlines in business, PIA, Aero Asia, Bhoja and Shaheen, though private companies (Hajvarai, Raji) open and close so fast that it is impossible to keep pace, so ask around for the latest information. Private airlines are usually about 20 percent cheaper than PIA, but offer only limited services between the major cities.

PIA offers a very extensive domestic network and flies to Bahawalpur, Bannu, Chitral, Dera Ismail Khan, Faisalabad, Gilgit, Gwadar, Hyderabad,

Tonga — Horse carriage, used for transport of people and goods

Islamabad, Jacobabad, Jiwani, Karachi, Khuzdar, Kohat, Lahore, Mianwali, Moenjodaro, Multan, Muzaffarabad, Nawabshah, Ormara, Panjgur, Pasni, Peshawar, Quetta, Rahimyar Khan, Rawalkot, Saidu Sharif, Sargodha, Sibi, Sindhri, Skardu, Sui, Sukkur, Turbat and Zhob. PIA produce a handy green timetable listing of all their flights. There is a late night 'coach' service between Karachi, Lahore and Islamabad which costs about 25 percent less than the normal fares.

Flights to Gilgit, Skardu and Chitral are extremely good value and, if bought in Pakistan, work out at about only three times the bus fare. However, all flights are on a standby basis as they operate only when visibility is good and so can be delayed for some days. For confirmation you should leave your ticket with PIA Rawalpindi, tel 567011, on the morning before you are booked to fly, pick it up at 3 pm, go to the airport the next morning and pray the weather is suitable. If the flight is cancelled, you are wait-listed for the next flight. Gilgit and Skardu flights leave from Islamabad; Chitral flights leave from Peshawar. You can fly to Swat from either Peshawar or Islamabad.

Journalists and groups are eligible for discounts. Apply to the public relations officer at the PIA offices in Karachi, Lahore, Rawalpindi, Peshawar, Multan or Quetta.

Always call PIA yourself to confirm your ticket. For the telephone numbers see under useful numbers for each city.

By Train This is the best way to get around if you have enough time, though the trains are very crowded so you must book well in advance, especially for sleepers. The trunk lines run from Karachi to Peshawar via Multan, Lahore and Rawalpindi, and from Karachi to the Iranian border via Sukkur and Quetta. There is an extensive network of branch lines. Trains run frequently, but they are slow, unpunctual and crowded. Train classes are express, mail and ordinary; compartment classes are air-conditioned, first, economy and second. Air-conditioned and first class have sleeper compartments, and there are special ladies' compartments recommended for women travelling alone. Air-conditioned class is almost as expensive as flying. Most passengers bring their own bedding, but it can sometimes be hired at major stations. As buying a ticket can be time-consuming and frustrating, ask an agency or hotel employee to handle it for you. If all else fails, you can pay a station porter (recognisable by his red turban and armband) to buy you a ticket and find you a seat.

Groups can hire a luxurious tourist car complete with dining and sitting room, which can be attached to certain trains and detached at any railway station for as many hours as the group wishes. The cost is reasonable if shared by a large group. Contact the Divisional Superintendent's Office, Pakistan Railways, Karachi.

Foreign tourists can get a 25 percent discount (50 percent for students) on most rail fares. To apply you need patience. First get a tourist certificate from the local PTDC (Pakistan Tourism Development Corporation) tourist officer. Show this to the Divisional Railway Superintendent at Karachi, Lahore, Rawalpindi, Peshawar, Quetta, Sukkur or Multan railway stations with your passport and student card (these offices are not easy to find). He will give you the necessary concession order which you then show at the ticket window when you buy your ticket. Indians and visiting Pakistanis are not eligible.

By Road (Useful Hints) Buses, coasters, minibuses, wagons and jeeps generally all leave from different stations, so be very specific when asking directions to the station.

Pakistani women never travel alone by road: it is better to travel in pairs or with a male companion who you say is your husband, brother, father or son. There is no danger in travelling alone, but it offends good Muslim males to see women so immodest as to travel unaccompanied. I have never had any problems on the few occasions when I have travelled alone, but I wear local dress and wrap up in a large shawl and try to find an older wagon driver who speaks some English. I then buy the two front seats for myself, and sit and read until he is ready to leave. Pakistani men can be acutely uncomfortable sitting beside a strange woman. Pakistani women travel only on the front or back seats, and often suffer from travel sickness. A supply of plastic bags to pass around is welcomed by all.

Buses Buses are the cheapest but most uncomfortable and dangerous way to travel in Pakistan. The Government Transport Service (GTS) buses go everywhere possible and run to fixed schedules. Bus stations are usually near the railway station, if there is one, or near the bazaar in smaller places. On longer journeys, buses make scheduled stops for food, but it is wise to take some food (especially fruit) and drink with you. Seats cannot always be reserved in advance.

Several private air-conditioned **luxury bus** services, with noisy videos, ply the routes between the major cities. They usually leave from their own company offices.

Coasters, minibuses and wagons, with about 15 to 20 seats, are faster, more comfortable and only slightly more expensive than government buses.

Seats can usually be booked in advance, but in bigger towns, the vehicles, both government and privately owned, just leave when full in a continuous stream.

Suzuki pickups with 10 or so passengers sitting in two rows knee to knee are the usual transport for short distances in towns. Just flag one down, pay Rs2 and pound on the roof or floor when you want to get off.

Jeeps Passenger-cargo jeeps are the public transport in the northern valleys where the roads are too narrow for buses or wagons. The drivers are excellent, but the jeeps themselves are neither cheap nor comfortable, with as many passengers as possible perched on top of the cargo (usually sacks of grain or fertiliser) and crouched on the front and back bumpers. They run to no timetable and, in the remoter valleys, are quite rare.

The Northern Area Transport Company (NATCO) runs buses and jeeps up the Karakoram Highway and into some of the side valleys off the main road. They offer a discount to a limited number of Pakistani and foreign students on each vehicle.

Painted trucks: exterior and interior

Close to the Edge

Just watching had to do as entertainment. Men sat by roads in the mountains watching the trucks and buses go by, with people rocking and bumping and holding on for life itself on the roofs and sides and any little place they could squeeze in a hand or foot. I had the uncomfortable feeling that the spectators were waiting for something else to happen. An accident, perhaps — as the crowd at a circus is thrilled by the possibility of death from the trapezes.

The trapeze analogy seemed appropriate. The trucks and buses sped wildly on roads cut, not all that deeply, into the sides of the mountains, with spectacular views — and drops — off to the side. The driving was skilful and brave in Pakistan. We hired drivers, always, not only because they were cheap, but because I did not believe I could survive behind the wheel the way cars raced toward each other before swerving on narrow, broken roads. Foreigners closed their eyes and explained it to each other by mentioning hashish or Inshallah, the fatalism of men who believed their life was in God's hands — or, perhaps, they had a certain lack of respect for the power and danger of machines. Whatever the reasons, psychological or physical, the men and their machines regularly self-destructed, quite spectacularly. I kept track of small items about the buses in the English-language papers for a couple of weeks in July. Leaving aside the routine run of crashes and runnings-over, there were these: on July 1, twelve persons were killed and eight injured when two buses collided between Lahore and Rawalpindi, on July 3, three people were killed and twenty-five injured when a bus from Sialkot to Pasrur crashed into a tree; on July 9, four persons were killed and twenty injured when a bus from Mianchuan to Chickawatni overturned; on July 21, thirty-eight persons were killed and sixteen injured when a bus from Dir to Peshawar plunged one thousand feet into a gorge.

Richard Reeves, Passage to Peshawar, 1984

By Car It is easy and comparatively cheap to hire a car or jeep with driver in Pakistan. Nawaz Sharif, the Prime Minister, gave easy loans to individuals to buy **yellow cabs.** The country is now overflowing with them. They have meters, though the drivers prefer you to just bargain. Always ask around before you travel so you have some idea how much to bargain for. You can hire the cab for the day: worth it if you are on a paper chase round Islamabad offices. The drivers will probably only know the major hotels and big landmarks. If trying to reach an office or private house, it is best to telephone and ask them to give directions to your taxi driver.

Cars with drivers can be hired at big hotels. They are more expensive than yellow cabs (even more so if air-conditioned), but may be worth the extra cost as the drivers speak some English. The minor country and mountain roads are often impassable for ordinary cars, so four-wheel-drive vehicles with high clearance are recommended. You can hire jeeps in the street in the towns and even in some villages in the north. Stick to small 4WD vehicles in the mountains, as the roads and bridges are very narrow. The government-approved rate in Punjab, NWFP and on the Karakoram Highway is about Rs8 per kilometre and Rs100–200 overnight charge. In Gilgit, Chitral and Skardu ask the tourism officer and other officials for the going rate.

Self-drive vehicles are rarely available and not recommended. Driving Pakistani style takes skill and experience: no one observes the usual traffic rules, and unless you are used to driving in Asia and on the left, you may find it all just too harrowing and dangerous. The main Karachi–Lahore–Rawalpindi–Peshawar highway is always very crowded with particularly reckless drivers. Signposts are few and often only in Urdu, which makes finding your way difficult and frustrating — particularly in big cities. Driving at night is especially hazardous as trucks, bicycles and bullock carts rarely have lights.

It is perfectly safe to travel by road in most of Punjab, the Northern Areas and North-West Frontier Province (outside the tribal areas). But for their own security the authorities ask foreigners to avoid driving in most of Sindh and Balochistan.

Fuel There is a good network of fuel stations over most of the country, but in some areas you may need to carry extra fuel with you. It is worth keeping the tank fairly full as there may be unexpected shortages. The larger fuel stations have clean lavatories: ask the attendant for the key.

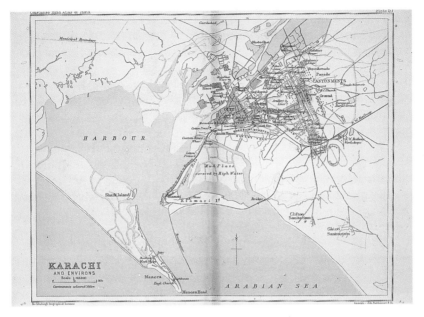

Nineteenth century map of Karachi

Maps

Good maps are not available first-hand in Pakistan, although you may be able to pick some up second-hand if you are lucky. Despite the wonders of satellite photography, the government is still paranoid about security, so all the old British maps of what is now Pakistan are restricted. The maps which are available to the general public, even the most modern, are very small scale and none too accurate. The best overall map is the Nelles Verlag/Apa Map of Pakistan, 1:1,500,000 (though it is hopelessly inaccurate in the north). A good alternative is the Bartholomew's 1:4,000,000 road map covering the entire subcontinent. Big English-language bookshops in Islamabad, Lahore and Karachi have some badly-drawn city and 1:1,000,000 provincial maps, with very little detail and no contours. There is also a 1:2,000,000 road map of Pakistan without contours. More generally useful — despite their faults — are the 1:1,000,000 contour maps issued by the Survey of Pakistan, if you can get hold of them. To do so, contact the Survey of Pakistan office on Murree Road in Faizabad, between Islamabad and Rawalpindi. (The office is about 200 metres from the intersection of Airport and Muree roads, on the right going towards Rawalpindi.) The Survey of Pakistan office in Karachi near the Metropole Hotel may also have them. You will need to show your passport and explain why you want a map. The Pakistan Tourism Development Corporation (PTDC), and the Tourism Development Corporation of Punjab (TDCP) publish small pamphlets with some helpful information but useless sketch-maps.

The best map for the Karakoram mountain range is the orthographical sketch-map in two sheets, produced by the Swiss Foundation for Alpine Research. Printed to the scale 1:250,000, it shows the main mountain ridges and gives contour lines every 1,220 metres, but does not show international boundaries with India and China. A similar map, scale 1:200,000, is published by Leomann Maps in four sheets.

The best contour maps are the American Military Service (AMS) U502 series, scale 1:250,00. However, road detail and village names are up to 50 years out of date. Also the cease-fire line between India and Pakistan is not marked, and the border with China has moved (in favour of China) so if you are trekking in Kashmir, Baltistan or Shimshal you must find out where it is. Take careful note of the relibility diagram on each map, rating it good, fair or poor.

The U502 maps are only available for northern Pakistan, namely: NJ 43–13 (Mastuj) for northern Chitral; NJ 43–14 (Baltit) for Hunza; NJ 43–15 (Shimshal) for Shimshal and Hispar; NI 43–1 (Churrai) for upper Swat; NI 43–2 (Gilgit) for Gilgit and Nanga Parbat; NI 43–4 (Mundik) for Skardu; NI 43–4 (Siachen) for Concordia and K2, and NI 43–6 (Srinagar) for the Kaghan Valley and Azad Kashmir. The maps covering the border area with Afghanistan (NJ 42–16 and NI 42–4) are restricted.

There are two superb 1:50,000 German maps — one of Nanga Parbat and one of the Minapin Glacier — drawn by the Deutsche Himalaya Expedition in 1934 and updated in 1980.

There is also an excellent Chinese map of the Batura Glacier on the scale 1:60,000. It was compiled in 1978 by the Institute of Glaciology, Cryopedology and Desert Research, Academia Sinica, Lanchow.

The aeronautical maps compiled and published by the Defense Mapping Agency Aerospace Center, St Louis Air Force Station, Missouri, scale 1:500,000 are fairly accurate for the heights of mountains, courses of rivers, and the names of major towns, but they show few roads and almost no villages, so are not particularly useful to the traveller.

You can order maps from any good map centre, such as Stanfords, 12 Long Acre, London WC2, tel 01 836 1321, or the Library of Congress Geography and Map Division, Washington DC.

I have included some general sketch-maps in this volume which give a fair idea of the country.

Accommodation

Karachi, Islamabad, Rawalpindi, Lahore and Peshawar have expensive **international-class hotels**, but good accommodation outside these major cities is in short supply. The situation is improving, however, with the Serena chain building and taking over hotels at Quetta, Faisalabad, Swat and Gilgit, and the Shangrila chain opening in the north at Nathiagali, Kaghan, Chilas and Skardu. These hotels are all comfortable but are also relatively expensive. The best hotels are usually heavily booked, especially in Islamabad and Lahore, so advance reservation is essential.

The **Pakistan Tourism Development Corporation** runs motels and guest-houses at the most popular tourist sites and resorts all over the country, especially in the northern valleys and along the Karakoram Highway. They are often the oldest hotel in the area, usually on the best site. The government have just embarked on a much-needed renovation and extension programme, and are building 22 new PTDC motels and tourist complexes plus a number of roadside facilities and restaurants. These are detailed throughout the text and in the hotel listing at the end of this book. Rooms are moderately priced, and the PTDC staff are usually extremely helpful. For booking contact the PTDC Motel Reservation Office in Islamabad, Block 4 B, Jinnah Super Market (near Taj Mahal Restaurant) F-7 tel (92-51) 920 8948-9 or 111 555 999, fax (92 51) 921 8233.

Every town has a wide range of **locally run hotels** varying greatly in price (US$1–100) and standard. Many are cheap by Western standards and give adequate accommodation. Some are exceptionally good value, but it is usually prudent to check the room and sanitary facilities before signing in.

Cheaper local hotels usually provide only a bottom sheet and a well-used blanket, so you may want to carry your own sheet and pillowcase (or sleeping bag liner), and certainly a towel and soap. In winter or in the mountains, you will need a sleeping bag.

At the bottom end are *musafir khanas*, local inns in which a *charpoy* (rope bed) is provided without bedding in a communal dormitory or a courtyard.

These local inns and the really cheap hotels usually refuse foreigners, except in very remote areas where there is no other accommodation. (See the Health section on bed bugs and fleas, page 22.)

The Pakistan Youth Hostel Association (PYHA) has its head office in Islamabad, on Garden Road, G–6, near Aabpara Market, and runs a dozen **youth hostels** for PYHA or International YHA members only. You can join at Islamabad and make advance bookings for the hostels at Islamabad, Lahore and Peshawar; plus four in the Kaghan Valley at Balakot, Sharan, Naran and Batakundi; two in the Murree Hills at Bhurban and Khanspur; one in the Salt Range at Ketas, one at the ancient ruins of Taxila and one at Abbottabad at the south end of the Karakoram Highway. The hostels are excellent value at less than one US dollar a night and are even cheaper if you hold a student card. You can buy a temporary membership. They are all very popular and crowded in summer when you may only stay three nights consecutively. The Lahore hostel even has a swimming pool. You can camp in the gardens and use the cooking and shower facilities: everyone is expected to help with cleaning.

There are barrack-like **YMCA hostels** at Karachi and Lahore, and more home-like YWCA hostels at Karachi, Lahore and Rawalpindi, where you can pay a temporary membership fee to stay.

Railway retiring rooms, a hold-over from the British Raj, are rooms with beds for passengers holding air-conditioned or first-class tickets. These are excellent value costing about one US dollar a night and are available at Karachi City and Cantonment, Lahore City, Multan Cantonment, Rawalpindi Cantonment, Faisalabad, Sargodha, Taxila, Bahawalpur and Quetta.

Islamabad has the only official campsite in Pakistan, but **camping** is often possible in the gardens of small hotels, rest-houses and youth hostels, with access to their facilities. Camping by the roadside, in tribal areas or in some parts of the northern valleys is prohibited. It can also be uncomfortable to camp in the open, as the local/people are very curious and in some areas hostile.

Tipping

It is part of the Muslim ethic that the rich distribute some of their wealth among their poorer neighbours. A few rupees go a long way in spreading goodwill and should be handed out to anyone who does you any special service. Tucking a note in a man's breast pocket saying 'Something for your children' will avoid any embarrassment about being tipped by a woman or a 'foreign guest'. A good alternative to rupees in return for village hospitality is a photo of your family, or a postcard of, for example, the Shah Faisal mosque in Islamabad. Posh restaurant waiters expect the usual 10 to 15 percent on top of the bill.

Never give sweets, biscuits, pens, cash or any little present to children or anyone who has not rendered a service. This encourages begging of the 'one pen' type that is so demoralising in Nepal. This is not hard-hearted: begging lowers the self-esteem of the people, and giving sweets and biscuits to children is actually cruel as there are no dentists to fill their cavities.

Unleavened bread, roti or naan

Begging

An Islamic poor tax or *zakaat* is automatically collected out of everyone's bank account. This is used to take care of the destitute, so there is less street begging in Pakistan as compared with India.

Food and Drink

The best Pakistani food is varied and delicious. Chicken, mutton and beef are on the menu in most restaurants, served with *daal* (lentils), *subzi* (vegetables) and *dahi* (yoghurt), and scooped up with *roti* (bread) either *chapatis* or *naan* (two types of unleavened bread, usually made with wheat flour). Lahore is famous for its Mughlai cuisine, Karachi for its seafood, and Peshawar for its kebabs, *naan* and green tea. Pakistani curries are usually not as hot as Indian curries, and many dishes have no chillies at all, though they are well-seasoned with other spices. Pakistani food at its worst is extremely monotonous: vegetables stewed for hours and a layer of oil over everything.

Chinese restaurants of varying standard can be found in the major cities, and international-class hotels serve European dishes. All restaurants are moderately priced by international standards: six to ten US dollars for a meal in a top hotel or restaurant.

Visitors should be sensible about what they eat. It is easy to avoid an upset stomach by taking a few simple precautions. Many seasoned travellers in Asia feel they have developed some immunity, but don't be fooled. You may be slower to react, but you are still susceptible to all the parasites, bacteria and viruses that affect a new arrival. Avoid eating anything that has not been freshly cooked, especially salads. Remember: 'Boil it, bake it, peel it or forget it!'

Buffet meals in first-class hotels are particularly risky, as food kept warm for long periods may be contaminated.

Food from roadside stalls is usually perfectly safe, but make sure it comes from a boiling pot on to a clean, dry, uncracked plate. *Chapatis* and *daal* make a good, cheap, high-protein meal and are available anywhere. Eat where the crowds are, as the most popular stalls have the best and — freshest — food.

To save on meat consumption, Tuesdays and Wednesdays are designated meatless days in most areas. Most restaurants serve only chicken, fish and vegetables on these days.

Fruit is particularly good in Pakistan, but peel it with a clean knife. (You can buy a good pocket knife in the bazaar.) Cut fruit, fruit juices and ice cream sold in the bazaar spell danger to all.

Avoid drinking water that has not been boiled or purified. Avoid ice everywhere, even in major hotels, as it is made with unboiled water. Tea is usually safe if it is poured into a clean, uncracked, dry cup. It is a Pakistani custom to boil milk, so that too is safe in your tea. International-class hotels claim that their water is safe because it is filtered, but it is wiser not to risk it — only very expensive filters correctly used will eliminate the giardia parasite which is endemic in Pakistan. Bottled water, soft drinks and fruit juices in cardboard cartons, are safe and are available in all major towns and many smaller ones.

I always carry a light plastic iodine water filter cup called Penta Pure travel cup, made by WTC Industries, Plymouth, Minnesota, USA, which kills everything, including giardia, leaves the water tasting pleasant, is small enough to carry in your handbag or pocket, and is good for 600 cups.

Clothes – What to Wear

In Pakistan you will be judged by your clothes. Pakistanis are extremely fashion-conscious, but dress conservatively and are always as neat and clean as their circumstances allow. Both men and women wear the national costume, *shalwar-kameez*: baggy trousers with a draw-string waist and a long loose shirt down to the knees. Some men wear Western shirt and trousers to the office, but women only wear the national dress. For your own comfort, and out of sensitivity to Pakistani opinion, it is wise to wear some loose-fitting outfit that hides the shape of your body and covers most bare flesh. Even inside wealthy Westernised homes, Pakistani women are modestly covered (often in flowing, couturier designed, hand-printed silks).

As a courtesy to Islam, visiting women should keep their legs and shoulders covered in public at all times. Most Pakistanis are extraordinarily tolerant and hospitable, so, unlike in Iran or the Arabian peninsula, no one would arrest you or say anything directly to you if you chose to wear a dress, or even shorts or a halter top in public, but the men would make ribald comments in their mother tongue, which fortunately you will not under-stand. Strict Muslims will screw their faces up in disgust, think you a whore and turn away to spit discretely to get the bad taste out of their mouths.

Anyway, clothes of loose cotton, or some new breathable synthetic fabric are healthier in hot weather, and it is actually cooler if you shade your skin from direct sunlight. A comfortable summer outfit is cotton trousers (not blue jeans which are too hot and sticky) and a long loose man's shirt with tails, or an extra-large tee-shirt with sleeves that come down to your elbows, worn outside the trousers to completely cover your bottom.

Businessmen are expected to wear a shirt and tie or a smart safari suit in summer and an ordinary suit in winter. Business-women can wear a suit with a loose top worn outside a longish skirt that is not too tight, or a modest dress or blouse with a loose skirt falling below the calves. A knotted scarf round your neck can play the role of a Pakistani shawl. In summer it is too hot to wear stockings; in winter, north of Lahore the days are crisp and a long jacket over a longish, loose skirt with stockings and boots make a smart, all-covering outfit.

Pakistan's major export is cotton, and in Karachi, Lahore and Islamabad you can buy big tee-shirts for US$1.50 and a readymade *shalwar-kameez* for between US$5 and US$20, depending on the quality. Elsewhere, a dressmaker can run one up quickly and inexpensively. Even a couturier silk outfit costs less than US$100.

Different style of veils

The light-weight scarf or *dupatta* (usually two metres long and half a metre wide) worn by Pakistani women, is handy to drape around your shoulders and head in remoter areas, and when visiting mosques and shrines. They cost about US$1 in the bazaar.

In winter and in the mountains you will need sweaters and something to fend off wind and rain. Pakistanis wear a large cotton or woollen shawl day and night in winter, which is an idea worth copying.

Men should wear shorts only while playing sports and should wear a track suit to and from the sports ground.

What to Take

A packing check-list includes: loose cotton trousers or middle-length full skirt and shirts, loose underwear that wicks-away moisture, sneakers, sandals, flip-flops (to wear in the shower) and some sort of headgear to protect against the sun and dust (Pakistani women and most men keep their heads covered at all times), sunglasses, sunscreen, lip-salve, water-purifying tablets or a water filter (such as the iodine filter Penta Pure travel cup mentioned on page 24) and a plastic or metal water bottle (I swear by the half-litre plastic bottles sold in airport duty-free shops full of brandy, scotch, vodka or gin — they are tough, flat and easy to pack and make excellent water bottles once you remove the labels — and are just the right size to carry in your handbag). You will only need a swimsuit if staying in first class hotels, or have access to a private pool.

A small zippered shoulder bag to keep out the dust (and itchy fingers) is useful for carrying your cameras and other possessions, and enough money for one day. A small backpack might be less secure if you have to take it off when you sit down. A little waistpack may be ideal for carrying small items and money, but on a woman it looks a little strange over the long loose shirt — the shoulder bag is more elegant, and can be worn in front for security. A secure money-pouch that you wear inside your clothes is essential for your travellers' cheques, foreign exchange and important documents. These should never leave your person, even at night. I prefer a light breathable pouch with velcro flap and thin shoelace strap which I wear knotted round my waist (not around my neck). It is completely invisible under loose clothes. A full size, buckle-on money belt can get very hot and itchy in the humid Pakistani summer.

You will need a pocket knife for peeling fruit and vegetables, and a small torch (flashlight) as there are frequent power cuts in the cities and many remote villages have no electricity at all. You can also buy torches, candles, matches and batteries in Pakistan. If you are using cheaper hotels, take a universal plug for washbasins, soap, towel, insect powder, and sheets or a sleeping bag (see the Health section, page 22, for bed-bugs and fleas).

Women should take a complete supply of sanitary tampons and their favourite moisturising cream, as these are only available in Islamabad. However, good chemists in Karachi, Islamabad and Lahore sell imported insect repellent, shampoo, good toilet soap, shaving cream, razor blades, toothbrushes and toothpaste, and pills such as lomotil to steady an upset stomach. Toilet paper is available in most towns.

It is wise to take a small medical kit with you, or put one together at a good chemist shop in Pakistan. Band-aids, bandages, cotton wool, sterile pads, antiseptic ointment, sore-throat pastilles, vitamins, antibiotics and oral rehydration salts are all available at all chemists shops in Karachi, Lahore and Islamabad. All these are cheap in Pakistan, and you can give them away before you leave, but it is more convenient to arrive with everything prepared, unless you are planning to spend your first day shopping for clothes and essentials.

Take several photocopies of the front pages of your passport, Pakistani visa, travellers' cheques receipt, air ticket and any other documents, plus some passport photos, and pack at least two sets in different places in your luggage. You will need three photocopies of your passport and visa to give to emigration on departure.

Finally, carry a good wad of family photos and postcards to help when making conversation and to give as presents

Visiting Mosques and Shrines

Tourists are welcome in mosques and shrines, provided they remove their shoes, show respect and are suitably dressed with legs and arms covered. Princess Diana shocked the Islamic world in 1991 by visiting the Lahore Badshahi mosque wearing a tight knee-length skirt that rode up above her knees when she sat down. The *maulana* quickly gave her a shawl to hide her knees, but later some fundamentalists tried to prosecute the *maulana* for having allowed her into the mosque when incorrectly dressed. The judge sensibly threw the case out of court. Women should drape their heads and shoulders with a shawl. A pair of socks (or the little bootees that airlines hand out in business class) will keep your feet off the stones, which can get painfully hot in summer. Women are not allowed into the inner sanctum at some shrines but may look in through a side window. Many mosques close their doors to tourists half an hour before prayers. Have a few rupees handy to pay the man who minds your shoes and to give as an offering.

Shopping – Best Buys

Pakistan has some fine handicrafts. Specialities include rugs and carpets, leather goods, furs, embroidered and appliquéd bedspreads and table linen, hand-block printed and tie-dyed cotton and silk, woollen shawls, pottery, copper and brassware, onyx ornaments, carved woodwork, gold and silver jewellery, seed pearls from China and precious and semi-precious stones. Prices are controlled in government-sponsored handicraft shops, and you must bargain in the bazaars. There are more ideas in the hotel, restaurant and shopping section at the end of the book.

Business Hours

Sunday is the weekly holiday, when all offices and most shops are closed. Most offices are closed on Saturday and all have a short day on Friday. **Government office** hours are 8 am to 2.30 pm in the summer, Monday to Thursday, and 8.30 am to 3 pm in the winter. All offices close at noon on Friday. 9.30 am to noon is the best time to find the more senior officials at their desks. **Business office** hours are officially 7.30 am to 2.30 pm in summer and 9 am to 4 pm in the winter, but many private offices are open 9 am to 1 pm and 2 or 3 pm to 5, 6 or 7 pm. **Banks** are usually open 9 am to 1 pm, Monday to Thursday, and

9 to 11.30 am on Friday and Saturday. **Large post offices** (GPO) open Monday to Thursday from 8.30 am to 2 pm, and from 2.30 to 7.30 pm in summer, half an hour later in winter; 8.30 to noon on Friday. **Branch post offices** do not reopen in the afternoon. The **main telephone exchanges** in larger towns are open 24 hours. Shops open between 9 and 10 am, and close between 6 and 8 pm. During Ramazan, the Muslim month of fasting, less work is done.

National Holidays

23 March — Pakistan Day, celebrating the 1940 resolution of the Muslim League of India to create the independent Muslim state of Pakistan

1 May — International Labour Day

1 July — Bank holiday (banks only)

14 August — Independence Day, celebrating Pakistan's separation from India in 1947

6 September — Defence of Pakistan Day

11 September — Anniversary of the death of M A Jinnah, the Quaid-e-Azam, founder of the nation

9 November — Allama Muhammad Iqbal Day to honour Pakistan's greatest poet–philosopher (1876-1938) who, in 1930, conceived the idea of a separate Muslim state

25 December — Birthday of the Quaid-e-Azam

31 December — Bank holiday (banks only)

Religious Holidays

These occur on different dates each year, as the Muslim calendar is ten to 12 days shorter than that of the West. Muslims use a lunar calendar. The year is divided into 12 months, alternately 29 and 30 days long. The year has either 354 or 355 days (11 years out of every 30 have 355 days, an extra day being added at the end of the year). The Muslim months shift in relation to the seasons, falling back 10 or 11 days each Western year. Every 30 years a cycle is complete. The 12 months are: Moharram, Safar, Rabi-ul-Awwal, Rabi-ul-Sani, Jumada-ul-Awwal, Jumada-ul-Sani, Rajab, Shaban, Ramazan, Shawwal, Ziquad and Zilhaj.

Ramazan is the fasting month, when Muslims do not eat or drink from sunrise to sunset. The approximate dates of Ramazan for the next few years are listed in the **When to Go** section, page 16.

The other most important Muslim dates are:
First day of Moharram which is New Year's Day.
Ninth and tenth of Moharram: Shias commemorate the massacre of
Hussain (the Prophet's grandson) at Kerbala, Iraq, by self-flaggelation
in mourning.
Twelfth of Rabi-ul-Awwal: Milad-ul-Nabi, or the birthday of the Prophet
Muhammad, born in AD 570.
First of Ramazan: beginning of the month of fasting.
Twenty-first of Ramazan: Shab-e-Qadr, or Night of Prayer.
First of Shawwal: Eid-ul-Fitr, a three-day festival to celebrate the end of
Ramazan, marked by the new moon.
Tenth of Zilhaj: Eid-ul-Azha, two-day festival commemorating the sacrifice
of Ismail (Muslims believe it was Ismail, not Isaac, that Abraham offered
to sacrifice). Pakistanis sacrifice animals on this occasion, and this is the
time Muslims make their pilgrimage to Mecca.
The Muslim calendar begins on 16 July AD 622, the date of the Hijra,
when the Prophet Muhammad migrated from Mecca to Medina. AH stands
for Anno Hijrae.

Other Festivals

The last week of February and early March are the main festival times.
The **camel fair in Sibi** in Balochistan, the **Sindh horse and cattle show**
in Jacobabad, the Jashan-e-Larkana in Larkana in Sindh and the **national
horse and cattle show in Lahore** all take place at the end of February with
dancing camels and horses, traditional music, games and handicraft
exhibitions combined with the usual show and sale of livestock.

Basant, the kite-flying festival of Lahore, is an ancient celebration of
spring when everyone wears yellow clothes and the young fly kites from the
rooftops. Ground glass coats the kite strings to cut down rivals, and
excitement reaches fever pitch in the kite battles.

Spring comes later in the mountains and **Nauroze** (new day) is
celebrated in Gilgit, Hunza and Skardu at the spring equinox on 21 March
with polo games, folk music and dancing.

Mela Chiraghan, the festival of lights, brightens up the tomb of
Hazrat Madho Lal Hussain near the Shalimar Gardens in Lahore on the last
weekend of March.

The prayer hall, Badshahi Mosque, Lahore

The **Shandur polo match** between Chitral and Gilgit takes thousands of supporters from both sides to the Shandur Pass sometime in late June or July.

Lok Mela, a folk festival of music, dance, craftsmen at work and a handicraft exhibition and sale, enlivens the Lok Virsa Institute of Folk and Traditional Heritage in Shakarparian Park in Islamabad every October.

Gilgit Festival or Jashan-e-Gilgit, on 1 November, marks the day in 1947 when the Gilgit Scouts mutinied against the Maharaja of Kashmir and joined Pakistan. The Northern Areas celebrate with a week of polo tournaments.

Time

Pakistan is five hours ahead of GMT (four hours ahead of British Summer Time). When it is noon in Pakistan it is 7 am (8 am in summer) in London; 2 am (3 am) in New York, and 5 pm (6 pm) in Sydney. Sunrise is about 4.45 am in June and 7.00 am in December. Darkness falls at about 5 pm in winter and 7.30 pm in summer.

Electricity

Electricity is 220–240 volts, 50–60 cycles AC. Since supply is insufficient for the demand, there is a power-sharing system in operation. Each area in rotation has half hour power cuts throughout the day at prearranged times. Some hotels have their own generators, others supply oil lamps, or candles and matches. Tourists should bring their own torch (flashlight). In the north, the electricity supply is more erratic and there are brown outs down to a few volts. Electric hair-dryers and razors are usable only in large cities. Most plugs are two-pin with round holes.

Post and Telecommunications

The postal system is reasonable for international mail. I have dropped postcards into tiny red mailboxes nailed to trees all over the Northern Areas and Chitral, and they have all arrived in Europe about a month later. In towns, to avoid stamp theft, you can ask the post office *wallah* to franc your letters in front of you. Airmail letter-forms to Europe take four or five days from Islamabad and are the most reliable.

Parcels must be sewn in cloth (quickly done in the bazaar), and need a customs declaration and postal inspection, so take a needle and thread to the post office and finish the sewing job there. Any parcel with a declared value over Rs500 needs an export permit.

Post Restante is held at the General Post Office in each town. Those with an American Express card or travellers' cheques can have mail held for a month at the American Express Offices at Karachi, Islamabad, Lahore or Rawalpindi. Have the letters addressed to, eg SHAW, Mrs Isobel. If addressed to Mrs Shaw they will be filed under M, or Isobel Shaw under I.

Telephone, Fax, Telex and **Telegraph** The cheapest way to call home is to book a three minute call, about US$5, to the USA from Public Call Offices (PCOs) which have mushroomed all over Pakistan. Usually privately owned, they stay open long hours and offer instant international dialling and fax services worldwide. Government telephone and telegraph exchanges stay open 24 hours in larger towns, the staff are efficient and always helpful, but only the larger offices have fax machines. It is much more expensive to telephone from a hotel.

Newspapers and Periodicals

Pakistan publishes about 15 English-language dailies: the best are *The News* and *Dawn* from Karachi. *The Pakistan Times* and *Nation* published in Lahore, contains less foreign news coverage and *The Muslim* is published in Islamabad. Peshawar runs its own *Frontier Post*, an interesting read, and Quetta is served by *The Balochistan Times*. Foreign newspapers and periodicals are available at large bookstalls and the big hotels, as are English-language books.

The weekly *Friday Times* and monthly *Newsline* and *Herald* make informative reading.

Numbers, Weights and Measures

Pakistanis count large numbers in lakhs (100,000) and crores (10 million). The country is officially metric, but some milestones are still in place from British times, and many Pakistanis confuse miles with kilometres. Short distances are measured in British furlongs (220 yards an eighth of a mile, or 201 metres); land is measured in *kanals*, one *kanal* is equivalent to a twentieth of a hectare or an eighth of an acre; cloth is still measured in yards and gold is weighed by the *tola* (about 11.7 gms). Meat and vegetables are often sold by the seer (0.933 kg).

Sports and Activities

Pakistanis are sports mad and play all sorts of ball games. They excel at **cricket, field hockey, badminton** and **squash.** They are also famous for **polo** and, in the northern areas, play a local variety of the game that is faster and more exciting than ste stadier international game. In Islamabad there is a good **horse riding** school in Shakarparian Park, and in many other areas tourist can hire horses. Some of the international standard hotels have **tennis** and **squash** courts, **swimming pools** and **gyms.**

Fishing   There is excellent deep-sea fishing off Karachi and equally good freshwater fishing in the northern rivers and streams which were stocked with trout by the British. The trout season runs from March to October. Fishing permits are compulsory and costs about US$2 a day for foreigners (or Rs20 for Pakistanis) and can be obtained from the local fishing authority or fishing warden.

In conversation

Bird- and Game-watching Over 740 species of birds have been identified in Pakistan. The Indus is one of the most important migration routes of the world, so the lakes and reservoirs of the Punjab and Sindh are alive with migrant birds during the winter months. The coastline and deserts are also good places to see unusual birds. Pakistan has seven national parks, 72 wildlife sanctuaries and 76 game reserves.

Golf There are 36 golf courses in Pakistan, many virtually unused.

Trekking The Himalaya, Karakoram and Hindu Kush offer some of the best trekking in the world: see *Pakistan Trekking Guide* by Isobel Shaw and Ben Shaw, Odyssey, 1993.

Mountaineering Pakistan has five peaks over 8,000 metres (26,250 feet) and over 100 higher than 7,000 metres (23,000 feet), some of which are still unclimbed. Fifty to sixty mountaineering expeditions climb in Pakistan each year. Applications for permission to climb K–2 must be made two years in advance, and applications for other peaks a year in advance. For regulations

Village house with a large grain container

Muhammad Maqsood alias Pappu Pehalvan at his school Akhara
Pappu Pehalvan, Lahore

*Wrestlers show their stuff in Lahore outside
the walls of Lahore Fort near Masti Gate*

and application forms, write to the Tourism Division, College Road, F-7/2, Islamabad, or to any Pakistani Embassy or Pakistan International Airlines office.

Rafting and Kayaking These sports are permitted on the Indus, Hunza, Gilgit, Swat and Kunhar (Kaghan) rivers, but the sport is in its infancy. The best guide is *Paddling the Frontier — Guide to Pakistan's Whitewater* by Wickliffe W Walker published by the Islamabad travel agent Travel Walji's. Apply to a good travel agent (see listing) for more details.

Cycling Mountain biking is becoming increasingly popular in Northern Pakistan and you can rent mountain bikes in Gilgit (see list page 304). You can take your bike by bus to the top of the Khunjerab Pass (that's at about 4,700 metres, so make sure you are acclimatised first) and cycle back down the black-topped Karakoram Highway (KKH) through Hunza to Gilgit (there are some strenuous uphill sections). Another popular ride is along the dirt road from Gilgit to Chitral across the Shandur Pass.

Hunting Boar is the only officially sanctioned game animal.

Skiing You can ski at Malam Jabba in the Swat Valley, NWFP. Facilities are basic with two short slopes, a chair lift, skating rink and a 50-room hotel run by the PTDC. The resort boasts stunning views over the Swat Valley to the distant Karakoram mountains. See page 216.

Desert safaris Travel agents can arrange camel safaris in the Cholistan Desert.

Jeep safaris This is the most popular way to see most of the Northern Areas, North-West Frontier Province and Balochistan. Walji's, Hindu Kush Trails, Sitara, Indus Guides and Rakaposhi Tours (see list page 275, 284, 285 and 289) are the main specialists, with reliable vehicles. But any Pakistani travel agent can advise you.

Asian Study Group This Islamabad organisation runs excellent trips every week for members only. If you are going to be in Islamabad for some time it is well worthwhile joining. Their address is 80 West Shahrah-e-Quaid-e-Azam, Malik Complex, 1st floor, almost opposite Saudi-Pak tower in the Blue Area, tell 815891. They are open Monday to Friday, 3 to 5 pm, plus Tuesday and Thursday, 11 am to 1 pm. President Mrs Perveen Malik, tel 278027.

Photography

Pakistan and its people are superbly photogenic, but the noonday sun tends to flatten subjects and rob colours of their brilliance. Though few travellers have time to wait for perfect light, they should remember that the best results are achieved before 10 am and after 3 pm in winter, and before 9 am and after 4 pm in summer. Underexposing midday shots by half a stop or more can help as will the use of a polarising, daylight or haze filter, but the colours in the resulting pictures may still be disappointing.

Colour print film is available in many towns, but it is sometimes old and heat damaged, so check the expiry date. Film for colour slides and black and white prints is only available in Karachi, Lahore and Islamabad and is expensive. Enthusiasts should take all the film they need with them and store it in as cool a place as possible, preferably a fridge. For the best results I would also recommend that you take your exposed film home to have it developed.

Customs regulations stipulate that you can only take one camera and five rolls of film into Pakistan. I have never had any problems when carrying two cameras and 20 rolls of film. Professionals with a lot of equipment should obtain a registration document from their home customs so that they do not have to pay duty when they return home, and this is useful to wave at Pakistani customs should questions be asked.

Photographing military installations, airports and bridges is forbidden. People like to be asked before being photographed, at which point men usually assume manly poses and stare straight into the camera. If you take that shot, you might get your candid a few seconds later. Also, a telephoto lens can be useful for spontaneous shots, but remember that a foreigner in Pakistan does nothing in public completely unobserved. Men should not attempt to photograph women, though female photographers usually have no problem at all, especially if there are no men around to disapprove and if a little time is first spent making friends and asking permission.

Women Travellers

Women are respected and cherished in Pakistan. It is a pleasure to walk to the head of a queue, or to be given the last available seat which rarely happens at home. But a woman's life is more restricted in Pakistan than we are used to in the West. A Pakistani woman rarely travels alone. Indeed, many may never even leave their house unless accompanied by a family member, friend or servant. Foreign women are therefore advised not to travel alone in Pakistan, not because it is dangerous, but because it can upset or even offend a good Muslim male to see a woman so immodest as to travel unaccompanied.

Geography

The Indus River forms the axis of Pakistan and, with its tributaries, drains the whole of the country, except for the sparsely populated western province of Balochistan.

The Indus is also one of the four riverine cradles of early civilisation. Like the Nile and the Tigris–Euphrates, it flows across the vast arid zone that spans North Africa and Asia from Morocco to Mongolia. (The Yellow River, in northern China, flows out of this zone to the east.) Almost the entire zone has long since converted to Islam, providing a common culture and identity to the many desert peoples who live here.

Pakistan stretches from the Arabian Sea to the high mountains of Central Asia over a maximum length of 1,800 kilometres (1,120 miles). It covers an area of about 888,000 square kilometres (350,000 square miles), making it nearly four times as large as Great Britain or one-third the size of India. About 9 percent (84,000 square kilometres/33,000 square miles) of this is the Northern Areas and Azad Kashmir, part of the disputed area claimed by India, but administered by Pakistan since 1949.

Pakistan is bordered by Iran on the west, Afghanistan on the northwest, China on the northeast and India on the east. Its southern coastline on the Arabian Sea is nearly 1,000 kilometres (about 600 miles) long.

Politically, Pakistan is divided into four provinces: Sindh, Balochistan, Punjab and North-West Frontier Province (usually abbreviated to NWFP). In addition, there are two other regions, the Northern Areas, which include Gilgit, Hunza, Chilas and Skardu, and Azad (Free) Kashmir and Jammu. These regions are claimed by India on the strength of the maharaja of Kashmir's accession to India in October 1947, but are on the Pakistani side of the line of control. They are administered directly from Islamabad, with the local inhabitants enjoying only limited voting rights.

Geographically, Pakistan comprises three main regions: the mountainous north, where three of the world's great mountain ranges meet (the Hindu Kush, the Karakoram and the Himalaya); the enormous but sparsely populated plateau of Balochistan in the southwest, which covers 43 percent of the country's total area; and the Punjab and Sindh plains of the Indus River and its four main tributaries. Apart from these irrigated plains, Pakistan is largely barren mountains and arid plateaux.

(previous spread) Minarets in silhouette at Badshahi Mosque in Lahore

As vast as Balochistan is, it is not described in this guide because it is off the normal tourist route. Foreign tourists need permits to travel anywhere in the province except the capital, Quetta. For further information on Balochistan see *Pakistan Handbook* by Isobel Shaw.

The Himalaya and Karakoram are the youngest mountain ranges in the world. About the time the dinosaurs became extinct, the northward-drifting Indian Geological plate collided with the Asian plate, its northern edge was forced under the Asian plate and about 55 million years ago began to push up the mountains. The Indian plate is still driving northwards at about five centimetres (two inches) per year, causing the mountains to rise about seven millimetres (1/4 inch) each year. Pakistan has the largest concentration of high mountains in the world, with 121 peaks over 7,000 metres (23,000 feet) within a radius of 180 kilometres (112 miles). It also claims the longest glaciers outside the polar regions.

But it is the Indus River that gives Pakistan life; together with its tributaries it provides water for the largest irrigation system in the world. Many of the canals were dug in the last century, but since Independence many new dams and canals have been built, providing water not only for irrigation but also for generating electricity. The dam at Tarbela in northern Punjab, built in the 1970s, is the largest earth-filled dam in the world, both in terms of the amount of earth used and its electricity-generating capacity.

The Indus River is 3,200 kilometres (2,000 miles) long, making it the third-longest river in Asia after the Yangtzi and Yellow rivers. It rises near Mount Kailash in Tibet, passes through Ladakh in eastern Kashmir and enters Pakistan in the Northern Areas before flowing northwestwards between the Himalaya and Karakoram mountain ranges. It plunges through some of the world's deepest gorges as it twists among the mountains, eventually finding an exit south to the plains of Punjab and Sindh. The river then meanders, becoming as wide as 30 kilometres (20 miles) in places as it splits into numerous channels separated by large islands before it finally oozes into the Arabian Sea through a giant delta 150 kilometres (100 miles) long and 250 kilometres (150 miles) wide stretching east from Karachi to the Indian border. On its journey it deposits millions of tons of silt each year.

The river floods every summer, when the melting of the mountain snows coincides with the monsoon in Punjab. In recent years the flooding has been largely controlled, but in past times the force of the floodwaters frequently caused the Indus to change course in Punjab and Sindh. Many ruined cities in the desert of Sindh were once flourishing riverside commercial centres until the Indus abandoned them.

Climate

Pakistan offers great variety in its climate, from cool mountain pastures beside the glaciers, through windy plateaux, to warm river valleys and burning deserts. Arriving at Karachi, Islamabad or Lahore the first impression is of tree-lined streets and well-watered gardens. But only the central strip of Pakistan, from Lahore to the mountain slopes north of Islamabad, is favoured with refreshing natural rain and moderate temperatures; most of Pakistan's agricultural land is the result of extensive irrigation.

Central Pakistan is blessed by the annual monsoon which blows in across the northern Punjab from India, causing sudden summer downpours from July to September, and dropping 500 millimetres (19.5 inches) of rain a year. The monsoon usually reaches Islamabad about a week after arriving in Delhi. Occasionally, rain comes to this area from the west in winter.

The rest of the country, the north, west and south, are deserts dependent on irrigation from the five great rivers, the Indus, Jhelum, Chenab, Ravi and Sutlej. Over three-quarters of Pakistan receives less than 250 millimetres (9.8 inches) of rain annually and a quarter of that area less than 120 millimetres (4.7 inches) a year.

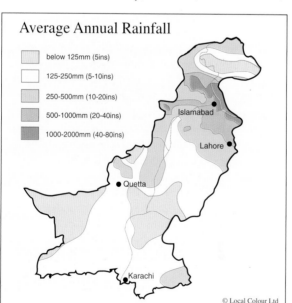

Average Annual Rainfall

below 125mm (5ins)
125-250mm (5-10ins)
250-500mm (10-20ins)
500-1000mm (20-40ins)
1000-2000mm (40-80ins)

Islamabad
Lahore
Quetta
Karachi

© Local Colour Ltd

June and July are the hottest months, with midday temperatures over 40 degrees Celsius (over 100 degrees Fahrenheit) in most places. In upper Sindh and neighbouring Balochistan, the temperature occasionally goes into the 50s° Celsius (over 122° Fahrenheit).

Naturally, it is cooler at higher altitudes, especially in the mountain valleys of Swat and Kaghan, and around Murree where there is rain, but it can get very hot in summer along the dry northern valleys of the Indus and Gilgit rivers, where the heat radiates off the bare mountains. Above 2,000 metres (6,500 feet), temperatures are usually pleasant during the day and cool at night.

December, January and February are the coldest months. At this time, Sindh, southern Punjab and the lower areas of Balochistan are cool, with daytime temperatures of 10–25 degrees Celsius (50–77 degrees Fahrenheit). Islamabad in winter is crisp during the day and cold at night. Above 1,500 metres (5,000 feet), days are cold and nights are very cold.

Population

In 1999 Pakistan's population was estimated at 140 million. the ninth largest in the world and increasing by 3.1 percent a year — one of the highest birth rates in Asia. In 1901 there were only 16.6 million people in what is now Pakistan.

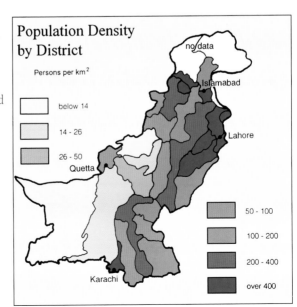

Population Density by District

Persons per km²

below 14

14 - 26

26 - 50

50 - 100

100 - 200

200 - 400

over 400

no data

Islamabad

Lahore

Quetta

Karachi

A third of Pakistan's population live in the big cities, the biggest being Karachi (population about 11 million), Lahore (eight million) Faisalabad and Rawalpindi–Islamabad (three million each) Hyderabad, Multan Gujranwala and Peshawar (two million each), and Sialkot, Sargodha and Quetta (one million each), About three-quarters of all Pakistanis live in the Indus Valley, leaving the desert areas virtually uninhabited.

Fertile Punjab is by far the most populous province with about 80 million inhabitants, followed by Sindh with over 35 million, NWFP claims over 16 million, Balochistan 7 million and over a million live in the Northern Areas.

Though united by Islam there are many ethnic groups speaking over 20 languages, the major ones being Punjabi in Punjab; Sindhi and Seraiki in Sindh; Balochi, Pushtu and Brahui in Balochistan; Pushtu, Hindko, Kashmiri, Khowar, Kohistani, Gujar and Kalashi in the North-West Frontier Province, and Balti, Shina, Burushaski and Wakhi in the Northern Areas. The linguistic picture is further complicated by the multiplicity of tribal dialects that have evolved in isolated valleys.

Of the above, Burushaski belongs to no known language family, and Brahui is an ancient Dravidian tongue, now mainly restricted to South India. Balochi belongs to the Iranian sub-family of Indo–European languages and Balti is ancient Tibetan. Kashmiri, Khowar, Kohistani, Kalashi and Shina are all Indo-European Dardic languages, while Sindhi and Seraiki, Punjabi and Urdu show a much simpler pattern of Indo–Aryan languages.

The *lingua franca* of Pakistan is Urdu, which means 'army' or 'camp', reflecting that the language was formed from a mixture of Hindi, local languages, and the Persian, Arabic and Turkish spoken by invaders from the North. Though Urdu is the mother-tongue of only a fraction of the population, it is the medium of education in schools and the majority understand at least a few words. English is also taught in some schools and the more educated people are reasonably fluent — there is no difficulty in making yourself understood in the larger towns.

Economy

Agriculture

Pakistan's economy is heavily dependent upon agriculture, which accounts for a quarter of the gross domestic product (GDP) and employs over half the population. Most of the agriculture relies on water supplied through some

64,000 kilometres (40,000 miles) of irrigation canals, almost all of which are on the Indus plain. Rising salinity, caused by poor drainage, is a growing problem, affecting about half of all irrigated land. Wheat is the principal food crop, followed by rice, millet, maize, barley and pulses. Cotton is by far the most important cash crop and accounts for five percent of world production. High-quality Basmati rice, grown mainly in Lahore Division, is also a major export. Other major crops include sugar-cane, oil-seeds (mustard, rape, sesame, linseed and castor), tobacco, fodder, fruit (citrus, mangoes, bananas, pomegranates, apples and apricots, among others), and vegetables such as potatoes, onions and chillies.

Industry
Cotton yarn and textile manufacture is Pakistan's most important industry, followed by light engineering (electrical goods, metal working, precision equipment), food processing (vegetable oils, sugar, drinks), cement, pharmaceuticals, leather and rubber. Pakistan has a substantial fertiliser industry, and Russia helped to build an iron and steel works near Karachi. Industry is concentrated around Karachi, Hyderabad and Lahore, and employs 13 percent of the workforce.

Energy
Hydro-electric generation is Pakistan's largest source of energy, mainly at the giant Tarbela and Mangla dams, but demand outstrips supply and lack of power hampers the development of industry in many areas. Balochistan has large reserves of natural gas while oil is found on the Potwar Plateau and in southern Sindh which supplies about one-third of the country's needs. The rest is imported, principally from Kuwait.

Remittances
In the early 1980s about three million Pakistanis worked in the Gulf States, sending home some 2,000 million US dollars annually in remittances. This income was essential to the poorer Pakistani families, most of whom had at least one member working overseas. The drop in oil prices in the mid-eighties drastically reduced this income, but since the 1991 Gulf War when the Pakistanis sent soldiers to protect the holy land of Saudi Arabia, Pakistanis have been given more of the available jobs. Now nearly 1.5 million

workers send home about 1,500 million dollars annually. According to the latest figures the average annual income per person in Pakistan is under US$400, but adjusted to real purchasing power in Pakistan, where the cost of living is low, and taking into account that many people grow their own food, the figure jumps to US$1,900 a year, about US$300 higher than that in India.

Pakistan's tourism industry remains largely undeveloped, in spite of the great potential it holds.

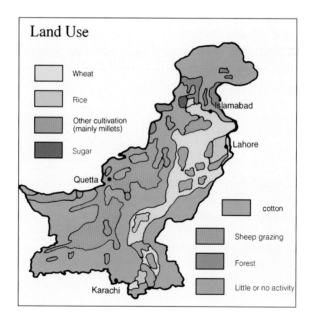

(opposite page) Harvest time at Khaplu in Baltistan

History

The story of Pakistan divides into six distinct periods: prehistory; the ancient empires, from about 3000 BC to the sixth century AD; the coming of Islam, from 711 to the late 14th century; the Mughal period, from 1526 to the 18th century; the British period, from the mid-18th century to 1947; and Pakistan since Partition and Independence.

Prehistory

Ten million years ago, the common ancestors of both men and apes roamed the open woodland south of what is now Islamabad. Our own genus, *Homo*, a meat-eater and user of stone tools, evolved here about two million years ago. Modern man, the species *Homo sapiens*, has been living here for at least 50,000 years, according to the carbon dating of fossils liberally scattered along the banks of the Soan River. About 9,000 years ago, man learned to tame and husband animals and to cultivate crops, and farming villages dating from 6,000 BC have been excavated in Balochistan, North-West Frontier Province and Punjab.

The Ancient Empires

These farm communities were the forerunners of the great **Indus Civilisation,** which developed at roughly the same time as the Mesopotamian and Egyptian empires, around 3000 BC. The Indus Civilisation was a well-organised urban society and developed a (still-undeciphered) pictographic form of writing and united the Indus Valley under a strong central government. The sites of the two major excavations of this civilisation are at Moenjodaro in Sindh and Harappa in Punjab, though there were about 400 sites in all.

In about 1700 BC, **Aryans** swept down from Central Asia in horse-drawn chariots. Though culturally less advanced than the Indus Civilisation, their Vedic religion developed into Hinduism. They raised and venerated cows, spoke an Indo–European language, and composed the Rigveda, the oldest religious text in the world, which describes battles against people living in cities. They also composed the great epic poems, the Ramayana and Mahabharata.

Buddhism evolved in the sixth century BC, at about the same time that **Gandhara**, in northern Pakistan, became the easternmost province of the Achaemenid Empire of Persia, then at its height under Darius the Great. Gandhara was a semi-independent kingdom with capitals at Pushkalavati (now called Charsadda) and Taxila, where, from the fourth century BC, there existed one of the greatest universities of the ancient world.

Alexander the Great conquered the region between 327 and 325 BC, taking Gandhara and visiting Taxila before marching across the Salt Range (south of modern Islamabad) to the Beas River. He then sailed down the Beas to the Indus and continued south to the sea. He finally returned to the West by marching across the Makran Desert in Balochistan.

Alexander's empire was short-lived, and in 321 BC, Chandragupta founded the **Mauryan Empire,** which took in modern Pakistan but had its capital far to the east at Patna, on the Ganges River. His grandson, Ashoka, promoted Buddhism and built Buddhist shrines all over the empire.

History records little of Sindh and Balochistan from the third century BC to the sixth century AD, these provinces being effectively lost at the western

Tomb of Bibi Jawindi in Uch, Punjab

edge of Indian influence and the eastern edge of Persian influence. Northern Pakistan, on the other hand, has a fully documented history. Wave after wave of invaders from Persia, Afghanistan and Central Asia entered through the passes of the North-West Frontier and swept across Punjab towards Delhi.

The **Bactrian Greeks,** descendants of Alexander the Great's soldiers in Bactria (now Balkh, in north-central Afghanistan), arrived in 185 BC, about 50 years after the death of Ashoka. They built new Greek cities at Taxila and Pushkalavati and were followed in 75 BC by the **Scythians** (Sakas), Iranian nomads from Central Asia, and in about AD 20 by the powerful **Parthians,** from east of the Caspian Sea.

The Parthians defeated the Romans in 53 BC by waving silken banners, from which the Roman soliders fled, thinking that such fine, lightweight fabric must be the product of sorcery. The Parthians by then had grown rich as middlemen in the trade that developed along the Silk Road between China and the Roman Empire.

The **Kushans,** from Central Asia, overthrew the Parthians and assumed their position at the centre of the lucrative silk trade. By the second century AD, the Kushans had reached the height of their power, with an empire that extended from eastern Iran to the Chinese frontier and south to the Ganges River. They made their winter capital at Peshawar and their summer capital north of Kabul. Under their most famous king, Kanishka (ruled *c* 128–151), Buddhism prospered and thousands of monasteries and stupas were built in the Peshawar plains and nearby Swat. Gandhara became the Buddhist holy land and a centre of pilgrimage. The Gandharan school of art developed, named after the commercial and spiritual centre of the empire. It combined the artistic traditions of East and West to produce a style so dynamic that it flourished for five centuries.

As the Kushans declined, the northern reaches of their empire were absorbed by the Sassanian Empire of Persia, and the southern areas by the Gupta Empire. In the fourth century, a new dynasty of Kidar (Little) Kushans came to power, with their capital at Peshawar.

In about 455, the **White Huns** (Hephthalites) invaded Gandhara from the northwest and sacked its cities. The White Huns worshipped Shiva and the sun god Surya. Buddhism declined, though it continued in altered form for many centuries and did not finally die out in the Swat Valley until the 16th century. The White Huns were converted to Hinduism and may have become the Rajput warrior class.

The Sassanians and Turks overthrew the Huns in 565, but by late in the sixth century Hindu kings ruled again what is now Pakistan: the **Turki Shahi** rulers of Kapisa in Afghanistan controlled the area west of the Indus, including Gandhara; the raja of Kashmir ruled east of the Indus and in northern Punjab; and numerous small Hindu kingdoms occupied the rest. Brahmanical Hinduism spread at the expense of Buddhism.

In 870, **Hindu Shahis** from Central Asia overthrew the **Turki Shahis** and established their capital at Hund on the Indus. They ruled an area from Jalalabad in Afghanistan to Multan, and extending east to include Kashmir, until 1008.

The Coming of Islam

Islam reached Pakistan from both south and north. In 711, an Arab naval expedition under **Muhammad bin Qasim** arrived to suppress piracy on Arab shipping and ended up establishing control over the Indus Valley as far north as Multan. Most of the local rulers remained in power but now paid tribute to the caliph of Baghdad.

In the 11th century, the Turkish rulers of Afghanistan began the Islamic conquest of India from the northwest. **Mahmud of Ghazni** (979–1030) led a series of raids against the Rajput kingdoms and wealthy Hindu temples. Gandhara, Punjab, Sindh and Balochistan became integral parts of the Ghaznavid Empire, which had its capital at Ghazni in Afghanistan. The Ghaznavids developed Lahore as their centre of Islamic culture in Punjab, and mass conversions to Islam began at this time.

The Ghaznavid kingdom was destroyed near the end of the next century by the Ghorids, the Turkish Muslim rulers of Ghor in Afghanistan. **Muhammad of Ghor** swept down the Indus into India, defeated the Rajput confederacy there in 1192 and captured Delhi the following year. This marked the beginning of the Sultanate Period, which lasted for over 300 years, with five dynasties of Muslim sultans succeeding one another in Delhi. The Mongol, **Genghiz Khan**, harried the Delhi sultans during the 13th century, never succeeding in overthrowing them. **Tamerlane**, the great Turkish conqueror who had his capital at Samarkand, penetrated India soon after in 1398–9 and sacked Delhi.

(following pages) The Court of the Shish Mahal, in Lahore Fort, with Badshahi Mosque and the Tomb of Ranjit Singh in the background

The Mughal Period

In the early 16th century **Babur,** a descendant of Tamerlane and Genghiz Khan, raided Punjab from Afghanistan, finally defeating the last of the Delhi sultans, the Lodis, at the battle of Panipat in 1526. That laid the foundation of the Mughal Empire (the word Mughal derives from Mongol, meaning anyone from Central Asia).

Four years later, Babur was succeeded by his son **Humayun,** who proved to be more an intellectual than a statesman and was ousted by a Pathan, **Sher Shah Suri,** who ruled the empire until his death in 1545. Humayun returned from exile in Persia and regained the throne in 1554, but died two years later after failing down his library stairs.

He was succeeded this time by his son, **Akbar,** the greatest of the Mughal emperors. By the time of his death in 1605, his empire stretched from central India to Kashmir, and included Sindh and Rajasthan. Akbar improved Sher Shah Suri's centralised administrative system and was a great patron of Mughal art and literature.

Mughal art and architecture reached its height under Akbar's son, **Jahangir,** and grandson, **Shah Jahan,** who between them left a legacy of magnificent mosques, palaces, forts and gardens embellished with luxurious and delicate decorations.

Aurangzeb, who ruled from 1658 to 1707, was a pious man and an efficient administrator, but within a few decades of his death the empire disintegrated into several independent principalities and Muslim power declined.

Then, in 1739, **Nadir Shah** of Persia invaded the subcontinent and sacked Delhi, but annexed only the territories west of the Indus. After his death, **Ahmad Shah Durrani** founded the kingdom of Afghanistan and acquired the Indus territories, Punjab and Kashmir.

Early in the 19th century, the martial **Sikhs,** whose religion split from Hinduism in the 16th century, asserted themselves in Punjab and, by the 1830s, had pushed the Afghans back across the Indus and as far northwest as the Khyber Pass. **Ranjit Singh,** their greatest leader, consolidated Sikh power in Punjab and ruled from his capital at Lahore from 1799 to 1839.

The British Period

The British, meanwhile, had arrived in the subcontinent some two centuries earlier, at the beginning of the 17th century. British East India Company traders started as humble petitioners, soliciting concessions — first from local rulers and later from the Mughal emperors — to trade in cotton, wool, opium, indigo, sugar, jute, diamonds and anything else on which they thought they could turn a profit. Slowly, through force, bribery, usury and intrigue, they consolidated their trading privileges.

By the middle of the 18th century, the British (in the guise of the British East India Company) had become deeply enmeshed in the politics of India and, after the battle of Plassey in 1757, began the systematic conquest of the sub-continent. As Mughal power waned, the Sikhs rose to power in Punjab and the north, while the British rapidly extended their influence over the rest of the country. By 1843, Sindh was in British hands, taken because it was a useful corridor to Afghanistan. British territories met those of the Sikhs at the Sutlej River in Punjab. In 1845, the British defeated the Sikhs in the First Anglo–Sikh War and set up a British political resident at Lahore. Four years later, the British won the Second Sikh War and annexed Punjab and the North-West Frontier area.

After the First War of Independence in 1857 (also called the Indian or Sepoy Mutiny), the British government assumed sovereignty over the lands of the British East India Company, bringing half a century of steadily increasing government control to its logical conclusion in the British Raj — raj meaning 'rule'. Queen Victoria's Indian realm continued to expand, until Hunza, the remote kingdom bordering China, fell into British hands in 1891, bringing expansion to an end.

The frontier separating British India from Afghanistan was delineated by the British in 1893. The resulting Durand Line cut straight through the tribal area of the Pathans. (There are now about 13 million Pathans on the Pakistani side of the border and about a third as many in Afghanistan.) The British left the tribal areas to govern themselves under the supervision of British political agents, a system still used by the Pakistani government.

In other ways also, the influence of the British Raj persists in Pakistan: elements of the colonial administration and legal systems, reflecting the traditions of Great Britain survive to this day. The British mapped the country, demarcated its borders and supplied it with impressive networks of roads, railways and canals. Not only the English language, but also British culture, art and architecture are still in evidence. The architecture is concentrated in the separate cantonments the British built for themselves beside most major towns. These cantonments feature wide, tree-lined avenues and imposing public buildings that are a curious mixture of Victorian Gothic and classic Mughal styles.

The Emergence of Pakistan

Following the unsuccessful First War of Independence in 1857, the British resolved to suppress and weaken the Muslims, whom they held primarily responsible for the uprising. Sir Syed Ahmed Khan (1817–98), one of the first to set about restoring Muslim status, founded the Aligarh Movement, later to evolve into the Muslim League. The League was initially part of the Indian National Congress, which had been founded in 1885 to promote political freedom for all communities of the subcontinent. The Muslims broke away, however, because they felt that the Congress neglected their interests.

In 1930, the great Muslim poet and philosopher, Dr Muhammad Iqbal, proposed the creation of a separate Muslim state comprising those areas of the subcontinent with a Muslim majority. His goal was adopted by Muhammad Ali Jinnah, a British-trained lawyer who was to lead the struggle for Pakistan and become its first head of state. When the British realised that they had to relinquish their imperial hold over the subcontinent, they tried to keep the country intact by suggesting that there be autonomous Muslim states under a central government. They failed, however, to devise a plan acceptable to both the Muslim League and the Hindu-dominated Congress. The British finally agreed that the subcontinent should be partitioned into two states upon Independence in 1947.

The division of the subcontinent proved a difficult task. It had to be executed within a limited period of time to coincide with separation from Great Britain. Pakistan was to consist of the Muslim-majority areas of the northeast and northwest, while India would retain the predominantly Hindu central region. The most explosive problem area was the fertile Punjab, where Hindu, Muslim and Sikh populations were inextricably mixed. At Independence, an estimated six million Muslim refugees, mainly from Punjab, streamed across the border into Pakistan, while some four and a half million Sikhs and Hindus went the other way. This migration was accompanied by some of the most grisly communal violence of modern times, resulting in the loss of perhaps half a million lives.

The accession of hundreds of princely states scattered over the subcontinent provided considerable scope for disagreement between India and Pakistan. Though the vast majority were Hindu and readily acceded to India, control of two Hindu-majority states under Muslim rulers was achieved only by sending in the Indian army.

(opposite page) Minar-e-Pakistan in the park near Badshahi Mosque, Lahore

It was in Muslim-majority Kashmir that war broke out. The Hindu maharaja of this beautiful and strategic state had let the Independence Day accession deadline pass without joining either Pakistan or India — an apparent bid for independence or at least a favourable autonomy arrangement. Two months later, the Pakistanis invaded Kashmir, and the maharaja turned to India for help. This led to a military stalemate and the division of Kashmir. Both Pakistan and India still claim the whole of Kashmir, which remains the prime bone of contention between the two countries. The conflict is unlikely to be resolved until India makes good its 45-year-old promise of a plebiscite to determine the wishes of the Kashmiris now living under Indian rule.

The Muslim-majority states that acceded to Pakistan were Khairpur (in Sindh), Bahawalpur (in Punjab), Kalat and Las Bela (in Balochistan), Dir, Swat and Chitral (in North-West Frontier Province) and Gilgit, Hunza, Punial, Ishkoman, Gupis and Yasin (in the Northern Areas).

Another problem of Partition was that the headwaters of all of Pakistan's main rivers lie in India, requiring a bilateral agreement on water rights for irrigation. A solution was not found until 1959, when the World Bank facilitated the drawing up of a treaty.

Pakistan after Independence

Muhammad Ali Jinnah, the Quaid-e-Azam (pronounced kai-day-AAH-zam) or Father of the Nation, became Pakistan's first Governor-General, but he died thirteen months later on 11 September 1948 of tuberculosis. His friend Liaquat Ali Khan became prime minister, but was assassinated three years later, leaving no suitable successor. Both men wanted to keep Pakistan a secular state.

The greatest difficulties facing the new, effectively leaderless, Pakistan were that it consisted of two parts — West and East — separated by nearly 2,000 kilometres (1,250 miles) of hostile Indian territory and that its two divisions were ethnically distinct, with little in common except religion. East Pakistan had the larger population and provided most of the country's export earnings from its jute and tea, while West Pakistan dominated politically and had greater military strength.

The writing of the first constitution took nearly a decade. It was promulgated in March 1956 to declare Pakistan an Islamic Republic with a parliamentary form of government. Almost immediately, in 1958, the constitution was abrogated by the martial law government of General Ayub Khan, who in 1969 was succeeded by General Yahya Khan.

All the while, East Pakistan was becoming increasingly dissatisfied with its position in the power structure. Things came to a head in 1970, when conditions in the East where exacerbated by a disastrous cyclone. In December that year, elections resulted in wins for the Pakistan People's Party (PPP), led by Z A Bhutto, in the West, and Sheikh Mujib's Awami League in the East, which had the overall majority. The dispute over which party would form the government led first to strikes in East Pakistan, then to outright revolt. With a declaration of war by West Pakistan, India supported the creation of a separate Bangladesh in the territory constituting East Pakistan. Bangladesh became independent in January 1972 and was recognised by Pakistan in 1974.

Zulfikar Ali Bhutto remained prime minister of what was left of Pakistan until 1977, pursuing a policy popular with the urban masses and rural poor, especially in Sindh. He nationalised basic industries, banks and insurance, began to democratise the civil service and initiated reform of the health and education systems. He also strengthened ties with China in an attempt to balance the threat from India and started building the Karakoram Highway linking the two countries. Bhutto's downfall came after the general elections in 1977, which opposition parties alleged were rigged in Punjab.

General Zia-ul-Haq took over the administration of Pakistan, and the state charged Bhutto with the murder of the father of a political opponent. His conviction was followed by a retrial and a second conviction. Bhutto was hanged on 4 April 1979.

Under martial law there was steady economic growth favouring the private sector, and some effort was made to Islamise the political, legal and economic structures. Zia's regime was greatly helped by the Soviet invasion of Afghanistan in December 1979, after which the USA donated vast amounts of military equipment and aid to Pakistan to fight the Soviets and help the four million Afghan refugees who crossed into Balochistan and North-West Frontier Province (NWFP).

In February 1985 Zia allowed non-party National Assembly elections and, later that year, legalised political parties and lifted martial law. In May 1988 he dismissed his prime minister, Muhammad Khan Junejo, and called for elections in November, but on 17 August 1988 he was killed in a plane crash in Bahawalpur along with five senior generals and the American Ambassador who joined his party at the last moment. The cause of the crash has never been disclosed.

Benazir Bhutto's campaign poster

Elections were held as scheduled in November, and the Pakistan People's Party was returned to power with Benazir Bhutto (the daughter of Zulfikar Ali Bhutto) as prime minister, but after 20 months, in August 1990, she was accused of corruption and dismissed.

Elections two months later put an Islamic Democratic Alliance in power, with Mian Nawaz Sharif, the powerful Punjab chief minister as prime minister. This government was in turn dismissed for corruption in June 1993, and Benazir Bhutto and the PPP were re-elected to power the following October only to be dismissed for corruption in November 1996. Mian Nawaz Sharif was reelected as Prime Minister in 1997.

Afghan Refugees and Drugs

After the Soviets invaded Afghanistan in December 1979, an estimated four million Afghan refugees fled to Pakistan during the 1980s. Following the Soviet withdrawal from Afghanistan in February 1989, some of the Afghans returned home, but with the continuing civil war in Afghanistan, there are still some two to three million refugees living in Pakistan.

Their impact on Pakistan is enormous: billions of dollars of foreign aid and arms flowed into the country in the 1980s, and thousands of foreign aid workers arrived. The drug problem soared: in the early 1990s there were about two million drug addicts in Pakistan, three out of four of them addicted to heroin; in Karachi alone one out of eleven males between the ages of 15 and 45 is addicted to heroin.

Historical Dates

3000–1500 BC	Indus Civilisation
1700 BC	Aryans invade from Central Asia in horse-drawn chariots
516 BC	Northern Pakistan becomes the easternmost province of the Achaemenid Empire of Persia. Gandhara is a semi-independent kingdom
327–325 BC	Alexander the Great invades Pakistan
272–236 BC	Mauryan Emperor Ashoka promotes Buddhism
185 BC	Bactrian Greeks conquer northwest Pakistan
75 BC	Arrival of Scythians (Sakas) from Central Asia
20 AD	Parthians conquer northern Pakistan
60 AD	Kushans from Central Asia overthrow the Parthians
3rd century	Kushans decline and are dominated by the Sassanian Empire of Persia
4th century	Kidar (Little) Kushans come to power
455	White Huns invade Gandhara and are converted to Hinduism, possibly as the Rajput warrior caste
565	Sassanians and Turks overthrow Huns.
Late 6th–7th century	Turki Shahis control area west of Indus, including Gandhara
711	Muhammad bin Qasim conquers Sindh and southern Punjab
870	Hindu Shahis arrive from Central Asia
1001–26	Mahmud of Ghazni invades. Mass conversions to Islam
1034–1337	Sindh ruled by Sumrahs, a Sindhi tribe
1150	Ghaznavid Kingdom destroyed by Ghorids
13th century	The consolidation of the Muslim Sultanate of north India
1221	The Mongol, Genghiz Khan invades Punjab
1337	Sammah Rajputs overthrow the Sumrahs in Sindh
1398–9	Tamerlane invades from Central Asia
15th century	Decline of the Delhi Sultanate. Founding of the Sikh religion
1524	Babur, first Mughal emperor, raids Punjab
Early 16th century	Sindh conquered by Shah Beg Arghun from Kandahar. Amir Chakar Rind unites Balochi tribes and defeats Sammahs
1526	Babur defeats the Lodis, the last of the Delhi sultans, and establishes the Mughal Empire
1530–56	Humayun, Babur's son, is emperor, but is forced into exile in Persia by Sher Shah Suri
1545	Death of Sher Shah Suri. Tarkhans capture power in Sindh
1556–1605	Akbar, son of Humayun, is emperor
1605–27	Jahangir is emperor
1627–58	Shah Jahan is emperor

1658–1707	Aurangzeb is emperor. Sikhs organise as a warrior sect
1736	Founding of Kalhora Dynasty in Sindh
1739	Nadir Shah of Persia invades the subcontinent
1747–73	Ahmad Shah Durrani founds the Kingdom of Afghanistan and acquires Indus territories, Punjab and Kashmir
1760s–1830s	Sikhs become dominant force in Punjab
1789	Talpur Balochis overthrow Kalhora Dynasty in Sindh
1799–1839	Ranjit Singh rules Punjab from Lahore
1843	British annex Sindh. First British–Afghan War
1845–6	First British–Sikh War
1848–9	The British defeat the Sikhs in Second Sikh War, annex Punjab and NWFP
1857	First War of Independence (Indian or Sepoy Mutiny)
1858	British government assumes direct rule of British East India Company lands, establishes British Raj
1887	All districts of Balochistan in British hands
1889	British establish Gilgit Agency
1891	British conquer Hunza and Nagar
1906	All India Muslim League founded
1930	Muhammad Iqbal proposes creation of separate Muslim state
1947	Independence and Partition
1948	Muhammad Ali Jinnah dies. Indo–Pakistani clash over Kashmir
1949	UN sponsors ceasefire in Kashmir
1958	General Ayub Khan sets up military government
1965	17-day Indo–Pakistan War. UN sponsors ceasefire
1969	General Yahya Khan takes over government
1970–7	Pakistan People's Party government under Z A Bhutto
1972	East Pakistan becomes Bangladesh
1977	General Zia-ul-Haq takes over government
1988	General Zia-ul-Haq killed in plane crash. Benazir Bhutto elected as prime minister
1990	Benazir Bhutto dismissed. Nawaz Sharif elected as prime minister
1993	Nawaz Sharif dismissed. Benazir Bhutto returned as prime minister
1996	Benajir Bhutto's government dismissed
1997	Nawaz Sharif reelected as prime minister
1998	Pakistan explodes nuclear devices

Religion

There is something mystical about the Indus Valley. It gave rise to one of the first great civilisations, and lent its name to India and Hinduism. Mahayana Buddhism also developed here under the Gandharans as did the Sikh religion under Guru Nanak.

Pakistan was created in the Indus Valley specifically to provide the Muslims of India with a state of their own, and there are few countries where religion plays such an important role in the lives of its people. Islam pervades every facet of society. The muezzin's call to worship from the minarets of the mosques; men bowed in prayer in the fields, shops and airports; *qibla* (Urdu for 'the direction of Mecca') marked in every hotel bedroom; the veiled women in the streets — all constant reminders of the devotion and religious fervour of the Pakistanis.

Muslims make up over 98 percent of the population of Pakistan, of which roughly 80 percent are Sunni and 20 percent Shia. About one percent of the population is Christian with slightly more Protestants than Catholics. The Hindus, mostly nomads living in the south, account for less than one percent. In Karachi, Lahore, Rawalpindi and Quetta there are small communities of Buddhists, Parsis (descended from Persian Zoroastrians) and Baha'is (a religious movement founded in 1844, seeking world unity). There is also a tiny group of animist Kalash living in Chitral on the Afghan border.

Islam

Islam — Arabic for 'submission to God' — was founded by the Prophet Muhammad, who was born in the Arabian city of Mecca in AD 570 and died in Medina in 632. As a prophet, Muhammad was convinced that there was but one God and that there should be one community of believers, while as a statesman he possessed an unparalleled ability to unify the Arab nation. As a prophet and a statesman, he is one of the towering figures of history.

The Prophet Muhammad started life as a poor orphan in Mecca, a town on the west coast of Arabia, strategically placed on the international south-north trade route that controlled the trade from both Africa and the Indian Ocean to the Mediterranean. Traders of many religious persuasions passed through the town: monotheistic Jews and Christians from the north and Arab tribal people who followed their own gods and worshipped idols in desert sanctuaries. The most important shrine was the Kabah in Mecca itself which contained 360 pagan idols, worshipped by dozens of separate tribes and clans. The Prophet Muhammad's tribe, the Hashemites, were the traditional guardians of this shrine, which was believed to have been built by Adam himself at the beginning of time. Mecca grew rich as the passing traders made offerings at the shrine.

From the age of 12, the Prophet Muhammad travelled with his uncle on long trading trips where he worked as a camel driver. Gradually he became known as *al Amin* — the Trusted One — for being fair in his dealings and honouring his obligations. He was charismatic, gentle and honest. Tradition relates that on a trip to Syria, the Prophet was recognised by a Christian monk as the non-Jewish person mentioned in Genesis 49 verse 10:

'The sceptre shall not pass from Judah,
nor the mace from between his feet,
   until **he** come to whom it belongs,
to whom the peoples shall render obedience.'
The Jerusalem Bible, 1966

At the age of 25, the Prophet Muhammad was employed by a rich widow, Khadijah, to run her trading business which prospered under his stewardship. The 40-year-old widow Khadijah asked the Prophet to marry her and he became instantly rich. They had one daughter Fatima. The Prophet had about 12 other wives married for tribal and treaty reasons, but his other children all died in infancy.

Beginning in AD 610, when he was 40, the Prophet Muhammad received 114 revelations from God. The first of these came to him as he meditated alone in a cave known as Hira on top of Mount Jabal Nur, a few miles from Mecca. Some later revelations came to him in Medina (Madinah). The first messages were repeated warnings, addressed directly to the pagans, Jews and Christians of Mecca, that they must renounce paganism, accept Allah as the One God of all mankind and live according to his laws. The longer and later Medinan revelations stress Allah's merciful nature more fully, with much practical advice on personal and family matters.

In 613, the Prophet Muhammad began preaching in public, rejecting all other religions and demanding the removal of the idols from the Kabah. As the Kabah was the central shrine of the area, this threatened the trade with desert tribes who worshipped there. Though many followed the Prophet's new preaching, he was unpopular with the shrine guardians and, in 622, he fled to Medina, 400 kilometres (250 miles) to the north, where he converted virtually all the tribal leaders, many of whom were Jews. The flight to Medina is known as the *hijra* or migration. The Muslim calendar is counted from this migration. AH stands for Anno Hijra. The faithful who followed Muhammad into exile were called *muhajirs* or refugees.

The Prophet Muhammad was a brilliant military leader and persuasive politician and in less than ten years managed to unite the desert tribes into a powerful army that marched with the people of Medina against Mecca. The force was so overwhelming the city was taken without resistance. The conquest of Mecca also gave the Prophet conrol of the Kabah where he smashed the idols and resumed his preaching to pagan pilgrims as they visited the shrine telling them of the one true God in whose eyes all mankind is equal.

After the Prophet's death, the 114 revelations were assembled into a book, the Quran (or Koran), not in the order in which they were received, but according to their length, the longest first. Besides the Quran there is another primary source of Islam known as the *Sunna*, the Way of the Prophet, which consists of the Prophet's reported actions and sayings. These have been collected into what is known as the Hadith Literature (the Muslim equivalent of the Christian gospels).

The Quran and Sunna lay down the whole philosophy of Islam and its moral code. As the exact word of God as revealed through the Prophet Muhammad, the Quran is infallible; it is the supreme authority to which a Muslim looks for guidance. The Quran and Sunna describe a complete way of life: rules are laid down for washing and eating, for waging war and conducting politics, for buying and selling, marriage and divorce, inheritance, banking, how to calculate taxes and excise. Islam does not distinguish between the divine and the secular; the rules for religion, politics and ordinary daily life are combined. These rules constitute the Sharia, the path — the Islamic law. To break the Sharia is to offend God as well as society. The Sharia is not so much law in the Western sense, rather it offers divine guidelines for everyday living.

Muslims believe that all the basic teachings of Islam were first revealed at Creation, and that prophets have been sent from time to time to reconvey God's word. These divinely inspired prophets (124,000 in all) are the same ones found in Jewish and Christian religious texts such as Abraham, Moses, Isaiah and David. Jesus too is revered as a great prophet, though not regarded, as he is by Christians, as divine in himself. (Muslims view as polytheism the Christian belief in the Trinity: Father, Son and Holy Spirit — three manifestations of the one God.) Muslims call those who follow the prophets — that is to say, Jews and Christians as well as Muslims — *ahl-e-kitab*, or 'people of revealed books'.

Islam teaches that, despite the words of the early prophets, man has continually erred and the prophecy has become obscured and overladen with false interpretations. The Prophet Muhammad was sent to restore purity and bring to mankind the true word of God. He was the last of all the prophets. He brought up to date the message of all who preceded him, to be followed only by the Messiah himself.

Each Muslim or adherent of Islam, has five fundamental religious duties, called the Pillars of Islam. He must recite the creed, 'La illaha ill' allah Muhammad Rasul allah' ('There is no deity but Allah, and Muhammad is his messenger'). He must also pray five times a day, fast during the month of Ramazan and give alms (zakat) for distribution among the poor. Finally, when all other worldly obligations are fulfilled, he must, if possible, make a pilgrimage to Mecca.

Islam suffered a major split almost from its beginning. The Prophet Muhammad died without clearly designating a successor, and there followed a struggle for power, with the result that most of the early leaders of Islam suffered violent deaths. Two main sects of Islam emerged: the larger sect, the Sunnis, followed elected leaders called caliphs (khalifa is Arabic for 'successor'); the smaller sect, the Shias (or Shi'ites), followed a line of hereditary leaders called Imams, who were descended directly from the Prophet Muhammad through Fatima, his daughter, and Ali, his son-in-law and cousin. This line, in the major Shia sect, ran to 12 generations of Imams who were regarded as infallible interpreters of God's word. The last Imam went into hiding in about 870 and is known as the 'Hidden Imam'. One day he will return to earth as the Mahdi or Messiah, when he will herald in a new perfect state where there is no injustice or oppression.

The Ismailis, the followers of the Aga Khan, who are very active in Pakistan, are an offshoot of the Shias. In 765 they chose to follow Ismail as their 7th Imam. Traditional Shias believed Ismail to have died and followed his younger brother. The present Aga Khan, Karim, is the 49th Imam, directly descended from the Prophet through Ismail.

Today, most Pakistanis are orthodox Sunnis; most of the rest are Shias, with a smaller number of Ismailis. There are also a few Ahmadis (or Ahmediyas), adherents of a new sect which is branded as heretical by other Muslims. The Ahmadis are also called Qadianis, after the Punjabi town of Qadian where the sect was founded in 1908.

Despite the problems of succession, the Islamic empire expanded rapidly and, within a century, stretched from Spain to India. Islam arrived in Pakistan 80 years after the Prophet Muhammad's death with the Arab conquest of Sindh in AD 711. (The ruins of a mosque dating from 726 have been found at Banbhore, near Karachi.) Holy men subsequently travelling to the subcontinent were able to convert many to Islam, as the new religion offered greater hope of salvation than Hinduism, with its fatalistic cycle of reincarnation and its rigid caste structure. In the 11th century, Mahmud of Ghazni brought Islam into the north from Afghanistan, and Islam became the dominant religious force in all the areas of modern Pakistan.

Today, Islamic principles guide the development of Pakistani society, from the government's introduction of interest-free banking and the systematic collection of *zakat* (the welfare tax prescribed by Islam) to the ban against the purchase of alcohol except by permit-holding non-Muslims.

Sufism

Sufism is Islam's mystical tradition, and Sufis are Muslim holy men who develop their spirituality through prayer and meditation. Sufi comes from the Arabic *safa*, meaning 'purity', so Sufis are those whose hearts and souls are pure.

The first Sufis were ascetic wanderers in the ninth century who, through fasting, meditation and self-denial, found nearness to God. They wandered around the Islamic world, through Persia and Afghanistan and into the sub-continent, preaching a message of love, peace and brotherhood, and teaching by pious example. Many were scholars, poets and musicians able to attract large followings to their gentle form of Islam. Some of Pakistan's finest music and literature were written by Sufi saints: verses set to music that extol the love of God, and morality stories in which virtue receives its reward. The saints portrayed life at its most perfect, embodying the noblest moral teachings of Islam.

The places where Sufi saints settled and died have become important centres of pilgrimage, attracting devoted followers who admire their piety and hope for their intercession to secure God's grant of health, fertility, peace or success. In this way, the saints have given hope to the poor and sick for over a thousand years.

The greatest saints in Pakistan, each with hundreds of thousands of devotees, are Lal Shahbaz Qalandar, whose shrine is in Sehwan Sharif, Data Ganj Baksh of Lahore, Baba Farid Ganj-e-Shakar of Pakpatan, Shah Latif of Bhit Shah near Hala in Sindh, Pir Baba of Buner near Swat, Bari Imam of Nurpur near Islamabad and Shah Shams Tabrez of Multan. All over the country, hundreds of other shrines draw pilgrims who come to pray and make offerings.

Foreign visitors are always welcome at Sufi shrines, provided they remove their shoes, cover their heads and otherwise show respect. The shrines are centres of religious, cultural and social interest. Rich and poor alike come to pray. The most interesting time to go is on Thursday evening, when the shrines are crowded and there is often devotional singing and dancing. Some Sufi followers use music, dancing and incense to reach a trance-like state of communion with God.

Every shrine has a festival (*urs*) each year on the anniversary of its saint's death. The shrine then becomes a fairground, with musicians playing traditional instruments and singers performing mystical folk songs, while dervishes and mendicants dance themselves into a devotional frenzy. Trade fairs also take place, as do sports competitions and, at the larger festivals, exhibition matches of such traditional martial arts as wrestling, swordsmanship, riding, fighting with daggers, and tent-pegging (in which horsemen riding at full gallop pluck wooden pegs from the ground with lances, which derives from attacks on enemy encampments).

Hinduism

Pakistan has played an important role in the historical development of Buddhism and Hinduism, the latter taking its very name from the Indus River, along the banks of which it evolved sometime after the Aryan invasion in 1700 BC. About four million Hindus left Pakistan at Partition in 1947, and fewer than 1.5 million remain in the country today.

Buddhism

Buddhism developed in the Ganges Valley and spread to the Indus Valley in the third century BC, about 230 years after the death of the Buddha. From the second to the fifth century AD Gandhara, in northern Pakistan, was Buddhism's most important northern centre. Here Mahayana Buddhism developed and, in the Swat Valley, tantric Buddhism evolved. Padmasambhava, the great tantric master and sorcerer, was born in Swat in the eighth century. Trisong Detsen, the king of Tibet from 755 to 795, invited Padmasambhava to Tibet where he used his magic to overthrow the old Bon priests and founded the Nyingma order (recognisable by their red hats). From Tibet, Mahayana Buddhism spread to Mongolia, China, Korea and Japan.

Only a few Buddhists remain in Pakistan today, but the museums are full of Buddhist art dating from the first to the seventh century. These works, mostly statues of the Buddha and scenes from his life carved in stone or modelled in plaster, were excavated from archaeological sites all over the country.

Siddhartha Gautama, the Buddha, was born in Nepal in 624 BC. The son of a wealthy prince, he led a sheltered existence until the age of 29 when, at his first sight of human suffering, he resolved to renounce all worldly pleasures. He left his wife and young son and surrendered himself to the search for peace. He tried fasting and penance without success, finally receiving enlightenment through meditation. He then devoted the rest of his life to teaching the way of righteousness and truth. He died at the age of 80 in 544 BC in Gorakhpur, an Indian town just across the border from his Nepalese birthplace.

Buddhists do not believe in a supreme god, but look instead to the Buddha, the teacher of truth, to guide them along the Middle Path, between worldliness and asceticism, to perfection and a higher life. Buddhists endeavour to avoid suffering by suppressing their sensual passions, depending on themselves and their own efforts to purify their lives through charity, compassion, truthfulness, chastity, respect and self-restraint. The final goal is nirvana, a state of mind beyond human existence, beyond sin and care.

When the Buddha died he was cremated and his ashes divided up and buried under stupas at various places across northern India. Several of the stupas in Pakistan are thought to have once contained his ashes.

Though the Buddha did not visit Pakistan during his final incarnation, he is believed to have been there in some of his earlier lives. The legends of these former lives are told in the Jataka stories, and Buddhist shrines, several of which are near Peshawar, were built at the places described in them.

Sikhism

The founder of the Sikh religion, Guru Nanak (1469–1538), was born near Lahore. Taking some elements of Hinduism and Islam, and combining them with new ideas, he preached a monotheistic religion with no caste system. The religion evolved over two centuries and, through confrontation with the Mughals, became a strong military brotherhood. The Sikhs achieved the height of their power under Ranjit Singh at the beginning of the 19th century, when they controlled an empire centred on Punjab, with Lahore as their temporal capital and nearby Amritsar (in India) as their religious capital.

At Partition, the Sikhs migrated *en masse* to India, where they are now agitating for a separate Sikh state in the Indian part of Punjab. Their shrines in Pakistan are maintained by the government and are visited at festival times by Sikh pilgrims.

(Following spread) Enjoying the cool of the Talpur Mausoleum in Hyderabad, Sindh

Sindh

The southern province of Sindh takes its name from
Sindhu, an old Sanskrit name for the Indus River
which flows down its centre making fertile an
otherwise arid, barren land. The province has three
distinct landscapes: the lush, irrigated plains along
the river, the sparsely populated deserts on either
side of the irrigated belt, and the mangrove swamps
of the Indus delta. It is flat except at its western edge, where the Kirthar Hills
form its border with Balochistan. The climate is pleasant in winter, with
temperatures ranging from 10° to 30°C (50° to 85°F), and hot in summer,
when the mercury moves between 25° and 50°C (75° and 120°F).

The irrigated alluvial soil forms some of Pakistan's best farmland. As far
as canals can carry water from the Indus, farmers grow wheat, rice, millet,
pulses, oil-seeds, cotton, sugar-cane, chillies and such fruits as bananas,
mangoes, dates and varieties of citrus. Most of the 70 percent of Sindh's rural
population that live by agriculture are tenant farmers tilling soil belonging to
feudal landlords of Balochi descent. Their mediaeval way of life has changed
little over the centuries, despite some mechanisation. The tenants dare not
vote against their landlords in elections and little gets done without the
consent of the strong landowning families such as the Bhuttos.

The deserts begin immediately the irrigation ends, the line between green
fields and sandy scrubland strikingly abrupt. Desert tribes, some settled around
wells, some nomadic, eke out a bare subsistence by breeding camels and goats,
growing pulses and millet, and hiring themselves out as migrant labourers.

The Indus delta is a vast marshy tract stretching southeast from Karachi
to the Indian border some 250 kilometres (150 miles) away. Through its
myriad sluggish channels meandering around thousands of mangrove
islands, the Indus empties into the Arabian Sea. Each year, the river
deposits millions of tons of silt in the coastal waters, extending the delta
and enriching the marine food chain. Fishing is the principal occupation
on the coast, providing Karachi's restaurants with the seafood for which
they are justly famous.

The history of Sindh goes back some 5,000 years to the Indus
Civilisation, which was contemporaneous with the better-known civilisations
of Mesopotamia and Egypt. Archaeologists have identified some 400 Indus
Civilisation cities, scattered from Kabul to Delhi. The most famous of these,

the capital Moenjodaro, on the right bank of the Indus in Sindh, was one of the great cities of the ancient world. It had a remarkably advanced urban organisation and archaeologists believe that the whole empire was controlled and administered from here.

Alexander the Great arrived in Sindh in 326 BC and captured the main towns along the river. In the third and second centuries BC, Sindh was part of the great Mauryan Empire of India and embraced Buddhism. Between the sixth and eighth centuries AD Buddhism was gradually supplanted by Hinduism, and a caste system was introduced.

In AD 711 , an Arab expedition under the 17-year-old Muhammad bin Qasim conquered Sindh, which marked the beginning of the Islamic era in the subcontinent. The province was governed until 874 by the Abbassid Caliphate, the leaders of the Sunni Muslims who ruled from Baghdad and whose court is so vividly described in *The Thousand and One Nights*.

From the ninth to the 19th centuries, seven different dynasties ruled in Sindh: the Sumras, Sammahs, Arghuns, Tarkhan, Mughals, Kalhoras and the Talpurs succeeded one another. The capital city moved whenever the summer flooding of the Indus carried the river away into a new channel, causing old cities to be abandoned and new ones to be built. Mansura, Thatta, Alor, Sehwan, Khudabad and Hyderabad were each at one time or another the seat of government — each at one time or another situated on thr banks of the river.

In 1843 the British defeated the Talpurs at the battle of Miani and ruled the territory until Independence in 1947. It was under the British that Karachi grew from a small fishing village to a large industrial city.

The cultural life of Sindh revolves around the shrines of the Sufi saints (see pages 82 and 151), where religious music and devotional singing constitute a major part of the traditional ceremonies. The Sufi saints are also responsible for the best of Sindhi literature, having written poetry and narratives of great beauty and intensity that are recited and sung all over Pakistan. Sufi shrines are everywhere, and the people who come to them do so in the faith that the saints will intercede with God for the granting of some favour — be it health, fertility or success in some endeavour.

Religion is intensely important to Sindhis, who mark out prayer areas beside their homes and along the roads. These areas are about two metres square and surrounded by stones, with the *mehrab* or prayer niche oriented towards Mecca. Anyone can stop, remove their shoes and pray. (Tourists should be careful not to inadvertently step into one of these areas while wearing their shoes.)

The Sindhi language, which has its own script based on the Arabic alphabet with additional letters, is only one of several spoken in the province. Some of the other languages are Thari spoken in the Thar Desert, Kutchi in the Rann (Marsh) of Kutch, Lari in Lower Sindh, and Seraiki in Upper Sindh. Karachi, the capital, is not representative of the rest of the province, as most of the inhabitants are the Urdu-speaking descendants of the Mohajirs (immigrants) who came from India at Partition in 1947.

Sindh is celebrated for its handicrafts, particularly its textiles, pottery and lacquered woodwork. Patchwork quilts and fabrics with woven stripes or block-printed designs are available in bazaars all over the province. Blue-glazed tiles from Sindh decorate most shrines and mosques in Pakistan, and the town of Hala has developed into a centre for the woodwork industry.

The Sindhis are the most colourfully and variously dressed people in Pakistan, with men in the centre of the province favouring turbans in shocking pink. Others wear embroidered caps set aglitter by tiny mirrors, colourful long-tailed shirts worn over *lungis* (men's sarongs), and traditional embroidered slippers with long, pointed, upturned toes. Women of the desert dress in red skirts cut long and flowing, and in bright, tie-dyed shawls.

Industry, both rural cottage industries and large-scale factories, is now developing rapidly in Sindh. For some 4,000 years cotton and textiles have been Sindh's major export (cloth in ancient Greek was *sindonion*, and in Latin *sindon*), and textiles and carpets are still the province's most important industries. More recently sugar, oil, flour and rice mills have been joined by factories producing steel, fertilisers, cement, electrical goods, pharmaceuticals and rubber.

Since the early 1990s there has been a security problem in Sindh. Groups of bandits (dacoits) sometimes controlled by the feudal landlords, hold up buses and trains, and highjack cars. Tourists are asked not to drive out of Karachi without an armed escort. The Pakistan Tourism Development Corporation (PTDC) or a good tour agent such as Walji, Rakaposhi, Zeb or Sitara (see listing page 266) can arrange this for you. Frequent bus tours go to all the sites along the National Highway to Thatta and there are daily air tours to Moenjodaro. Speak to your consulate or to PTDC for the latest security news.

(facing page) Clockwise from upper left: Afridi chieftain in the Khyber Pass; Kalash girl; bagpiper of the Khyber Rifles; merchant of Islamkot in the Thar Desert in Sindh; young Balochi girls.

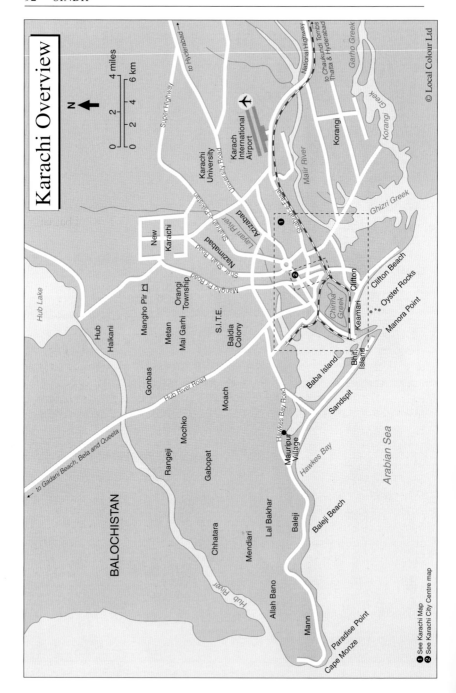

Karachi Overview

N

0   2   4 miles
0   2   4   6 km

to Hyderabad

to Chaukundi Tombs
Thatta & Hyderabad

© Local Colour Ltd

Super Highway

National Highway

Garho Creek

Korangi Creek

Korangi

Malir River

Karachi
University

Karachi
International
Airport

University Road

Shahrah-e-Faisal

Ghizri Creek

New
Karachi

Azizabad

Lyari River

Nazimabad

Sher Shah Road

Clifton

Clifton Beach

Oyster Rocks

Manora Point

Keamari

Mangho Pir

Orangi
Township

Metan

Mai Garhi

S.I.T.E.

Baldia
Colony

China Creek

Bhit
Island

Hub Lake

Hub
Halkani

Gonbas

Hub River Road

Moach

Baba Island

Sandspit

Mochko

Rangeji

Gabopat

Hawkes Bay Road

Mauripur
Village

Hawkes Bay

Arabian Sea

to Gadani Beach, Bela and Queeta

BALOCHISTAN

Chhatara

Mendiari

Lal Bakhar

Baleji

Baleji Beach

Allah Bano

Mann

Hub River

Paradise Point

Cape Monze

❶ See Karachi Map
❷ See Karachi City Centre map

❶

❷

Karachi

With a population of eleven million, Karachi is by far the largest city in Pakistan. A century ago, however, it was a small, isolated collection of fishermen's huts clustered on the three islands of Manora, Bhit and Baba in what is now Karachi harbour. The British built Karachi up and made it the capital of Sindh and, since the creation of Pakistan in 1947, the city has grown into an international port and the commercial and industrial hub of the country. It boasts an unusual mixture of modern skyscrapers and solid, 19th century Victorian Gothic buildings, tree-lined boulevards and narrow, dusty alleys. Because it is a comparatively new city, it has no Mughal mosques or tombs. Its principal attractions are, instead, its colourful bazaars, its modern monuments and the sea.

Getting to Karachi

Karachi has an international airport and a harbour, and is connected to the rest of the country by rail and two major roads, the National Highway and the Super Highway. Most visitors arrive at the new international terminal which is efficient, with banks that are always open to change travellers' cheques and foreign currency. Fixed-price porters are on hand and transport to town readily available. It is easier to pre-pay your taxi fare at the counter inside the terminal, saving you from being mobbed outside (or at least find out how much the pre-paid fare is so you know what to bargain for in the free-for-all outside). The terminal is ten kilometres (6 miles) from the Saddar Bazaar (the city centre), a journey costing Rs120–180 by taxi.

Because of security problems, Karachi is sometimes under curfew. Check with your embassy for the latest security information.

When to Go

Karachi is best during the winter months from mid-November to mid-February, when the daytime temperature is 15°–20°C (60°–70°F). In summer the temperature hovers at 35°–45°C (100°–115°F). The city is very humid, though little rain falls during the monsoon season in July and August.

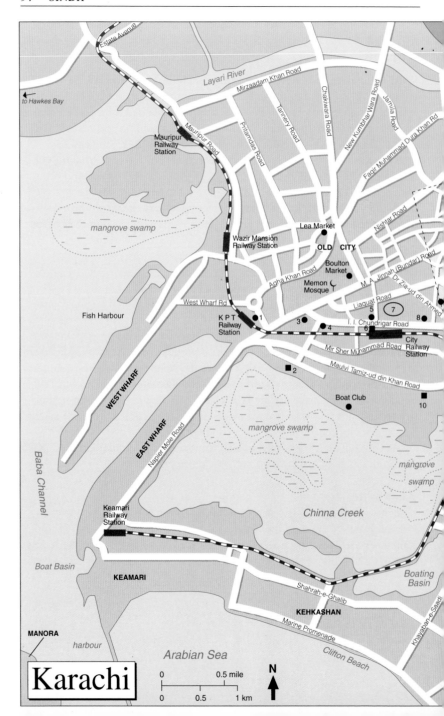

to Hawkes Bay

Layari River

Mirzaadam Khan Road

Estate Avenue

Mauripur Railway Station

Mauripur Road

Pritamdas Road

Tannery Road

Chakiwara Road

New Kumbhar Wara Road

Faqir Muhammad Dura Khan Rd

Jamila Road

Nishtar Road

mangrove swamp

Wazir Mansion Railway Station

Lea Market

OLD   CITY

Boulton Market

Agha Khan Road

Memon Mosque

M. A. Jinnah (Bundar) Road

Dr Zia-ud din Ahmed

West Wharf Rd

Liaquat Road

5

7

Fish Harbour

K P T Railway Station

1

3

4

6

I. I. Chundrigar Road

8

City Railway Station

Mir Sher Muhammad Road

Maulvi Tamiz-ud din Khan Road

2

WEST WHARF

EAST WHARF

Napier Mole Road

Boat Club

10

mangrove swamp

mangrove swamp

Baba Channel

Chinna Creek

Keamari Railway Station

Boat Basin

KEAMARI

Shahrah-e-Ghalib

Boating Basin

KEHKASHAN

Marine Promenade

Khayaban-e-Saadi

Clifton Beach

MANORA

harbour

Arabian Sea

Karachi

0   0.5 mile

0   0.5   1 km

N

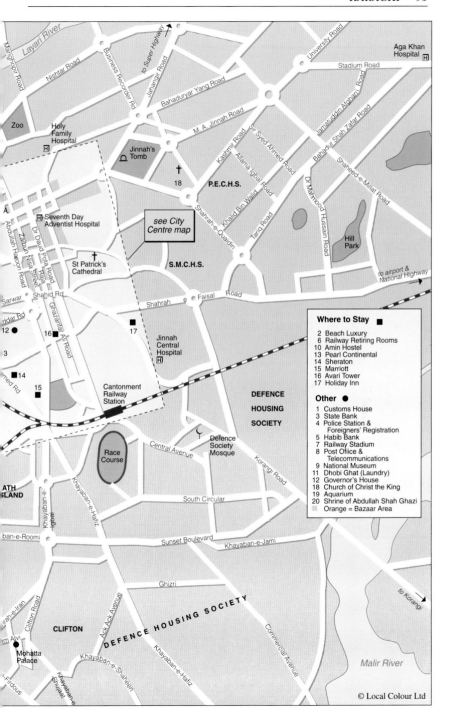

Where to Stay ■

2 Beach Luxury
6 Railway Retiring Rooms
10 Amin Hostel
13 Pearl Continental
14 Sheraton
15 Marriott
16 Avari Tower
17 Holiday Inn

Other ●

1 Customs House
3 State Bank
4 Police Station &
  Foreigners' Registration
5 Habib Bank
7 Railway Stadium
8 Post Office &
  Telecommunications
9 National Museum
11 Dhobi Ghat (Laundry)
12 Governor's House
18 Church of Christ the King
19 Aquarium
20 Shrine of Abdullah Shah Ghazi
■ Orange = Bazaar Area

© Local Colour Ltd

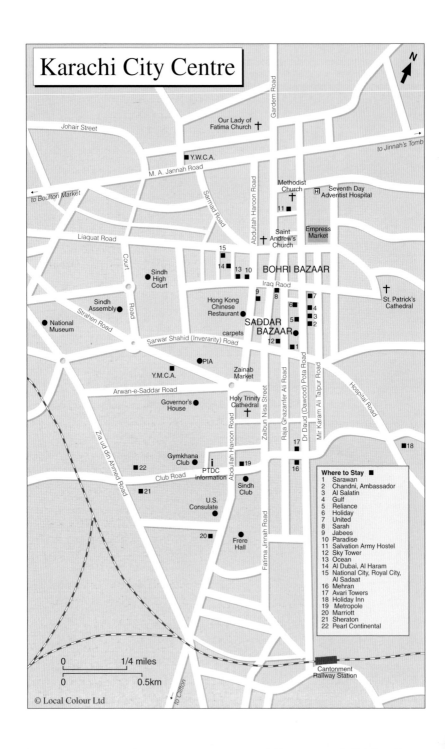

Sights

The Bazaars

One safe attraction not to be missed, even by those with only a few hours in Karachi, is the sprawling bazaar in the **old city** north of M A Jinnah (Bundar) Road, behind Boulton Market. Hindu women wearing bright, full skirts over baggy trousers, and tribal Balochi men in huge, colourful turbans jostle with camel and donkey carts in the narrow streets. Closer to the market's heart, the alleyways become too narrow for carts and are crammed instead with tiny box-like shops where each lane specialises in a different commodity.

To get there, ask the driver to drop you in **Sarafa (jewellery) Bazaar,** where exquisite old tribal silver jewellery is sold by weight.

Enter a narrow lane opposite a shop called Bombay Jewellery Mart to get to the heart of the bazaar. At the end of Sarafa Bazaar, you come to **Bartan Gali,** where pots and pans of copper, aluminium and steel in all sizes stand stacked against the walls. They, too, are sold by weight. Tinsmiths sit on the ground in front of their stalls coating the copper pots with tin, as the copper is poisonous and must be coated before it can be used for cooking.

Next comes the wholesale cloth bazaar, the most colourful of all. Gold and red, turquoise and blue, the lengths of cloth festoon the alleys. This is the best place to buy traditional Sindhi fabrics: *sussi,* a striped hand-loom; *ajrak,* with block-printed geometric designs; and *bandini,* which is tie-dyed.

There follows a wider area, the **Khajoor (date) Bazaar,** where tarpaulin awnings flap in the wind over piles of dried fruit. Hawkers wander up and down offering everything from embroidered Sindhi hats and coloured pyjama cords to strips of walnut bark for cleaning the teeth.

Further east, **Saddar Bazaar,** modern Karachi's central shopping area, stretches for about a kilometre (half a mile) from north to south between the two main streets, Abdullah Haroon (Victoria) Road and Zaibunnisa (Elphinstone) Street.

Saddar (pronounced 'suther') is divided into several distinct markets. First on the right, as you go north along Abdullah Haroon Road is **Zainab Market,** with dozens of little shops selling new copper- and brass-ware, onyx, inlaid wood, lacquer-work, hand-printed cloth and appliqué bed-spreads or *rillis.* Look for the shops with excellent old embroidered Sindhi cloth, traditional wedding dresses with mirror embroidery work and old tribal silver jewellery. (Village Handicrafts and Crown Handicrafts are recommended.) Also available at Zainab Market are very good and extremely cheap cotton shirts, ready-made *shalwar-kameez* (women's national costume), Western clothes, export rejects and tee-shirts that proclaim, 'I caught crabs in Karachi'.

A little further up Abdullah Haroon Road are carpet shops selling new Pakistani carpets and old tribal rugs from Balochistan, Afghanistan and Iran.

Bohri Bazaar, down the side lanes north of the carpet shops, is another cloth bazaar offering a wide selection of fabrics. It is usually full of women dressed in traditional purdah shopping elbow to elbow with thoroughly modern Karachi ladies.

Empress Market, further north and dating from 1889, is a huge Victorian Gothic structure crowned by a clock tower 50 metres (165 feet) high. Inside are hundreds of stalls selling fruit, vegetables, meat, fish and other groceries. Housewives hire assistants to haggle for the best produce (for a small commission) and carry their shopping bags. A stall behind the market sells hookahs of every shape and size.

For more shopping ideas see the shopping section page 262.

The Harbour

The most romantic way to spend an evening in Karachi is to go crabbing in Karachi's harbour in a traditional lateen-sailed craft, an activity that begins at sunset and ends with a crab feast under the stars.

To hire your boat go to **Keamari Harbour,** a 15-minute ride by minibus or taxi from central Karachi. At the end of the wharf, dozens of boatmen clamour for your attention. A private boat seats about ten people – bargain hard. Aim to set sail about an hour before sunset and plan to stay out three to four hours. Before you leave, check that your boatman has on board potatoes, onions, seasonings and — well — crabs, in case your luck is bad. Bring your own drinks.

The wharf business settled, a boy shins up the mast to unfurl the sail and the boat slides out into the harbour. The captain finds a spot to drop anchor, and passengers receive handlines and bits of fish to use as bait. Meanwhile, the crew fry up the potatoes and onions and heat a pot of water. The crabs can then be either boiled or fried with spices.

As the sun sets, dangling V-formations of cormorants wing westward to their roosts and flamingos fly close to the shoreline.

If there is a moon to light your way, a romantic sail further up the harbour takes you to **Sandspit,** the nine-kilometre-long (six-mile) sandbank that divides the sheltered harbour from the open sea. Wade ashore and walk about 100 metres over the spit to the seaward side, where from July to November giant sea turtles lumber ashore to lay their eggs in the sand. To find them, look along the shoreline for their tracks, which resemble tractor tracks about a metre and a half (five feet) wide. Follow these up the beach. The turtle is extremely sensitive while she is digging her nest, but once she starts laying her eggs, you may approach nearer. However, keep very quiet and do not use a flashlight or take flash photos or she will return to the sea without completing her laying and will die. The turtles, both *Chelonia mydas* and *Lipidochelys olivacea* are endangered species.

In season, 2,000 to 3,000 turtles lay on all the sandy beaches from the mouth of the harbour west to Cape Monze. The Sindh Wildlife Management Board arranges guided tours of the turtle projects at Sandspit and Hawkes Bay (see Karachi listing on page 263).

Daytime visitors to Keamari Harbour can chug around in public launches that cast off when they are full. The crossing to Manora Point or to the islands of Bhit or Baba takes about ten minutes from Keamari. Photography is forbidden in the harbour area.

Manora Point, once an island and the site of the original fishing village of Karachi, is now joined by Sandspit to the modern city. Manora is less than an hour by car from central Karachi, but going by boat is easier and more fun. Once there, travel is by public Suzuki or on foot. The beach is neither clean nor safe enough for swimming. Kilometres of sand beg to be walked across, and there are even camel rides. Manora also has a large naval base, a lighthouse, two British Raj-era churches and a ruined Hindu temple.

The harbour islands of **Bhit** and **Baba** are still inhabited by descendants of Karachi's original fishing population. They are members of the dark-skinned Mohana tribe (related to the fishermen on Manchar Lake and at Sukkur), and are very friendly.

Other daytime options at Keamari include bird-watching in the swampy creeks between Karachi and the mouths of the Indus and deep-sea fishing.

The **fish harbour** is at the end of West Wharf Road, where hundreds of fishing boats with coloured sails or outboard motors bring their daily catch. The wharf is always bustling with men unloading fish or loading ice, and with children sluicing down boats and sitting in circles peeling shrimps. Further upstream, boat builders work *shisham* wood with bow drills and hand adzes and saws. No metal is used in the boats; hull planks are pegged to the ribs with wooden dowels.

Oriental Carpets

by Kent Obee

Pakistan is an excellent place to shop for oriental carpets from neighbouring countries or from Pakistan itself, which is now ranked among the top four producers of hand-knotted carpets in the world.

The carpet industry developed in Pakistan only after Partition, so Pakistani carpets are all 'new' and mostly copies of Persian and Turkoman designs. At their best, however, they are as well made as the Iranian or Afghan originals — only less expensive. They are a sensible choice for the buyer wishing to avoid the uncertainties of older rugs or interested in coordinating the carpet with a particular colour scheme.

Pakistan is also an entrepôt for carpets from Afghanistan, Iran and Chinese Turkestan (Xinjiang). Afghan carpets are the most readily available, and doubly so in recent years as a result of the upheaval in that country. Most Afghan carpets are 'tribal' pieces made by either Turkoman or Baloch weavers — though many of the newer carpets are actually made in refugee camps in Pakistan. Smuggled Iranian carpets are available in smaller numbers in the major cities at prices as high or higher than the same carpets would fetch in Europe or America. Tribal carpets from Chinese Turkestan have become increasingly available on the market since the opening of the Karakoram Highway.

Any one of Pakistan's major cities — Karachi, Islamabad, Peshawar, Lahore or Quetta — is a good place to shop for carpets. Lahore is the manufacturing and wholesaling centre of the indigenous carpet industry. Peshawar and Quetta are entry points for goods coming from Afghanistan and Iran, but the better pieces soon make their way to the markets of Islamabad and Karachi, drawn by the more numerous foreign buyers and the resulting higher prices.

Caveat emptor is the golden rule of carpet buying in Pakistan. Although many dealers are well informed and genuinely interested in sharing their enthusiasm for their wares, others are neither particularly knowledgeable nor above duping a gullible tourist with a story that a chemically washed product from a refugee camp is a hundred-year-old Bokhara. Shops in the major tourist hotels can be especially bad in this respect. The collector's knowledge (or that of a friend) of carpets and the current market is the best guarantee of making a worthwhile purchase.

The prospective buyer should be prepared to bargain — and bargain, hard. The amount dealers come down varies greatly from shop to shop; it can be as little as five or ten percent, or it might be 50 percent. Many residents of Islamabad, when shopping at the popular Juma (Friday) Market, use as a rule of thumb a reduction of a third.

While there are inherent risks, there are also genuine carpet bargains to be had in Pakistan. Few antiques or museum pieces appear on the market, but the discerning shopper can find carpets of true quality and artistic merit. The pursuit of these can be enjoyable and educational — even addictive.

The Beaches

The most popular outing for tourists with children is **Clifton Beach,** about five kilometres (three miles) south of central Karachi along Abdullah Haroon (Victoria) Road, only ten minutes by taxi or thirty by bus numbers 10 or 20 from Shahrah-e-Iraq (Iraq Road). The beach has a well-stocked aquarium and an amusement park with a roller-coaster, ferris wheel, merry-go-round and dodgem cars. Visitors can also ride camels and horses along the beach or sample the not very appetising fare at the many food stalls. The water, however, is too polluted for swimming.

Clifton was once a tiny coastal village. Attracted by the cool sea breeze, the British developed it in the 19th century into a health resort for the military. Along its tree-lined streets survive many graceful old colonial houses set in spacious, shaded gardens.

Clifton View-point, atop the hill beside the amusement park, overlooks the whole of Karachi. In the foreground stands **Mohatta Palace,** a turn-of-the-century Mughal-Gothic pile of red sandstone complete with domes and cupolas. Jinnah's sister, Fatima, lived here until she died in 1978, but it is now empty. The seaward view has Oyster Rocks protruding from the water halfway to Manora Lighthouse, and to the right (west) you can see the tops of the loading cranes at Keamari Harbour.

At the top of the hill near Clifton View-point is the **Shrine of Abdullah Shah Ghazi.** Its tall, square chamber and green dome are typical of Sufi shrines everywhere in Pakistan. Abdullah Shah Ghazi was a ninth-century saint descended directly from the Prophet Muhammad. He is revered as the patron saint of Karachi and has one of the largest followings in Pakistan, with devotees flocking to his shrine at a rate of 1,000 per day or as many as 10,000 at weekends. His intercession with God is considered particularly beneficial to women with marital problems, such as an inability to conceive.

Foreigners are welcome in the shrine if they are suitably dressed (heads, legs and arms covered) and remove their shoes at the entrance. The most interesting time to visit is Thursday evening, when Sindh's most celebrated devotional singers gather for the *qawwali* ceremony, the singing of mystical songs. Many devotees spend the night in the shrine wrapped in their shawls.

This shrine, like others, is well supplied with beggars, who are attracted by the distribution of free food. They provide the faithful with the opportunity of gaining a blessing through the giving of alms.

Beaches clean enough for swimming stretch west for hundreds of kilometres along the coast of Sindh and Balochistan to the Iranian border, but only those near Karachi are open to foreigners.

Hawkes Bay, 25 kilometres (16 miles) from central Karachi, offers beach huts with cooking facilities, bathrooms and changing space. The swimming is particularly good in March and April, and in winter the sea is cold but still pleasant. However, from May through October the sea is dangerously rough, making swimming inadvisable. Bikinis should not be worn, but a modest swimsuit or tee-shirt and shorts are fine. Pakistani women go in fully dressed in *shalwar-kameez*. Camel rides and other seaside amusements are available. PTDC is building a restaurant on the beach, and other private hotels have planning permission to build.

Baleji Beach, about 45 minutes west of Karachi, is a succession of secluded bays divided by rocky outcrops. **French Beach** is the most popular, and there most foreigners and rich Pakistanis picnic and swim. There is no greenery or shade of *any* kind, apart from that provided by beach umbrellas or private huts. The rock pools are interesting, and body surfing is good, though swimmers should beware of the undertow.

Beyond Baleji Beach is Karachi Nuclear Power Plant (KANUPP) and, for security reasons, the police may stop you from going further. The road detours round KANUPP for about three kilometres (two miles), returning to the coast at **Paradise Point.** Here the waves crash through a rock with a hole in it — the most photographed rock in Pakistan. From here on, the road follows the top of a low cliff with quiet little coves along its base. From December through March, the snorkelling here is very good, but there is a problem with security. **Cape Monze**, about 25 kilometres (15 miles) beyond the nuclear power plant, has a lighthouse and some more isolated coves.

Gaddani Beach, about 50 kilometres (30 miles) from Karachi across the Hub River in Balochistan, is famous as the world's biggest shipbreaking yard. Ships displacing up to 20,000 tons are beached by running them full speed on to the sand at high tide. They are then taken apart with a minimum of mechanisation. Foreign visitors in private cars are occasionally turned back at the checkpoint at the bridge over the usually dry Hub River unless they have a permit obtainable (not very conveniently) from the provincial government of Balochistan in Quetta. After the bridge, turn left to the Japanese project and continue to Gaddani along the beach, thus avoiding the main road and any further checkposts. You can also get there in about three hours by public bus from Lee Market in Karachi, leaving in the morning and afternoon.

National Museum

One of the few museums in Pakistan, the National Museum, located off Dr Zia-ud-din Ahmed Road, is open 10 am to 5 pm. It houses a fairly well-displayed collection of 4,500-year-old Indus Civilisation artefacts, impressive 1,500-year-old Gandharan Buddhist stone sculpture, tenth-century Hindu sculpture from Bangladesh and Muslim *objets d'art*. There is also an interesting ethnological gallery, especially the Kalash exhibition, a room of coins and illustrated manuscripts, and a special exhibition hall.

Architecture

The Tomb of Muhammad Ali Jinnah is Karachi's most impressive monument. Jinnah, called the Quaid-e-Azam (pronounced kai-day-AAH-zam) meaning Great Leader or Father of the Nation, led the movement for a separate Muslim state, which started in the 1930s. At Partition in 1947, he became the governor-general of Pakistan, an office he held for little more than a year before dying of tuberculosis. The square tomb stands on a hill at the east end of M A Jinnah Road, from where there is a good view over the city. The crystal chandelier inside is a gift from the People's Republic of China, the blue-tiled ceiling comes from Japan and the silver railing was

given by Iran. The colourful ceremony of the changing of the guard takes place every two hours, at 10 am, noon, 2 pm, and so on: every 15 minutes the four soldiers on duty move round one corner to take turns to stand in the shade.

Masjid-e-Tooba, or **Defence Society Mosque,** Karachi's largest and best-known modern mosque, built in the 1960s from local subscription, is an elegant, flattened dome, 72 metres in diameter, balanced on a low surrounding wall with no central pillars. It has excellent acoustics, enabling the unamplified voice of the *maulana* to be heard clearly by 5,000 worshippers.

Holy Trinity Cathedral, on Abdullah Haroon Road north of the Metropole Hotel, was built as the garrison church in the mid-19th century and survives as an example of colonial church architecture. Its many brass and marble memorials set round the inside wall recall the history of British life in Sindh.

Several other 19th-century churches survive in Karachi, including **St Patrick's Cathedral** and **St Andrew's Church** where there are English language services on Sunday evening. There are no graveyards near the churches; all Christians are buried in the Christian cemetery near the airport and in the War Graves Commission cemetery near the Aga Khan Hospital.

The **Sindh Club,** on Abdullah Haroon Road, is of interest to enthusiasts of British social history. Founded in the mid-19th century exclusively for the enjoyment of British civil servants, the club did not accept Indian or Pakistani members until the early 1950s, some years after Independence. Though only members and their guests may eat at the club (and, in the evening, only if attired in dark suit and tie), well-dressed, casual visitors may wander in to gawk at the spacious halls and wide verandahs overlooking beautifully tended gardens. Particularly evocative are the billiards and reading rooms.

Frere Hall, set in the spacious Jinnah Gardens opposite the Marriott Hotel, is a singularly charming Victorian Gothic hotchpotch. Built as a social and cultural centre in 1865, it is now a public library. The ceiling was recently painted by Sadequain, an eminent Pakistani artist.

The **Sindh High Court,** on Court Road, is a 19th-century red sandstone assemblage of cupolas, balconies and pillars. Opposite is the **Sindh Assembly Building,** which was built late in the 19th century in typical British colonial style with wide verandahs and high ceilings.

A drive west on 11 Chundrigar Road takes one past the vast **Cotton Exchange Building** and the new **Habib Bank Plaza,** an elegant round tower. Further along on the left is the 19th-century, Greek-porticoed **State Bank of Pakistan,** beside which stands the new **State Bank Building.**

Trips from Karachi

You are advised not to leave Karachi without and armed guard. Any tour operator can make all the necessary arrangements for you.

National Highway to Thatta (see map page 108)

A day trip along the National Highway to Thatta takes one past Chaukundi, Banbhore and Makli Hill on a tour of scenic and historical interest.

Chaukundi Tombs

The **Chaukundi Tombs** are the first stop, 27 kilometres (17 miles) east of Karachi, where acres of stone tombs stretch along the crest of a low ridge. Built between the 15th and 19th centuries by Balochis (a tribe originating in Syria) and Burpats (who arose from a cross of Balochis and Rajputs), the tombs are of various sizes and designs but fall into two basic types: some support roofs on pillars, but most consist of solid, oblong pyramids standing two to four metres (seven to 14 feet) high and completely covered with finely carved geometric designs. The small rosette is a frequent motif that may have some forgotten connection with pre-Islamic sun-worship, as may the sunflowers, wheels and chrysanthemums, which also suggest the sun. Squares, diamonds, triangles, swastikas, herringbones, zig-zags and crosses are also used in every possible combination. The same patterns also appear on local wood carvings and textiles.

Men's graves are those surmounted by a stylised turban atop a pillar carved with weapons and sometimes horses and riders, a design that may have originated in the Rajput custom of temporarily burying a fallen soldier at the battlefield and marking his grave with his upright sword capped by his turban. At any rate, such representation of animals and people is extremely rare in Muslim culture and bespeaks pre-Muslim influence.

Women's graves are often decorated with stylised jewellery, the earrings, bangles and necklaces resembling those still worn today. Similar groups of tombs exist at over 100 sites along the coast of Pakistan and as far inland as Sukkur.

Banbhore

Banbhore, an archaeological excavation with a museum, lies 62 kilometres (39 miles) from Karachi on the north bank of Gharo Creek and a few kilometres south of the highway. The foundations of a mosque and the city wall both date from the eighth century, making the mosque the earliest yet found in the subcontinent. It was about 40 metres (130 feet) square and consisted of an open courtyard surrounded by covered cloisters on three sides and the prayer chamber on the fourth. The roof of the prayer chamber was supported by 33 pillars arranged in three rows. The city wall was built of limestone blocks and had semi-circular bastions at regular intervals and three gates, the main gate opening south to the creek. The other gates, on the north and east sides, led to a lake that served as the city's main water supply.

Once a port near the mouth of the Indus, Banbhore may have been founded by Alexander the Great in 325 BC; certainly, Greek-style pottery dating from the first century BC has been found here. For the next 700 years, Buddhists and Hindus ruled the town as it grew in size and importance.

Banbhore has been identified with Debal, the port taken in AD 711 by the first Arab invader of the subcontinent, Muhammad bin Qasim. Sent by the caliph of Baghdad, the 17-year-old conqueror arrived by sea with a force of 15,000 infantry augmented by cavalry mounted on horses and camels. Weapons included rockets, firearms and five catapults, the biggest of which, called 'Wee Bride', took 500 men to operate and had been used by the Prophet Muhammad himself. The catapult destroyed the Hindu temple at Debal, and when the garrison surrendered, Muhammad bin Qasim ordered beheaded every man over 18 — an age he himself would never attain.

The precocious conqueror then went on to take Neroon (now Hyderabad), before marching up the Indus, killing King Dahir, packing off the king's two daughters to the caliph of Baghdad, taking Brahmanabad–Mansura, fighting a fierce battle at Alor and proceeding on to Multan.

King Dahir's two spirited daughters, meanwhile, conspired to avenge their father's death by telling the caliph that Muhammad bin Qasim had defiled them before fobbing them off on him. The caliph was furious and sent an order to Muhammad bin Qasim to have himself sewn up in the skin of a freshly killed cow and returned to Baghdad. Ever obedient, Muhammad did as he was ordered and died within three days. The girls subsequently confessed their lie and suffered an even nastier death.

Banbhore was destroyed in the 13th century, when it was sacked and burnt by the Afghan invader, Jalal-ud-din. The coastline has since inched forward in a march that is estimated to have pushed back the sea by at least 80 kilometres (50 miles) since Alexander's time. Also, silting and earthquakes have directed the Indus into different channels, leaving the ruins high and dry.

The coin and pottery displayed in the little museum at the site give an idea of what the port was like in its heyday, indicating that Banbhore

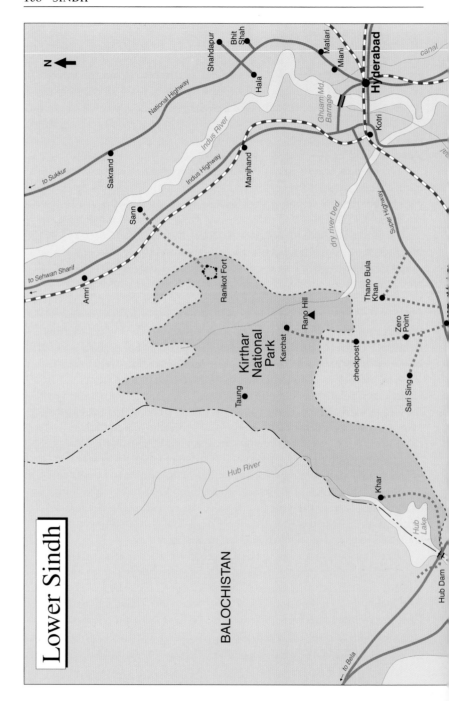

Lower Sindh

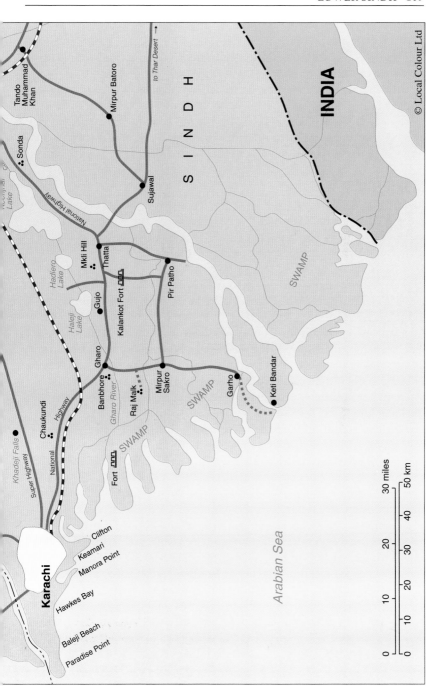

© Local Colour Ltd

had trading links with the Muslim countries to the west and with lands as far east as China.

Haleji Lake, 87 kilometres (54 miles) from Karachi, is a nature reserve. In the winter months, birds migrate from the north and settle here in their thousands. On a good day between October and February, bird-watchers can expect to see 100 species here, including flamingos, pelicans, kingfishers and up to 20 different species of birds of prey.

Makli Hill

Makli Hill (Makli means 'Little Mecca') is reputedly the largest necropolis in the world. With a million graves, tombs and mausoleums, it is an impressive and eerie place. For over ten centuries, the Sindhi people have held Makli sacred, and a spiritual atmosphere persists to this day.

Makli was the graveyard for the nearby town of Thatta, which was the capital of Lower Sindh from the 14th century to the 17th, a prosperous port and a great centre of Islamic learning. Here lie the remains of Thatta's élite: kings, queens, generals, saints, scholars, philosophers and poets. The hill is long and low, stretching for about eight kilometres (five miles) north to south and bisected by the National Highway. Some of the tombs, which vary in size and grandeur, are of stone decorated with delicate carving, while others are of brick covered with beautiful tiles glazed blue and white. The most interesting mausoleums are in two groups: the relatively recent **tombs of the Tarkhan kings,** the rulers of Sindh from 1545 to 1614, lie near the highway, and the older **tombs of the Sammah kings** are clustered three kilometres (two miles) away along the ridge to the north. Permission to take a car to the Sammah tombs can be obtained from the Archaeological Office to the left of the main gate. Accommodation is available at the Archaeological Department Rest House and should be booked through the Archaeological Office in Karachi (see Karachi listing on page 263).

Starting at the gate on the National Highway and working north along the ridge, first visit the unusual **well** surrounded by a white wall on the left. Half-way down the well is a pillared gallery where soldiers stood guarding the water.

The first tomb on the right is that of **Jani Beg Tarkhan,** the last independent Tarkhan ruler of Sindh, who died in 1601 (the dates on the signs at Makli are not always correct). His octagonal brick tomb stands on a terraced platform in the centre of a courtyard surrounded by a brick wall. Alternate layers of dark blue and turquoise glazed tiles and red unglazed bricks decorate the walls. Inside, the cenotaph (empty sarcophagus) of Jani Beg is inscribed with verses the Koran. THe actual body, as in all Muslim tombs of this sort, is in another sarcophagus underground. The mosque set in the western wall of the enclosure has an exquisitely decorated *mehrab*, the prayer niche facing Mecca.

The tomb of **Tughril Beg Tarkhan**, a general who served the Mughal Emperor Aurangzeb and died in 1679, has a small square pavilion with a conical dome supported by 12 delicately carved stone pillars with honeycombed capitals. Lotus blossoms and sunflowers decorate the niches. The wall mosque to the west has three elegant *mehrabs* in the centre and solid raised minarets at each end.

The tomb of **Baqi Beg Uzbek**, who died in 1640, is an open brick court with a raised central platform supporting three graves. The mosque in the west wall has a domed chamber with a brick ceiling patterned in zigzags.

The finest tomb on Makli Hill, that of **Isa Khan Tarkhan II**, is a magnificent two-storey stone building in the centre of a square courtyard surrounded by a high stone wall. Isa Khan II died at the age of 90 in 1644, having served as governor of Gujarat (in India) under the Mughal emperor Shah Jahan, then as governor of Thatta for a year. The tomb has a high dome surrounded by a two-tiered verandah, the upper tier being roofed with small domes and reached by stairs going up the east side. The tomb is decorated inside and out with delicate tracery like that at Akbar's palace at Fatehpur Sikri, near Agra in India. Floral and geometric designs surrounding a lattice window decorate the *mehrab* of the wall mosque in the west wall of the enclosure.

The tomb of **Jan Baba**, son of Isa Khan I and father of Isa Khan II, was built in 1608 and stands in a stone enclosure entered through an elegant portico built later. Under a pillared pavilion lie seven graves in a row. The walls are covered in carved tracery that looks like fine brown lace; one wall hides the two ladies' tombs in the northeast corner. The east door offers an excellent view of Thatta.

One of the best-preserved tombs at Makli is that of **Dewan Shurfa Khan,** a revenue collector who died in 1638. (The richness of the tomb indicates where much of the revenue went.) The square brick building, with heavy round towers at its corners, is placed in the centre of a walled court. When Sir Richard Burton (later to become famous for his discovery of the source of the Nile River) saw it in 1876, he found the tiled dome 'gaudy, with more the appearance of a pleasure house than a mansion of the dead'. In the richly decorated interior (Burton continues) 'your eye rejects the profuseness of square and circle, spiral and curve, diamond and scroll work, flowers, border pattern and quotation from the Koran'. Perhaps time has softened the effect, for a century later the blue, red and white zigzags of the ceiling and the ornate decoration on the cenotaph delight the eye.

The paved road then twists and turns for a kilometre (about half a mile) among thousands of graves of every description before reaching the **Shrine of Abdullah Shah Ashabi**, which is surrounded by the usual food and souvenir stalls catering for pilgrims. The colourful clothes and lively bustle of the saint's devotees make a welcome change after all the empty tombs.

A dirt road leads from the shrine north along the ridge for another 2.3 kilometres (1.5 miles) to the **Sammah tombs**. The Sammahs ruled Sindh from 1337 to 1524 and reached the peak of their power under **Sultan Jam Nizam-ud-din** (1461–1509), whose square stone mausoleum is the most impressive of the group. The walls are decorated inside and out with bands of medallions, diamonds, sunflowers, calligraphy and, on the north side, even a row of ducks. The loveliest part of the tomb is the richly carved projection of the *mehrab* on the outside of the west wall, with its arched balcony above showing Gujarati Hindu influence. (Possibly the Muslim architects employed Hindu stonesmiths who carried over habits acquired when building Hindu temples.) The tomb remains open to the sky because the architects were unable to build a big enough dome. Stairs lead to the top of the walls, which offer a commanding view of the surrounding countryside.

Next to the tomb are the ruins of a mosque with a view north across the ravine to the next section of Makli Hill. The white shrine in the distance is that of **Ali Shah Shirazi,** a popular saint who died in 1572.

Thatta

Thatta, about 100 kilometres (62 miles) east of Karachi, was once called Pattala, and it was here that Alexander the Great rested his troops in 325 BC before marching across the Makran Desert in Balochistan. Thatta, the capital of lower Sindh from the 14th century through the 16th, became part of the Mughal Empire in 1592 and prospered for another 150 years as a port famous for its cotton weaving and wood carving. The city finally fell into decline in the 18th century, not only because the Indus shifted its course away from the town, but also because Britain's newly developed textile industry began to export cotton *lungis* to India that were better and cheaper than the once famous Thatta product. By 1851, the population had fallen from a high of 300,000 to 7,000. The beautiful wooden houses have rotted away, leaving now only about a dozen near the bazaar.

Thatta's **Jami Mosque** (sometimes called **Shah Jahan Mosque** after its imperial Mughal builder) dates from 1647 and is built of red brick tempered with the cool blues and greens of glazed tiles. The mosque consists of a central court surrounded by brick arcades covered with 93 domes. These domes have the acoustical effect of enabling prayers said in front of the *mehrab* to be heard in any part of the building. The domes over the entrance and the *mehrab* are completely lined with glazed tiles of blue, turquoise and white arranged to represent the sun surrounded by stars.

The story of the origin of the mosque is that Shah Jahan, as a young man, took refuge in Thatta when his father, Jahangir, was displeased with him for some reason lost to history. Later, when he became emperor, he built the mosque in gratitude to the people of Thatta for harbouring him.

Thatta Bazaar, behind the mosque, is a good place to buy *sussi* (striped hand-loom) and *ajrak* (hand-block-printed) cloth and to see some old houses with wind-catchers on their roofs and balconies of carved wood hanging over the street. **Khizri Mosque,** a small brick structure dating from 1613 in a tiny courtyard behind a high wall just before the bazaar on the right, also has wind-catchers on the roof to funnel cool air to the faithful below.

Dabgir Mosque is about one kilometre (half a mile) south of Shah Jahan Mosque on the road to Sujawal. Now well out of town, this mosque once stood in the heart of the much bigger Thatta of old. It was built in 1588 by Khusro Khan Charkas, a finance officer who escaped punishment for embezzlement when the governor suddenly died. He atoned for his crime (and disposed of its proceeds, perhaps) by building the mosque.

The **Yahya Khan Bridge,** the last to span the Indus before it reaches the sea, is eight kilometres (five miles) beyond Dabgir Mosque toward Sujawal. The bridge is about one kilometre (half a mile) long. For two or three kilometres on either side, the road runs along a high embankment laid across the flood plain and overlooking surprisingly dense riverine forest.

Keenjhar Lake, lying 22 kilometres (14 miles) from Thatta on the road to Hyderabad, has developed into a resort offering sailboats for hire, fishing facilities and excellent bird-watching. It is crowded on Fridays but quiet during the rest of the week. The bare Sindh Department of Culture and Tourism motel is bookable through the SDCT or PTDC offices in Karachi (see Karachi listing on page 263).

Beside the lake is the **Tomb of Noori,** a fisher-girl of the Mohana tribe who married King Jam Tamachi of the Sammah Dynasty and thus became the subject of a romantic rags-to-riches story very popular in Sindh. Jam Tamachi is buried on Makli Hill.

Geometric patterns in the Jami Mosque in Thatta (left) contrast with the floral design of a mosque in Lahore.

Sonda Graveyard, on the east side of the National Highway, 14 kilometres (nine miles) beyond the entrance to Keenjhar Lake, has some excellent Chaukundi-style tombs, almost all of which are decorated with a carving of a horse and rider or of jewellery. The Engineering Department bungalow on the embankment behind the graveyard overlooks, on the one side, the white sands of the Indus flood plain and, far in the distance on the other, Keenjhar Lake.

North of Karachi

Another day trip from Karachi, this time to the north, takes in Mangho Pir, Hub Dam and Khar Wildlife Preserve.

Mangho Pir

Mangho Pir, 18 kilometres (11 miles) north of Karachi, is the Shrine of Pir Mangho, a 13th-century Sufi saint. It stands on a low hill beside two sulphurous hot springs guarded by crocodiles. These crocodiles are the snub-nosed variety, as distinct from the long-snouted gavial (*gharia*) of the Indus, and are considered particularly dangerous.

An amusing legend is attached to their origin. When Pir Mangho first came from Arabia, he inadvertently brought the crocodiles in his hair, where they travelled in the form of lice. Soon after his arrival, there sprang from the desert two oases around hot springs gushing from a clump of date palms. The 'crocodiles' jumped into the springs and have lived there ever since. (Zoologists, for their part, suggest that the crocodiles became stranded in the springs when the Hub River changed course.)

On Fridays the shrine is thronged with pilgrims seeking blessings and cures, particularly for rheumatism, skin diseases and leprosy. They used to enter the pool containing the crocodiles, but now use a separate bathing place built nearby. Supplicants offer goats to the crocodiles and believe that, if the meat is eaten, their prayers will be answered. The five crocodiles currently in residence consequently spend most of their time stuffed to bursting and immobile, with shreds of meat dangling from their jaws. A connection begs to be made between this gorging of crocodiles and the worship of crocodiles in ancient Egypt, a land with which the people of the Indus conducted trade as long as 5,000 years ago.

From Mangho Pir, a paved road runs northwest for 33 kilometres (20 miles) to the **Hub Dam**. The escarpment overlooking the Hub Valley from the west is the home of several groups of Baloch tribespeople, and small, temporary settlements of wattle houses surrounded by thorn hedges cluster along the top of the ridge. Men may not approach these settlements, but foreign women are welcome to enter and meet the Balochi women within.

The Hub Dam is almost five kilometres (three miles) long and holds back a shallow lake trapped between low, barren hills. A sandy track passable only by 4WD vehicles continues past the dam for about 20 kilometres (12 miles) along the edge of Kirthar National Park to **Khar Wildlife Preserve,** where there is a guest-house bookable through the Sindh Wildlife Management Board (see Karachi listing on page 263).

In winter, Hub Lake is alive with birds. Swimming is inadvisable, as the lake is also alive with crocodiles. Monitor lizards inhabit the rocks around Khar, and the wildlife complex is a breeding centre for blackbuck, peacocks and urial sheep.

Kirthar National Park

A four-hour drive northeast from Karachi, off the Super Highway (for 4WD vehicles only) takes the visitor deep into the heart of Kirthar National Park, a game preserve measuring over 3,000 square kilometres in the Kirthar Hills and a good destination for a three-day trip if the bandits are brought under control. October to February is the most comfortable — that is, coolest — time to go, but the flowers bloom during the (relatively) wet monsoon in August.

Five furnished rest-houses with cooking facilities and running water are situated on the edge of a wide valley in the centre of the park at **Karchat.** They are bookable through the Sindh Wildlife Management Board, which also hires out tents to those who wish to camp. Some food is available if ordered well in advance, but it is better to take your own food, drink and bedding.

The rolling valleys and contorted, rugged lines of the Kirthar Hills form a natural haven for urial sheep, ibex and *chinkara* gazelle. Jungle cats, desert cats and even the occasional leopard or desert wolf also prowl the park, but you would be extremely lucky to see them. Pangolins (scaly anteaters), porcupines and monitor lizards are more in evidence.

Other attractions in the park are the 18th-century Chaukundi-style tombs at **Taung** and the prehistoric archaeological remains at **Koh Tarash.** The enormous **Ranikot Fort** is also within the park, two hours by jeep from Karchat. Ranikot is about four hours from Karachi via the Super Highway and Indus Highway.

Moenjodaro

The 4,000-year-old brick ruins of the Indus Civilisation city of Moenjodaro, which means 'Mound of the Dead', stand on the west bank of the Indus in upper Sindh, one hour and 20 minutes from Karachi by air.

The Indus Civilisation flourished from 3000 to 1500 BC, making it contemporary with the ancient civilisations of Egypt and Mesopotamia. At its height, it comprised at least 400 cities and towns along the Indus and its tributaries, covering most of present-day Pakistan and stretching northwest as far as modern Kabul and east as far as modern Delhi. The waterways were the main highways connecting the empire, and flat-bottomed barges almost identical to those still used today plied the rivers from city to city. Few of the cities have been excavated; what little we know of the civilisation comes mostly from Moenjodaro and Harappa, the latter being 550 kilometres (342 miles) to the north, near Lahore.

The Indus people had a strong central administrative system. The cities appear to have been built according to a single, highly organised plan, with a raised citadel in the west and streets laid out in neat blocks defined by wide avenues intersecting at right angles. Much like modern Islamabad, different sectors were reserved for different functions, so that there was an administrative sector, a residential sector for the wealthy, another for the working class and separate sectors for various kinds of artisans and tradesmen.

A priestly class probably governed the people, collecting taxes in the form of grain, which was stored in state granaries, the period equivalent of modern banks. Weights and measures were standardised throughout the empire. Indeed, regulation was so pervasive that even the dimensions of building bricks were universally prescribed, 28 by 14 by 7 centimetres.

The first prerequisite of an urban civilisation is a well-organised agricultural system able to produce the surpluses necessary to feed its cities, and the Indus Civilisation developed from an aggregate of settled farming communities using relatively advanced farming techniques. Irrigation was probably practised even though the climate at the time was slightly wetter than now, resulting in forested, highly fertile land along the Indus. Crops included wheat, barley, sesame and vegetables. By 2000 BC, cotton had become a major trade commodity — a status it retains today — and all the draught animals and livestock now seen in the subcontinent had been domesticated. That cats and dogs were also tamed is evidenced evocatively by a certain brick on display in the museum at the site. Before baking, the brick was imprinted with the footprints of both animals, thus becoming posterity's record of a dog chasing a cat.

The elaborate and efficient system of waste drainage used in the Indus cities has excited considerable interest. Drains from each house flowed first into cesspits, in which solid matter settled, then liquid waste flowed on through the carefully graded, brick-lined drains that ran down the centre of each street under a cover pierced at intervals with inspection holes. The sewers eventually emptied into the river.

Bathrooms in the homes of the wealthy had floors of snugly fitting bricks. Some houses had separate lavatories, and most had their own brick-lined wells. Many even had rubbish chutes running through the wall to rectangular brick rubbish bins outside.

Sentry-boxes stood at intervals in the streets to shelter the city police from the sun and rain.

An hour at **Moenjodaro Museum** provides some idea of what the ancient city probably looked like, and of the cultural and economic basis of the whole civilisation.

Two large murals show a reconstruction of the city, with its high outer walls narrowing at the top, along which soldiers patrol from one square watch-tower to the next. Down by the river, cargoes of cotton and grain are unloaded from boats into two-wheeled ox carts like those still used today. In the carts, the grain is transferred to the state granaries, as priests mill around the palace and its great bath nearby. Two-storey, flat-roofed houses stretch into the distance across the prosperous city.

One of the more interesting exhibits shows the **traders' seals**, which demonstrate the great artistic talent of the Indus people. These seals are exquisitely tiny, generally two to four centimetres (0.8–1.6 inches) square, and fashioned from steatite, a soft, easily-carved stone. Each is delicately and realistically engraved with such animals as roaring tigers and rough-skinned rhinoceros or renderings of deities and fighting demons. Across the tops of most seals are inscriptions in Indus Civilisation script, presumably naming the merchants who owned them. As no extensive writings have survived and these proper names are complemented by only a few short inscriptions found on bits of pottery, philologists hoping to decipher the script appear to face a hopeless task.

Though the evidence in hand suggests that the Indus Civilisation was both larger and better organised than either its Egyptian or Mesopotamian counterpart, we know less about it. (In the case of Egypt, the ancient way of life is known from artefacts preserved in the dry atmosphere sealed within the pyramids and royal tombs.) We do know, however, that trade among the three civilisations and the surrounding tribes was extensive. Merchants from the Indus carried cotton by camel and horse caravan across the hills to

Mesopotamia (where cotton came to be called *sindu*, just as in Greece, cloth was called *sindonian*). What they received in return must have been perishable, for no trace remains, but on the way back through Balochistan, merchants picked up steatite for their seals, bitumen and alabaster.

Silver, lead, tin, turquoise and lapis came from Persia and Afghanistan, red iron oxide pigment from the islands of the Persian Gulf, and copper and various semi-precious stones from India.

Mother goddesses moulded of clay were common throughout the ancient world, and those found in Moenjodaro show that the people here were as devoted to these fertility deities as anyone else. There are, however, no definitive clues regarding the nature of the state religion, though the famous little statue of a haughty **priest-king** (the original is on display in the National Museum in Karachi) indicates the existence of a ruling class of clergy, and the many elaborate baths suggest ritual bathing similar to that practised today by both Hindus and Muslims.

The **bronze dancing girl,** pert and provocative (and a copy of the original kept but not displayed in Delhi), indicates either a tradition of temple girls or a familiar and lively sense of fun. Some of the numerous terracotta figurines are undeniably phallic, suggesting a coarse sense of humour.

The figurines and jewellery displayed show that the women of the Indus Civilisation wore short skirts and dressed their hair in high, complicated coiffures. They loved jewellery and wore hairpins, earrings and multiple strings of beads made of carnelian, agate, faience, ivory, cowrie shells and gold. Priests' robes were worn over one shoulder, like those worn by Buddhist monks today, and priests either wore their hair short or gathered it in a bun held at the back of the head by a headband.

The **pottery** in the museum is not of great beauty, reflecting efficient mass production rather than a striving for elegance. Potters in the village nearby are still churning out the same designs.

Moenjodaro was abandoned around 1500 BC, although the civilisation lingered on in places for another five centuries. The decline probably resulted from a combination of factors. Climatic change (perhaps a slight easterly shift in the monsoon) compounded the effects of overgrazing and the felling of trees for fuel, causing impoverishment of the soil, which was also becoming saline. A parallel problem on a different plane was general political deterioration. Towards the end, the building of fortifications became fast and furious, presumably to defend the city from the waves of warlike Aryan nomads who started invading the subcontinent from Central Asia around 1700 BC. We know from the Rigveda, the religious hymns of the Aryans, that they overthrew a people with flat noses and a strange language; a people who lived in walled cities. The Rigveda also describes breaking a dam and flooding a city. Some of the more striking finds at Moenjodaro are skeletons lying in contorted positions, as though they lay precisely where they had been slain. However, the picture of the city dying overnight as the result of the slaughter of its inhabitants is probably more dramatic than accurate.

Excavations have uncovered only parts of the city, which was about five kilometres (three miles) in circumference. An embankment for flood control ran 1,500 metres (5,000 feet) along the river bank, but today the river is five kilometres to the east and controlled by a modern embankment.

From the front of the museum and looking south, the visitor first notices the remains of a **Buddhist stupa** built at the highest point and dominating the other ruins. Built 2,000 years later than the Indus Civilisation city, it sits atop the ruins of the ancient acropolis, or fortified citadel, that once crowned the 15-metre (50-foot) high artificial hill. Moenjodaro's administrative and religious buildings — the public bath, state granary, palace and assembly hall — are just to the west of the stupa.

The **great bath**, more than two metres (seven feet) deep and sealed with a bitumen lining, was probably used for ritual bathing. It has been restored with new brick, so it appears rather as it did to those who used it. Broad steps lead down into the water at either end, and a neatly arched and brick-lined drain accommodates the overflow. A cloister surrounds the bath, and on three sides are a series of small rooms, possibly private baths for the priests. In one of these is a well.

Beside the bath is the **state granary**, the 'treasury' where taxes in the form of wheat, barley and sesame were stored. Twenty-seven high brick platforms in three rows of nine are separated by ventilation channels. Wooden storage bins were built on these foundations. On the north side, but crumbled so that it is hard to make out, is the loading bay, where the ox-drawn carts pulled up to load and unload.

The **palace**, or priests' college, is north of the bath and consists of a cloistered court surrounded by rooms. The assembly hall is about 100 metres (yards) to the south and survives as the foundations of a large, square, pillared room adjacent to a portion of the city fortifications. No temple building has been uncovered, but if there is a great temple it is probably buried under the Buddhist stupa.

The secular and unofficial part of the city lies east of the citadel area and is laid out in a neat, chessboard pattern. Wide thoroughfares divide the city into 12 regular blocks, with narrower side streets leading off to give access to the individual houses.

Only a fraction of the square kilometre (four-tenths of a square mile) that this area covered has been excavated, but the **residential district** for the wealthy, which has been unearthed, is the most exciting part of **Moenjodaro.** Here you stroll down narrow side streets between high, forbiddingly blank walls, the shadows of which are cool — but eerie. Even when the city was alive, these alleyways must have been dark and claustrophobic. Periodically, a set of steps leads to a door, but the front of the house is windowless. Inside are the remains of about ten rooms of different sizes opening onto a central courtyard. Most of the houses had two storeys, and a staircase led up to a (probably) wooden balcony that encircled the courtyard and provided access to the upper rooms. Still-visible holes in the walls presumably held the wooden beams that supported the second floor. The only windows were small and high up and, though looking onto the courtyard, were protected by wooden or stone grilles.

Odd as it seems, the brick linings of **wells** tower into the air like factory chimneys, but the explanation is quite simple. As the centuries passed and old houses fell down, new ones were built on top of them, thus raising the general level of the ground. As excavators have worked their way down through the levels and further into the past, they have left standing the well linings thus exposed. The workmanship near the top of the wells, which was added as the ground level rose, is coarser than the older work showing lower down, illustrating the decline of the civilisation.

On the east side of the wealthy residential area is a wide avenue leading south, and this is where the **shops** were. Each commodity was sold in its own specific street: jewellers congregated in one street, fabric merchants in the next, coppersmiths occupied a third street and potters yet another.

The smaller **houses of the working class** are about 300 metres south, along the main street. In the northwest corner of this area is a block of 16 single-storey cottages in two rows of eight, one row facing a street, the other a narrow lane. All are identical, comprising two small rooms, and share a nearby well.

Moenjodaro and the knowledge of the civilisation that built it lay undisturbed for thousands of years until it was rediscovered in 1922 by Sir John Marshall, a British archaeologist. Now the ruins are under threat. Years of irrigation in an area with inadequate drainage have raised the water-table and made the water salty. Moisture is creeping up the brick walls of Moenjodaro, softening them so that they crumble to the touch. With the water-table now only a few metres from the surface, the remains of the earliest years of the city's existence are already many metres below it. UNESCO has provided money to pay for pumping water out in an attempt to lower the water-table, but irreparable damage has already occurred, and the earliest remains are probably lost forever.

Derawar Fort in the Cholistan Desert of southern Punjab

Punjab

Punjab, its name meaning 'Land of Five Rivers', is the richest, most fertile and most heavily populated province of Pakistan. (Originally the five rivers referred to the Jhelum, Chenab, Ravi, Sutlej and Beas — but the last is now in Indian Punjab only, so the Indus is now included as Pakistan's fifth river). In Punjab live nearly 80 million people — more than half the population of the entire country. Geographically, it is a land of contrasts, from the alluvial plain of the Indus River and its tributaries to the sand-dunes of the Cholistan Desert, from the verdant beauty of the pine-covered foothills of the Himalaya to the strangely convoluted lunar landscape of the Potwar Plateau and the Salt Range.

Monsoon rains fall on northern Punjab, making the belt from Lahore to Rawalpindi–Islamabad and continuing north into the foothills, the only part of Pakistan to get more than 500 millimetres of rain a year. Further south, the five rivers provide adequate water for irrigating most of the land on the alluvial plains that separate and surround them.

Punjab grows most of Pakistan's wheat, rice, barley, maize, pulses, oil-seeds, sugar-cane and tobacco. The area around Multan is the cotton-growing centre of the country. Cotton is Pakistan's most important cash crop, exported in raw form, as yarn and in fabrics and clothing. Punjab is also the home of much of Pakistan's industry. Textiles, steel, chemicals, sporting goods, electrical appliances, surgical instruments and fertilisers are all made here, mainly around the large cities of Faisalabad, Multan, Sialkot, Gujranwala and the provincial capital, Lahore. Punjab is also rich in mineral resources, including salt, gypsum, coal, oil and gas.

Geographical position and the fertility of its soil have made Punjab an important centre of human endeavour from prehistoric times. Man lived on the banks of the Soan River 50,000 years ago, and the Indus Civilisation flourished at Harappa and other sites as early as 2500 BC. Taxila, near modern Islamabad, was a centre of culture and learning for a thousand years from 500 BC to AD 500. When Alexander the Great visited Taxila in 326 BC, it was known through-out the ancient world for its university. Islamic learning and architecture developed at Uch and Multan during the 13th and 14th centuries.

In the 17th century, Lahore became one of the greatest Mughal cities in the subcontinent. A town near Lahore was the birthplace of Guru Nanak, the

15th-century founder of the Sikh religion, and Lahore was the capital from which Maharaja Ranjit Singh ruled his 19th century Sikh Empire. The British coveted this fertile region, and overthrew the Sikhs in 1849, annexing Punjab to their Indian dominions, with Lahore as its provincial capital. Finally, it was in Lahore that the All India Muslim League passed, on 23 March 1940, its Resolution for the Creation of Pakistan.

At Partition, which came about seven years later, wealthy Punjab, like Bengal in the east, was itself partitioned, its multicommunal population of Muslims, Hindus and Sikhs precluding its total inclusion in either India or Pakistan. At the same time, no line drawn through the province could fail to place many millions of people on the wrong side of the border. The result was a nightmare of massacres and mass-migrations.

When the Pakistanis decided to build a new capital from scratch, it was in Punjab, the fertile heart of the country, that a site was chosen. The construction of Islamabad began in 1962 near the most beautiful part of the province, the Murree Hills, adjacent to Rawalpindi and the Grand Trunk Road, Pakistan's east–west axis. Islamabad is no longer considered part of Punjab, forming its own capital territory, but I describe it in this chapter.

The best time to visit northern Punjab is in the spring, from February to April, and in the autumn, from September to November. Southern Punjab is extremely hot in summer, so Multan is at its best in winter, from November to February.

Lahore

Lahore is Pakistan's most interesting city, the cultural, intellectual and artistic centre of the nation. Its faded elegance, busy streets and bazaars, and wide variety of Islamic and British architecture make it a city full of atmosphere, contrast and surprise. Lahore looks south to the great civilisation of the Mughal emperors; Peshawar looks north to Central Asia. Those who visit both cities gain some understanding of the cultural influences that have shaped Pakistan.

Getting to Lahore

Air, rail and road links tie Lahore to the other cities of Pakistan. PIA operates domestic flights from 18 towns in Pakistan to Lohore, and international flights direct from India, the Far East, Middle East, Europe and the USA land at Lahore's airport, which is some eleven kilometres (seven miles) from the city centre. Buses cover the 280 kilometres (174 miles) from Islamabad–Rawalpindi along the new motorway in three hours, and along the old Grand Trunk Road in five to six hours. The same journey takes five or six hours on the safer and more comfortable train. From Karachi to Lahore takes two to three days by road or 17–21 hours by train. There is a choice of four classes of compartment, air-conditioned sleeper, first class sleeper, first class seats and second class, and a choice of express or ordinary train. The Grand Trunk Road crosses the Indian border 29 kilometres (18 miles) from Lahore at Wagah (see General Information for Travellers on page 15 for border open times).

When to Go

October to March is the best time to visit Lahore. Because it is only 213 metres (700 feet) above sea level, it is hotter than Islamabad and can get very hot in summer.

History

Lahore has been the capital of Punjab for nearly a thousand years, first from 1021 to 1186 under the Ghaznavid Dynasty, founded by Mahmud of Ghazni, then under Muhammad of Ghor, and then under the various sultans of Delhi. It reached its full glory under Mughal rule from 1524 to 1752. The third Mughal emperor, Akbar, held his court in Lahore for the 14 years from 1584 to 1598. He built the massive Lahore Fort on the foundations of a previous fort and enclosed the city within a red brick wall boasting 12 gates. Jahangir and Shah Jahan (who was born in Lahore) extended the fort, built palaces and tombs, and laid out gardens. The last of the great Mughals, Aurangzeb (1658–1707), gave Lahore its most famous monument, the great Badshahi Mosque.

In the 18th and 19th centuries the Sikhs also had their capital at Lahore. They took little interest in the gardens and actually dismantled many of Lahore's Mughal monuments, from which it is said they took enough marble to build the Golden Temple at Amritsar twice over.

When the British took over in 1849, they erected splendidly pompous Victorian public buildings in the style that has come to be called Mughal–Gothic. The Lahore Cantonment, the British residential district of wide, tree-lined streets and white bungalows set in large, shaded gardens, is the prettiest cantonment in Pakistan.

Since Independence in 1947, Lahore has expanded rapidly as the capital of Pakistani Punjab. It is the second-largest city in the country and an important industrial centre.

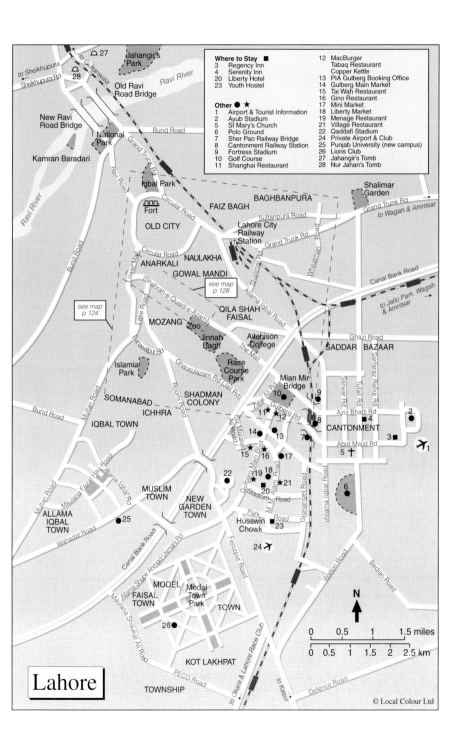

Where to Stay ■
3 Regency Inn
4 Serenity Inn
20 Liberty Hotel
23 Youth Hostel

Other ● ★
1 Airport & Tourist Information
2 Ayub Stadium
5 St Mary's Church
6 Polo Ground
7 Sher Pao Railway Bridge
8 Cantonment Railway Station
9 Fortress Stadium
10 Golf Course
11 Shanghai Restaurant

12 MacBurger
  Tabaq Restaurant
  Copper Kettle
13 PIA Gulberg Booking Office
14 Gulberg Main Market
15 Tai Wah Restaurant
16 Gino Restaurant
17 Mini Market
18 Liberty Market
19 Menage Restaurant
21 Village Restaurant
22 Qaddafi Stadium
24 Private Airport & Club
25 Punjab University (new campus)
26 Lions Club
27 Jahangir's Tomb
28 Nur Jahan's Tomb

to Sheikhupura
Sheikhupura Rd
to Gujranwala
27
28
Jahangir's Park
Ravi River
Old Ravi Road Bridge
New Ravi Road Bridge
National Park
Kamran Baradari
Ravi River
Ravi Road
Grand Trunk Rd
Bund Road
Iqbal Park
Circular Road
Fort
OLD CITY
FAIZ BAGH
BAGHBANPURA
Shalimar Garden
Grand Trunk Rd
to Wagah & Amritsar
Sultanpura Road
Lahore City Railway Station
Grand Trunk Rd
Wheatman Road
Circular Road
NAULAKHA
ANARKALI
GOWAL MANDI
see map p 128
Shalimar Rd
Allama Iqbal Road
Canal Bank Road
to Jallo Park, Wagah & Amritsar
Lower Mall
(Shahrah-e-Quaid-e-Azam)
QILA SHAH FAISAL
see map p 124
MOZANG
Zoo
Jinnah Bagh
Aitchison College
Ghazi Road
SADDAR BAZAAR
Bahawalpur Rd
Lake Road
Race Course Park
The Mall
Islamia Park
Ghausulazam Rd (Jail Rd)
SHADMAN COLONY
Mian Mir Bridge
10
9
Sarwar Rd
Tufail Rd
Sarfraz Rafiq Rd
2
Bund Road
SOMANABAD
ICHHRA
IQBAL TOWN
Rohini Road
Zafar Ali Rd
11
★12
14
15
★
16
17
Gulberg Rd
Ferozepur Road (Mall Road)
Isd Mardan Road
13
★19
18
16
★
8
7
Aziz Bhatti Rd
CANTONMENT
4
3
Abid Majid Rd
5
1
Mullan Road
Maulana Fazal Haq Road
Allama Iqbal Rd
MUSLIM TOWN
NEW GARDEN TOWN
22
Gulberg Main Blvd
21
20
M M Alam Road
Gulistan Road
6
ALLAMA IQBAL TOWN
25
Wahdat Road
Canal Bank Road
Park Road
Husswin Chowk
23
24
Walton Road
Bedian Road
MODEL FAISAL TOWN
Model Town Park
TOWN
26
Maulana Shabir Ahmad Usman Rd
Maulana Shaukat Ali Road
Ferozepur Road
to Okara & Lahore Race Club
to Kasur
Defence Road

N

0   0.5   1   1.5 miles
0 0.5 1 1.5 2 2.5 km

KOT LAKHPAT
TOWNSHIP
PECO Road

Lahore

© Local Colour Ltd

Sights

Except for the old town and the British-built Lahore Central Museum, all the most impressive sights in Lahore date from the Mughal period. These include Badshahi Mosque, Lahore Fort, Wazir Khan's Mosque, Shalimar Garden and Jahangir's Tomb.

The Tourist Development Corporation of Punjab (TDCP) runs two three-hour tours daily around Lahore, starting at 8.30 am and 2.30 pm, with pick up points at National, Faletti's, Holiday Inn, Pearl Continental and Avari hotels. The morning tour visits the Badshahi Mosque, Lahore Fort, Jahangir's Tomb and the Lahore Museum. The afternoon tour goes to the Shalimar Garden, Wazir Khan Mosque in the old city and the government-owned Pakistan Handicraft Shop. TDCP also run very popular trips to Northern Pakistan — Chitral, Swat, Kaghan, Gilgit and Hunza, and inter-city air-conditioned buses. TDCP, Information Centre, 4A Lawrence Road, tel 6360553, 6369687, fax (92 42) 6369686.

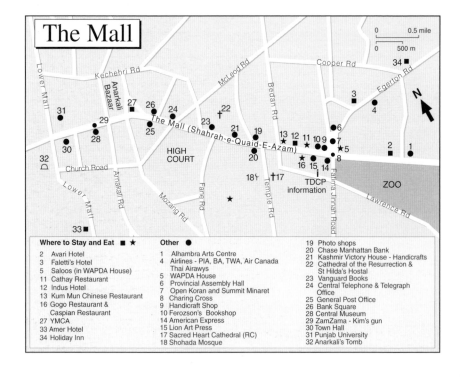

The Mall

Where to Stay and Eat ■ ★
2 Avari Hotel
3 Faletti's Hotel
5 Saloos (in WAPDA House)
11 Cathay Restaurant
12 Indus Hotel
13 Kum Mun Chinese Restaurant
16 Gogo Restaurant &
Caspian Restaurant
27 YMCA
33 Amer Hotel
34 Holiday Inn

Other ●
1 Alhambra Arts Centre
4 Airlines - PIA, BA, TWA, Air Canada
Thai Airawys
5 WAPDA House
6 Provincial Assembly Hall
7 Open Koran and Summit Minaret
8 Charing Cross
9 Handicraft Shop
10 Ferozson's Bookshop
14 American Express
15 Lion Art Press
17 Sacred Heart Cathedral (RC)
18 Shohada Mosque

19 Photo shops
20 Chase Manhattan Bank
21 Kashmir Victory House - Handicrafts
22 Cathedral of the Resurrection &
St Hilda's Hostal
23 Vanguard Books
24 Central Telephone & Telegraph
Office
25 General Post Office
26 Bank Square
28 Central Museum
29 ZamZama - Kim's gun
30 Town Hall
31 Punjab University
32 Anarkali's Tomb

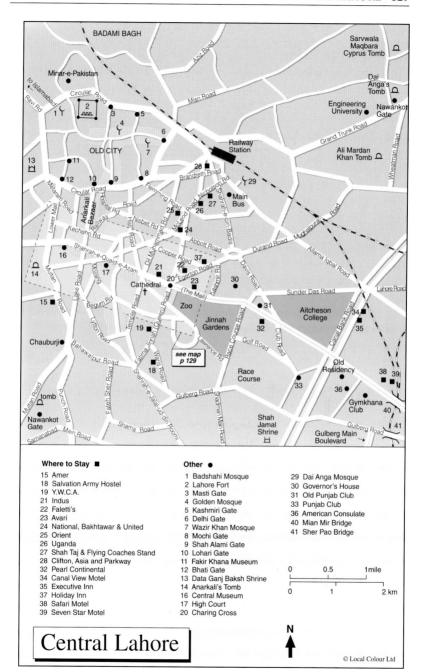

BADAMI BAGH

Sarvwala Maqbara Cyprus Tomb

Minar-e-Pakistan

To Islamabad

Dai Anga's Tomb

Engineering University

Nawankot Gate

Aziz Road

Circular Road

Misri Road

Ravi Rd

2

1

3

5

4

6

Grand Trunk Road

Ali Mardan Khan Tomb

Railway Station

Wheatman Road

OLD CITY

7

13

11

12 10 9

8

28

Brandreth Road

Nicholson Rd

29

Main Bus

Dai Anga Mosque

Flemming Road

Sharah-e-Din-Badis

Mcleod Road

27

26

25

Nisbet Rd

24

Abbott Road

Durand Road

Mughalpura Road

Allama Iqbal Road

Meleran Road

Circular Road

Anarkali Bazaar

Hall Road

Railway

Road

Kechehri Rd

Lower Mall

16

Shahrah-e-Quaid-e-Azam

17

21

22

37

Cooper Road

Dil Muhammad Road

Egerton Rd

Kalami Rd

Davis Road

Sunder Das Road

Aitcheson College

34

35

14

Multan Road

Lake Road

Mozang

20

23

Cathedral †

Zoo

30

31

Jinnah Gardens

32

Golf Road

Club Road

Canal Bank Road

Lahore Road

15

Begum Rd

Lytton Road

Temple Road

19

Fatima Jinnah (Queen) Road

Race Course Road

Lawrence Rd

see map p 129

Chauburji

Bahawalpur Road

Fateh Sher Road

Shahrah-e-Jalal-ud-din Room

18

White Road

Gulberg Road

Jackman Main Road

Race Course

33

Old Residency

36

38 39

Gymkhana Club 40

41

tomb

Multan Road

Punch Road

Nawankot Gate

Shama Road

Main Road

Samanabad

Shah Jamal Shrine

Gulberg Main Boulevard

Gulberg Road

see map p 129

Where to Stay ■

15 Amer
18 Salvation Army Hostel
19 Y.W.C.A.
21 Indus
22 Faletti's
23 Avari
24 National, Bakhtawar & United
25 Orient
26 Uganda
27 Shah Taj & Flying Coaches Stand
28 Clifton, Asia and Parkway
32 Pearl Continental
34 Canal View Motel
35 Executive Inn
37 Holiday Inn
38 Safari Motel
39 Seven Star Motel

Other ●

1 Badshahi Mosque
2 Lahore Fort
3 Masti Gate
4 Golden Mosque
5 Kashmiri Gate
6 Delhi Gate
7 Wazir Khan Mosque
8 Mochi Gate
9 Shah Alami Gate
10 Lohari Gate
11 Fakir Khana Museum
12 Bhati Gate
13 Data Ganj Baksh Shrine
14 Anarkali's Tomb
16 Central Museum
17 High Court
20 Charing Cross

29 Dai Anga Mosque
30 Governor's House
31 Old Punjab Club
33 Punjab Club
36 American Consulate
40 Mian Mir Bridge
41 Sher Pao Bridge

0		0.5		1mile

0		1		2 km

Central Lahore

N

© Local Colour Ltd

Lahore Central Museum

This is the best museum in Pakistan, tel 7662669, with 19 galleries displaying collections of Buddhist stone sculpture from the Gandharan period, including the haunting fasting Buddha, Islamic, Hindu and Jain wood carving, and Islamic works such as illustrated manuscripts, Korans, rugs and metalwork. Paintings are arranged in chronological order to show the development of miniatures from Jain through Indian, Persian, imperial and provincial Mughal, Rajasthani and Pahari to Sikh, and in the adjoining gallery are modern Pakistani paintings. The ceiling is decorated by Sadequain (a well-known Pakistani artist) to illustrate a line from one of Iqbal's (see page 131) poems, 'Constellations beyond the stars: passions beyond love itself'.

The prehistory gallery is excellent, with artefacts from Moenjodaro and other Indus Civilisation cities, and the coin collection is the most complete in the country, as is the ethnographic display. But nothing has been changed for 30 years so everything is now faded and dusty, the reserve collections in the storerooms are never displayed.

The museum is housed in a Mughal–Gothic structure opened in 1894 (the foundation stone was laid in 1890 by Prince Albert Victor, Prince of Wales — the prince suspected of being Jack the Ripper — who died the following year). A regal bronze statue of Queen Victoria wearing her Honiton lace apron, which was cast for her diamond jubilee in 1897, now stands in the museum. The wedding ring was forgotten by the artist and was added as an afterthought at Princess Alexandra's insistence. The statue used to be in Charing Cross on The Mall where an open Koran now stands.

The museum is open 9 am to 5 pm in summer and 9 am to 4 pm in winter, except Wednesdays and the first Monday of each month. There is a small extrance fee and a photography fee. Free guided tour daily from 10 am to 12 noon.

Lahore museum's first curator, and the collector of most of its treasures, was John Lockwood Kipling, Rudyard's father and no doubt the writer's model for the kindly 'white-bearded Englishman' who was curator of the old Lahore Museum in his book 'Kim'.

Badshahi Mosque

(Open 5 am to 9 pm) With the simple grace of its lines, its pleasing proportions and its airy spaciousness, this mosque, built by Emperor Aurangzeb in 1674, represents the very best of Mughal architecture. It is a huge, walled square with minarets at each corner and a monumental gate at the top of a broad flight of steps. The courtyard is paved with red sandstone – which gets very hot under bare feet in summer. A square marble fountain stands in the centre of the courtyard, while an arcade of white arches lines its perimeter on three sides. The fourth side, opposite the gate, is the prayer chamber, which is crowned by three elegant marble domes. The ceilings inside the prayer chamber are decorated with carved plaster-work and floral frescos in subdued colours.

You can climb to the top of one of the minarets for an excellent bird's-eye view of the mosque, the fort opposite and the old city of Lahore. The minarets have 204 steps and are exactly one-third as tall as the courtyard is wide. (see pictures pages 12–13, 45 and 68–69).

Hazuri Bagh

This garden (*bagh*) lies in the square area between Badshahi Mosque and Lahore Fort. Aurangzeb built it as a *serai* (a kind of rest-house) and used it for reviewing his troops. The two-storey building by the south gate served as a boarding house for scholars studying at the mosque. The north gate, through which nobles passed when visiting the palaces inside the fort, is called Roshnai Darwaza ('Gate of Light') because it was brightly lit at night. Ranjit Singh's grandson was killed by failing masonry, (probably murdered), while passing here *en route* from his father's cremation to his own coronation.

Hazuri Bagh Baradari, the marble pavilion in the centre of the garden is one of the few surviving Sikh monuments in Lahore. It was built by Ranjit Singh in 1818 using marble taken from various Mughal tombs and the floor of the fort's royal bathhouse. Its elegant pillars of carved marble support delicately cusped arches. Ranjit Singh held court under the mirrored ceiling of the central area. The pavilion had a second storey until it was damaged by lightning in 1932.

The **Tomb of Allama Muhammad Iqbal**, the great poet–philosopher who lived from 1873 to 1938 and conceived the idea of Pakistan as a separate Muslim state, is on the left as you face the gate of Badshahi Mosque. Built in 1951, this small tomb is constructed of red sandstone. The window grilles, door-frames and entire interior are of carved white marble. The translucent marble headstone, a gift from Afghanistan, is inscribed with two of the poet's couplets condemning racial discrimination.

Lahore Fort

The massive walls of Lahore Fort, built by Akbar in the 1560s, tower over the old city of Lahore, and the huge rectangle they define, 380 by 330 metres (1,250 by 1,080 feet), is filled with buildings from a variety of periods. A complete tour of the fort takes about two hours.

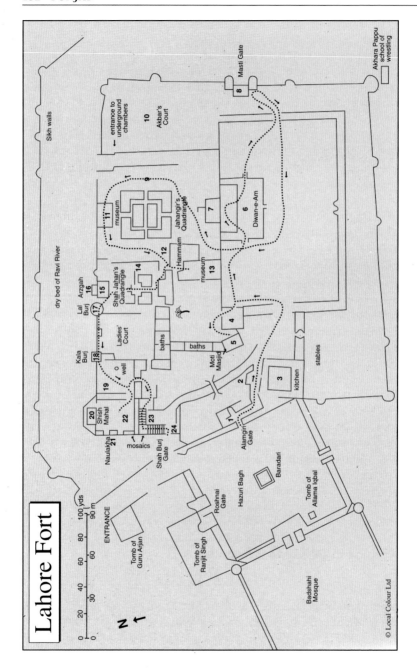

Lahore Fort

The entrance is through Alamgiri Gate (1), built by Aurangzeb at the same time as Badshahi Mosque in 1674. A ramp leads from Alamgiri Gate to the old Musamman Burj Gate (2) on the left and, on the right, to the royal kitchens (3), which are now occupied by the police and closed to the public. (Note that ground level within the walls is much higher than that outside. The intervening space is filled with many levels of dungeons, all windowless except the rooms against the walls.)

The **Maktab Khana** (Clerks' House) (4) is a small cloistered court surrounded by arcades in which clerks sat recording the names of visitors. The inscription outside tells that it was built by Jahangir in 1618.

The **Moti Masjid** (Pearl Mosque) (5) is entered via steps rising from the corner of the large courtyard north of the Maktab Khana. This little gem was built by Shah Jahan in 1644, ten years before he built a similar mosque in the Red Fort at Agra and 18 years before he built the most exquisite pearl mosque of all in the Red Fort at Delhi. All three are faced in white marble and are charmingly intimate, making their impact through their delicate proportions and purity of line.

The **Diwan-e-Am** (Hall of Public Audience) (6) is an open pavilion with 40 pillars built by Shah Jahan in 1631 to shelter his subjects when they appeared before him. The original building collapsed in 1841 when it was shelled by Sikhs from the top of one of the minarets of Badshahi Mosque. Credit for this poor reconstruction goes to the British, who used it as a hospital and covered the spacious lawn in front with barracks and offices. The pillars have been replaced upside down.

The marble pavilion and red sandstone balcony at the back of the Diwan-e-Am are originals built by Akbar. Here the emperor appeared daily before the public — who, in his day, crowded under a canvas awning. The serpentine sandstone brackets are typical of Akbar's commissions, with the depiction of animals showing Hindu influence and reflecting Akbar's policy of religious tolerance. His two-storey **Diwan-e-Khas** (Hall of Private Audience) (7), built in 1566, is behind the balcony and is reached by stairs on the right. Visible inside are traces of the original painted and gilded stucco work, and the marble work here is the oldest in Lahore.

Masti (or **Masjidi**) **Gate** (8) is east of the Diwan-e-Am. It was the original main gate to the fort built by Akbar in 1566 and receives its name from the Masjid (Mosque) of Maryam Zamani just outside. The gate is defended by heavy octagonal bastions equipped with battlements, loopholes and machicolations from which attackers were targeted with missiles and boiling oil.

Jahangir's Quadrangle (9), north of the Diwan-e-Am, and one of the fort's most attractive areas, was started by Akbar in 1566 and finished by Jahangir in 1617. The buildings on the east, west and south sides of the court reflect typical Akbari style, with richly carved red sandstone columns and elaborate animal-shaped brackets. Behind the buildings to the east is **Akbar's Court** (10), now housing the fort administrative offices and, in the underground rooms, conservation laboratories.

The **Khwabgah-e-Jahangir** (Jahangir's Room of Dreams — or, more prosaically, his sleeping quarters) (11) is the main building running the length of the north side of Jahangir's Quadrangle and is typical of Jahangir's period in its austerity. It is now a museum, containing a huge ivory model of the Taj Mahal (returned from England in 1950), some excellent illustrated manuscripts (including the *Akbar Nama*, the daily chronicle of Akbar's reign), some beautiful calligraphy, good miniature paintings and a collection of Mughal coins.

The **Hammam** (12), Jahangir's bathhouse, is in the southwest corner of the quadrangle. It was once quite luxuriously paved with marble and had delicate floral frescos covering the walls. A cascade of water flowed over the carved sandstone of the niche in the south wall. The bath was remodelled (and its floor stripped of marble) in Sikh times. The British used it as a kitchen. It is now closed to protect it, but you can enter with special permission.

The new **museum** (13), west of the bath, contains a fine collection of Mughal and Sikh arms and paintings dating from the Sikh period. Stairs outside the building run to the second floor, where more Sikh paintings are hung.

From the museum you again enter the quadrangle of the Moti Masjid. **Shah Jahan's Quadrangle** (14) is to the north, the first building on the left (south side) is Shah Jahan's sleeping quarters, which consist of five connecting rooms built in 1633. The middle room features lattice screens, door-frames and a central fountain, all of marble. The fresco of Radha and Krishna dates from the Sikh period.

Shah Jahan's Diwan-e-Khas (Hall of Private Audience) (15) is the graceful arcaded pavilion of marble on the north side of the quadrangle, which the emperor built around 1645. Delicately carved marble lattice screens overlook the now dry bed of the Ravi River, and the floor is paved with coloured marble in geometric patterns. The central fountain was once decorated with *pietra dura* (semi-precious stones) inlay. The British converted the pavilion into a church.

Below the pavilion, at the foot of the fort wall, is the ruined **Arzgah** (16), where nobles assembled every morning to pay their respects to the emperor. Here, on the outer wall, are some particularly fine tile mosaics of blue dragons, the emblem carried before the emperor.

The Lal Burj (Red Tower) (17) is the octagonal summer pavilion in the northwest corner of Shah Jahan's Quadrangle. Built between 1617 and 1631 by Jahangir and Shah Jahan, it forms part of the north wall of the fort. The tower is decorated with beautiful tile mosaics and filigree work. The paintings inside date mostly from the Sikh period, as does the third storey of the structure. The floor was originally of marble, and the water channels, fountains and central pool must have made it delightfully cool in summer. On the staircase in the northeast corner survive remains of a gilded and painted honeycomb cornice, indicating how lavishly decorated the whole pavilion once was.

Adjacent is the **Zenana Sehan** (Ladies' Courtyard), built by Shah Jahan in 1633. All that remains is a small marble pavilion overlooking the river in the middle of the north side of the courtyard. This pavilion was reserved for the emperor when he came to visit the ladies of his harem. Only the foundations of the ladies' apartments and their private mosque survive. The remains of the *hammam* (bathhouse) is on the south side of the courtyard. It was built in the Turkish style, with a dressing room, warm bath and hot bath. The marble floor is still intact in the southwestern room. Note here the terracotta water pipes built into the wall. The water heater was at the western end beside the original *baitul khala* (lavatory).

The **Kala Burj** (Black Tower) (18), a twin summer pavilion to the Lal Burj, is in the northwest corner of the ladies' court. The building's decoration is completely gone, and its central portion is closed, but it still serves as passage to the **Garden Court** (19), the ladies' private garden.

The **Court of the Shish Mahal** (Palace of Mirrors) (20) is the best-preserved and most interesting place in the fort. The Shish Mahal was built by Shah Jahan in 1631 as private apartments for his empress, and it was here that the British chose to assume sovereignty over Punjab in 1849. The whole of the interior is covered with mirror mosaics, carved and gilded plaster-work and *pietra dura* inlay. The ceiling is original Mughal work; the walls, with frescos and shards of blue and white china, date from Sikh times. The main hall of the palace is open at the front, with five cusped arches supported on delicate fluted double pillars. *Pietra dura* inlay decorates the base of each pillar and the tops of the arches. The graceful vine pattern over the two outer arches is particularly fine. The floor is a geometric mosaic of marble.

Surrounding the main hall is a string of nine connecting rooms with views through exquisite marble screens to the dry river bed. Here, the ladies could look out without being seen and enjoy the cool breezes off the then-flowing river. The easternmost room is covered in frescos and offers excellent views along the outer walls of the fort, showing the windows of the underground rooms and the remains of the brilliantly coloured tile mosaics of animals, people and geometric designs that once decorated the arched niches on the outer face of the wall.

The **Naulakha** (21), named after the nine *lakhs* (hundred-thousand) of rupees it cost to build in 1631, is the small marble pavilion on the west side of the court styled after a Bengali bamboo hut with a curved roof. This dainty pavilion was decorated with the finest *pietra dura* inlay in Lahore; the carefully selected bits of jade, carnelian, lapis, agate, jet and other semi-precious stones were set into the marble in delicate floral and geometric designs. At the top of the double pillars supporting the archway, in one tiny niche, 102 minute pieces of stone were inlaid to make one floral pattern. The view through a lovely marble screen takes in the Badshahi Mosque, Ranjit Singh's Tomb, the golden dome of Guru Arjan's Memorial and the Minar-e-Pakistan. (see pictures pages 68–69).

On the south side of the court is a row of rooms (22); on the rear wall of the central one is a water cascade. The water once rippled down this wall and filled the water channels and fountains in the courtyard.

The exit is around to the left (east) behind this wall and down the broad, shallow steps of the **Hathi Paer** (Elephant Path) (23). This was the private entrance of the royal family and leads straight to the **Shah Burj Gate** (24). In the western wall above the path are niches from which eunuchs observed and a crier announced the comings and goings of royalty. Servants stood in attendance in the gallery above.

As you leave through the Shah Burj Gate, look to your right along the wall at the 350-year-old **mosaics** set in the outer face of the fort wall. This use of glazed ceramic tile is of Persian origin and became popular in the reign of Shah Jahan as a practical means of decorating brick monuments in Punjab, where stone is scarce. The mosaics decorating the west and north walls of Lahore Fort are unique in style and variety of design, for here the geometric patterns are liberally interspersed with animal and human figures which, like Mughal miniature paintings, illustrate the ways and amusements of the Mughal court, a curious blend of barbarism and refinement. Vigorous scenes in which elephants, camels and bulls are pitted against each other jostle with depictions of a polo game and of *paris*, Persian winged fairies wearing robes inflated by flight. Decorating the north wall are blue dragons and numerous scenes peopled by courtiers.

Lahore is famous for its **wrestlers**. The most famous school is **Akhara Pappu Pehalvan**, just outside the walls of Lahore Fort near Masti Gate. Here you can watch the wrestlers practising both morning and evening. (see pictures pages 50–51).

Sights near Lahore Fort

The **Minar-e-Pakistan** (Tower of Pakistan), which looms in the park near Badshahi Mosque, marks the spot at which the Muslim League on 23 March 1940 passed the resolution calling for the creation of the independent Muslim state of Pakistan. For Rs2 visitors can climb to the top for an excellent view of Lahore Fort, Badshahi Mosque and, outside the walls, the tombs of Guru Arjan Mal and Ranjit Singh.

The **Tomb of Guru Arjan** has elegant fluted domes covered in gold leaf. Guru Arjan was the fifth Sikh guru and is remembered for compiling the *Adi Granth*, the original Sikh holy book, which is now across the Indian border in Amritsar.

The **Samadhi** or **Tomb of Ranjit Singh** (in the same compound as Guru Arjan's tomb) is a splendidly ornate example of Sikh architecture, with gilded, fluted domes and cupolas, and an elaborate balustrade around the top. It is lined with marble taken from various Mughal monuments in Lahore. The ashes of this greatest Sikh ruler, who controlled Punjab and Kashmir from 1799 to 1839, are in the lotus-shaped urn sheltered in the centre of the tomb under a marble pavilion inlaid with *pietra dura*. Known as 'the one-eyed lion of the Punjab', the illiterate maharaja ruled his empire with a firm hand and was fond of horses and beautiful women. Other tiny urns in the tomb contain the scanty remains of his four wives and seven concubines who threw themselves on his funeral pyre.

Wazir Khan's Mosque, Lahore

Old City and Wazir Khan's Mosque

The old city is the best part of Lahore; don't worry about getting lost — people will direct you and there are rickshaws on the wider lanes if you get tired.

At the time that Akbar built the fort at the northwest corner of Lahore, he enclosed the city within a high brick wall with 12 gates, six of which still stand. A circular road allows motor traffic to bypass the old city. You can take a rickshaw tour of the old gates, driving anti-clockwise round the city.

Wazir Khan's Mosque is in the old city, 300 metres (yards) from **Delhi Gate**. It is on the left in a narrow lane lined with tiny shops selling everything from paper money garlands to rat traps. On the way you pass **Wazir Khan's Hammam** or bath house, just inside Delhi Gate on the left.

Wazir Khan's Mosque is unique and is one of the most beautiful in Pakistan. It was built in 1634 by Hakim Ali-ud-din, popularly known as Wazir Khan, who was governor of Punjab under Shah Jahan. Craftsmen from the Punjabi city of Chiniot, from where Wazir Khan hailed and which is still celebrated for its wood-carvers, were brought in to do the work. The mosque is built of brick and faced with mosaics of brightly coloured glazed tiles in Mughal floral motifs on a background of clear yellow. Its frescos and enamel mosaics have been carefully restored by Pakistan's few remaining craftsmen able to do so. The effect is very fine, particularly the mosaic calligraphy, including a Persian inscription over the entrance which translates as: 'Remove thy heart from the gardens of the world/And know that this building is the true abode of man.'

The prayer hall has five chambers, each surmounted by a dome. Octagonal minarets stand at each corner of the courtyard. The custodian will unlock one so that visitors can climb up the 69 steps to the muezzin's gallery for an excellent panorama of the old city. Entombed in the courtyard is Syed Muhammad Ishaq, a saint otherwise called Miran Shah, who died in the 14th century. To the left of his grave is a well.

The **Sonehri Masjid** (Golden Mosque), named for its three gilt domes, dominates a square some 500 metres (about a quarter of a mile) west of Wazir Khan's Mosque. The way through the bazaar is along a narrow lane overhung by precarious wooden balconies. You pass all the sights sounds and smells of an Asian bazaar: in the alleys to the left are spices, dried fruit and nuts — all the ingredients for Mughal cooking. The Golden Mosque was built in 1753 by Bokhari Khan, a favourite of the powerful widow of Mir Mannu until (it is said) he displeased the lady and was beaten to death by her female attendants, who used their slippers for the purpose.

In the courtyard behind the mosque is a large well with steps leading down to the water. This is credited to Guru Arjan, the fifth Sikh guru.

Take the alley that runs beside the left (south) wall of the mosque, and continue along a very narrow lane in which are sold pots and pans in all sizes and shapes. This is the **brass bazaar**. The pots and pans are sold by weight, but some fine antique brassware still rewards a search. A shop I can recommend is the tiny, two-storey place called Kashmiri Museum. After 200 metres (yards), you come out at a tonga (horse cart) and motor rickshaw stand in a wide street. Either vehicle will take you cheaply from the old city via **Shah Almi Gate**. Where the gate used to be is now an abandoned Hindu temple.

Further to the west is **Bhati Gate**, shaded by a huge banyan tree. About 500 metres (about a quarter of a mile) into the old city from Bhati Gate, on the right, is **Fakir Khana Museum**. This modest house with big wooden doors contains a charming collection of family relics, including miniature paintings, local *objets d'art*, carpets, Gandhara statues and semi-precious stones, to be viewed by appointment only, tel 7660645.

Mubarik Haveli, about 50 metres past Fakir Khana Museum, is a 19th century house set round a courtyard, aesthetically restored by Kamal Khan Mumtaz (one of Pakistan's best architects) and an interesting living example of local building techniques used for restoration. For viewing contact Mr Bahauddin, tel 7656482. Continue from here through to the Hazuri Bagh, or retrace your steps to the Bhati Gate.

About 500 metres outside the old city's Bhati Gate is the **Mausoleum of Data Ganj Baksh**, and beside it the Data Durbar Mosque with its two slender towers capped by gilt cones, beside it is a hospital. This complex is the shrine of Syed Ali Abdul Hasan bin Usman, popularly known as Data Ganj Baksh meaning 'he who gives generously'. This Sufi saint came from the Afghan city of Ghazni to Lahore in 1039 and died here in 1072. He was a great scholar — the author of the *Kashful Mahjub*, a basic text in Persian on the fundamentals of Sufism — and is one of the most popular saints in Pakistan. Hundreds of pilgrims flock to his shrine every day to pray for favours, and it is said no one leaves empty-handed. Foreign visitors are welcome, with Thursday being the most interesting and crowded day to go (see pages 82 and 151). Data Ganj Baksh's *urs* (death festival) — almost a national event — spans the 18th and 19th days of the month of Safar.

Jahangir's Tomb

This second cluster of Mughal monuments is on the Grand Trunk Road about five kilometres (three miles) towards Rawalpindi from the centre of Lahore. Take a picnic and plan half a day here — you can buy soft drinks and snacks outside the main gate. Bus numbers 6 and 23 take about 20 minutes from Lahore Railway Station. After you have crossed the toll bridge over the Ravi River, a dome and minarets become visible over the palm trees. Turn right about 700 metres (yards) beyond the toll booth. If on foot, follow the path across the railway line. If driving, follow the road for 600 metres before turning left to cross the railway level crossing. About 700 metres further on is the massive Mughal gateway leading into the tombs. The small entrance fee covers the three tombs together.

The fresco-covered gateway of plastered red brick leads into **Akbari Serai,** built by Shah Jahan in about 1637 as a travellers' hotel. It is a spacious garden quartered by footpaths and planted with huge *chinar,* plane, *shisham* (rosewood), peepul and banyan trees. Around the four sides are 180 small rooms with verandahs.

On the east side, a handsome red sandstone gateway inlaid with marble leads into the **Tomb of Jahangir,** who died in 1627. The tomb was built by his son, Shah Jahan of Taj Mahal fame. It stands in the centre of a large garden divided by paths and water channels into 16 square sections and filled with gracefully spreading mature trees. The flat-roofed mausoleum is low and square, with each corner featuring a tall, octagonal minaret decorated with a zigzag design and crowned with a marble cupola. The minaretts slope outwards in case of an earthquake.

The red sandstone walls are inlaid with marble in intricate geometric patterns. Inside, the floors are of highly polished variegated marble, and the walls and ceilings of the surrounding arcade and its 30 rooms are covered in geometric and floral frescos. Four passages lead into the centre, where the white marble cenotaph (empty tomb) stands on a plinth decorated with *pietra dura* inlay in delicate floral designs.

The Ninety-nine Attributes of God are inlaid in black marble. The south side of the cenotaph is inscribed: 'The Glorious Tomb of His High Majesty, Asylum of Pardon, Nur-ud-din Muhammad, the Emperor Jahangir', followed by the year of his death. Marble lattice screens fill the arches on all four sides.

A staircase within each of the five-storey minarets leads up to the roof, which is surrounded by a balustrade and paved with white marble inlaid with geometric patterns in yellow and black. (Ask for the key at the ticket office.) The marble cenotaph surrounded by a marble railing that once occupied the centre of the roof was removed by the Sikhs to Amritsar.

A certain General Amise, a French officer in Ranjit Singh's army, actually converted Jahangir's tomb into a residence. After his death the tomb was lived in by Sultan Muhammad, the brother of the Afghan ruler Amir Dost Muhammad.

The passage leading through to the **Tomb of Asaf Khan** is left of the handsome red sandstone mosque that stands on the west side of the Akbari Serai, opposite the gate of Jahangir's Tomb. Its bulbous dome is visible from the *serai* as it looms over the mosque.

Votive threads attached to a marble screen

Asaf Khan enjoyed close marriage ties with the ruling family. He was brother-in-law to Jahangir through Nur Jahan and father-in-law to their son, Shah Jahan, through Mumtaz Mahal, the lady of the Taj Mahal. Shah Jahan built this huge mausoleum for his father-in-law upon his death in 1641, nearly a decade and a half after Asaf Khan had provided crucial support in his struggle for the succession.

The tomb, which reflects classic Mughal design, is set at the centre of a large walled garden. A particularly graceful, high-pointed dome crowns an arched octagonal base. The whole must have been a glorious sight when the arches were fully faced with glazed-tile mosaics of blue, green, yellow and orange, and when its dome was sheathed in shining white marble. The marble cenotaph within, once inlaid with *pietra dura*, still lists the Ninety-nine Attributes of God in black inlay, but the fountains on the plinth marking the four cardinal points are gone. The northernmost of the two massive gates leading to the garden still retains some of its glazed tiles.

The **Tomb of Nur Jahan**, west of the railway, is reached via the road outside the south wall of Asaf Khan's Tomb. Follow it west, then turn left to cross the railway line, at which point the tomb is immediately on your left.

Nur Jahan lived until 1645, surviving by 18 years her husband, Jahangir, through whom she wielded considerable power. She filled her years of forced retirement by building herself a magnificent square tomb similar in design to that of her husband. Unfortunately, the monument was stripped to its brick core by the Sikhs, but it has been restored recently with new sandstone facing inlaid with marble. The four minarets and the garden wall have collapsed, and the frescos inside survive only in traces. The marble cenotaphs of Nur Jahan and her daughter, Lakli Begum, and the marble platform supporting them are 20th-century replacements, the originals having disappeared.

To return to the Grand Trunk Road, drive on past Nur Jahan's Tomb and turn right.

The **Kamran Baradari** on a wooded island just down river from the toll bridge is a restored marble pavilion with twelve arches (*baradari*) built in 1540 for Kamran, Emperor Humayun's brother. The island park is crowded on Fridays, but makes a pleasant picnic place during the rest of the week, accessible by boat from the Lahore side of the river.

Shalimar Garden

This impressive Mughal monument, the most complete Mughal garden in the entire Indian subcontinent, is on the Grand Trunk Road, five kilometres (three miles) towards the Indian border from the centre of Lahore. Wagon number 12 takes 20 minutes from the railway station. If going by car from Jahangir's Tomb, bypass the city by taking Bund Road after crossing the toll bridge over the Ravi River. Make an effort to be at Shalimar Garden when the fountains are playing, which is daily 10 to 11 am and 4 to 5 pm in summer, and 11 am to 12 noon and 3 to 4 pm in winter. The flowers are at their best in February and March.

Shah Jahan built the Shalimar Garden in 1642 for the pleasure of the royal household, which often stayed here for days or weeks at a time. In design, it conforms to the classic Mughal conception of the perfect garden and consists of three terraces of straight, shaded walks set around a perfectly symmetrical arrangement of ponds, fountains and marble pavilions, all surrounded by flower beds and fruit trees and enclosed within a wall. (In its rigid symmetry, it is similar to gardens laid out in 17th century Europe.) Incredibly, the whole garden took less than 18 months to build. The problem of creating sufficient water pressure to feed the hundreds of fountains was solved by carrying water from the Royal Canal into raised tanks outside the garden.

The garden was designed to be entered at the lower terrace, which was open to distinguished members of the public. Honoured guests then moved against the flow of the cool waters to discover new and greater delights at the middle terrace, which was used for entertaining. Only intimates of the royal family were permitted to experience the supreme serenity of the upper terrace, the royal inner sanctum.

These days, visitors lose this effect by trooping straight on to the upper terrace from the Grand Trunk Road. The terrace is divided into quarters by ponds splashed by fountains and has nine buildings, including the octagonal towers at each corner. The emperor's sleeping quarters were in the building at the centre of the south wall, just to your left as you enter. The building's three rooms, the walls and ceilings of which were once covered with frescos, open on to a wide verandah overlooking the garden through five gracefully cusped arches.

The empress's sleeping quarters are at the centre of the west wall, across from the Hall of Public Audience, which juts through the wall and out of the garden. The emperor walked through this hall daily to show himself to the public gathered in a separate walled garden outside. The arcaded pavilion on the north side of the terrace is the Grand Hall, which was once covered with frescos and used for ceremonial functions. The little house in the northeast quarter, built by the Sikhs early in the 19th century, was used as a guest-house. William Moorcroft, the prodigious English explorer, stayed here in 1820.

The middle terrace is four metres (13 feet) down and reached by two flights of steps on either side of the Grand Hall. Between them, a cascade carries water down from the upper ponds to the great central pond: a broad square of water upon which play 150 fountains. Between the cascade and the pond, and surrounded by a marble railing, is the emperor's marble throne, where he sat in the moonlight listening to his musicians play and watching his nautch girls dance.

The Turkish bathhouse is set against the wall in the southeast corner of the terrace. Its changing room and cold and hot baths were once decorated with *pietra dura* inlay.

Two pavilions on either side of a waterfall guard the steps between the middle and lower terraces. In rows along the marble wall behind the waterfall are hundreds of little cusped niches. Flowers in golden vases occupied them by day, and lamps by night, so that, when viewed from the lower terrace through a double row of five cusped arches, the waterfall was a shimmering sheet of light.

The lower terrace, the least exciting, has two gates decorated with glazed-tile mosaics, two corner towers and a hall in the centre once decorated with white marble and frescos.

Trips From Lahore

Hiran Minar

Emperor Jahangir enjoyed hunting in the area around Sheikhupura, about 30 kilometres (19 miles) from Lahore. There, in 1616, he built a hunting pavilion at the centre of an artificial lake and the Hiran Minar, a tower in memory of his pet deer. Three years later he built the massive brick fort still standing at **Sheikhupura.**

Buses run frequently between Lahore and Sheikhupura. If driving yourself, turn left 700 metres (yards) past the toll gate on the bridge over the Ravi River and go west along Sheikhupura Road. After two kilometres (1.3 miles), take the right fork on to the dual carriageway, an excellent road that goes straight across flat farmland for 30 kilometres (19 miles), to Sheikhupura.

The Hiran Minar and an artificial lake are in a deer park four kilometres (2.5 miles) beyond Sheikhupura toward Sargodha. Turn right where the dual carriageway ends, just past the railway level crossing.

The waters of the large, square lake are held within a brick wall and well stocked with fish. A little arched pavilion stands at each corner of the lake, and steps lead down to the water. An arched causeway leads out to the three-storey octagonal pavilion in the centre, where Jahangir sat in the shelter of the graceful arcade and watched the wild animals drawn to the water. Near the end of the causeway stands the Hiran Minar, dedicated to the memory of the deer Jahangir called Mansaraj. Visitors can climb the 99 steps to the top. An old well is concealed in the bushes near the tower, and boats are for hire on the lake.

Chhanga Manga Wildlife Reserve

This park in a huge forest 70 kilometres (43 miles) southwest of Lahore and halfway to Sahiwal features two small steam trains that pull deer-watchers along narrowgauge tracks through the woods to large fenced pens stocked with several species of deer. There is a lake with boating, a restaurant and accommodation that is good value.

Harappa

An important excavation of the Indus Civilisation, Harappa is just west of Sahiwal towards Multan. The Archaeology Department Rest House is comfortable, with rooms bookable through the Director of Archaeology at Lahore Fort (see Lahore listing on page 275).

The Fortified City Railway Station, Lahore

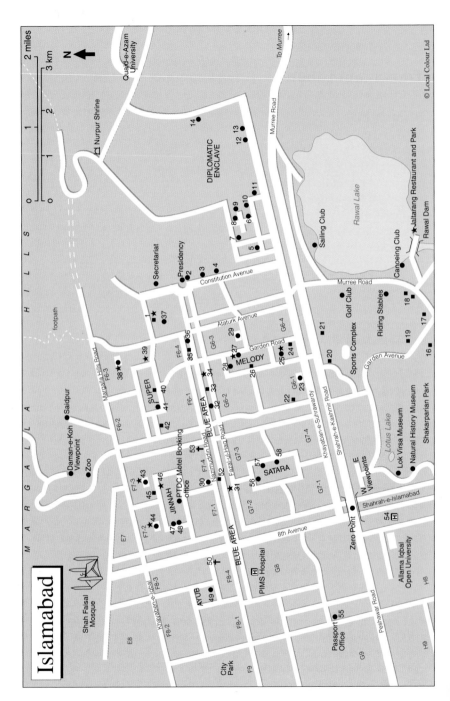

Islamabad

M A R G A L L A   H I L L S

2 miles
3 km

N

Shah Faisal Mosque

Nurpur Shrine

Quad-e-Azam University

Daman-e-Koh Viewpoint
Saidpur
Zoo

footpath

Secretariat
Presidency
2
3
4

14

Constitution Avenue

DIPLOMATIC ENCLAVE

12 13
11
8 9
10
7
6
5

Murree Road

Rawal Lake

Sailing Club

Canoeing Club

Jaltarang Restaurant and Park
Rawal Dam

Margalla Hills Road

38 ★
39 ★
1 ★
37
36
35
SUPER
41 40
42
F6-3
F6-2
F6-4
F6-1

Ataturk Avenue

29
27
26 ★ 25 ★ 24
MELODY
28
G6-3
G6-4
G6-2
G6-1
22
23

Garden Road

21
20

Golf Club
Sports Complex
Riding Stables
18
19
17
16
Garden Avenue

Murree Road

BLUE AREA
32 33 34
52
53
30
31
56
57
SATARA
58
G7-4
G7-3
G7-2
G7-1

PTDC Motel Booking office

Nazimuddin Road
Fazal-ul-Haq Road
Khayaban-e-Suhrawardy
Shahrah-e-Kashmir Road

F7-3 ★ 43
45 ★ 46 ★
JINNAH
47
48
44
F7-2
F7-1
E7

Zero Point
W
E
Viewpoints

Shahrah-e-Islamabad

54 H

Lotus Lake

Lok Virsa Museum
Natural History Museum
Shakarparian Park

8th Avenue

BLUE AREA
50
F8-4
PIMS Hospital H
G8

Khayaban-e-Iqbal
E8
F8-3
F8-2
F8-1

AYUB
49

City Park
F9

Passport Office
55
G9

Peshawar Road

Allama Iqbal Open University
H8

H9

© Local Colour Ltd

Islamabad

Islamabad, Pakistan's new capital, nestles against the Margalla Hills, the foothills of the Himalaya in northern Punjab. Technically it is not part of Punjab, but forms its own Capital Authority. Modern, spacious and carefully planned, Islamabad is a city of wide, tree-lined streets, large houses, elegant public buildings and well-organised bazaars. Traffic jams and crowds are rare, and narrow lanes and slums are few and far between. Sidewalks are shaded and safe behind rows of flame trees, jacaranda and hibiscus. Roses, jasmine and bougainvillaea fill the many parks, and scenic viewpoints show the city to its best advantage.

The decision to replace Karachi with a new capital in the centre of the country near the hills was made in 1958. Doxiadis Associates, a Greek firm, drew up plans for a huge triangle with its apex towards the Margalla Hills. Within the triangle is a grid divided into eight zones designated governmental, diplomatic, residential, commercial, educational, industrial and so on. The city has no real centre and is very widely spread out, each sector having its own shopping area and its own open space. Construction began in 1961, with the first residents moving in two years later.

Getting to Islamabad

Islamabad is about 15 kilometres from Rawalpindi and three roads connect the two cities, Murree Road, Airport Road and Peshawar Road. The international airport, railway station and two bus stations are all in Rawalpindi.

A taxi from the airport to Islamabad takes about 15 minutes. Wagons and buses are not allowed into the airport, but wait on the road outside. To get from the airport to Islamabad by wagon, walk outside the airport compound, turn right outside the gates and catch a wagon for Raja Bazaar, Rawalpindi from near the petrol station. Change at Committee Chowk. The journey takes more than an hour but costs very little. Wagons, minibuses and buses connect Rawalpindi to Islamabad. Wagon numbers 1 and 6 start from the Saddar Bazaar GPO and end via different routes at the Secretariat in Islamabad. Wagon number 3 starts in Raja Bazaar and ends at Bari Imam's shrine in Nurpur.

There is a tourist information centre opposite the international arrival lounge.

When to Go
At 518 metres (1,700 feet) above sea level, Islamabad is at its best from October to March, when days are crisp and nights are cold. Spring is short but intense, with flowers producing a riot of colour in March. The hottest months are May and June, before the monsoon, but even they are not oppressive. Abnormally hot weather can be escaped by taking a trip to Murree, a hill resort 2,240 metres (7,400 feet) above sea level, about an hour's drive away.

Getting Around
This can be a problem. The city is divided into sectors two kilometres square and numbered east to west, 5, 6, 7, 8, 9, 10 and 11 (numbers 1–4 have not yet been built). Going north to south the sectors have letters E, F, G, H and I, so, for example there are sectors E-9, F-9, G-9, H-9 and I-9. Each sector is divided in four quarters numbered 1, 2, 3 and 4, starting in the southwest quarter and progressing round clockwise. Within each sector the streets have numbers. A typical address may read like this, House 2, Street 67, F-7/3. An added complication is that Sectors E, F and G have been given names, so 'E' is also known as 'Mehran', 'F' as 'Shalimar' and 'G' as 'Ramna', so the above address might also be written 2, St 67, Shalimar 7/3. Only the main roads between the sectors have been given names, everything else is numbered. There are big markets in the centre of each sector, and small markets in the centre of each quarter.

Maps are also a problem. The Survey of Pakistan *Islamabad/Rawalpinidi Guide Map,* scale 1:30,000 is useless — only the main streets are labelled. The new PTDC and TDCP maps are the same. Apparently the editor thought all those numbered streets looked too messy! The only good street map I have found is that produced by KM Raffi Property Consultants, available in London Bookshop in Kohsar Market. This is excellent, and gives details of the main markets on the back, including banks, hotels, businesses and shops.

The next problem is transport. Islamabad is too spread out for walking, and public transport runs on only three or four of the main streets. The wagons, minibuses and buses start in Rawalpindi (see above) and go either via Ayub (F–8), Jinnah (F–7) and Super Markets (F–6) to the Secretariat building, or past Aabpara and through the Diplomatic Enclave (where most of the embassies are) to the Nurpur shrine. Other wagons start at Aabpara and go past Melody and Super Markets.

Yellow cabs and taxis can be hired for about Rs100 per hour. But taxi drivers only know the main landmarks, so if you wish to get to a specific address you will have to direct them. If you do not have a map, the only way is to telephone your destination and have someone there direct your taxi driver.

One great blessing is that the Margalla Hills to the north of the city are visible from everywhere, so you can always orient yourself by looking at the hills.

Sights

Daman-e-Koh Viewpoint is halfway up the **Margalla Hills** and gives the best bird's-eye view south over Islamabad, with the President's Palace, the Legislative Assembly and the Secretariat offices dominating the east end of the city (to your left) and the huge Shah Faisal Mosque pressed against the hills to the west. In the distance are Rawal Lake and Rawalpindi. On a clear day after rain, you can see far out over the Potwar Plateau beyond Rawalpindi to a horizon serrated by the Salt Range.

The **zoo** and **children's adventure playground** are at the bottom of the hill below Daman-e-Koh Viewpoint. The road rising behind the view-point leads to the top of the ridge and then east towards Murree.

From the end of Margalla Hills Road, near the Marriott Hotel, you can walk to the top of the Margalla Hills on an easy, well-engineered path in 30 minutes, for a stimulating view of Islamabad, particularly at dawn or dusk. The Asian Study Group, tel 815891, (see page 282) publishes an excellent guide, *Trekking in the Margalla Hills* by Hans van Hoeflaken, with maps detailing all the many routes on the hills.

Shah Faisal Mosque, superbly sited at the foot of the Margalla Hills, resembles an eight-sided Bedouin tent surrounded by four 90-metre-high (300-foot) concrete minarets. The walls hang from four giant concrete girders and are faced with white marble. The interior is decorated with blue mosaics by the Pakistani artists Gulgee and Sadequain, and a spectacular golden chandelier hangs from the centre. Designed by Vedat Dalokay, a Turkish architect, and financed largely by donations from Saudi Arabia, it is the world's biggest mosque, with room for 15,000 worshippers inside and another 85,000 in its raised courtyard. Below the courtyard are two storeys housing an Islamic research centre, library, museum, press centre, lecture hall, cafeteria and the offices of the Shariat faculty of the Islamic University. Open 8 am to 3 pm, you can arrange guided tours by calling 851205. The mosque is closed to tourists at prayer times.

Shakarparian Park, centred on two low hills between Islamabad and Rawalpindi, has paved paths winding through gardens and past fountains and young trees planted by visiting dignitaries. The hills are crowned by **East and West Viewpoints,** which offer photogenic views of Islamabad against the backdrop of the Margalla Hills. A plan of the city has been laid out in a sunken garden at East Viewpoint, with hedges cleverly trimmed to resemble the hills.

Lok Virsa (the Institute of Folk and Traditional Heritage), also in Shakarparian Park, displays a large collection of art, handicrafts and musical instruments from around the country and has an open-air exhibition of wood carvings. Closed on Mondays.

Rawal Lake is the large reservoir surrounded by forest, northeast of Shakarparian Park. It is a protected reserve offering excellent bird-watching, with many migrating birds resting here *en route* between their summer breeding grounds in the north and winter homes in Sindh and India. About 300 species have been spotted in the Islamabad area.

Nurpur village and the Shrine of Syed Abdul Latif Shah, a 17th century saint, are in the foreground of the Margalla Hills and near Quaid-e-Azam University at the northeastern edge of town. The saint has an enormous following throughout the country, and a visit to his shrine speaks volumes about the intensity of religious devotion in Pakistan. Invalids who have come to pray for recovery pull threads from their clothing and cut off locks of their hair to hang from the banyan tree in the courtyard, while others anoint their foreheads or wounds with ashes from the sacred fire. The best time to go is on Thursday evening, when the shrine is alive with pilgrims and there is usually *qawwali* (devotional singing). Take the minibus from Aabpara Market.

The **Holy Man's Cave,** where the saint lived and meditated for 12 years, is a 45-minute climb up the hillside just behind Nurpur.

Sufism — Muslim Mystics and Saints

By Isobel Shaw

The atmosphere in the shrine is hushed, tense and emotional. The crowd shuffles slowly forward to caress the silver railing round the saint's tomb. Reverently, the pilgrims touch the doorpost, the pillars, the stone that once hung around the saint's neck. They slip their offering into one of the locked collection boxes and anoint themselves with holy oil from one of the many lamps.

A man helps his wife, barely able to walk, to the railing, and as she clutches it she cries, her lips moving in prayer. The procession swirls past her. Young women pray for a child, men for success, the poor for strength, the troubled for peace. In the further recesses of the dim tomb sit men and women with Korans open on their crossed knees, fingers tracing the lines of Arabic as they recite from memory, the intensity of their devotion, lifting them from the world, blotting out the profane.

Sufi shrines, the tombs of Sufi saints, are scattered in their hundreds all over Pakistan. Thousands of devotees flock to each shrine to beg their favourite saint to intercede with God and secure the granting of some favour.

The mystic side of Islam emerged in the ninth century, when wandering holy men from Arabia, Iraq, Persia and Afghanistan set out from their native lands, carrying messages of love — love for God, love for the Prophet Muhammad and love for one's neighbour. For the next 700 years, wandering ascetics filtered into the subcontinent, spreading their brand of Islam. Each chose an area in which to settle and preach, and many opened kitchens to feed the hungry. (Most shrines still offer free food and shelter.)

The Sufis preached a love for God that went beyond simple obedience. Their teaching was geared to the common man who did not understand Arabic or complicated theological concepts. The Sufis used the local vernacular — be it Punjabi, Sindhi, Balochi or Pushtu — and composed haunting music, lyrical poems and popular romantic stories to carry their message to the masses. Tales of love and longing, and songs of solace and hope could be easily understood by all. Many used dance, moving feverishly to the driving beat of drums to reach a trance-like state of union with God. These mystics were known in the West as Whirling Dervishes.

The spiritual strength and traditions of the Sufis have survived through the centuries, and the shrines are as active now as in the days of their founders. Each shrine has an annual festival to commemorate the death of its saint with three days of music, devotional singing and prayer. Outside the shrine, the amiable chaos of a fairground prevails, complete with performing animals, street theatre, transvestite dancing, acrobatics and wrestling alongside the food and souvenir stalls. Wildly dressed fakirs mingle with the crowds, receiving food and coins in return for blessings.

Nothing better reveals the spiritual life of Pakistan than a visit to a shrine during its festival (urs), or on a Thursday evening when the singing and praying continues all night.

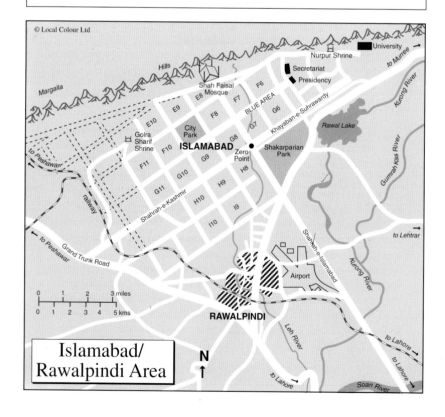

Ralawpindi

Ralawpindi is a lively, bustling city with lots of local colour in its crowded streets and bustling bazaars, though it lacks the grand monuments you can see in some other Pakistani cities of its size. The city, developed under the British Raj as a regional military headquarters, is now the supreme headquarters of the Pakistani army with a large garrison stationed here. The cantonment is typical of residential areas built by the British all over the subcontinent.

Getting to Ralawpindi

Rawalpindi is on the Grand Trunk Road 280 kilometres (174 miles) from Lahore and 173 kilometres (108 miles) from Peshawar. It shares an international airport, a railway station and two bus stations with Islamabad. Murree Road, Airport Road and Peshawar Road connect Rawalpindi and Islamabad. A taxi from the airport to central Rawalpindi costs about Rs70. Wagons and Suzukis wait 100 metres away outside the airport gates and cost very little to Saddar and Raja bazaars.

For the budget traveller, good public transport and a broad range of cheaper hotels and restaurants make Rawalpindi an easier place to stay than Islamabad (unless you plan to camp or stay in Islamabad's Youth Hostel). A steady stream of buses and minibuses cover the 15 kilometres between the two cities in about as many minutes. Alternatively, you can take a taxi from Rawalpindi for a half-day tour of Islamabad.

Sights

The best way to see Rawalpindi is on foot, walking the alleys in the old city and wending through its bazaars, but you should orient yourself before setting out. The city has two main roads: the Grand Trunk Road runs roughly from east to west and is known as The Mall as it passes through the cantonment; Murree Road breaks north from The Mall, crosses the railway and brushes the east end of the old city on its way to Islamabad. The two main bazaar areas are Raja Bazaar in the old city and Saddar Bazaar, which developed as a cantonment bazaar, between the old city and The Mall.

The Old City

The old residential city, once surrounded by walls, is a maze of narrow twisting alleyways hiding Hindu and Sikh temples, Muslim shrines and old carved houses. It is best to take a guide, enter from **Banni Chowk** and walk south from there. You enter the original Hindu quarter with carved balconies

Rawalpindi Old City

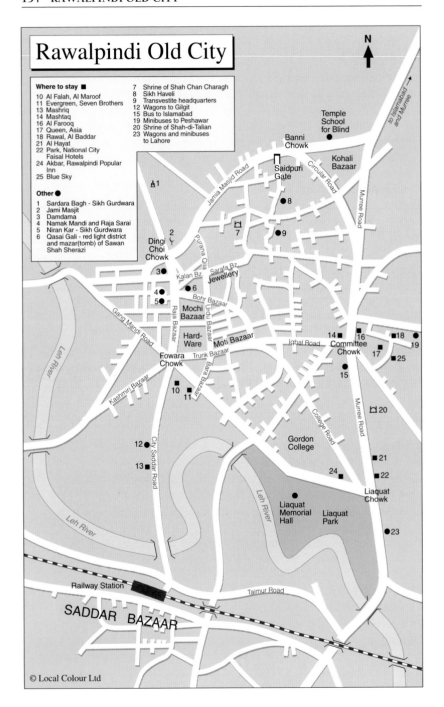

Where to stay ■

10 Al Falah, Al Maroof
11 Evergreen, Seven Brothers
13 Mashriq
14 Mashtaq
16 Al Farooq
17 Queen, Asia
18 Rawal, Al Baddar
21 Al Hayat
22 Park, National City
    Faisal Hotels
24 Akbar, Rawalpindi Popular
    Inn
25 Blue Sky

7   Shrine of Shah Chan Charagh
8   Sikh Haveli
9   Transvestite headquarters
12 Wagons to Gilgit
15 Bus to Islamabad
19 Minibuses to Peshawar
20 Shrine of Shah-di-Talian
23 Wagons and minibuses
    to Lahore

Other ●

1   Sardara Bagh - Sikh Gurdwara
2   Jami Masjit
3   Damdama
4   Namak Mandi and Raja Sarai
5   Niran Kar - Sikh Gurdwara
6   Qasai Gali - red light district
    and mazar(tomb) of Sawan
    Shah Sherazi

N

Temple
School
for Blind ●

Banni
Chowk

Saidpuri
Gate

Kohali
Bazaar

Circular Road

Murree Road

Jamia Masjid Road

●8

A1

2

●9

7

Dingi
Choi
Chowk

Purana Qila

Sarafa Bz.
Jewellery

3●

Kalan Bz.

●6

4●
5●

Bohr Bazaar

Urdu Bazaar

Raja Bazaar

Mochi
Bazaar

Gang Mandi Road

Hard-
Ware

Moti Bazaar

Fowara
Chowk

Trunk Bazaar

Bara Bazaar

14■ 16

■18 ●
19

Committee
Chowk 17

■25

Iqbal Road

15

Leh River

Kashmiri Bazaar

10■

11■

☐20

12●

13●

City Saddar Road

Murree Road

College Road

Gordon
College

24■

■21

■22

Liaquat
Chowk

Leh River

Liaquat
Memorial
Hall

Liaquat
Park

●23

Leh River

Railway Station

Taimur Road

SADDAR BAZAAR

© Local Colour Ltd

to Islamabad and Murree

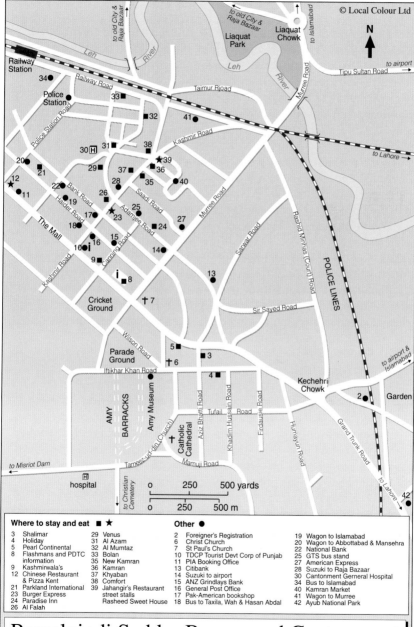

© Local Colour Ltd

Rawalpindi Saddar Bazaar and Cantonment

Where to stay and eat ■ ★

3	Shalimar	
4	Holiday	
5	Pearl Continental	
8	Flashmans and PDTC information	
9	Kashmirwala's	
12	Chinese Restaurant & Pizza Kent	
21	Parkland International	
23	Burger Express	
24	Paradise Inn	
26	Al Falah	

29	Venus
31	Al Azam
32	Al Mumtaz
33	Bolan
35	New Kamran
36	Kamran
37	Khyaban
38	Comfort
39	Jahangir's Restaurant street stalls Rasheed Sweet House

Other ●

2	Foreigner's Registration
6	Christ Church
7	St Paul's Church
10	TDCP Tourist Devt Corp of Punjab
11	PIA Booking Office
13	Citibank
14	Suzuki to airport
15	ANZ Grindlays Bank
16	General Post Office
17	Pak-American bookshop
18	Bus to Taxila, Wah & Hasan Abdal

19	Wagon to Islamabad
20	Wagon to Abbottabad & Mansehra
22	National Bank
25	GTS bus stand
27	American Express
28	Suzuki to Raja Bazaar
30	Cantonment Gerneral Hospital
34	Bus to Islamabad
40	Kamran Market
41	Wagon to Murree
42	Ayub National Park

Rawalpindi Saddar Bazaar and Cantonment

over the alleyway. A few hundred metres into the city is **Soojan Singh's** *haveli* (a traditional house set around a courtyard), built in 1893. Before Pakistan's independence in 1947 this *haveli* was one of the richest and tallest houses in the city. Its high rooms have painted and carved wooden ceilings and the balcony around the central courtyard is supported on wrought iron pillars from Glasgow, Scotland. A bridge-like balcony connects the *haveli* with the house opposite across the alleyway. Two towers, five storeys high with brick *jalis* (grills) give a view over the rooftops of the old city. You can see the spires of five Hindu temples, the Sardara Bagh (a Sikh gurdwara or temple), the Jami Mosque, and the towers of other old Hindu and Sikh houses. The Margalla Hills rise to the north beyond Islamabad, and you can see the airport to the east. The house was burned at Partition and is awaiting restoration.

Deeper into the old town is the headquarters of the Pakistani transvestite community run by their elected queen. This is an accepted tradition in Pakistan. The transvestites dance at weddings and births and are always seen around holy shrines. They walk through the streets with their tambourines and drums.

Shah Chan Charagh Shrine nearby is the burial place of the patron saint of Rawalpindi, and the elder brother of Bari Imam of Islamabad. The green–domed inner sanctum is closed to women who may pray on the right side and look in through a grill.

The **Purana Qila** (Old Fort), on the highest point in Rawalpindi, on the edge of Raja Bazaar has all been destroyed except for the double arched entrance, dated 1896. **Sardara Bagh** further up the street is the Sikh gurdwara (temple) built by Bahadur Sardar Soojan Singh in the 1890s. There is rumoured to be an underground passage connecting the temple with Soojan Singh's *haveli*.

Qasai Gulli (or Butchers Lane), is Rawalpindi's red light district. The girls live upstairs and sit in the windows at night. Originally they served their clients dinner, so the best butchers in town worked in the same street. Ask for the **Mazar of Sawan Shah Sherazi**. You will be shown into a narrow shop selling plastic buckets and crockery under a huge peepul tree. In the back of the shop is the shrine of Sawan Shah Sherazi, the patron saint of prostitutes. The legend relates that the saint was banished by his guru and told to sit in the street of the prostitutes and dancing girls to atone for his sins. He preached so sympathetically to the girls that they became his devoted followers. (Though today most of Pakistan's prostitutes are devoted to Bari Imam of Islamabad.)

The next alley is **Mochi Bazaar** selling hardware, followed by **Namak Mandi**, the salt market, where you will find the **Raja Serai**, the oldest *serai* or travellers' inn in Rawalpindi. Opposite the Raja Serai stands the **Gurdwara Niran Kar**, built in 1822. Niran Kar was a strict orthodox Sikh who founded a 'Puritan' sect of Sikhism here in about 1811.

Other Bazaars in the Old City

Raja Bazaar is made up of many smaller bazaars, each a labyrinth of small alleys. As is typical in Asia, shops selling the same items are grouped together. (This was true also in 14th-century European cities, in which trade guilds each had their own area.) To get to Raja Bazaar from Murree Road, turn west into Liaquat Road. On your left you will see **Liaquat Park,** where Liaquat Ali Khan, Pakistan's first prime minister, was shot while speaking at a rally of the Muslim League in October 1951. The park's **Liaquat Memorial Hall** is Rawalpindi's principal concert hall and the venue for visiting troupes and popular Pakistani singers. On the right, just after the conspicuous and recently renovated mosque is the main street of **Bara Bazaar** (or Smugglers' Bazaar), where imported electrical goods and crockery, cutlery and cloth are on sale. Turn right down Bara Bazaar, and at the end turn right again for the **Trunk Bazaar**, where all shapes and sizes of trunks and suitcases are sold. About 100 metres along on the left is a very narrow alleyway with a sign reading **Moti Bazaar** in English over the entrance. This is the ladies' bazaar, and shawls, woollen goods, make-up, false hairbraids, beads, etc are all sold here. The whole alley is shaded by awnings from one end to the other. To the north are the medicine shops of **Bohr Bazaar.**

Back on the main Liaquat Road, from the entrance to Bara Bazaar to the roundabout, are **music shops** were you can buy brass and woodwind instruments or hire a band. Above the music shops is a row of old carved wooden balconies. At the end of Liaquat Road, five roads meet at a large roundabout where huge billboards display garish movie posters. The first road left, City-Saddar Road, leads from the old city to Saddar Bazaar and the cantonment area.

Raja Bazaar Road, the fourth road leading off the roundabout, is a dual-carriageway. Here a second-hand clothes market is followed by a vegetable wholesale market halfway down on the right, and a market selling dried fruits, nuts, lentils and spices in the alleys off to the left. Conical mounds of red chilli, orange turmeric, orange and yellow lentils and green dried peas evoke all the bazaar scenes in the *Arabian Nights*.

At the end of Raja Bazaar turn right down a narrow street into **Kalan Bazaar:** shoes and stockings are on display on the left, and bales of cloth, chiffon scarves, hats, hair and beauty oils, and blockprint bedspreads on the right. A narrow but motorable street selling knives, scissors and whips, and overhung with old wooden balconies, branches up the hill to the left. At the top of the hill is the **Purana Qila Bazaar** and a small Hindu temple. Purana Qila means Old Fort, though there is no trace of a fort here now. This is where you can buy wedding dresses, fancily embroidered cloth and heavy gold braid.

Kalan Bazaar runs into **Sarafa Bazaar,** the jewellery market. On your left is a 19th-century red British postbox, Rawalpindi's first. The jewellery bazaar sells gold and silver, and is the best place to hunt for antique tribal silver, some of which is very lovely. (Most of these jewellers also have smarter shops on Murree Road.) Then come the brass shops selling household utensils made of copper, brass, tin, aluminium and stainless steel. Muhammad Shafi and Sons, on the right, is well- known for its antique brass- and copper-ware, and also has a storeroom down an alleyway behind the shop where you can rummage for treasures. Most of the ware is still coated in tin, but the piece of your choice will be expertly polished for you in a few days. Aim at bargaining down to about two-thirds of the asking price, and check that all the vessels are waterproof. Any holes can be soldered while you wait. If you continue on down Sarafa Bazaar, you will come out on to Murree Road again.

The Cantonment
The Leh River and the railway line mark the boundry between the old city and the cantonment. The cantonment evokes the British Raj, with its Christian churches and cemetery, spacious bungalows, club, cricket ground, mall and the colonial-style Flashman's Hotel. Behind Flashman's is **Saddar Bazaar,** the centre not only for shopping but also for hotels, banks, airlines and travel agents. The heart of the bazaar is along Kashmir Road and Massey Gate.

The **Army Museum,** near the Pearl Continental Hotel, has a fine collection of weapons, uniforms and paintings depicting Pakistan's military history. Hours are 9 am to 3 pm in winter, 8 am to noon and 5.30 to 7 pm in summer.

The **Army Chief of Staff's House** is behind high walls at the east end of The Mall. Beyond it, along the Grand Trunk Road towards Lahore, are the jail, Murree Brewery (a Parsee-owned firm that makes whisky and excellent beer for sale to non-Muslims) and **Ayub National Park.** The park has a lake with boats, children's amusement park and playground, mini-golf course, zoo and restaurants, in addition to walkways and bridle paths through the trees.

Trips from Islamabad–Ralawpindi

Whatever the season, there are numerous full and half-day trips you can make using Islamabad or Rawalpindi as a base (see map page 183). You can explore Pakistani history at a number of archaeological excavations and 16th-century forts; visit the hill stations, dams or lakes; explore the national parks by car or on foot; or go walking, bird-watching or picnicking in the forest. Some trips are accessible by public transport, others require a private car.

Air Safari

On alternate Saturdays, PIA runs a special tourist trip flying low over the Himalaya and Karakoram mountains. This must be the most spectacular flight in the world — a five star attraction — you swoop along the giant glaciers, circle K–2 and Nanga Parbat, and skim the summits of 100 peaks over 7,000 metres (23,000 feet).

Murree and the Galis

Murree, at 2,240 metres (7,400 feet), is only an hour's drive northeast of Islamabad. Its cool pine forest, amidst magnificent mountain scenery, make it the first choice for a day's outing from the capital. The Galis are a string of hill resorts along the ridge between Murree and Abbottabad, on the Karakoram Highway (see map page 183).

Founded as a hill station by the British in 1851, Murree was the summer headquarters of the government of Punjab until 1876, when the honour was transferred to Simla. Murree remained, however, a little bit of England, complete with a mall for promenading, parks, churches, schools, clubs and cafes. Since Independence, Murree has once again become the summer retreat of the governor of Punjab and, since Islamabad became the capital of Pakistan in 1962, has expanded rapidly.

Murree is lovely all year round. In summer it is cool — even chilly in the evening — and rain is common. In winter, the snow is piled high along the sides of the streets. But it is extremely popular with Punjabis escaping the heat of the plains in summer, so is too crowded for comfort from late May to early September, especially at weekends. To beat the crowds and still enjoy the walks, the best time to go is April–May and September–October.

Getting to Murree

TDCP (Tourist Development Corporation of Punjab) tel (051) 564824, fax (92 51) 568421, runs daily buses from their office in Rawalpindi on the corner of The Mall and Kashmir Road. Ordinary bus and minibus services run frequently from Saddar and Pir Wadai bus stations in Rawalpindi. Visitors going by car can return to the capital on the back road via Patriata and Karor which, like the main road, climbs steeply through mature pine forest but takes about an hour longer. Another option is to make a loop from Islamabad to Murree, through the Galis to Abbottabad and back to Islamabad via the Karakoram Highway, Taxila and the Grand Trunk Road. This loop takes five or six hours driving time.

Sights

Murree spreads along the top of a ridge for about five kilometres (three miles). At the northeast end is **Kashmir Point**, with views across the valley of the Jhelum River into Azad Kashmir. At the southwest end is **Pindi Point**, looking back towards Rawalpindi and Islamabad. Between the two runs **The Mall**, at the centre of which is the main shopping area, where most people congregate. Numerous roads leave The Mall and either follow the contours of the ridge or descend to the principal road. Promenading and shopping are Murree's main amusements, or riding in the new chair-lifts, one from Bansara Gali (below Murree) to Pindi Point, the other to the top of Patriata hill (on the road to Karor); both rides cost about Rs50 and take half an hour with a change from open chair-lift to the enclosed bubble in the middle.

Good buys in Murree are cashmere shawls, furs, walking sticks, fruits and nuts. Murree's pistachio nuts are reputed to be the best in Pakistan.

Bhurban is a minor resort eight kilometres (five miles) from Murree on the road leading northeast to Kohala and the Jhelum Valley. The **golf course** here is open only to members. From near the Pearl Continental hotel you can take one of the many delightful paved walks through the woods.

The Galis

The **Galis** are in the North-West Frontier Province (NWFP), but are included here for convenience). The Galis (*gali* meaning 'lane' in the local dialect, or 'pass' in Hindko) are perched along the crest of the ridge on the road that runs north from Murree to Abbottabad. The hill stations are Barian, Sawar Gali, Khaira Gali, Changla Gali, Dunga Gali and Nathiagali (usually written as one word), this last being the most popular. The road follows the ridge through forests of giant pines and offers on the rare very clear day, superb views of the snow-covered Pir Panjal Range in Indian-held Kashmir and the 8,125-metre (26,660-foot) Nanga Parbat, 170 kilometres (100 miles) away to the northeast.

Regular bus and minibus services connect Murree with Abbottabad, with stops at the various Galis along the way. The road is surfaced but narrow, with steep drops into the valley below. Running mostly at altitudes of 2,000–2,500 metres (7,000–8,000 feet), the road may be blocked by snow from December until the beginning of May.

Numerous footpaths cut through the forest, and horses are for hire in some villages. At **Ayubia National Park**, between Changla Gali and Dunga Gali, is a chair-lift to the top of the ridge.

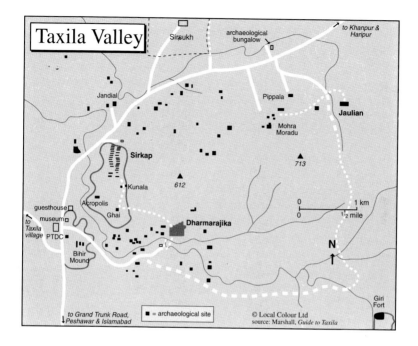

Nathiagali, about an hour's drive from Murree, is the most popular of the Galis. Nathiagali is the summer retreat of the governor of NWFP (while his Punjabi counterpart is at Murree) and it has a small timbered church, bungalows, park and magnificent governor's lodge. This is the best place to stay for those who like walking, being smaller and far pleasanter than Murree. Walks include following the water pipe from the Shangrila Pines Hotel, eight kilometres (five miles) through Dunga Gali to Ayubia or climbing the highest peak along the ridge, the 2,981-metre (9,780-foot) Miranjani, or nearby Mukshpuri (2,817 metres or 9,243 feet).

Islamabad to Peshawar

Along the Grand Trunk Road from Islamabad–Rawalpindi, west to Peshawar are some of Pakistan's most important historic sites. Trade routes from the east, west, north and south come together in this area, and all the great invaders of the subcontinent passed this way. Every major epoch of Pakistani history has left its mark here: the ruins of the great civilisations of the three cities of Taxila; the Mughal caravanserai at Attock; Hasan Abdal, one of the spiritual centres of the Sikhs; and the modern Tarbela Dam.

Buses ply continuously between Rawalpindi and Peshawar, with passengers free to alight anywhere along the way. The railway runs parallel to the road.

Taxila

Taxila, about 35 kilometres (22 miles) from Islamabad, is one of the subcontinent's most important archaeological treasures, with the remains of three great cities and dozens of Buddhist monasteries dating from 600 BC to AD 600. Situated at the meeting place of trade routes linking China, India, Central Asia and the West, Taxila was incorporated in many empires and became the cultural crossroads of the ancient world.

It was the principal university town of Gandhara, a kingdom of northern Pakistan from the sixth century BC to the 11th century AD. Students at Taxila studied mathematics, law, history, medicine, social sciences, the arts, astronomy and military science. The level of knowledge was remarkably high for the period, especially in the fields of mathematics, medicine and astronomy. Alexander the Great of Greece arrived in 326 BC and held philosophical discussions with the resident intellectuals. He left a garrison at Taxila, but his empire quickly disintegrated following his death in Babylon at the age of 33.

Ashoka, before he inherited the whole of the Ganges-centred Mauryan Empire in about 275 BC, was viceroy at Taxila. He introduced Buddhism to Gandhara, from where the religion spread to Central Asia, Tibet and China. Ashoka died in 232 BC, and soon afterwards his empire declined.

Gandhara was then ruled by Bactrian Greeks from northern Afghanistan, who built a new city at Taxila. Now called Sirkap, the city was laid out in a regular grid, with streets crossing at right angles. The Sakas and Parthians followed the Greeks. Gondophares, one of the greatest of the Parthian kings, played host at Taxila to St Thomas the Apostle, the first Christian missionary to India.

In about AD 60, the Kushans arrived from Afghanistan and ousted the Parthians. They brought the Gandharan Empire to its greatest height in the second century AD, when it extended from eastern Iran to the Ganges valley. The Kushans built a new city at Taxila, which was a regional capital.

The Kushans were also great patrons of Buddhism, which from the first to the fifth centuries AD was the majority religion. Thousands of stupas were built all over the kingdom, with more than 50 in Taxila, one atop every hill. This was the great period of Gandharan Buddhist art; images of the Buddha and scenes from his life worked in stone and plaster decorated every stupa and monastery. Most of the Buddhist sculpture in Taxila Museum is Kushan (see page 194).

Around AD 455, disaster struck Taxila in the form of the White Huns, hordes from Central Asia related to Attila, who was ravaging Europe at about the same time. Taxila never really recovered.

Taxila may at first disappoint those unused to older archaeological sites, appearing as nothing more than heaps of stones and the odd wall dotted about the valley. Visiting the museum helps enliven the ruins.

Taxila Museum is open daily 9 am to 12 pm and 2 to 4 pm in winter and 8.30 am to 12.30 pm and 2.30 to 5 pm in summer, cosed on the first Monday of every month. It houses one of the best collections of Gandharan Buddhist art in Pakistan, an interesting coin collection and a display of artefacts — utensils, weights, jewellery and coins — illustrating the daily life of the inhabitants of ancient Taxila. A contour map of Taxila Valley shows the layout of the cities and all the other archaeological sites.

Those with time for only one site should see Jaulian, even though it involves a short walk up a steep hill. Those with three hours should see, in order, Dharmarajika, Sirkap and Jaulian. (Only those who are quite fit should attempt to explore Taxila in the heat of summer, as there is little shade.)

Dharmarajika is the site of a Buddhist stupa and monastery. The stupa was probably the first built in Pakistan and is certainly one of the largest and most impressive. It was built by Emperor Ashoka in the third century BC to enclose a small relic chamber containing ashes of the Buddha. It was subsequently enlarged and restored over the centuries, and votive stupas and a monastery were added.

The **main stupa** is 15 metres (50 feet) high and 50 metres (165 feet) in diameter. The great slice cut into its west side is the work of treasure hunters searching for the golden casket containing the Buddha relics.

Originally, the stupa's entire dome was plastered and gilded, with a tall mast rising from its top supporting seven or more stone discs (like those on the stone umbrella in the museum). The dome was surrounded by painted and gilded carvings of the Buddha and scenes depicting his life. All the other buildings in the complex were plastered and painted in many colours. The forest of smaller stupas surrounding the main stupa were all topped by spires like those on modern Burmese or Thai pagodas.

Two processional paths lead round the stupa, with a flight of steps at each of the four cardinal points. To the left of the eastern flight of steps is the best-preserved section of the base of the stupa. This broad band of ornamental stone-work dates from the fourth or fifth century AD. Little niches that once contained sculptures of the Buddha are framed with trefoil arches alternating with portals.

Around the main stupa is a galaxy of smaller **votive stupas** built by wealthy pilgrims hoping to gain a blessing or merit. These monuments date from the first century BC to the fourth century AD. Beyond the ring of votive stupas to the south is a larger stupa dating from the second century AD. It is one of the best-preserved in the complex and is adorned with rows of Buddha images, atlantes (human figures supporting the structure) and elephants.

To the north is a **row of chapels** containing four huge lime plaster feet, the remains of two enormous sculptures of the Buddha, the larger of which must have been 11 metres (36 feet) high. On either side of the feet are the lower parts of other figures, some of which still show traces of red paint. All were once painted and gilded.

A large **monastery** lies on the northern edge of the complex, its five courtyards dating from the first century BC to the sixth century AD. In the centre of each courtyard is a stupa, and round the edges are the monks' cells. The largest (northernmost) court, with 104 cells on two storeys and a bath in the northwest corner, dates from the second or third century AD. In the centre of the monastery was the hall of assembly, and beyond the north wall was a sturdy watch-tower. Other ruins in the complex include a building that once housed a reclining Buddha figure, a water tank for bathing and an apsidal (round-ended) temple built in the first century AD.

From Dharmarajika, a footpath leads over the hill to Ghai Monastery, Kunala Stupa and Sirkap, the second city of Taxila. The city is 30 minutes away by foot, or 15 minutes if you go round by car to the main gate. A walk around the site takes at least 15 minutes, but even this can be uncomfortable in summer except in the very early morning.

Dharmarajika Stupa, Taxila

Sirkap was built by the Bactrian Greeks in 185 BC and used by the Sakas and Parthians until AD 80. The **city wall** ran five kilometres (three miles) round the roughly rectangular city, enclosing some rugged hills in the southeast, the isolated hill of the acropolis in the southwest and the large, level area of the city proper. The wall was about six metres (20 feet) thick, six to nine metres (20–30 feet) high and interspersed with tall, square bastions. A large hole excavated beside the wall about 50 metres (yards) to the right (west) of the north gate (by which visitors enter the city) bares construction from different eras. The neatly fitted Greek wall, dating from the second century BC, is at the bottom; the Saka wall, from the first century BC, is above it and is surmounted in turn by the Parthian wall, which dates from the first century AD. At the bottom of the hole is the original Greek drain.

The north gate leads into the wide **main street,** which is 700 metres (almost half a mile) long. The low walls that line the street are actually the foundations of the Parthian city; the upper parts of the buildings were made of mud and have long since disappeared. Down either side of the street was a row of small shops consisting of wooden platforms under colourful awnings. Behind the shops were two-storey private houses, the windowless walls of which were plastered and painted various colours.

The houses were entered through doors opening on to side streets. Each house had up to 20 small rooms on each storey arranged around a small court-yard, with a wooden balcony giving access to the upper rooms. Inside, the rooms were generally plastered and painted, but some had wooden panelling. The flat, mud-covered roof was supported by wooden beams.

Plaster statue of a bodhisattua, Taxila

In almost every block was a Jain or Buddhist stupa, with its gilded dome and crowning spire of umbrellas rising above the surrounding walls. (Mahavira, the founder of the Jain religion, was a contemporary of the Buddha.) The city had no wells, water being carried from the river outside the west wall. Sewage ran down the streets in open drains.

As one walks south from the north gate, the first block on the left contains a **stupa** set in a large court and overlooked by rooms on all sides. The relic chamber of this stupa once contained a Mauryan period (third century BC) crystal reliquary.

A large Buddhist **apsidal temple** occupies the whole of the fourth block left (east) of the main street. It was built on the ruins of an earlier temple following an earthquake in about AD 30. Two flights of steps lead up from the main street into the spacious courtyard around the temple. Immediately, on either side of the steps, are the small cells of the attendant monks. East of these are the bases of two small stupas, around which were found numerous stucco plaster heads and other decorative objects. These are now on view in the museum.

The temple has a round-ended nave with a stupa at its eastern end, around which ran a processional passage entered from the porch. The roof probably consisted of interlocking timbers covered with thatch and mud. The line of plain blocks of stone around the inside wall of the apse marks the level of the original timbered floor.

The **small stupa** in the next block dates from the first century BC, making it the oldest stupa at Sirkap. It has no base, but when unearthed its circular dome was decorated with acanthus flowers boldly modelled in lime stucco and painted. The stupa directly across the street has a double flight of seven steps leading up to it. Its plinth (square base) has thick stone walls radiating from the centre, suggesting to some a sundial, which actually were buttresses.

In the next block is the Buddhist **Shrine of the Double-Headed Eagle**, a first century AD stupa mixing classical Greek and Indian styles. The façade boasts a row of Corinthian pilasters alternating with decorated niches in three distinct styles. The pair of niches nearest the steps resemble the pedimental fronts of Greek buildings; the next pair feature ogee arches like Bengal roofs; the outer pair are shaped like early Indian *torans*, like those at Mathura, south of Delhi.

The double-headed eagle is perched atop the central niche. This motif, common to early Babylon and Sparta, was later adopted by the Scythians; later still, it was used in the imperial armies of Russia, Germany and Ceylon

(Sri Lanka). This stupa originally had a drum and dome topped by a tiered stone umbrella, the whole decorated with finely moulded stucco plaster, gilded and painted.

The small **Jain stupa** in the next block has a rectangular base with five decorative pilasters on each side. The drum, dome and umbrella have all disappeared, but the remains of two Persepolitan columns crowned with lions were unearthed in the courtyard, and parts of these now stand at the four corners of the plinth.

The **Royal Palace** and the houses of wealthy citizens and officials are further south along the main street on the left. The palace differs from private houses pnly in size. A Greek visitor in AD 44 described it as 'chaste in style', with wood-panelled rooms set around small courtyards.

Kunala Stupa is a ten-minute walk from the palace, crowning a hill in the southeastern part of the city beyond the end of the main street. The site offers an excellent bird's-eye view of the entire city.

Kunala was the faithful son of the third century BC Mauryan emperor Ashoka. It was his ironic misfortune to have eyes possessing such beauty that they captured the heart of his stepmother.Spurned by her stepson, the spiteful woman first tricked Ashoka into making him viceroy of Taxila, thus removing him far from the capital at Patna. She then sent a dispatch under Ashoka's seal, bringing accusations against him and ordering that his eyes be gouged out. The ministers at Taxila were loath to carry out the command, but the prince, believing it to have come from his father, insisted on its speedy execution.

The stupa was built at the very spot were the prince was blinded. Not surprisingly, it became a place of pilgrimage for the blind. (Taxila is still a haven for those suffering from eye trouble, as it has the best eye hospital in Pakistan.)

A curious feature of the stupa is that it was built over a smaller votive stupa (now exposed by excavators) because a stupa, once built, may not be moved or destroyed. When this little stupa was found in the way, it was simply incorporated into the structure. The smaller stupa dates from the first century BC, the surrounding one from the third or fourth century AD.

Kunala Monastery, also dating back to the third or fourth century, has an open courtyard surrounded by monks' cells. In each cell is a little arched niche in which the monk kept his lamp and books. The assembly hall is south of the courtyard.

Ghai Monastery crowns the next hill, which is still within the city walls. It is unusual in that the monks' cells surround, instead of an open court, a square hall with sloping windows.

Jaulian, with its monastery and stupa, is probably the best-preserved site at Taxila. It was built in the second century AD and burned by the White Huns in about AD 455.

The entrance leads into the **lower stupa court**, which is surrounded by alcoves or chapels that once contained statues of the Buddha. The south side of the court is wired off and roofed to protect the bases of five votive stupas built as offerings by pilgrims early in the fifth century AD. They are decorated with rows of plaster carvings of the Buddha with attendants, elephants, lions and contorted nudes. The inscription on the fifth stupa, titling the statues and naming the donors, is carved in Kharoshthi script, the national language of Gandhara.

The **main stupa court** is to the south, approached up five steps. The plaster Buddha images, bodhisattvas, attendants, animals and atlantes crowding around the bases of the central stupa and its 21 votive stupas are now protected by a flat roof. Once, though, the golden dome and umbrellas of the main stupa rose about 20 metres (65 feet) into the open sky, dominating the surrounding forest of gilded spires. The steps up the main stupa, which once led to the processional path round the dome, now give tourists access on to the modern roof.

Of particular interest is the Healing Buddha, the stone figure with the hole at its navel set in the north wall of the main stupa to the left of the steps. The faithful used to put a finger into the hole and pray for a cure. The Kharoshthi inscription below the Buddha images records that it was the gift of a certain Budhamitra who 'delighted in the law'.

Jaulian Monastery is west of the main stupa. The monastery courtyard, once decorated with statues of the Buddha and scenes from his life, is surrounded by 28 monks' cells. Access to each cell was through a low wooden door, and the lintels and doorjambs were also of wood. The walls above the doors were constructed of mud and small stones, but these have fallen down. In each cell is a small sloping window and a niche for the monk's lamp. In the fifth century AD, all the walls were plastered and painted. Another 28 cells once occupied the second storey, which was reached by a stone staircase in one of the cells. The upper cells all opened on to a carved wooden balcony that ran, supported by wooden pillars, around the court.

The shallow water tank at the centre of the court collected rainwater off the wooden roof during the monsoon; at other times, the monks carried water up from wells at the bottom of the hill. They bathed in the enclosure in the corner of the tank. The hall of assembly, kitchen, store-room, refectory, stewards' room and latrine are west of the monastery court.

Taxila to Peshawar

Hasan Abdal, 13 kilometres (eight miles) west of Taxila along the Grand Trunk Road, is the site of one of Pakistan's few active Sikh temples, some ruined Hindu temples and a Muslim shrine.

Tarbela Dam is on the Indus River, 45 kilometres (28 miles) north of the Grand Trunk Road. (The turn-off is about midway between Hasan Abdal and Attock.) Tarbela is the world's largest earth-filled dam in terms of the volume of earth used to build it and its electricity-generating capacity, and it boasts the two biggest spillways in the world. It is an impressive sight, particularly between July and September when the lake is full from the melting snows and the monsoon rains, and the main spillway is in use to carry the overflow. The dam is 2,743 metres (1.7 miles) long, 600 metres (2,000 feet) wide at its base and 143 metres (470 feet) high. You can no longer drive across the top of the dam unless you have a special permit.

Attock is about halfway between Islamabad and Peshawar, where the Grand Trunk Road crosses the Indus River. It was a small place of no importance until the 1540s, when Sher Shah Suri chose it as the crossing place for his new Shahi Road from Delhi to Kabul. Until then, everyone who crossed the Indus, from Alexander the Great to the Mughal emperor Babur, did so 20 kilometres (12 miles) further upriver at Hund.

The **Caravanserai of Sher Shah Suri** is the most impressive sight at Attock. It is just east of the new bridge and perched immediately above the south side of the road, from which it is accessible via a short, steep flight of steps. It was a 16th-century rest-house consisting of four rows of small rooms set around a huge courtyard. Its walls afford an excellent view of the river, the new bridge and **Attock Fort** which was built in the years 1581–6 by the Mughal emperor Akbar. (The fort serves as a prison so it is closed to the public.)

Readily visible just north of the bridge is the confluence of the Kabul and Indus rivers. The waters of the Kabul are a muddy brown, but those of the Indus are a clear blue, the silt having settled behind Tarbela Dam. The Indus here is a provincial boundary, and by the time you reach the western shore you have crossed from Punjab into North-West Frontier Province.

North-West Frontier Province

The North-West Frontier Province, or NWFP, runs for over 1,100 kilometres (680 miles) along the border with Afghanistan. Peshawar is its capital, and the Vale of Peshawar, fertile and well watered by the Kabul and Swat rivers, is its heart. This was also the heart of the ancient kingdom of Gandhara and is rich in archaeological remains.

The northern half of the province consists of five river valleys running roughly parallel, north to south: the Chitral, Dir, Swat, Indus and Kaghan. These valleys are on the northern edge of the monsoon belt, so are fairly green and partly wooded in their southern sections. Northern Chitral and the upper regions of the Indus Valley are mountainous deserts, where cultivation depends entirely on irrigation. The NWFP south of Peshawar is below the monsoon belt and consists of low, rocky mountains and wide, gravelly plains.

The **Tribal Areas**, which cover nearly half the province along its border with Afghanistan, are autonomous regions governed by tribal law under the supervision of the Pakistani government. Because the government cannot, however, guarantee the safety of people who enter these areas, they are closed to foreigners. Even Pakistanis need permission to enter. The increased cultivation of opium in the Tribal Areas in recent years has intensified the risks faced by outsiders who attempt to slip in for whatever reason.

The **Khyber Pass**, the route from Peshawar to Kabul in Afghanistan, is the feature of the province most widely known (and infused with romance) in the world beyond. To visit the pass you need a special permit from the Political Agent because of the tribal dangers and official sensitivity over drugs and guns. The PTDC at Deans Hotel run daily tours to the pass and make all the arrangements for permits and escort.

The warlike **Pathans** (or Pushtuns or Pukhtuns), who live in NWFP and the adjoining areas of Afghanistan, number about 17 million, making them one of the world's largest tribal societies. They have always considered themselves a race apart, a chosen people, and no one has ever managed to subdue them. The Mughals, Afghans, Sikhs, British and Russians have suffered defeat at their hands. The Pathans are divided into numerous sub-tribes and clans, each defending its territory and honour. In addition, the Pathans serve as Pakistan's first line of defence along the Durand Line, the border drawn in 1893 by Sir Mortimer Durand, then foreign secretary of British India.

About four million **Afghan refugees** flooded into Pakistan during the Russian occupation of Afghanistan from 1979 to 1988. Because of the continuing civil war in Afghanistan, many of them still live in Pakistan, mostly in NWFP and Balochistan.

Peshawar

Peshawar (pronounced pe-SHAH-wur), the capital of NWFP, is a frontier town, the meeting place of the subcontinent and Central Asia. It is also a place where ancient traditions jostle with those of today, where the bazaar in the old city has changed little in the past hundred years except to become the neighbour of a modern university, some modern hotels, several international banks and one of the best museums in Pakistan.

No other city is quite like old Peshawar. The bazaar within the walls is like an American Wild West movie costumed as a Bible epic. Pathan tribesmen stroll down the street with their hands hidden within their shawls, their faces half obscured by the loose ends of their turbans. (With his piercing eyes and finely chiselled nose, the Pathan must be the handsomest man on earth.) Afghan traders, many of them in Peshawar to sell drugs and buy arms, stride proudly past in their huge black and white turbans. Smuggling, drug-trading and arms-dealing are all in a day's work — as they have been in these narrow and crowded streets for centuries. Overlooking all are the massive Bala Hisar Fort — still a military installation — and the elegant Mahabat Khan Mosque — still a place of prayer.

On the other side of the railway line is the cantonment, its tree-lined streets wide and straight as they pass gracious administrative buildings and spacious bungalows commanding equally spacious gardens. Clubs, churches, schools, The Mall, Saddar Bazaar and the airport round out the British contribution to the modernisation of Peshawar. Further west is University Town, Peshawar's newest section and the site of Peshawar University.

A local book, *Peshawar, Historic City of the Frontier*, by A H Dani and published by Khyber Mail Press in 1969, makes a good first purchase. It provides a detailed account of Peshawar's history and a tour of its city walls and ancient monuments.

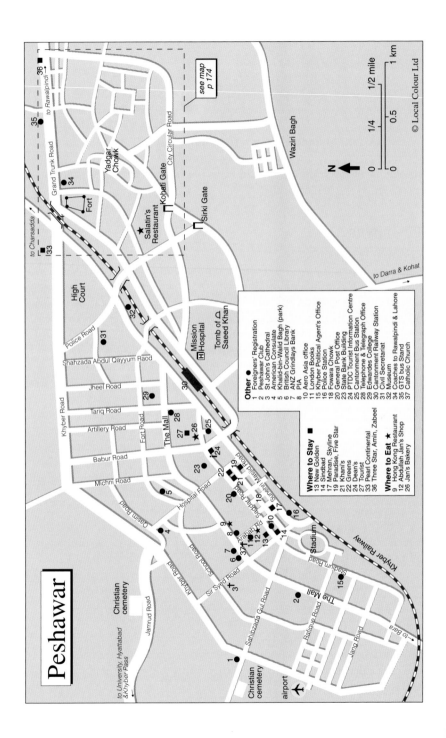

Peshawar

Other ●
1 Foreigners' Registration
2 Peshawar Club
3 St John's Cathedral
4 American Consulate
5 Khalid-bin-Walid Bagh (park)
6 British Council Library
7 ANZ Grindlays Bank
8 PIA
10 Aero Asia office
11 London Books
15 Khyber Political Agent's Office
16 Police Station
18 Fowara Chowk
20 General Post Office
23 State Bank Building
24 PTDC Tourist Information Centre
28 Cantonment Bus Station
28 Telephone & Telegraph Office
29 Edwardes College
30 Cantonment Railway Station
31 Civil Secretariat
32 Museum
34 Coaches to Rawalpindi & Lahore
35 GTS bus Stand
37 Catholic Church

Where to Stay ■
13 New Golden
14 Sindbad
17 Mehran, Skyline
19 Paradise, Five Star
21 Khan's
22 Greens
24 Dean's
27 Tourist
33 Pearl Continental
36 Three Star, Amin, Zabeel

Where to Eat ★
9 Hong Kong Restaurant
12 Abdullah Jan's Shop
26 Jan's Bakery

© Local Colour Ltd

Getting to Peshawar

Peshawar is linked by air to a dozen Pakistani towns and cities (including Karachi, Lahore and Islamabad–Rawalpindi), and even to Europe via Dubai. It is the last stop for tourists on the national rail system. Bus and minibus services run between Peshawar and Islamabad (three or four hours), the valleys of Swat, Dir and Chitral to the north and, for the adventurous, the desert towns to the south beyond Kohat. You should only visit Peshawar in cool weather; it is unpleasantly hot here from May through August.

History

The fortunes of Peshawar are inextricably linked to the Khyber Pass, the eastern end of which it guards. The pass seems to have been little used in prehistoric times, and even in early historic times it was generally shunned as too narrow and thus too prone to ambush. Not until the powerful Kushans invaded Gandhara and pacified the area in the first century AD did the Khyber become a popular trade route.

Peshawar owes its founding 2,000 years ago to these same Kushans. In the second century AD, Kanishka, the greatest of the Kushan kings, moved his winter capital here from Pushkalavati, 30 kilometres (20 miles) to the north. His summer capital was north of Kabul at Kapisa, and the Kushans moved freely back and forth through the Khyber Pass between the two cities, from which they ruled their enormous and prosperous empire for the next 400 years.

After the Kushan era, Peshawar declined into an obscurity not broken until the 16th century, following the Mughal emperor Babur's decision to rebuild the fort here in 1530. Sher Shah Suri, his successor (or, rather, the usurper of his son's throne), turned Peshawar's renaissance into a boom when he ran his Delhi-to-Kabul Shahi Road through the Khyber Pass. The Mughals turned Peshawar into a 'city of flowers' (one of the meanings of its name) by planting trees and laying out gardens.

In 1818, Ranjit Singh captured Peshawar for his Sikh Empire. He burned a large part of the city and felled the trees shading its many gardens for firewood. The following 30 years of Sikh rule saw the destruction of Peshawar's own Shalimar Gardens and of Babur's magnificent fort, not to mention the dwindling of the city's population by almost half.

The British crushed the Sikhs and occupied Peshawar in 1849 but, as much as Sikh rule had been hated, its British replacement aroused little enthusiasm. More or less continuous warfare between the British and the Pathans necessitated a huge British garrison. When the British built a paved road through the Khyber Pass, they needed to build numerous forts and pickets to guard it.

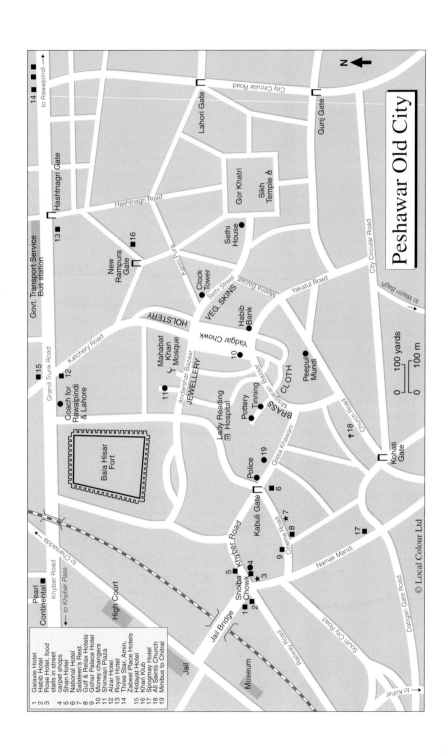

Peshawar Old City

N ←

to Rawalpindi →

Govt. Transport Service
Bus station

Hashtnagri Gate

Hashtnagri Road

New Rampura Gate

Grand Trunk Road

Katchery Road

Mahabat Khan Mosque

HOLSTERY

VEG. SKINS

Sethi Street

Clock Tower

Kaimi Pura

Meena Bazaar

Gor Khatri

Sethi House

Sikh Temple ⚑

Lahori Gate

City Circular Road

Gunj Gate

Yakatut Road

City Circular Road

to Wazir Bagh →

Habib Bank

Yadgar Chowk

Andarshar Bazaar

JEWELLERY

Lady Reading Hospital

Pottery

Tinning

Misgaran Bazaar

BRASS

CLOTH

Peepul Mundi

Qissa Khawani

Police

Kabuli Gate

Cinema Road

Namak Mandi

Church Road

Kohati Gate

Dabgari Gate Road

South City Road

to Kohati

Bala Hisar Fort

Coach for Rawalpindi & Lahore

High Court

Khyber Road

to Charsadda

to Khyber Pass

Jail Bridge

Railway Road

Museum

Jail

to Kohat

Shoba Chowk

0   100 yards
0   100 m

© Local Colour Ltd

Key:
1 Galaxie Hotel
2 Habib Hotel
3 Rose Hotel, food stalls in street
4 carpet shops
5 Shan Hotel
6 National Hotel
7 Salateen's Rest.
8 Gulf & Relax Hotels
9 Gohar Palace Hotel
10 Money changers
11 Shinwari Plaza
12 Aizar Hotel
13 Royal Hotel
14 Three Star, Amin, Zabeel Place Hotels
15 Hidayat Hotel
16 Khan Klub
17 Sopgmay Hotel
18 All Saints Church
19 Minibus to Chitral

Pearl Continental ■

Sights

Bazaar Tour

The most exciting part of Peshawar is its old city, elements of which date from Sikh, Mughal and even Buddhist times. It is a labyrinth of narrow lanes and colourful bazaars; a mosaic of traders, travellers, Pathan tribesmen and Afghans. In typical Asiatic style, shops selling similar wares are found together. They are generally open all day, every day, except during *juma* (Friday) prayers between noon and 2 pm. A tour taking in all the most interesting and picturesque bazaars and some of the specialist shops and workshops can be accomplished in two or three hours.

Khyber Bazaar Here you find many of Peshawar's cheaper hotels and, in the evening, food stalls selling excellent kebabs and fry-ups. Meat is sold by weight and then cooked while you watch. The main street, full of doctors, lawyers and dentists, features billboards depicting sets of false teeth of nightmarish proportions. **Kabuli Gate,** one of the walled city's 16 gates, is at the end of Khyber Bazaar. (The wall survived until the mid-1950s, and though the names remain, the gates and the wall have, for the most part, disappeared.)

Qissa Khawani (Story-tellers') Bazaar was described in the mid-19th century by the British Commissioner in Peshawar, Sir Herbert Edwardes, as 'the Piccadilly of Central Asia'. Towering over the street are tall, narrow buildings with intricately carved balconies and window-frames enclosing wooden shutters.

Brass and copper shops are in the street to the left (northwest) at the end of Qissa Khawani. These sell a range of new and old wares. Ali Brothers on the left is the best known and where all VIP visitors are taken. 'Poor Honest Ali', as he disarmingly calls himself, has Gardner Russian china as well as a selection of high-quality brass and copper. When Ali shows his testimonials from ambassadors and the photo of himself with Jackie Onassis, remember — bargain hard.

The Peshawar Pottery is down a side street on the left, immediately after the brass shops. Here you can watch the potters at work, 10 am to 4 pm except Fridays. The wide range of ornamental and utilitarian pottery is glazed in strong earth colours.

Tinsmiths work in the street leading to the pottery, using traditional methods to coat brass pots with tin to prevent the brass from poisoning food.

Back on the main street and beyond the copper market are shops selling **blankets and shawls** from the valleys of Swat and Kaghan. Made of hand-spun wool, they are predominantly red and black, with brightly patterned borders. The lane to the right (southeast), opposite the street to the pottery, leads to the **cloth bazaar.** Beyond that is the **basket bazaar,** which is full of baskets from Dera Ismail Khan, at the southern tip of the province. Here, also, is the **Banjara Bazaar**, which specialises in unusual decorative items such as bells, wooden beads and hair braids. Ask here for the way to **Peepul Mandi,** the main grain wholesale market, where there is a peepul tree believed to be descended from the tree beneath which the Buddha preached.

If you choose instead to continue on the main street towards Chowk Yadgar, you pass the **bird market,** where songbirds are sold as pets in small cages, as in China. To the left are more cloth shops selling all types of *chaders* (multi-purpose sheets) and block-prints.

Chowk Yadgar old Peshawar's central square, now developed, is the best place to leave your motor-rickshaw or car. The monument in the centre commemorates the heroes of the 1965 Indo–Pakistani War and is the traditional place for assembling political rallies and demonstrations.

A pottery in Peshawar

On the left (west) side of the square, money-changers squat on hand-knotted carpets with their safes behind them and their pocket calculators and mobile telephones at the ready. They will change any currency, but will accept only large notes.

From Chowk Yadgar are two interesting walks, one to the west and the other to the east. Running off the square to the west is **Andarshar Bazaar,** a narrow street of gold- and silversmiths selling jewellery (both tribal and modern), antique silver, old coins and military buttons and buckles. While you rummage through the boxes of treasures, trying on nomads' earrings, the shopkeeper plies you with cups of sweet green tea brewed in huge copper samovars. **Shinwari Plaza**, 70 metres beyond the Mahabat Mosque on the right, is a new plaza full of the best Afghan shops, happy hunting ground for jewellery and carpets and all things Afghan

Mahabat Khan Mosque is at the top of the hill to the right (north), its entrance a narrow gateway between jewellery shops. Built in the 1670s, this beautifully proportioned Mughal structure, named after a regional governor who served under both Shah Jahan and Aurangzeb, is orthodox in design. Its open courtyard has an ablution pond in the middle and a single row of rooms around the sides. The prayer hall occupies the west side, flanked by two tall minarets. According to the turn-of-the-century Gazetteer for NWFP, the minarets were frequently used in Sikh times 'as a substitute for the gallows'. A fire that raged through the Andarshar Bazaar in 1895 (the Gazetteer continues) failed to destroy the mosque thanks only to the 'unremitting efforts of the faithful'. The interior of the prayer hall is sheltered beneath three low fluted domes and is lavishly and colourfully painted with floral and geometric designs.

If you start again at Chowk Yadgar but go east this time, you pass fruit and vegetable stalls on the right and an alley full of hardware shops on the left before coming to **Cunningham Clock Tower.** It was built in 1900 'in commemoration of the Diamond Jubilee of Her Majesty the Queen Empress', but is named after Sir George Cunningham who came along somewhat later. Cunningham started his Asian career as the political agent assigned to North Waziristan (in the Tribal Areas) and advanced to become governor of NWFP in 1937–46 and again after Independence in 1947–8. The **leather and skins market** around the clock-tower features the skins of very young Karakul lambs, and many of the shops have tailors on hand to make Astrakhan hats.

The **Meena Bazaar,** for women, is down the alley to the right (south) of the clock-tower. Groups of black-tented women flit like ravens between the

(following pages) Street scenes in and around the bazaar, Peshawar

stalls shopping for beads, trimmings, machine-embroidery and trinkets. Visitors considering adopting purdah can buy their *burqa* (veil) here in a choice of colours.

Further up the hill from the clock-tower is the shoe bazaar, which is down an alley on the right. Next is the block-printing shop, where cloth is hand-printed using a variety of carved wooden blocks dipped in an array of dyes.

The way up the hill to the Mughal caravanserai is called **Sethi Street** because most of the old houses here belong to the Sethi family, one of the oldest merchant families in town. The Sethis once had offices in Czarist Russia and Shanghai; they imported silks and china and exported cloth, indigo and tea. The houses are tall and supplied with balconies. Beautifully carved wooden doors lead from the street to spacious courtyards, and cool cellars 15 metres (50 feet) deep provide a retreat from the heat of summer. Victorian glass chandeliers are a reminder of the family's vast wealth in the last century. A tour of one of the houses can be arranged through the PTDC at Dean's Hotel.

The **Gor Khatri** is a large Mughal caravanserai crowning the hill at the top end of Sethi Street. A huge Mughal gateway leads into a courtyard over 200 metres (650 feet) square, which was once surrounded on all four sides by rooms for travellers. The site has been considered holy for nearly 2,000 years. In the second century AD, it was a Buddhist shrine and monastery known as the Tower of Buddha's Bowl. With the decline of Buddhism, it became a Hindu shrine, and in Mughal times Shah Jahan's daughter built a mosque here and surrounded it with the caravanserai. The Sikhs knocked down the mosque during their 19th-century rule and replaced it with a temple to Gorakhnath. This still stands in the south eastern corner of the courtyard, with a shrine to Nandi beside it. The Sikhs closed the caravanserai and installed their governor in the compound. Since that time it has housed government offices.

Once again, start at Chowk Yadgar and follow Katchery Road (the main street going north), past a row of shops selling holsters for guns and bandoleers for ammunition, to the Grand Trunk Road. There, brooding over the highway to the north and the old city to the south, squats **Bala Hisar Fort**, which was built by the Sikhs in 1834 on the site of Babur's earlier fort. The army Frontier Corps still use it as their headquarters, so it is closed to the public.

The Cantonment

Peshawar's cantonment sprawls along the west side of the railway line and was laid out by the British as graciously and grandly as any other. Between the old city and the cantonment is the **Saddar Bazaar,** an area full of hotels, restaurants and shops stocked with antiques and carpets.

Peshawar Museum (tel 271310, 274452), formerly Victoria Memorial Hall, was built near the east end of The Mall in 1905. Its long hall, flanked by side galleries and with a raised platform at the end opposite the door, was the ballroom. The museum, open 8.30 am to 12.30 pm and 2.30 to 5 pm in summer, 9 am to 4 pm in winter, closed on Wednesday, has one of Pakistan's best collections of Gandharan art, and the pieces are well arranged and labelled, with sculptures illustrating the life of the Buddha placed in chronological order. The fasting Buddha here is even more haunting than the one in Lahore Museum. The ethnological section, the Hall of Tribes, has wooden carvings from the Kalash people in Chitral. There is also a Muslim Gallery. Guided tours can be arranged on request.

St John's Cathedral is the oldest in Peshawar, dating from 1851, the second year of the British presence. The Christian cemetery is not beside the church, however, being located instead at two places beyond the residential area on the road to the Khyber Pass. The oldest graves are cemented into the wall closest to the road and tell evocative tales of death on the frontier. One Lieutenant Colonel Walter Irvine was the chief medical officer of NWFP 'who lost his life in the Nagoman River when leading the Peshawar Vale Hunt, of which he was Master, 26 Jan 1919'. The Rev Isidor Lowenthal was a 'Missionary of the American Presbyterian Mission who translated the New Testament into Pushtoo and was shot by his Chokeydar [watchman], April 27 1864'. There are many sad tiny graves similar to the one for 'Our Little Mavis, born September 6th 1903, died May 1st 1904. The dearly loved child of Arthur and Maud Tyler.' Donations for the upkeep of the cemetery are welcomed by the bishop at St John's Cathedral.

The **Peshawar Club**, on Sir Syed Road near The Mall, is reserved for members and their guests, but anyone can go in to look around and browse in the library. The swimming pool is surrounded by large shade trees. In the morning, half of it is curtained off by a *shamiana*, behind which swim women in purdah. Bells ring loudly just before noon to warn the ladies that they are about to be exposed.

Edwardes College, one of Pakistan's prestigious boarding schools, was founded in 1855 as the Sir Herbert Edwardes Memorial School. It has splendid Mughal-Gothic buildings replete with ornate cupolas, baubles and pillars.

Khalid Bin Walid Bagh (affectionately known by foreign residents as the 'Kolly-Wolly-Beanbag') is the narrow park on The Mall, full of beautiful *chinar* trees. It is all that remains of an old Mughal Shalimar Garden.

University Town lies about seven kilometres (four miles) from the centre of Peshawar on the road to the Khyber Pass. Its oldest building is Islamia College, which was founded in 1913 to educate the sons of Pathan chiefs. If the elegant Mughal-Gothic hall looks familiar, you may have noticed it on the hundred-rupee note. The college formed the nucleus of the University of Peshawar when it was founded in 1950. Various research departments in the area include the Pakistan Academy for Rural Development and the Pakistan Forest Institute. The surrounding residential
area is a sprawling garden town of red brick buildings amidst watered lawns.

Hyattabad and **Karkhanai Bazaar,** the smugglers' bazaar, are beyond University Town on the road to the Khyber Pass. The smugglers' bazaar (moved down from Landi Kotal in the Khyber Pass), is a new shopping area full of imported electrical goods, fabrics, clothes and even a Marks and Spencers selling the real thing.

Islamia College, the nucleus of the University of Peshawar

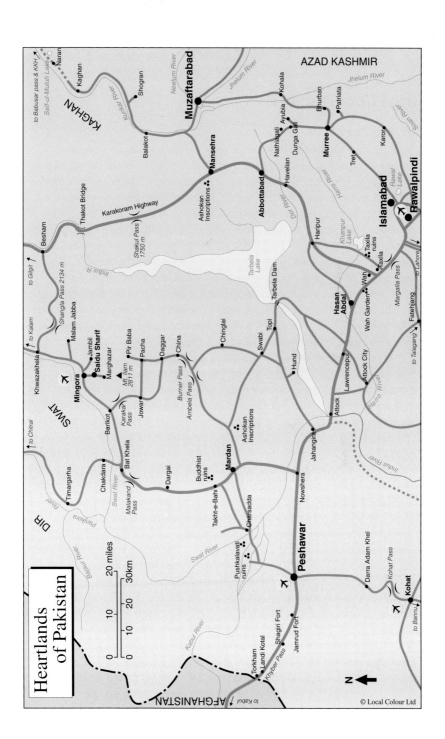

Trips from Peshawar

Khyber Pass

The legendary **Khyber Pass** is one of the great attractions for visitors to Peshawar. Tourists need a **permit** and an armed escort from the Political Agent in Stadium Road to visit the Khyber Pass. Residents in Pakistan get their Khyber permits from the Home Secretary at the Civil Secretariat. The permits are free and delivered immediately, but you can save yourself the hassle by joining one of the PTDC daily tours to the Khyber. Contact the **Tourist Information Centre,** PTDC, at Dean's Hotel, tel 279781-3, open 9 am to 1 pm and 2 to 4.30 pm, closed on Sunday and Friday afternoons. Gentle, friendly, Mr Salahuddin, has a mine of information at his fingertips and, should you prefer, will instruct you how to organise your own trip to the Khyber.

The Afghan border at Torkham is 56 kilometres (35 miles) from Peshawar, about an hour's drive. The road runs west from the cantonment and through University Town, Hyattabad and Karkhanai Bazaar, before and after which the fields on either side of the road are covered with refugee camps. After the camps are the compounds of Pathan tribesmen, their high mud walls furnished with turrets and gunslits, their entrances guarded by huge corrugated-iron gates.

Jamrud Fort, 18 kilometres (11 miles) from Peshawar and at the mouth of the Khyber Pass, is as far as you can go without a permit. The fort, coarsely constructed of stone daubed with mud plaster, was built by the Sikhs in 1823 on the site of an earlier fort. The famous Sikh general Hari Singh died and is buried here. The modern stone arch spanning the road dates from 1964.

The eastern end of the pass is wide and flat, bounded on either side by low, stony hills. Every small hillock in the area is capped with a picket manned by the Frontier Force. The road zigzags up, passing two viewing points that look back into the Vale of Peshawar, until it reaches **Shagai Fort** which was built by the British in the 1920s. It then starts down into a small valley in which stand fortified Pathan houses and the Ali Masjid. Perched high above this mosque on a commanding spur is the **Ali Masjid Fort,** which overlooks the entire length of the pass and guards the gorge that is its narrowest point. The road here hugs a narrow ledge beside the riverbed in the shadow of high cliffs on either side. Until the way was widened, two laden camels could not squeeze past one another, and even now the road is one way. (The return road and the railway follow separate ledges higher up on the opposite cliff, affording a less exciting view of the gorge.)

In the cemetery here are the graves of British soldiers killed in the Second Afghan War of 1879. Regimental insignia are carved and painted on to the rock faces at several places along the road, with the Gordon Highlanders, the South Wales Borderers, and the Royal Sussex, Cheshire and Dorset regiments standing in one doughty group.

After the gorge, the pass opens out into a wide fertile valley dotted with Pathan villages. True to form, however, these villages look more like forts, with high, crenellated mud walls running between watch-towers pierced with narrow gunslits.

Sphola Stupa, a Buddhist ruin dating from the second to the fifth centuries AD, stands to the right of the road and above the railway at the village of Zarai, 25 kilometres (16 miles) from Jamrud. The stupa has a high hemispherical dome resting on a three-tiered square base. Some beautiful Gandharan sculptures were found here when the site was excavated at the beginning of this century. Some of the finds are now in the Peshawar Museum. The side of the stupa facing the road has been restored.

Landi Kotal, at the end of the railway and eight kilometres (five miles) from the border, is still a smugglers' town. Electrical goods, cigarettes, guns and drugs are the main commodities in the bazaar below the road to the left, but since the Afghan War most trade has moved down to Karkhanai Bazaar outside Peshawar.

The road now forks: right to the Khyber Rifles' headquarters, left to the border. A viewing point beyond the town looks out across tank traps of closely packed cement pyramids to the border post at **Torkham**, the last oasis of green before the barren brown of the Afghan plain.

On a hilltop to the left of Torkham is the ruined **Kafir Fort**, a Hindu relic of the ninth century AD. On this ridge in 1919, the British and Afghans fought one of the last engagements of the Third Afghan War. The top of the hill is now Afghan territory, with a commanding view down on Pakistani installations and forts.

The Khyber Train

For rail enthusiasts, the Khyber Railway from Peshawar to Landi Kotal is a three-star attraction. The British built it in the 1920s at the then enormous cost of more than two million pounds. It passes through 34 tunnels totalling five kilometres (three miles) and over 92 bridges and culverts. The two or three coaches are pulled and pushed by two SG 060 oil-fired engines. At one point, the track climbs 130 metres in little more than a kilometre

(above) *The Buddha carved in stone, Peshawar Museum*
(opposite) *Camels out of their element at Taxila*

(425 feet in 0.7 miles) by means of the heart-stopping Changai Spur. This is a W-shaped section of track with two cliff-hanging reversing stations, at which train wheezes desperately before shuddering to a stop and backing away from the brink.

The Khyber train currently runs once a month to a fixed schedule. Ask for the dates from PTDC or any tour operator. Groups of 20 to 45 passengers can book the train for an all day outing to Landi Kotal and back, a ride lasting ten to eleven hours, for US$1,000. You can easily see the train at rest at Peshawar Station.

Darra Adam Khel

Darra is the gun factory of the Tribal Areas, located 40 kilometres (25 miles) south of Peshawar on the road to Kohat, a drive of about 40 minutes. To visit the gun factories, foreigners need a permit from the Home Secretary of NWFP whose office is in the Civil Secretariat on Police Road, but you can drive by bus or car through Darra without a permit provided you do not stop. The permit is free and issued while you wait, but you should get it the day before you plan your factory visit.

The Darra arms 'factory' fired up in 1897. In return for turning a blind eye to this illegal Pathan enterprise, the British were guaranteed safe passage along the main roads. In any case, the British believed it better that the Pathans have inferior weapons of their own making than stolen British-made guns.

Darra's main street is lined on either side with small forges at which guns are made by hand. The tools are astonishingly primitive, yet the forges turn out accurate reproductions of every conceivable sort of weapon, from pen pistols and hand-grenades to automatic rifles and **anti-aircraft** guns. The copies are so painstakingly reproduced that even the serial number of the original is carried over. Much of the craftsmanship is very fine, but the materials are sometimes wanting: gun barrels are often made from steel reinforcing rods diverted from the building trade. The main street constantly erupts with the roar of gunfire, as tribesmen step out to test prospective purchases.

Gandharan Remains

The three most interesting archaeological remains from Gandhara are Takht-e-Bahi (a ruined Buddhist monastery), the Ashokan edicts (two inscribed boulders) and Charsadda (an excavated mound that was once the capital city). These three places can be visited in a one-day outing from Peshawar or *en route* between Peshawar and either Islamabad or

Swat. An interesting loop takes in Charsadda and Takht-e-Bahi on the way up to Swat via the Malakand Pass, then the Ashokan edicts on the way down from Swat via the Ambela Pass.

The kingdom of Gandhara centred on the Peshawar area from the sixth century BC to the 11th century AD and enjoyed its high period from the first to the fifth centuries AD under the Kushan kings. This was a time of great international contacts, and Buddhist Gandhara was at the hub of Asia, trading with China, the Mediterranean and India. The kingdom is remembered chiefly for its Buddhist art. Museums all over the world display the fine stone and stucco sculptures of Gandhara; works that reflect a society that was mature, prosperous, advanced and (in the best Buddhist tradition) gentle.

The first capital of Gandhara was Pushkalavati — the Lotus City on the banks of the Swat River just north of its junction with Kabul, at a place now called Charsadda. Under the Kushans, the capital moved to Peshawar, and under the Hindu Shahi kings from the ninth to the 11th century the capital was at Hund, on the Indus. After Mahmud of Ghazni conquered the area and converted it to Islam in AD 1026, the name Gandhara disappeared. Only a few ruins and the civilisation's great art remain.

Though there is little to see, it is still exciting to stand on the mound where the Lotus City once flourished and to imagine Alexander the Great's army attacking in 327 BC, to read Ashoka's edicts of 260 BC at Shahbaz Garhi, and to visualise the life of a Buddhist monk at Takht-e-Bahi in the third century AD. These visits should only be made in cool weather from September to April.

Charsadda

Charsadda, the site of Pushkalavati, is 28 kilometres (17 miles) northeast of Peshawar. Pushkalavati was the capital of the ancient kingdom of Gandhara from about the sixth century BC to the second century AD. Even after the capital moved to Peshawar, Pushkalavati remained a centre of pilgrimage until the seventh century, thanks to the presence of an important Buddhist shrine.

The **Bala Hisar** is a mound about 800 metres (half a mile) to the left of the road from Peshawar, about a kilometre (half a mile) before Charsadda. It has been excavated twice, by Sir John Marshall in 1902 and by Sir Mortimer Wheeler in 1958. You can climb to the top. The millions of pottery shards amid the round, beautifully coloured stones at your feet are only the top layer of 2,500 years of debris, for the Bala Hisar was occupied from the sixth century BC to the 18th century AD.

In about 516 BC, Gandhara became part of the seventh province of the Achaemenid Empire and paid tribute to Darius the Great of Persia. According

A Pathan [Pukhtun] from the Khyber Agency

to Herodotus, the Greek historian writing in about 460 BC, Darius sent the explorer Scylax of Caryanda to sail down the Indus and find the sea. Scylax in all probability set out from Pushkalavati, as the river is navigable from here down.

Gandhara probably remained within the Achaemenid Empire for the next 200 years, until its overthrow by Alexander the Great in the fourth century BC. Alexander first captured Persia and Afghanistan, then in 327 BC he split his army, taking half of it north to subdue Swat. The other half he placed under the command of Hephaestion, with orders to go directly to Gandhara, capture the main towns, proceed to the Indus and build a bridge across it. The able Hephaestion laid siege to Pushkalavati and, after 30 days, took the city and killed its defender, Astes. He built his bridge by lashing together a line of boats from one bank to the other at Hund. He secured the surrender of Taxila through negotiations. By the time Alexander got to Gandhara, he owned it.

In 322 BC, Chandragupta Maurya rose to power, bringing Gandhara under his sway some years later. By this time Taxila, with its famous university, had grown more important than Pushkalavati. The Mauryan emperor Ashoka built stupas containing relics of the Buddha at both cities. The mound believed to enclose the stupa at Pushkalavati has not been excavated.

Gandharan detail from Butkara Stupa in Swat

The Bactrian Greeks were the next rulers of Gandhara. They arrived from Balkh in Afghanistan in about 185 BC and laid out new cities at both Pushkalavati and Taxila. The city at Taxila is now called Sirkap. The one at Pushkalavati, now called Shaikhan Dheri, is a kilometre (about half a mile) northeast of the Bala Hisar. From the top of Bala Hisar mound it is visible across the river; only dedicated archaeologists gain much by going to take a closer look.

Though the Bala Hisar had fallen into permanent decline by the second century BC, it was never entirely abandoned, and people continued to live here right up to the 18th century. It was used as a fort then, which is the meaning of hisar.

Charsadda is surrounded by hundreds of hectares of graves, all decorated with black and white stones in geometric patterns. The graveyard here is considered especially holy, like Makli Hill in Sindh (see page 110). The road running south from the crossroads at the centre of Charsadda leads to Prang, the site of several high, completely unexcavated mounds — the debris of thousands of years of occupation.

Takht-e-Bahi

The Buddhist monastery at Takht-e-Bahi, 14 kilometres (nine miles) north-west of Mardan on the road to Swat, is the most impressive and complete ruin of its kind in Pakistan. A visit here gives a good idea of what life as a Buddhist monk was like. The top of the hill behind the monastery affords a view of the Peshawar plains on one side and, on the other, the Malakand Pass and the hills of Swat.

To reach Takht-e-Bahi directly from Charsadda, turn left (north) at the crossroads in Charsadda. After exactly two kilometres (1.2 miles), turn right into a single-lane, surfaced road leading through rich irrigated farmland. Keep to the main road and after 22 kilometres (14 miles) come out on the main Mardan–Swat road. Turn left here and proceed one kilometre (about half a mile) to Takht-e-Bahi village.

To get to the ruins, cross the level crossing in the centre of Takht-e-Bahi and, after 500 metres (0.3 miles) turn right at the battered sign, 'Archaeological ruins of Takht-e-Bahi 3 km' (two miles). Cross the railway line, turn left at the gate of the sugar mill and, a little further on, turn right down a dirt road. Now you will see on top of the hill to the right the ruins of the large, eighth- to tenth-century Hindu Shahi Fort. Continue to the end of the track. The ruins of the monastery are straight ahead. It is a steep 500-metre walk up the hill to the site, and another 500 metres to the top of the hill.

The monastery and stupas at Takht-e-Bahi were founded in the first century AD and abandoned in the sixth or seventh century. On the ridge above the monastery to the south, and on the spurs to the east and west, are the ruins of private houses, some of which are three storeys high.

You approach the monastery from the east. On the right, just before the entrance of the main ruin, is a two-storey block of four monks' cells. In each cell are two niches for the monk's lamp and other belongings.

The **court of stupas** is the first you enter at the top of the path. Alcoves or chapels open to the court on three of its sides. Originally, these contained single plaster figures of the Buddha, either sitting or standing, the statues dedicated to the memory of holy men or donated by rich pilgrims. The largest statues must have been ten metres (33 feet) high, and all would have been gilded or painted. Carved friezes in high relief showing scenes from the life of the Buddha once ringed the walls of the chapels. Carved on slabs of stone, they were attached to the walls with iron nails.

The remains of 38 votive stupas and some more chapels are scattered haphazardly round the centre of the court. They also were built as offerings by pilgrims and were full of gilded and painted statues and reliefs depicting the Buddha and his life. One stupa is unusual in that it is octagonal.

The **monastery court** is north of the court of stupas, up some steps. It has monks' cells ranged round three sides, and a second storey once contributed another 15 cells. According to the Chinese pilgrim Xuan Zang, writing in 630 AD, the walls of the cells were plastered and painted different colours, and the wooden doorjambs and lintels were decorated with carvings. In each cell are two niches for the monk's lamp and belongings, and a small window.

The water tank stands in the southwestern corner of the court and was probably filled by rainwater draining from the roofs. The kitchen and dining-room are east of the monastery court, with stairs leading up from the kitchen to the second floor. On the outer wall of the kitchen are two projecting buttresses that may have been the latrine.

The court of the main stupa is south of the court of stupas up some steps. The single large stupa standing in the centre of the court was once about ten metres (33 feet) high, with its umbrellas projecting higher. The square base was surmounted by a hemispherical dome, and the entire structure would have been decorated with gilded and painted figures of the Buddha and scenes from his life. Like the court of stupas, this court had roofed alcoves on three sides, that once housed statues of the Buddha.

The **assembly court**, where the monks met together, is on the north-western corner of the complex and surrounded by high walls. The two cement water tanks in the centre of the court are modern.

Gandhara Art

by Isobel Shaw

Between the first and fifth century AD, the Buddhist kingdom of Gandhara in northern Pakistan enjoyed a period of unparalleled peace and prosperity. It stood at the hub of the trade routes linking China, India and the Mediterranean — a cultural and commercial crossroads. The heart of the kingdom was in the plains of Peshawar along the Kabul and Swat rivers, its capital near their confluence. The prosperity resulted in the growth of cities able to support a large community of Buddhist monks living in about 1,600 monasteries along the two rivers, always within easy reach of the towns where the monks went daily to beg.

Each monastery had its stupa, a solid domed structure (usually on a square base) representing the Buddha and sometimes containing some relic of the Buddha or of a revered Buddhist holy man. To facilitate their devotions, the monks decorated their stupas and monasteries with stone and plaster statues of the Buddha and scenes telling the story of his life. This Gandharan sculpture was so vivid and alive — and the kingdom so powerful — that the artistic tradition continued for five centuries.

The strength of Gandharan sculpture came from the depth of belief and devotion of the artists, whose work was their expression of veneration of the Buddha. They created an exciting new mix of Eastern and Western art, incorporating ideas from India, Persia, Greece and Rome. The various influences are evident in the Corinthian and Persepolitan capitals of pillars carved in relief, and in the centaurs, garlands, vine motifs and Atlas figures that ennoble piece after piece. The earliest sculptures refrain from direct representation of the Buddha in human form, resorting instead to symbols — a stupa, lotus, tree or wheel. In the second century AD, Kanishka, the greatest Kushan king, convoked a council on Buddhism, which decided to popularise Buddhism by encouraging sculptors to represent the Buddha, for the first time, as a man. The first Buddha figures had Greek faces and wore Roman-style robes, carved with deep folds. This Western look later gave way to a more mask-like expression, representing the inner serenity, the private ecstasy, achieved through deep meditation.

The Buddha is shown either standing, sitting cross-legged or lying on his deathbed. His hands are frozen in certain gestures recognised by the faithful as prayer, preaching, blessing or accepting gifts. His hair is wavy or curly and tied in a bun on top of his head, which was later mistaken for a protuberance from his skull. His earlobes are usually elongated, and the middle of his forehead bears a round mark. He is normally crowned with a halo.

The Buddha never visited Gandhara, but the Buddhist belief in reincarnation made it easy for sages to borrow from local oral tradition, turning the hero of any local legend into the Buddha living some previous life. Important shrines sprouted on the supposed sites of miracles performed by these earlier incarnations, each shrine decorated with scenes from the Jataka stories, as the legends came to be known.

Opposite the entrance to the assembly court, at its southeast corner, over the vaulted chambers, is a small chapel. It contains two tiers of ornamental trefoil panels divided by pilasters. This chapel may have housed a small stupa to commemorate an individual who was either especially holy or especially rich.

The ten vaulted chambers beneath this court, and reached through arched doorways, were used either for meditation or storage. Two more arched doorways lead west from these rooms out to a large open court, but what purpose this court served remains a mystery.

In the covered area south of the open court are two small stupas. Their elaborate decoration of red and gold paint was in perfect condition when they were excavated in 1910, but little decoration remains today, despite the protecting shed.

Private houses are scattered up the hill above the monastery and for more than a kilometre (about half a mile) along the ridge. Some houses have rooms set around a central court, but most are two-storey structures consisting of two small rooms, one above the other. Each is entered by a low door and lit by one small sloping window. Staircases run up the outside and consist of flat slabs of stone protruding from the wall.

Options from Takht-e-Bahi are to continue north up to Swat (see page 201) or to turn south to Mardan, 14 kilometres (nine miles) away, from where you can continue east along the ancient trade route.

Mardan

For nearly 200 years a major military base, Mardan was the headquarters of the élite Guides Corps, which was organised in 1846 to guide regular units in the field, collect intelligence and keep the peace on the North-West Frontier. British soldiers at the time wore uniforms of brilliant red and blue, making them easy targets for Pathan snipers. The Guides were the first to wear khaki, which is the local word for 'dust'.

The **Cavagnari Arch** in the centre of Mardan is dedicated to those Guides who died in Kabul in 1879. The plaque reads:

'The annals of no army and no regiment can show a brighter record of devoted bravery than has been achieved by this small band of Guides. By their deeds they have conferred undying honour not only to the regiment to which they belong, but on the whole British army.'

The Guides' cemetery and church are also worth a visit. For an account of the Guides in action, see Charles Miller's *Khyber* or M M Kaye's romantic novel, *Far Pavilions*. Mardan is now the home of the Punjab Regiment whom you must contact for an appointment to see the Guides' Church.

Ashokan Inscriptions at Shahbaz Garhi

Shahbaz Garhi is 13 kilometres (eight miles) east of Mardan on the road to Swabi. It was once an important city at the junction of three major trade routes: the main road from Europe, through Afghanistan to India via Pushkalavati; the more northerly route through Afghanistan via Bajaur, Dir and Swat; and the route from China via the Indus Valley and Swat. From Shabbaz Garhi, the combined routes continued east to cross the Indus at Hund.

(previous page) Making a point at the livestock market in Peshawar

The outline of the ancient city is now difficult to trace. Its centre was at the modern road junction, and the three modern roads pass over the sites of its three gates. Two Chinese pilgrims who visited in AD 520 and 630 wrote of a thriving Buddhist centre surrounded by stupas and monasteries.

The Ashokan inscriptions were written in the third century BC for the information and edification of travellers such as these. They are down a dirt track to the right (south), a few hundred metres (yards) before the left (north) turn to Rustam, the Ambela Pass and Swat. The inscriptions are on two rocks on a hill about 300 metres (yards) to the left (east) of the track and 400 metres (yards) from the main road.

They are the most important and complete of Ashoka's proclamations. Written 2,250 years ago, they are also the oldest historically significant writings extant in the subcontinent.

The Mauryan emperor Ashoka (272–231 BC) was one of the greatest monarchs the world has ever known, ruling over almost the whole of the Indian subcontinent from his capital at Pataliputra (now Patna) on the banks of the Ganges River in India. Tolerant of all religions, he may have been a Buddhist himself. He ordered that a series of edicts, announcing state policy and instructing his subjects, be inscribed on rocks and pillars all over his empire.

Ashoka's inscriptions were written in the script best understood by the people of the locality in which they were placed. Thus, the two in Pakistan (here at Shahbaz Garhi and at Mansehra) were in Kharoshthi, the Gandharan script derived from the Aramaic scripts of Iran. The inscriptions at Kandahar in Afghanistan were in Greek and Aramaic, and those in more southerly parts of the subcontinent were in Brahmi.

At Shahbaz Garhi are 12 edicts on the first rock and two on the second. They describe Ashoka's remorse at the terrible destruction and slaughter accompanying his overthrow of Kalinga in eastern India and announce that, in the future, his conquests will be achieved through 'righteousness and *dharma*' and thus infused with love. They go on to promise that wherever he may be — at table or in his ladies' apartments, on horseback or in his pleasure orchards — he is always available to hear petitions from his people. This is his duty.

The duties of his subjects are to honour their parents, relatives and friends, to give alms to the priests and the poor, and to eschew extravagance. The slaughter of animals is forbidden, with pilgrimage suggested as an alternative to hunting trips. Many religious rites are trivial and useless, the edicts warn, and the best ways of gaining merit are showing self-control, respect and generosity. All are commanded to show tolerance to people of other religious sects.

Finally, the edicts order that hospitals be founded for the treatment of both man and beast, and that medicinal herbs be planted to ensure a ready supply. Fruit trees should be planted and wells dug along the roadside for the refreshment of travellers.

A surfaced road leads from Shahbaz Garhi north to Swat via the Ambela Pass. The road east leads to **Swabi**, where it forks left to Tarbela dam and right to Attock. From Swabi to Islamabad is 119 kilometres (74 miles) via Attock, a drive of an hour and a half, and 137 kilometres (85 miles) via Tarbela dam, a drive of two hours, but you now need a permit to drive across the top of the dam, obtainable from Water and Power Development Authority (WAPDA) in Islamabad, tel (051) 568941-2, or through PTDC Islamabad. A ford before Tarbela dam could prove difficult for cars during the monsoon.

Hund

Hund is known to history priminary as the place to cross the Indus. Not the least of those to use this spot, Alexander the Great and his army of 50,000 men (35,000 of whom had come all the way from Europe) crossed with their animals over a bridge of boats. It was also the capital of Gandhara from AD 870 to 1001 under the Hindu Shahi kings, only to be utterly laid waste by their nemesis, Mahmud of Ghazni. The main crossing place moved 20 kilometres (12 miles) downstream to Attock in the 16th century. Now, Hund is a place for history enthusiasts only, as there is little to see.

Here, above Attock Gorge, the Indus sprawls lazily across the mountain-edged plain, flowing wide, slow and shallow. In winter, it can be forded on horseback, and even in summer, when it is swollen by melting snows and monsoon rains, it can still be crossed, albeit somewhat precariously, on inflated cow-skin rafts or upturned pots used as floats.

Among the Buddhist, Hindu and Muslim remains at Hund, the most noticeable are the walls of Akbar's fort, which were built in the 16th century and completely surround the modern village. The fort is square, with a gate at the centre of each wall. The road enters the village through the northern gate and exits by the south gate to the river, its cobblestones descending to the crossing place.

The Hindu remains have been badly damaged by the river, but still visible on the cliff at the river-bank is a section of the city wall with two square bastions of diaper masonry.

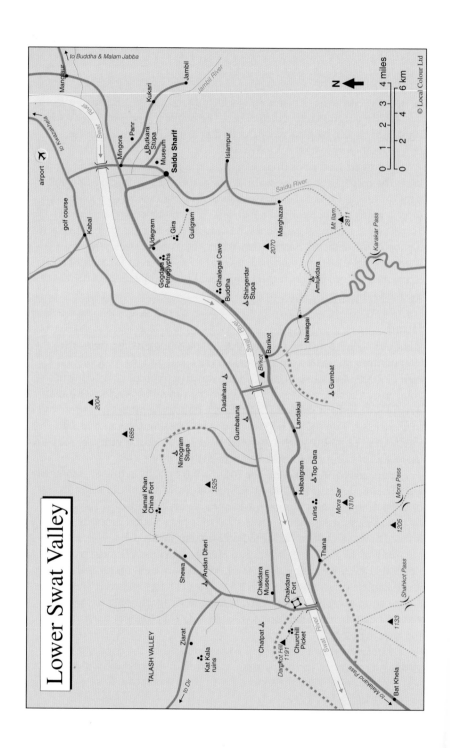

Lower Swat Valley

to Buddha & Malam Jabba

Mangaur

to Kwazakhela

Swat River

Panr

Mingora

Kukari

Jambil

Jambil River

airport

golf course

Kabal

Butkara Stupa

Museum

Saidu Sharif

Islampur

Saidu River

Udegram

Gira

Guligram

Marghazar

2070

Mt Ilam

2811

Karakar Pass

2004

Gogdara Petroglyphs

Ghalegai Cave

Buddha

Shingerdar Stupa

Amlukdara

Dadahara

Birkot

Barikot

Nawagai

1685

Gumbatuna

Swat River

Gumbat

Landakai

Kamal Khan China Fort

Nimogram Stupa

1525

Top Dara

Halbatgram

Mora Sar

1310

Mora Pass

1205

Shewa

Andan Dheri

Chakdara Museum

Chakdara Fort

ruins

Thana

Shahkot Pass

TALASH VALLEY

Ziarat

Kat Kala ruins

Chatpat

Dargkot Hill

1191

Churchill Picket

Swat River

1133

to Dir

to Malakand Pass

Bat Khela

N

0   1   2   3   4 miles

0   2   4   6 km

© Local Colour Ltd

Swat Valley

Swat is the most historically interesting valley in Pakistan. It is also one of the most beautiful — certainly much greener and more fertile than the valleys further north because it lies within the monsoon belt. In Lower Swat, the valley is wide, the fields on either side of the river are full of wheat and lucerne, and the villages are prosperous and surrounded by fruit trees. In Upper Swat, the river tumbles through pine forests hemmed in by snow-capped mountains. For the historian and amateur archaeologist, Swat offers several hundred archaeological sites spanning 5,000 years of history. For the sportsman and trekker, it offers good fishing and hiking.

Getting to Swat

Mingora is served daily by a 40-minute flight from Islamabad and a 35-minute flight from Peshawar. On Thursdays and Saturdays an unreliable afternoon flight connects Chitral to Islamabad via Swat, but it is often cancelled. Inexpensive bus and minibus services leave Peshawar every 15 minutes or so and take three hours to reach Mingora. Three roads lead to Swat, all passable by ordinary car (see map page 183). The shortest is via Mardan across the Malakand Pass, about 250 kilometres (150 miles) and four and a half hours from Islamabad, and about 120 kilometres (75 miles) and three hours from Peshawar. The most attractive route is via Shahbaz Garhi and the Ambela Pass to Buner, and thence across the Karakar Pass, about five and a half hours from Islamabad (see page 209). From Swat, the traveller can continue north across the difficult Lowari Pass to Chitral, or east on a paved road to the Karakoram Highway and thence to Gilgit and China.

When to Go

Ranging in altitude from 1,000 to 3,000 metres (3,300 to 9,800 feet), Swat is good to visit in all seasons. Ordinary cars can get most of the way up the valley in winter (depending on the snowfall) and, from April to December, to the very head of the valley. Monsoon rains fall from the end of July through August. The best months are September through December and March through May. Unfortunately for the tourist, Swat is now extremely popular with the Punjabis in summer, so it is uncomfortably crowded from June through August.

History

Stone Age people lived in Swat at least as early as 3000 BC. In 1700 BC, there arrived from Central Asia a wave of **Aryans,** forerunners of the Hindus and the composers of the Rigveda, the oldest religious text in the world. In one of the 1,028 hymns extant, a chief sings of a victory won on the banks of the River Suvastu, the Swat River.

In 327 BC, **Alexander the Great** invaded Swat on his way from Afghanistan to the Indus and fought four battles here.

From the second century BC to the ninth century AD, **Buddhism** flourished in the valley, leaving behind a legacy of beautiful sculpture and more than 500 monasteries. Here tantric Buddhism evolved and Padmasambhava, the great tantric master and sorcerer was born in Swat in the eighth century. Trisong Detsen, the king of Tibet from 755 to 795, invited Padmasambhava to Tibet where he used his magic to overthrow the old Bon priests and founded the Nyingma order (recognisable by their red hats). From Tibet, Mahayana Buddhism spread to Mongolia, China, Korea and Japan.

The **Hindu Shahi kings** built their fortified cities on the tops of many of the hills of Lower Swat from the eighth to the tenth century, and massive stone walls still crown the peaks on every side.

Mahmud of Ghazni took the valley in the 11th century after a fierce battle at Udegram, where his commander Kushal Khan was killed and buried. A mosque dating from the 11th century stands on the hill at Udegram. The Mughals came to Swat in the 16th century but failed to add it to their dominions. Babur at least gained a wife from Swat, but Akbar only suffered a disastrous defeat in the Karakar Pass.

The **Akhund of Swat,** who rose to power in the 19th century, was a Sufi ascetic with a highly charismatic and warlike personality. He united the Swatis around his capital at Saidu Sharif and has been immortalised in the West by the poem by Edward Lear (1812–88):

Who or why, or which, or what,
Is the Akhund of Swat?
Is he tall or short, or dark or fair?
Does he sit on a stool or a sofa or chair, or squat,
The Akhund of Swat?
Is he wise or foolish, young or old?
[... and plenty more in that vein]

The Akhund's death in 1877 inaugurated 40 years of tribal feuding until the Akhund's grandson, Miangul Wadud, aided by the British, was accepted as *badshah,* or king. The British acknowledged Swat as a sovereign state in 1926 and recognised Miangul Wadud as its *wali*, or ruler. Miangul Wadud abdicated in 1949 in favour of his son, Miangul Jehanzeb, who continued to develop the valley by building roads, schools and hospitals, and instituting land reform. Not until 1969 was Swat fully absorbed into Pakistan as Swat District, and Miangul's son, Aurangzeb, now represents Swat as an elected member of government aided by his son Adnan.

Suggested Itinerary

Three days and two nights from Islamabad by car
October to April — recommended months to visit:

Day 1   Drive up via the Malakand Pass, stopping *en route* to visit:
— Takht-e-Bahi, Buddhist ruins and monastery
— Chakdara Museum, collection of 1st to 7th century Buddhist sculptures
— Churchill's Picket
— Shingerdar Stupa, 3rd to 4th century Buddhist ruin
— 11th century mosque at Udegram and Raja Gira's castle
— Check into hotel at Saidu Sharif or Mingora
— In the evening, drive to Marghazar, 13 kilometres (eight miles) up the Saidu Valley

Day 2   Drive slowly up the valley as far as you can. Visit:
— Swat Museum
— Butkara Buddhist Stupa
— Stop for shopping in Khwazakhela, Madyan and Bahrain
Time allowing, explore more sites in Lower Swat:
— Birkot Hill
— Nimogram Stupa

Day 3   Drive slowly back to Islamabad via the Shangla Pass and Abbottabad. (Or, if that road is blocked by snow, via Ambela Pass.)

May to September — Beware — Swat is very crowded June through August

Day 1   Drive straight to Swat over the Ambela Pass. (It will be too hot to make any stops *en route* to Swat.) Spend the night in Miandam.

Day 2   Drive up to Kalam, stopping for shopping in Madyan and Bahrain. Continue beyond Kalam to the end of the road and walk. Spend the night at Kalam if you can find room.

Day 3   Drive back to Islamabad via the Shangla Pass.

(following page) A river, fed by mountain snows

To Saidu Sharif via the Malakand Pass

Go from Islamabad to Mardan via Attock and Swabi, or via Tarbela (if you have a permit) and Swabi. The quickest but least interesting route is via the Grand Trunk Road to Nowshera.

There is an unmarked bypass round Mardan to the west, but it is interesting to drive through the centre of Mardan to see the Cavagnari Arch (see page 197).

Takht-e-Bahi is 13 kilometres (eight miles) north of Mardan. As the climb to the Buddhist monastery is a steep 500 metres (0.3 miles) up a completely shadeless hill, this site should be visited only in cool weather.

The Malakand Pass begins at Dargai. The road over the pass is good, but is always crowded with a stream of trucks crawling up and careering down.

The view-point about a kilometre (half a mile) before the top of the pass overlooks the British-built Swat Canal, by which irrigation water is diverted from the Swat River through a tunnel under the Malakand Pass to the plains of Mardan. The old Buddhist road winding round the side of the hill about 15 metres (50 feet) below the modern road once led to a monastery below the pass. Unfortunately, the monastery was destroyed during the blasting of the canal tunnel.

Malakand Fort, on the left, at the top of the pass, guards the road. Here, 1,000 Sikh infantry under British command held off 10,000 tribal warriors led by the so-called Mad Mullah at the outbreak of the Pathan uprising in 1897, until reinforcements eventually arrived from Mardan. Stop here at the office of the Political Agent of Malakand, open 8.30 am to 2.30 pm, to get a permit if you wish to visit Churchill's Picket at Chakdara.

On the other side of the pass, the road descends through the thriving market town of Bat Khela and continues past the headworks of the Swat Canal to the Swat River. The first bridge across the river is at Chakdara, from which issues the road to Dir and Chitral.

Chakdara was an important centre for thousands of years, because it was here that the trade route from Afghanistan via Bajaur crossed the Swat River. (In 327 BC, Alexander the Great, *en route* to Taxila, crossed here with half of his 50,000-man army.) The area has many archaeological sites, including graveyards in use for 3,500 years and the remains of Buddhist monasteries from the first to the seventh century AD. Eighth to tenth-century Hindu Shahi forts crouch on the hilltops.

Chakdara Bridge, built in 1896 by the British, is guarded by Chakdara Fort, which was built the same year on the foundations of a 16th-century fort built by the Mughal emperor Akbar. The fort is still used by the army. Expect to be asked to show identification papers at the check-post at the bridge.

Damkot Hill overlooks the bridge and fort at Chakdara — and the entire valley from Malakand Pass to Barikot. The top of the hill is covered with excavated ruins from different periods, including a Buddhist monastery and Hindu Shahi fort. The newest building is **Churchill's Picket** (or *Piquet*), a small fort built in 1896. Winston Churchill served here during the Pathan uprising the following year and wrote with youthful exuberance in a dispatch to the *Daily Telegraph* (later included in *My Early Life*) that he had been sent to 'chastise the truculent assailants. The chastisement was to take the form of marching up the valley ... destroying all the crops, breaking the reservoirs of water, blowing up as many castles as time permitted, and shooting anyone who obstructed the process.'

If it is not too hot, the 15-minute walk up the path to the top is rewarding, both for the view and the sense of history. The army will check your permit before allowing you to climb the hill.

Chakdara Museum is in the village two kilometres (about one mile) from Chakdara Bridge along the road to Dir and Chitral, on the right at the junction. Its small but interesting collection of first to seventh-century AD Buddhist Gandharan sculpture from nearby sites is well-arranged and labelled. It is also of considerable importance, as many of the sculptures were found in their original positions in the Buddhist monasteries, allowing them to be chronologically dated. The museum also displays Hindu Shahi and local 19th- and 20th-century artefacts. The museum is open 8.30 am to 12.30 pm and 2.30 to 5 pm in summer, and 9 am to 4 pm from November through March; it is closed on Wednesdays.

There is a new PTDC restaurant near the museum.

Chakdara to Saidu Sharif

Haibatgram is a village on the main Malakand–Saidu road eight kilometres (five miles) from Chakdara Bridge, and overshadowed by an enormous Hindu Shahi fort of the eighth to the tenth century. Its walls cascade for more than two kilometres (about a mile and a half) to the village below.

Landakai, 12 kilometres (seven miles) from Chakdara Bridge, is the gateway to Swat. A rocky spur juts down from the hilltop to the river, forming a natural defence for the valley. Hindu Shahi forts crown each of the low ridges that run down from Landakai Spur to the eastern bank of the side stream. A barrier across the road marks the gateway to Swat.

Nimogram Buddhist Monastery and Stupa are across a bridge over the Swat River to the left, seven kilometres (four miles) from Landakai. The Nimogram remains are 21 kilometres (13 miles) away on the other side of the river and up a rough road. Nimogram is unique in that it has three main stupas, one for each of the three principles, or jewels, of Buddhism: Buddha the Teacher, *Dharma* (Truth) and *Sangha* (Order). A number of votive stupas surround the main stupas, and nearby is an unexcavated monastery. None of the Gandharan sculpture found here remains on the site.

Birkot Hill is the site of the ancient town of Bazira, which was sacked by Alexander the Great in 327 BC. It is on the left (north) side of the main road, just past the turning to Nimogram and just before the town of Barikot. The archaeological excavations at the base of the hill are clearly visible 100 metres to the left of the road.

It is an easy walk to the top of Birkot Hill from the excavations. There are no remains from Alexander's time on top of the hill, but there are the ruins of the eighth to tenth century Hindu Shahi fort, with one impressive stretch of defensive wall rising to a height of 15 metres (50 feet). This is visible in the distance from the main road beyond Barikot.

The road from the Ambela and Karakar passes joins the main Swat road at Barikot.

Mount Ilam, on the right-hand (south) side of the road (visible before Barikot, or from the other side of the river), is 2,811 metres (9,222 feet) high, making it the highest hill in Lower Swat. According to legend, it has been sacred since prehistoric times, when it was believed to be the seat of tribal deities and ancestors. At the top are big, square blocks of natural stone that may have been used as prehistoric altars. The mountain features prominently in the mythology of many religious groups, including the Buddhists, Lamas, Hindus and Muslims. It was probably the Mount Aornos described by the historians of Alexander the Great. (When Alexander defeated the Swatis, they fled to their mountain stronghold, the Rock of Aornos. Alexander pursued them and won a decisive victory at its summit.) An annual Hindu pilgrimage up the mountain to the 'throne of Ramachandra' was celebrated until Partition in 1947.

Shingerdar Stupa is on the right (south) side of the road, three kilometres (two miles) past Barikot. In the third and fourth centuries AD, the stupa's dome was covered with gold, and its base was plastered and painted, and surrounded with Gandharan carvings illustrating the life of the Buddha.

A large **Buddha** image is carved on the cliff face directly beside the road 1.5 kilometres (one mile) beyond Shingerdar Stupa. This dates from about the sixth century, and its face is very battered.

A flight of cement steps to the left of this image leads up to a natural grotto containing **more carvings**. These are also very battered, but you can just make out a bearded figure standing on a pedestal supported by lions and flanked by smaller figures. The central figure has a halo round his head and wears a long coat over Cossack trousers tucked into top boots. This Central Asian costume, still worn in China's westernmost city of Kashgar, was the same as that worn by the Kushan rulers, as shown by their coins of the first to the third century AD.

The **Gogdara rock engravings** are about six kilometres (four miles) past the carved Buddha image, about 100 metres (yards) to the right of the road just before the village of Udegram. The rock has recently been seriously defaced by local villagers, who have scratched their names all over it, but you can still see some of the engravings of stick figures driving two-wheeled war chariots (like those driven into Swat by the Aryans around 1700 BC), horses, ibex, leopards and oxen. Dating from about 1000 BC, these carvings are among the earliest petroglyphs found in Pakistan.

Buddhist carvings from the sixth or seventh century AD are higher up on the same rock, with more Buddhist carvings on a rock face on the right about 100 metres (110 yards) further along the path. These depict Padmapani, the lotus-bearing bodhisattva, seated with his right leg tucked up and flanked by two attendants.

Udegram is one of the most historically interesting villages in Swat. It was the site of the ancient town of Ora, where Alexander the Great fought one of his battles in 327 BC. It was also the capital of the Hindu Shahi rulers in Swat from the eighth to the tenth century. The massive Hindu ruins of Raja Gira's Castle are scattered up the hillside above the village. The earliest mosque in Swat, built in the 11th century at the time of Mahmud of Ghazni, was excavated in 1985 just below the Hindu Shahi fort.

For those who enjoy walking and exploring, there is plenty to see on the hillside above Udegram. It is worthwhile to go to the top of the hill, which takes about an hour and a half. The best time to go is in winter or, if during the summer, at dawn. It is too hot to climb during the heat of a summer day.

The first excavations, on the left near the modern village, date from the fourth century BC. This was the bazaar area of Ora, and most of the buildings were shops.

The **Shrine of Pir Khushab (or Khushal) Baba** is surrounded by a grove of trees at the foot of the hill. This is the grave of the commander of the army of Mahmud of Ghazni, who subdued Swat in the 11th century and introduced Islam. The commander was killed during the long siege of the fortress of Raja Gira, the last Hindu ruler of Swat. Arrowheads and human bones are scattered all over the hillside below the fortress.

The 11th-century **mosque** is on the centre of the hillside, about halfway between the saint's shrine and the main defensive wall of the fort. It is unlabelled, but ask any small boy for the *purana masjid*, and he will show the way. The south wall of the mosque, protected by the mountain, still stands about seven metres (23 feet) high. The west wall is also in quite good condition, with the arched *mehrab* (prayer niche facing Mecca) in the centre. The bases of the ten pillars that supported the roof over the prayer hall survive, as does the metre-deep (three-foot) ablution pool, which is surrounded by stone seats at the centre of the courtyard.

Massive, eighth to tenth-century AD defensive walls surround **Raja Gira's Castle**, which is entered up a monumental flight of steps eight metres (26 feet) wide. Inside the citadel are the foundations of many rooms separated by corridors. Nothing is labelled.

The walls of the town climb from the citadel for about one kilometre (just over half a mile) up to the crest of the hill, then follow the top of the sharp ridge separating the Swat and Saidu valleys. The view is magnificent in every direction, taking in Mount Ilam, the lower length of Swat Valley to Chakdara and the snow-covered mountains far to the north at its head. From the top of the hill the wall runs along a precipitous, rocky spur down the eastern side of the ruined town to a spring at the head of the gully. This spring was the town's sole water supply and was heavily defended. The water was brought from the well along a series of channels to holding tanks at the foot of the giant stairway. Italian excavators working the site lined one of these tanks with cement and filled it, using the existing system.

To Saidu Sharif via Ambela and Karakar Passes

This route to Swat is quieter and more scenic than the Malakand Pass. The roads are metalled the entire distance (see map page 183).

From Islamabad, go to Shahbaz Garhi either via Attock and Swabi or via Tarbela (only if you have a permit to cross the dam) and Swabi. There is a shorter road now open from Swabi north to Chinglai which joins the Rustam road near the Ambela Pass. From Peshawar, go to Shahbaz Garhi via Charsadda and Mardan, or via Nowshera and Mardan, this last route being the fastest but least interesting. At Shahbaz Garhi, turn north to Rustam, thence east across the Ambela Pass to Buner. See page 197 for the Ashokan Inscriptions at Shahbaz Garhi.

From **Ambela Pass** you can look across the Peshawar Valley. This was the scene of the Ambela Campaign in 1863, when British troops spent two foggy winter months trying to subdue 15,000 Mujahideen freedom fighters (or 'Hindustani fanatics', as the British called them) who had been raiding the Peshawar Valley from their hideout at Malka, in Buner. The ruins of several British forts still dot the pass.

The main road climbs up across the 894-metre (2,935-foot) **Buner Pass** and comes down to **China** (pronounced *cheena*). After four kilometres (2.5 miles) you come to **Daggar**, from where a newly repaired road leads left (west) to Jowar. If you have time, though, an interesting detour is north via Pacha to **Pir Baba**, the Shrine of Syed Ali, reputedly the grandson of the Mughal emperor Babur.

Pir Baba is one of Pakistan's most popular shrines, to which devotees flock by the thousand, particularly at the death festival of the saint. The path to the shrine is lined on one side with beggars and on the other with pretty boys and transvestites selling traditional cosmetics: kohl for the eyes and perfume. Behind the shrine is a separate mosque for women, and behind this the *baithak*, a place of meditation for fakirs and Sufi holy men.

The 45-kilometre (28-mile) road from Pir Baba to Barikot passes the sacred Mount Ilam (see page 207) on the right before rising through mature pine forests to the 1,336-metre (4,384-foot) **Karakar Pass**. Here, in 1586, the Mughal emperor Akbar lost most of his 8,000-man army in a vain attempt to invade Swat. From the top of the pass down to Barikot is a well-engineered road through pine forests.

For a description of the road from Barikot to Saidu Sharif, see page 207.

Saidu Sharif and Mingora

Saidu Sharif and Mingora are twin towns two kilometres (about one mile) apart. Saidu Sharif is the administrative capital of Swat Division, while Mingora is the district headquarters and main bazaar area. Both are 990 metres (3,250 feet) above sea level.

The **Tourist Information Centre** is in the new PTDC motel, tel 711205, near the Serena Hotel. Helpful Mr Fazal Rahim gives information on hotels of all grades, and has good ideas on how to organise your sight-seeing. Open in summer 9 am to 1 pm and 2 to 4.30 pm.

I can recommend Altaf Hussain of Falakser **rent-a-car** service at the Serena Hotel as a reliable driver–guide.

Mingora has been an important trading centre for at least 2,000 years. Its bazaars are interesting to explore for semi-precious stones, locally woven and embroidered cloth, and tribal jewellery. Saidu Sharif has, in addition to government buildings, the Swat Museum, the Tomb of the Akhund of Swat and the archaeological remains of the Butkara and Saidu Buddhist Stupas.

Places of interest nearby include, in addition to the places described below, Raja Gira's Castle (a distance of six kilometres (four miles), see page 209); Birkot Hill (16 kilometres (ten miles), see page 207); Chakdara (36 kilometres (22 miles), see page 205), and the Karakar Pass, briefly described on page 211. There is a golf course near the airport.

Swat Museum is on the east side of the street, halfway between Mingora and Saidu. Japanese aid has given a facelift to its seven galleries which now contain an excellent collection of Gandharan sculptures taken from some of the Buddhist sites in Swat, rearranged and labelled to illustrate the Buddha's life story. Terracotta figurines and utensils, beads, precious stones, coins, weapons and various metal objects illustrate daily life in Gandhara. The ethnographic section displays the finest examples of local embroidery, carved wood and tribal jewellery. A lecture and video hall complete the museum's facilities. You can buy books by the curator, Dr Ashraf Khan, illustrating the collection and describing the Buddhist sites in Swat. Hours are 9 am to 1 pm and 2 to 4 pm, October through March; 8.30 am to 12.30 pm and 2.30 to 5.30 pm, April through September, closed Wednesdays.

Butkara (Butkada) Stupa, one of the most important Buddhist shrines in Swat, is near the museum. Take the dirt track on the left (north) side of the museum for one kilometre (about half a mile). The stupa is 400 metres (about a quarter of a mile) across the fields to the left (north).

The stupa, which dates from the second century BC, was possibly built by the Mauryan emperor Ashoka to house some of the ashes of the Buddha. In subsequent centuries, it was enlarged five times by encasing the existing structure in a new shell. Italian excavators working in 1955 exposed the successive layers of the stupa, each layer illustrating a stage in the evolution of building techniques.

The stupa was enlarged three times before the birth of Christ. At the beginning of the third century AD, the peaceful rule of the Kushans brought unprecedented prosperity, and Buddhism in Swat approached its zenith. Butkara was a bustling shrine and centre for pilgrimage. The stupa was enlarged again and richly decorated with stone and plaster carvings of the life of the Buddha, and the whole was gilded and painted and capped by a stack of stone umbrellas

Most of the carvings have been removed, but two of green schist (a crystalline rock) dating from the fifth century have been left in place on the great stupa. One is a headless figure of the Buddha low down on the east side, and the other is a figure of the Buddha standing on a lotus flower between three rows of acolytes on the north side. A few other small fragments of statues still stand around the base of the stupa (see picture page 191).

Votive stupas were built around the main stupa by wealthy pilgrims hoping to gain merit. There were 215 of these, all decorated with statues, painted, gilded and crowned with stone umbrellas. Only the bases remain. The best-preserved ones are on the north side of the main stupa. You can still see some of the decoration: green schist columns, lions with full curly manes, eagles, stylised lilies, cupids on lotus flowers and a few traces of red and blue paint. Scattered all around the site and looking like millstones are circular stone umbrellas that have fallen from the various stupas. Some pilgrims preferred to erect columns surmounted by statuary, and the stone lions (some of limestone) crouching on their haunches east of the main stupa probably came from the tops of such columns.

The Jambil and Saidu rivers run on either side of Butkara and have often flooded the site, which is also frequently jolted by earthquakes since it sits on the fault line between the Indian and Asian geological plates. During times of plenty, the faithful repaired the damage, but in the seventh century devastating floods swept through the area, and the monastery was abandoned for a time. In the following century coarse repairs were made, but by this time the Hindu Shahi kings ruled the area and Buddhism had evolved into its tantric form. Butkara was soon abandoned.

Saidu Stupa and Monastery, above the road behind the Central Hospital and Serena Hotel, is an impressive first to fifth century site excavated in the late 1970s by the Italians. The stupa stands on a square base with steps up the north side. The large monastery, on a higher level to the east, contains monk's cells set around a central courtyard. A spacious assembly hall whose roof was originally supported on two wooden pillars is on the south-west corner. The many stone sculptures, coins and pottery found here are on display in the Swat Museum.

Marghazar is a small village at the top of the Saidu Valley, 1,287 metres (4,220 feet) above sea level and 13 kilometres (eight miles) from Saidu Sharif. Here the Saidu stream cascades down off Mount Ilam. The Marghazar Hotel was once the summer palace of the first Wali of Swat. Beside the stream behind the palace runs the old Hindu pilgrim path up Mount Ilam, a superb all-day hike to the top and back.

Islampur is a village two kilometres (about a mile) off the main Saidu–Marghazar road, where visitors can see handloom weaving and buy hand-woven shawls and blankets.

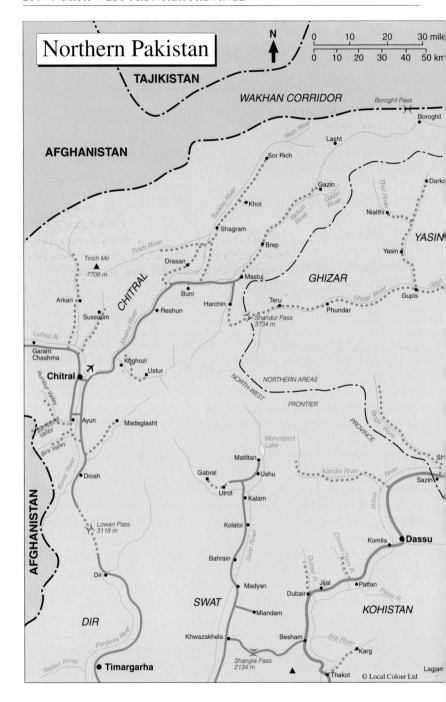

Northern Pakistan

N

0	10	20	30	mile
0	10	20	30	40	50 km

TAJIKISTAN

WAKHAN CORRIDOR

Boroghil Pass

Boroghil

AFGHANISTAN

Rich River

Lasht

Sor Rich

Tirikho River

Gazin

Darko

Khot

Gazin River

Thui River

Nialthi

Shagram

Yarkun River

YASIN

Brep

Yasin

Tirich River

Drasan

Tirich Mir
7708 m

Mastuj

GHIZAR

Buni

CHITRAL

Teru

Ghizar River

Gilgit

Arkari

Harchin

Phundar

Gupis

Reshun

Sussoom

Mastuj River

Shandur Pass
3734 m

Luthko R.

Garam
Chashma

Koghozi

Ustur

NORTH-WEST

NORTHERN AREAS

Rumbur Valley

Chitral

FRONTIER

Bumburet
Valley

Ayun

Madaglasht

PROVINCE

Tangir River

Birir Valley

Mahodand
Lake

Matiltan

Kunar River

Gabral

Ushu

Kandia River

River

Sh

Drosh

Utrot

Kalam

Sazin

Kolaloi

Swat River

Komila

Dassu

Lowari Pass
3118 m

Bahrain

Chowa Dara R.

Dubair R.

Jijal

Pattan

Palas R.

Lagjan

Dir

Madyan

Dubair

AFGHANISTAN

Miandam

KOHISTAN

SWAT

Khwazakhela

Besham

Alai River

Karg

DIR

Panjkora River

Shangla Pass
2134 m

Thakot

Bajaur River

Timargarha

© Local Colour Ltd

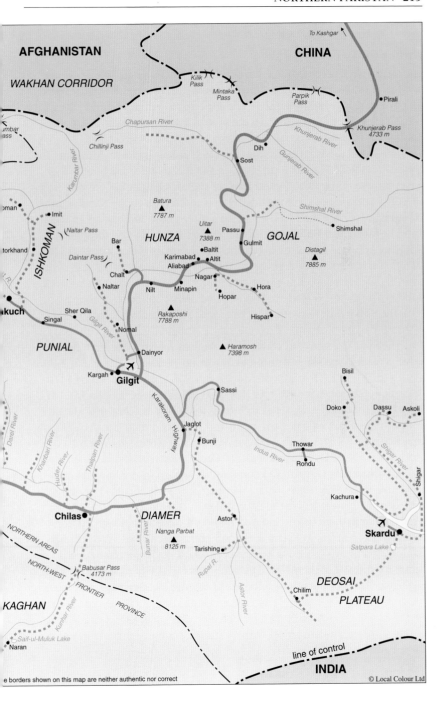

AFGHANISTAN

WAKHAN CORRIDOR

CHINA

To Kashgar

Kilik Pass

Mintaka Pass

Parpik Pass

• Pirali

Chapursan River

umbar ass

Chillinji Pass

Karambar River

Dih

Sost

Khunjerab River

Gunjerab River

Khunjerab Pass 4733 m

Batura 7787 m

Uitar 7388 m

Passu

Gulmit

GOJAL

Shimshal River

Distagil 7885 m

• Shimshal

oman

• Imit

Naltar Pass

Bar

HUNZA

Baltit

Altit

torkhand

Daintar Pass

Karimabad

Aliabad

Chalt

Nagar

Hora

ISHKOMAN

Naltar

Nilt

Minapin

Hopar

Hispar

kuch

Sher Qila

Singal

Nomal

Rakaposhi 7788 m

Gilgit River

PUNIAL

Dainyor

Haramosh 7398 m

Bisil

Kargah

Gilgit

Sassi

Doko

Dassu

Askoli

Karakoram Highway

Jaglot

Darel River

Khanbari River

Bunji

Thowar

Rondu

Shigar River

Thalpan River

Indus River

Kachura

Shigar

Chilas

DIAMER

Astor

Nanga Parbat 8125 m

Tarishing

Skardu

Satpara Lake

Huder River

Bunar River

NORTHERN AREAS

NORTH-WEST

Babusar Pass 4173 m

Rupal R.

Astor River

DEOSAI PLATEAU

KAGHAN

FRONTIER

PROVINCE

Kunhar River

Saif-ul-Muluk Lake

Naran

Chilim

line of control

INDIA

e borders shown on this map are neither authentic nor correct

© Local Colour Ltd

Upper Swat Valley

The Swat Valley becomes more beautiful the higher you go. In mid-winter it is sometimes blocked by snow above Bahrain, but in summer you can drive up beyond Kalam and from there trek north to either the Chitral Valley or the Gilgit Valley. From Khwazakhela, the road across the Shangla Pass to the Karakoram Highway is usually open only from April to December.

Minibuses to Kalam leave from the General Bus Station in Mingora. The fare is about Rs25 and the journey takes about two and a half hours. The buses from the New Road Bus Station are slightly cheaper but are very slow and dirty and are not recommended. Buses to Besham on the Karakoram Highway leave every half hour or so, take three hours and cost about Rs25.

The **Jahanabad Buddha** is three kilometres (two miles) off the main road, along the side road to Malam Jabba. The Buddha image is four metres (13 feet) tall and carved on a rock high on the mountainside on the other side of the river. It dates from about the seventh century AD and shows a serene-faced Buddha sitting cross-legged, his hands folded on his lap. To reach the carving, cross the river by the next bridge in Jahanabad village and walk back for about 20 minutes. Other carvings decorate a rock straight up from the bridge.

The metalled side road continues to **Malam Jabba**, a one-hour scenic drive. Malam Jabba **ski and summer resort** opened in 1998 at about 2,800 metres (8,700 feet). The 50 room hotel, tel (0936) 755588 is run by PTDC, or book in Islamabad at (051) 920 8948-9, 111 555 888, fax (92-51) 9218233. The resort boasts a chairlift offering stunning views over the Swat Valley to the distant Karakoram mountains. In winter there are two short ski runs and an ice-scating rink. You can rent ski and skating equipment. A recently excavated Buddhist monastery is a 15 minute walk from the hotel.

Khwazakhela is about 30 kilometres (19 miles) from Mingora on the east bank of the Swat River, where the road across the Shangla Pass to the Karakoram Highway leaves the Swat Valley. It is 69 kilometres (43 miles) from here to Besham on the Indus (a two-hour drive in a private car), and 70 kilometres (44 miles) to Kalam at the top of the Swat Valley. Well placed at the junction of two trade routes, Khwazakhela is the largest commercial centre in this part of the valley. The main street is worth exploring for silver tribal jewellery, locally woven and embroidered fabrics, carved wood, semi-precious stones and 'ancient' coins. The manufacture of fake ancient coins is a thriving business in Swat, so very few, if any, of the coins for sale are as old as they appear. Similarly, most of the 'antique' wood-carvings are newly carved and blackened.

The richly carved **Mata Mosque** is across the bridge, a fifteen-minute drive away on the other side of the Swat River. The ornate scroll capitals to its pillars are similar to those in Kalam.

Miandam is a small summer resort at 1,800 metres (6,000 feet), ten kilometres (six miles) up a steep side valley and 56 kilometres (35 miles) from Saidu Sharif, making it an hour's drive. The metalled road passes small villages stacked up the hillside, the roofs of one row of houses forming the street for the row of houses above. Tiny terraced fields march up the hillside right to the top.

Miandam is a good place for walkers. Paths follow the stream, past houses with beehives set into the walls and good-luck charms whitewashed around the doors. In the graveyards are carved wooden grave posts with floral designs, like those used by Buddhists 1,000 years ago.

Madyan is a tourist resort at on the Swat River. At 1,321 metres (4,335 feet) above sea level, it is neither as cool nor as beautiful as Miandam, but it is a larger town and has many hotels in all price ranges and some good tourist shopping. Antique and modern shawls, traditional embroidery, tribal jewellery, carved wood and antique or reproduced coins are sold along the main street. This is the last Swati village, offering interesting two- and three-day walks up to the mountain villages — ask in the bazaar in Muambar Khan's shop for a guide. North of Madyan is Swat Kohistan where walking is not recommended without an armed guard.

The central mosque at Madyan has carved wooden pillars with elegant scroll capitals, and its mud-plastered west wall is covered with relief designs in floral motifs. Both bespeak the Swati's love of decoration.

Bahrain is ten kilometres north of Madyan and only slightly higher, at about 1,400 metres (4,500 feet). It is another popular riverside tourist resort, with bazaars worth exploring for their handicrafts. Some of the houses have carved wooden doors, pillars and balconies. These show a remarkable variety of decorative motifs, including floral scrolls and bands of ornamental diaper patterns almost identical to those seen on Buddhist shrines and quite different from the usual Muslim designs.

At **Kalam**, 29 kilometres (18 miles) from Bahrain and about 2,000 metres (6,800 feet) above sea level, the valley opens out, providing room for a small but fertile plateau above the river. On this plateau are administrative offices, the police station, the PTDC motel and information office, the old Falaksir and many new hotels. Down by the river are about 30 more hotels (some of which are cheaper) see Swat Hotels page 299. Across the river in the old village the **mosque** features some excellent wood-carving. Gigantic scrolls form the capitals of the pillars, and some of the beams are ten metres (over 30 feet) long. Kalam is cool in summer and is packed with Punjabis escaping the heat of the plains.

Beyond Kalam the road divides. Dirt roads follow the Ushu and Utrot rivers, both passable in ordinary cars in summer. The modern **Muslim graves** in this area are surrounded by intricately carved wooden railings. There are rest-houses at **Utrot, Gabral, Ushu** and **Matiltan**. From Matiltan, the road is jeepable almost to **Mahodand Lake**, the 'Lake of Fishes'. It is not safe to camp in the grassy fields by the lake; though the walking and fishing are excellent, it is not safe to wander here without an armed guard. A fishing permit is required. Bring your own tackle.

Chitral Valley

Chitral is an isolated valley about 300 kilometres (190 miles) long in the northwestern corner of Pakistan (see maps page 183 and 214). It is dominated by Tirich Mir, the highest mountain in the Hindu Kush, which separates Chitral from the narrow Wakhan Corridor in Afghanistan and Tajikistan beyond.

The tourist season is April to November. At some 1,500 metres (5,000 feet) above sea level, Chitral town is snowbound in winter, but not too hot in summer.

Getting to Chitral

The easiest way to reach Chitral is by air from Peshawar. There are three flights most days, provided the weather is clear, which it often isn't. Book several days in advance and be prepared for cancellation (see page 28 on how to confirm your booking). The flight takes 55 minutes and costs Rs475 one way if booked in Pakistan or US$40 if booked overseas (plus Rs30 airport tax). The view is spectacular.

The drive to Chitral town from Peshawar or Islamabad over the 3,118-metre (10,230-foot) **Lowari Pass** takes 10 to 12 hours. The road is blocked by snow from November to May. Driving from Chitral town to Gilgit over the 3,734-metre (12,250-foot) **Shandur Pass** takes two days — if the jeep road is open. The only motorable route from Upper Swat to Chitral is back via Mingora, Chakdara, Timargarha, Dir and the Lowari Pass. Frequent buses run from Mingora to Timargarha where you must change for Dir.

All visitors to Chitral must **register with the police** on arrival. You can do this from 8 am to 2 pm in summer, 8.30 am to 2.30 pm in winter, closed at noon on Friday and Saturday and all day on Sunday. To visit the Kalash valleys you buy your permit for about Rs50 at the entrance to the valley. To see the Kalash women dance you pay the headman of the village concerned. Ask at PTDC for the latest rules on permits and fees.

Sights

The main attractions of Chitral town are the bazaar, the fort and the mosque by the river. The summer palace of the ex-ruler of Chitral is on the hilltop above the town.

The **Kalash people** are the tourist attraction for which Chitral is most famous. This non-Muslim and culturally distinct tribe live in three valleys close to the Afghan border, about an hour's drive from Chitral town. They are the last unconverted survivors of the Kafir ('heathen') tribes that so fascinated the first European visitors to what was then called Kafiristan. Kalash women are of particular interest, as they are not in purdah, but wear instead extraordinary head-dresses decorated with cowrie shells and buttons and,

Young girls in Hunza

around their necks, countless strings of red beads set off by their black robes. (*Kalash* means black. The other Kafir tribes that used to live in Afghanistan wore red robes and were called Red Kafirs.)

About 3,000 Kalash live in about 20 villages in the three valleys of **Birir**, **Bumburet** and **Rambur**. They make offerings to several gods, each of which protects a different aspect of life and livelihood: animals, crops, fruits, family and so on. They build their houses of stone and timber, and fill in all the cracks with mud and pebbles. In summer, the women sit on a wide verandah on the second storey to cook, spin and weave. In winter, they cook inside, the smoke escaping through the central hole in the cantilevered wooden ceiling. The wooden temples of the Kalash are often elaborately carved, especially around the doors, pillars and ceilings. Some of the holy places are closed to women, both Kalash and foreign. The dead are left in wooden coffins above ground in Kalash graveyards, where the lids often fall off, exposing skeletons to view.

The Kalash love music and dancing, and perform different dances for their various festivals, which are celebrated in May, August, November and December.

Garam Chashma (Hot Springs) is a town 45 kilometres (28 miles) from Chitral town along a spectacular drive up the Lutkho River through a deep and narrow gorge. The sulphurous hot springs are believed to cure skin diseases, gout, rheumatism and headaches.

Upper Chitral Valley

The main jeep track up the Chitral Valley follows the Mastuj River for 107 kilometres (66 miles) to **Mastuj** and, from there, jogs south to cross the **Shandur Pass** into the Gilgit Valley. Tourists need a permit from the Deputy Commissioner if they wish to deviate from the main road.

For more information on Chitral see *Pakistan Handbook* by Isobel Shaw and *Pakistan Trekking Guide* by Isobel Shaw and Ben Shaw.

Kaghan Valley

The Kaghan Valley was the old summer route to the Northern Areas before the advent of the all-weather Karakoram Highway (see maps page 183 and 214). It is over 160 kilometres (100 miles) long and climbs from about 900 metres (3,000 feet) at its mouth to 4,173 metres (13,690 feet) at the **Babusar Pass**. A jeep road over the pass (open July to September) connects with the

Karakoram Highway at Chilas. The narrow, green Kaghan Valley is terraced from river to hilltop and clothed in forests of huge Himalayan pines. Just on the edge of the monsoon belt, it is wet enough for cultivation without irrigation. There is no Kaghan River, the Kunhar River (not to be confused with the Kunar River in Chitral) flows the full length of the valley to join the Jhelum at Muzaffarabad. The name Kaghan comes from an unimportant village halfway down the valley.

Getting to Kaghan

Balakot, the gateway to the Kaghan Valley, is about a four-hour drive, without stops, from Rawalpindi–Islamabad (though in NWFP, Kaghan is closer to Islamabad than to Peshawar). Buses, minibuses and wagons leave Rawalpindi continuously for Mansehra on the Karakoram Highway and take about three hours. Change at Mansehra for Balakot and Naran. There is also a more scenic route via Murree and Muzaffarabad, though this takes longer and is more difficult on public transport.

    Naran, the main tourist centre in the valley, is 82 kilometres (51 miles) from Balakot. At 2,427 metres (7,963 feet) above sea level and furnished with a PTDC motel and many local hotels, this is the most popular place to stay. Being a green valley, like Murree and Swat, it is extremely crowded with Punjabis from June through early September. The best time to go is April through June and September–October, though the Babusar Pass is closed by snow some of this time.

    Fishing and walking are the main attractions, in addition to scenic side trips to **Shogran** and **Saif-ul-Muluk Lake**. Walking, trekking and camping is safe in Kaghan, and being wet and green it is much cooler here in summer than further north in the dry Northern Areas, or upper Chitral. For those interested in flora and fauna, this is a better choice than further north, though there are no glaciers or high snow-capped mountains in the valley. It is unbelievably crowded in summer, though relatively easy to escape the masses if you go camping.

    From Naran to the top of Babusar Pass is 66 kilometres (41 miles), a jeep drive of about five hours. The 37 kilometres (23 miles) from the top of the pass down to Chilas zigzags across difficult scree at first, then follows a green and fertile valley down to the dry, barren Indus, deprived by the mountains of the monsoon rains.

    For more information on Kaghan see *Pakistan Handbook* by Isobel Shaw and *Pakistan Trekking Guide* by Isobel Shaw and Ben Shaw.

(following spread) Baltis pole a raft made of inflated skins across the Shyok River

The Karakoram Highway

The Karakoram Highway, or KKH, is the greatest wonder of modern Pakistan and one of the most spectacular roads in the world (see maps page 183 and 214). Connecting Pakistan to China, it twists through three great mountain ranges — the Himalaya, Karakoram and Pamir — following one of the ancient silk routes along the valleys of the Indus, Gilgit and Hunza rivers to the Chinese border at the Khunjerab Pass. It then crosses the high Central Asian plateau before winding down through the Pamirs to Kashgar, at the western edge of the Taklamakan Desert. By this route, Chinese silks, ceramics, lacquer-work, bronze, iron, furs and spices travelled West, while the wool, linen, ivory, gold, silver, precious and semi-precious stones, asbestos and glass of South Asia and the West travelled East.

For much of its 1,284 kilometres (799 miles), the Karakoram Highway is overshadowed by towering, barren mountains, a high altitude desert enjoying less than 100 millimetres (four inches) of rain a year. In many of the gorges through which it passes, it rides a shelf cut into a sheer cliff face as high as 500 metres (1,600 feet) above the river. The KKH has opened up remote villages where little has changed in hundreds of years, where farmers irrigate tiny terraces to grow small patches of wheat, barley or maize that stand out like emeralds against the grey, stony mountains. The highway is an incredible feat of engineering and an enduring monument to the 810 Pakistanis and 82 Chinese who died forcing it through what is probably the world's most difficult and unstable terrain. (The unofficial death toll is somewhat higher, coming to nearly one life for each kilometre of road.)

The **Karakoram** and the **Himalaya,** the newest mountain ranges in the world, began to form some 55 million years ago when the Indian subcontinent drifted northwards and rammed into the Asian land mass. By this time the dinosaurs were already extinct. India is still trundling northwards at the geologically reckless rate of five centimetres (two inches) a year, and the mountains are still growing by about seven millimetres (1/4 of an inch) annually. The KKH runs through the middle of this collision belt, where there is an earth tremor, on average, every three minutes. *Karakoram* is Turkish for 'crumbling rock', an apt description for the giant, grey, snow-capped slag heaps that tower above the gorges cut between them.

The **Indus River** flows northwest, dividing the Himalaya from the Karakoram, before being knocked south by the Hindu Kush. The KKH hugs the banks of the Indus for 310 kilometres of its climb north, winding around the foot of Nanga Parbat, the ninth highest mountain in the world and the western anchor of the Himalaya. The highway then leaves the Indus for the Gilgit, Hunza and Khunjerab rivers to take on the Karakoram Range, which boasts 12 of the 30 highest mountains in the world. By the time the road reaches the 4,733-metre (15,528-foot) Khunjerab Pass, it has earned the name of the highest metalled border crossing in the world.

From Islamabad to Kashgar is a four-day journey (about 30 hours non-stop driving time), provided that there are no rockfalls. A second option is to fly the 603 kilometres (375 miles) to Gilgit, from which the remaining 681 kilometres (423 miles) to Kashgar can be covered in two or three days. The Khunjerab Pass is open to tourists from 1 May to 30 November (weather permitting), though the Chinese authorities usually stop allowing access from their side two or three weeks earlier.

The flight from Islamabad to Gilgit must be one of the most exciting in the world. The PIA pilot of the small Fokker Friendship plane flies by sight up the Kaghan Valley and over the Babusar Pass, then skirts round the shoulder of 8,125-metre (26,660-foot) Nanga Parbat for a peek at the 'sleeping beauty', who is fancied to be lying on her back across the top. The mountain is so massive that the plane takes fully ten minutes to fly past it. The pilot invites passengers into the cockpit to see Pakistan's 121 peaks over 7,000 metres (23,000 feet) which stretch, range after range, as far as the eye can see. The sharp triangle of K–2, the second highest mountain in world, is clearly visible on the horizon. As the flight can operate only in clear weather, it is often cancelled.

Distances

Islamabad	— Abbottabad	121 km	(75 mls)	2	hours
Abbottabad	— Besham	151 km	(94 mls)	4	hours
Besham	— Komila/Dassu	74 km	(46 mls)	2	hours
Komila/Dassu	— Chilas	129 km	(80 mls)	3	hours
Chilas	— Gilgit	128 km	(79 mls)	3	hours
Gilgit	— Aliabad/ Karimabad	105 km	(65 mls)	2	hours
Aliabad/ Karimabad	— Passu	56 km	(40 mls)	1	hour
Passu	— Sost	35 km	(22 mls)	40	minutes
Sost	— Khunjerab	62 km	(39 mls)	2.5	hours
Khunjerab	— Pirali	32 km	(20 mls)	40	minutes
Pirali	— Tashkurgan	96 km	(60 mls)	2	hours
Tashkurgan	— Kashgar	295 km	(183 mls)	7	hours

Suggested Intineraries
Four days

Day 1	Drive from Islamabad to Chilas, eleven hours without stops
Day 2	Chilas to Karimabad, five hours (plus lunch stop in Gilgit)
Day 3	Karimabad to Tashkurgan, seven hours
Day 4	Tashkurgan to Kashgar, seven hours

Five Days

Day 1	Drive from Islamabad to Saidu Sharif in Swat via Buner
Day 2	Saidu Sharif to Chilas via the Shangla Pass
Days 3–5	As above

Six Days

Day 1	Drive from Islamabad to Nathiagali
Day 2	Nathiagali to Besham
Day 3	Besham to Gilgit
Day 4	Gilgit to Karimabad, Passu or Sost
Days 5–6	To Tashkurgan and Kashgar

All of the above itineraries involve long days of driving. The most beautiful area is between Gilgit and Sost. It is a good idea to break your journey at least at Karimabad. Do not be tempted to rush through Northern Pakistan in your haste to reach China. The scenery is more beautiful along the Pakistani portion of the highway, and the tourist facilities are better developed.

When to Go

The Khunjerab Pass is closed at least from 1 December to 30 April. Gilgit and Hunza are most beautiful in April, when the fruit trees bloom, and October, when the autumn colours reach their brightest. July is very hot in Gilgit and along the Indus Valley.

Islamabad to Gilgit

The first day's journey up the KKH passes through Hazara, a long, narrow district between the Indus and Jhelum rivers, with its capital at Abbottabad.

Abbottabad, at 1,220 metres (4,000 feet) is named after James Abbott, a British administrator who served in Hazara in the 1840s and '50s. It is a military town, full of soldiers exercising, parading, playing polo and practising the bagpipes. The cantonment area, a reminder of the British era, is full of spacious bungalows surrounded by gardens and pine trees, in addition to a church and a club at the top of the hill.

Mansehra, 24 kilometres (15 miles) from Abbottabad was an important junction of ancient trade routes. The roads from Kashmir (now closed) and Kaghan meet the KKH here, and there is a set of **Ashokan edicts,** like those at Shahbaz Garhi, outlining the Mauryan emperor's state policy and providing his subjects with moral instruction (see page 197).

The Karakoram Highway climbs through pine forest to a pass at 1,750 metres (which is higher than Gilgit), before dropping down to join the Indus River about 100 kilometres (60 miles) from Mansehra. The Chinese-built bridge across the Indus is decorated with moulded lions, lanterns, butterflies and flowers.

Besham, (pronounced bèh-SHAAM) a small bazaar on the west bank of the Indus 28 kilometres (17 miles) beyond the bridge, is halfway between Islamabad and Gilgit, and a good place for an overnight stop. The road from Swat joins the KKH here, and Besham can be very crowded in summer, so book in advance if you want to stay in the PTDC motel. (see page 303).

From Besham, the KKH follows the Indus River round the base of Nanga Parbat and through one of the wildest and most inhospitable areas of Pakistan. The men here are armed and sullen, the women never seen — it is not wise to wander off the KKH or cycle alone along this stretch of road.

This is the area where the Indian geological plate noses under the Asian plate, pushing up the mountains at an annual rate of seven millimetres (a quarter of an inch). The heaving and settling of the mountains makes this the most geologically unstable part of Pakistan. Rockslides frequently block the road, but the army usually has them cleared within a few hours. This area is particularly interesting to geologists, for crushed and tilted northwards between the two large continental plates is a small island plate. The Hunza, Gilgit and Indus rivers cut a section through this plate, from its lower face near Pattan to its upper face at Chalt, near Hunza. The KKH provides convenient access.

Chilas, (pronounced chè-LAAS), another recommended overnight stop, is a small bazaar town that was once an important junction on the ancient trade route. The jeep track over the Babusar Pass from the Kaghan Valley joins the KKH here. The town itself is three kilometres (two miles) south of the KKH, out of sight of the road, but the Shangrila and other hotels, police (frontier constabulary) post and petrol pump are right on the highway. The sun radiates off the barren mountains and makes it extremely hot here in summer.

Petroglyphs, rock carvings and inscriptions cover hundreds of rocks along the banks of the Indus at Chilas. They date from the first century BC to modern times and were carved by invaders, traders, pilgrims and local

inhabitants. The earliest drawings show warriors on horseback and lifelike leopards and antelopes. Later, Buddhist pilgrims and missionaries travelling to and from China carved thousands of Buddha images and stupas as prayers for safe journeys. They wrote inscriptions in various languages, often giving the date, their destination and the purpose of their journey. The inscriptions and drawings of different periods are all jumbled together, often with inscriptions in four different languages and written centuries apart sharing a single rock.

The two most interesting groups of drawings are down a jeep track before the Shangrila Hotel on the south (left) bank and down another jeep track leading to the bridge to Thalpan a little after the petrol station. The best carvings face the river, and there are some particularly good ones on the north bank, across the Thalpan bridge, both up and down river for about a kilometre. From the first century BC, a warrior with a huge knife slaughters a goat that he holds up by the back leg, and a snow leopard attacks an ibex. On some rocks, whole scenes are portrayed: drinking parties, a ruler with captives, a horse festival (or polo game), a ploughman and a royal couple. Buddha images and stupas are numerous and of various types.

East of Chilas, the Indus and the KKH pass through a desert at about 1,200 metres (4,000 feet). North of the river, barren mountains rise as high as 5,000 metres (16,000 feet) and, south of the river, Nanga Parbat looms a dizzying 3,000 metres (10,000 feet) higher than that, thus towering an awesome 7,000 metres (23,000 feet) above the river. Within the gorge, the scenery looks just like Tibet. High mud cliffs studded with round boulders, glacial remains and flood debris flank the road, while huge sand-dunes, untouched by monsoon rains, roll down to the river. Summer is cruelly hot, and biting winds howl through the gorge in winter.

The best views of Nanga Parbat are looking back from about ten kilometres beyond the bridge that crosses the Indus at Raikot. The mountain's massive bulk rises serene and white in the distance. Ahead is a clear view of the triangular points of Rakaposhi and Domani. To the east, on the other side of the river, towers the snow-covered Haramosh Range. Just a bit upriver is the confluence of the Indus and Gilgit rivers. The KKH leaves the Indus and follows the Gilgit — and then the Hunza — towards China.

A metalled road follows the Indus River southeast through narrow gorges to **Skardu**, the capital of Baltistan, sometimes called Little Tibet. Also accessible by air, Skardu is the starting point for some of the world's best mountaineering. Nowhere else is there such a concentration of high

(previous page) Askandria Fort holds a commanding position above the Indus River in Skardu

mountains, about 100 of which are over 7,000 metres (23,000 feet), culminating in the 8,611-metre (28,250-foot) K–2.

See *Pakistan Trekking Guide* by Isobel Shaw and Ben Shaw for a complete description of Skardu and Baltistan.

Gilgit

Gilgit, the capital of Pakistan's Northern Areas, is a thriving frontier town that has expanded rapidly since the Karakoram Highway opened in 1978. It sits in a wide, irrigated bowl 1,500 metres (5,000 feet) above sea level, surrounded by barren mountains. The Northern Areas enjoy very little rainfall, so all agricultural land must be irrigated by water from the melting snows of higher altitudes. The tiny, terraced fields and fruit groves stack one upon the other up the lower slopes of the mountains around Gilgit, their greenery contrasting vividly with the surrounding desert.

Getting to Gilgit

Three flights are scheduled most days from Islamabad to Gilgit, taking 70 minutes. The best views are on the right going north and the left going south (see page 225). The plane flies only in clear weather, and cancellations can lead to a backlog. Confirm your return flight on arrival (see page 28 for how to confirm your bookings). Northern Areas Transport Company (NATCO) buses and various private buses, minibuses and wagons ply the road daily between Rawalpindi and Gilgit, taking 15 to 20 hours.

NATCO and PTDC run public buses and minibuses further up the KKH to the Chinese border. Other companies run wagons and jeeps all over the region, and Suzuki vans go wherever the road is suitable.

Public jeeps up the Gilgit Valley leave morning and afternoon from the Punial Road bus-stop beyond the Aga Khan Polo Ground. They tend to be very crowded. NATCO buses, wagons and jeeps leave from NATCO in the main bazaar. Check for their schedule. The Sargin wagon services up the Hunza Valley leave from near the Nasim Cinema. NATCO, PTDC, Walji/Avis, Mountain Movers and many others have private jeeps for hire.

History

Gilgit has been inhabited for thousands of years. The various waves of invaders that passed through lower Pakistan also reached Gilgit, bringing their customs and religions with them. The animism of the early inhabitants gave way to fire worship brought in from Iran, which was replaced in turn by Hinduism following the Aryan invasion. From the first century BC, Gilgit, like Kashgar, was an important staging post on the Silk Route from China, and the Chinese wielded considerable influence in the area.

Inscriptions and pictures carved on rocks throughout the region give snatches of its history, as does the collection of the 6th to 11th century Buddhist manuscripts discovered in Kargah, ten kilometres west of Gilgit, in 1931.

From the 4th to the 11th century AD, Gilgit was mostly Buddhist. According to the Chinese Tang Annals, Gilgit and Yasin together were called Little Bolor (Xiao Po-lu), with its capital in Yasin. (Baltistan was known as Great Bolor.)

Early in the eighth century, three great powers — China, Arabia and Tibet — jostled for control. A rock in Dainyor lists the Tibetan kings who ruled in the seventh and eighth centuries. In 725, according to the Dainyor rock, the kingdoms of Great and Little Bolor merged into one under Tibetan suzerainty. There was a Chinese interlude (747–51) when 10,000 Chinese troops invaded across the Boroghil and Darkot passes and took Yasin before being driven back by the Arabs from the West.

Less than a hundred years after the Prophet Muhammad's death in 632, Arab Muslim forces invaded Pakistan from the south by sea, simultaneously reaching Xinjiang in the north by land. Muhammad bin Qasim was successful in the south, but the northern invasion was repulsed. Kashmir was an up-and-coming power at about this time, and the Tibetans enlisted the Kashmiris in an alliance strong enough to keep the Muslim Arabs out of northern Pakistan.

The tenth century brought the invasion of the Shins, a Europoid people who spoke Shina (pronounced She-NAA), still the language of the main Gilgit Valley, and drove the native Burushaski speakers up into Hunza, Nagar and Yasin. The Shins may have been Hindu, as were the Hindu Shahi kings, who then ruled upper Pakistan from their capital at Hund on the Indus, just below the modern Tarbela Dam.

It was not until early in the 11th century that Mahmud of Ghazni invaded from Afghanistan, overthrowing the Hindus at Hund and finally winning the plains of Pakistan for Islam. At the time, Gilgit was part of the powerful independent mountain stronghold of Dardistan. Gradually, central power waned, and each isolated valley became a small kingdom speaking its own language and following its own customs. There were seven different kingdoms along the Gilgit and Hunza rivers alone (Gilgit, Punial, Ishkoman, Ghizar, Yasin, Hunza and Nagar), speaking at least four distinct languages (Shina, Khowar, Burushaski, and Wakhi). Each tiny kingdom was autonomous and usually at war with the next. Indeed, Marco Polo, who passed through Badakhshan (northeastern Afghanistan) in about 1273 called the area 'noisy with kingdoms'. The better-situated of these grew rich by taxing the traffic to and from China.

Sometime after the 15th century, the entire area gradually converted to Islam. Pathan Sunnis came up the Indus from Swat in about the 16th century, and Shia Muslims spread into Baltistan from Kashmir before the 17th century. Finally, early in the 19th century, the *mir* (king) of Hunza, Silum Khan III, who had been in temporary exile in Badakhshan, was converted to the Ismaili creed by a *pir* (religious leader) there. Most of his subjects in Hunza and Gojal (upper Hunza) followed suit. Ishkoman, Yasin and the top end of Chitral are now mostly Ismaili, followers of the Aga Khan.

Though northern Pakistan is virtually 100 percent Muslim, the people still hold a strong belief in fairies, witches and *jinns* (wizards), and there survive vestiges of pre-Islamic planting and harvesting ceremonies.

In 1846, the British sold Kashmir, Ladakh, Baltistan and Gilgit to Gulab Singh, the raja of Jammu, and appointed him the first maharaja of Kashmir. But the maharaja's Hindu soldiers could do little to subdue the Muslim tribesmen, despite repeated campaigns in the 1850s and 60s.

Socialising in Gilgit's main square

The British became interested in the region because of its strategic importance near Russia and China and, in 1877, set up the Gilgit Agency, the most isolated outpost of the British Empire, to guard against a possible Russian thrust through the mountains to the Vale of Kashmir. This was the world of Kipling's Kim and the 'Great Game' (see page 238).

Totally cut off by snow for eight months of the year, the first British agency was not a success: it was too small and too remote to make its presence felt, and it ended abruptly in 1881 when it was nearly overrun by the Kohistanis. The second agency, established in 1889, fared better. By then the route from Srinagar via Astor had been improved, there was a telegraphic link, and the agency included a full compliment of British soldiers. There followed a series of campaigns to subdue the surrounding kingdoms: in 1891, led by Algernon Durand, they overran Hunza and in 1893, they strengthened the fort at Chilas to defend the new road over the Babusar Pass against the Kohistani tribes.

In 1913 the British formed the Gilgit Scouts, a force of 600 men raised to guard against invasion and to maintain peace. The scouts were mostly the sons of royalty from the seven kingdoms, commanded by a *subedar major,* usually the brother of one of the kings, under the direction of the political agent. The Scout's bagpipe band wore the Black Watch tartan and, even today, practices in Chinar Bagh near the river. In 1935 the airfield was built.

At Independence in 1947, British India was divided into Hindu-majority India and Muslim-majority Pakistan. One of the many vexing problems brought about by the split was what to do with the hundreds of princely states, which theoretically had the right to remain independent. The vast majority were Hindu and were easily persuaded to join India, and the Muslim states in Pakistan were absorbed by Pakistan. The rub was Kashmir, a Muslim-majority state ruled by a Hindu maharaja.

Maharaja Hari Singh let the Independence Day accession deadline pass without joining either Pakistan or India — an apparent bid for independence or at least a favourable autonomy arrangement. Two weeks before the 14 August Independence Day, the political agent of Gilgit handed over power to a new Kashmiri Hindu governor, Ghansara Singh. The Gilgit Scouts were left in the charge of Major William Brown, a British officer who had volunteered to see them through Independence.

In Punjab grisly bloodshed marked Partition, as ten million Hindu, Sikh and Muslim refugees fled in opposite directions across the new border. Gilgit waited in suspense while the maharaja dithered.

On 26 October, Pathan tribesmen from the North-West Frontier Province invaded Kashmir, declaring a jihad (holy war). Hari Singh fled to Delhi and begged for help, agreeing to accede to India, subject to a general referendum. In Gilgit, Subedar Major Babar Khan, brother of the *mir* of Nagar and commander of the Scouts, and Mirzada Shah Khan, brother of the *mir* of Hunza, arrested Governor Ghansara Singh on 31 October with the connivance of their commander, Major William Brown. The next day Gilgit was declared 'the independent Republic of Gilgit', which later acceded to Pakistan. The Gilgit Scouts and Muslim soldiers of the Kashmiri army then joined the war against India, winning Baltistan for Pakistan. There is a memorial to Babar Khan in Chinar Bagh; Mirzada Shah Khan is still alive.

The first war for Kashmir ended in January 1949, with a United Nations-sponsored ceasefire. Pakistan retained the Northern Areas (Gilgit, Hunza, Diamer and Baltistan), and Azad (Free) Kashmir, while India held the Kashmir Valley and Ladakh. The Kashmir question remains the core issue behind most of the disputes between India and Pakistan since Independence. The two countries declared war in 1965 and 1971, and in 1985 fighting flared again on the Siachen Glacier.

Until 1974 the seven feudal principalities along the Gilgit and Hunza rivers remained more or less autonomous, with the *mirs* or rajas in control of the administration, police and justice. Between 1970 and 1974, the Pakistani government relieved the rulers of most of their powers, and the principalities were incorporated into Pakistan. The Northern Areas are now divided into five administrative districts: Diamer (administered from Chilas, Baltistan (Skardu), Ghanche (Khaplu), Ghizar (Gakuch) and Gilgit (Gilgit town, which is also the headquarters of the chief administrator of the Northern Areas). Hunza is part of Gilgit district which has a population of nearly 300,000 — a threefold increase since Independence.

The referendum promised in 1947 was never held. Pakistan is loath to make the Northern Areas a province of Pakistan, as this would be construed as permanent acceptance of the ceasefire line. Officially, the region is called a 'federally administered area' and is looked after by a special ministry in Islamabad.

Because of its sensitive position bordering China and Afghanistan — and a stone's throw across the Wakhan Corridor from the former Soviet Union — Pakistan has made a concerted effort to develop the area, improving the irrigation and road networks, building schools, hospitals and medical centres, and developing training and marketing programmes. But signs painted on walls and rocks saying 'We want the vote' illustrate the underlying frustration of people barred not only from voting, but also from appealing to the

Pakistan Supreme Court. The people of the Northern Areas fought to join Pakistan, and now they feel excluded and exploited.

There is also smouldering religious tension. In May 1988, the Sunnis of Chilas attacked the Shias of Gilgit, ostensibly because the Shias finished the Ramazan month of fasting one day ahead of the Sunnis. Hundreds were killed. In November 1989, Sunnis again attacked Shias, leaving several dead.

Sights

Gilgit is the only market town for hundreds of kilometres in every direction and the meeting place for traders from Central Asia, Punjab and Sindh. Mountain men from the remotest valleys walk for days to bring their goats to market. Except on Fridays, the bazaars are always bustling and photogenic. The single-storey, box-like shops sell an extraordinary range of goods, from paraffin lamps and camp stoves to fragile porcelain and lustrous silks from China, from powdered milk and iodized salt to tough climbing boots and ice axes. Bakeries and bookshops do brisk business, as do the markets selling vegetables, fruit, meat and spices.

The **polo tournaments** in June, August and November are engaging and exciting. Polo originated in the Northern Areas, and the version still played here is much less staid than the international game. The field is unusually long and narrow, and the ponies are small and vigorous. Six players make up a team (instead of four), and the same ponies are used throughout the match. If a player manages to catch the ball in his hand, he can charge through the goalposts to score. The spectators become wildly involved, shouting and jeering in a solid mass. But drowning out all else are the excruciatingly loud *surnai* (clarinets) and the *damal* and *dadang* (drums) of the band, a carry-over from the days when kings directed their troops in battle by signalling with different tunes. The band now relays musical messages from the coach. In addition, each player has his own signature tune. These, as well as the commands, are readily recognised by the crowd, and the women, confined to their houses, can follow the game and know who has the ball and who has scored a goal.

Trips from Gilgit

A visit to the **Kargah Buddha** is the most popular outing from Gilgit (see map page 214. The Buddha is carved halfway up a cliff face at Kargah Nullah, ten kilometres (six miles) west of Gilgit on the road to Punial. You can drive to the channel cut along the hillside; an easy two-hour stroll through fields, groves and villages featuring magnificent views down over Gilgit and the valley. The channel ends near Serena Lodge, from where you can catch a Suzuki back to Gilgit for Rs2.

The three-metre (ten-foot) Buddha figure was carved in the seventh century. A monastery and three stupas about 400 metres (a quarter of a mile) upstream from the Buddha were excavated in 1938–9, following the discovery of the so-called **Gilgit manuscripts** in 1931. Written in Sanskrit, the manuscripts contain Buddhist texts and the names and dates of some of the rulers of the area and the more illustrious pilgrims. More manuscripts were found in 1939 and 1956, and all are now divided among the British Museum, Rome, Delhi and Karachi.

Jutial Nullah is a valley starting behind Serena Lodge. Follow the irrigation channel behind the hotel to the cleft in the cliff-face, then take the goat path into the gorge, keeping the stream on your left. Like most valleys in the Northern Areas, Jutial is very narrow at its mouth and considerably wider further up. A six-kilometre (four-mile) walk along the stream, through a steep-sided gorge, takes you in one and a half hours to pine forests and pastureland.

Naltar is the loveliest full-day outing from Gilgit. About a two-hour drive away, it is an area of alpine meadows and pine forests 3,000 metres (10,000 feet) above sea level and surrounded by snow-capped mountains. The road up from Nomal climbs steeply through a rocky gorge to emerge on the fertile, high-altitude pastures. Those who wish to stay can choose among the Public Works Department rest-house, the very basic local hotel, or camping. Naltar is the perfect base for gentle walks through the forest or up to Naltar Lake, where the fishing is excellent. The village is also the starting point for more energetic treks across the 4,000-metre (13,000-foot) **Naltar Pass** to the Ishkoman Valley, or across the 4,800-metre (15,700-foot) **Daintar Pass** to Chalt. The two ski-lifts at Naltar are reserved for army use.

West to Chitral

The jeep road to Chitral across the Shandur Pass follows the Gilgit River west for 240 kilometres (150 miles), a tortuous 12-hour journey not recommended for the faint-hearted. The dirt track — barely wide enough for a jeep — is cut

The Great Game

by Peter Fredenburg

The second half of the 19th century saw intense rivalry between Russia and British India for domination of the high ground of Central Asia, an unmapped sprawl of mountains from Afghanistan in the west to Tibet in the east. While the Russians probed for a route through this no man's land to the markets and warm-water ports of the subcontinent, the British sought to remove the threat of a Russian invasion by establishing hegemony over a string of buffer states in the mountains. In this contest, information was everything.

The blanks on the maps that so perplexed and distressed military strategists energised explorers, who risked (and often lost) life and limb gathering the information needed to fill them in. The 'pundits', native graduates of the spy school run at Dehra Dun by Captain Thomas Montgomerie, posed as holy men to penetrate and map Tibet, where no European could go. Afghanistan and Chinese Turkestan — and the tangled knot of mountains in between — were explored by British and Russian military men, either active or 'retired', some travelling with official status, others without, maintaining for their government (to use the modern phrase) 'plausible deniability'. The world they uncovered was as complex ethnologically as it was topographically, to the delight of anthropologists and linguists but the exasperation of the soldiers and civil servants whose job it was to bring the myriad mountain kingdoms — isolated, backward and fractious — under imperial sway.

Kipling fictionalised the Game in Kim and The Man Who Would be King, but the real world of such players as Nikolai Prejevalsky and Francis Younghusband was hardly less entertaining to the armchair adventurers who immersed themselves in the geography and intrigues of the Karakorams, the Pamirs and the Hindu Kush, convinced that the fate of empires hinged on events in narrow clefts with names like Ladakh, Baltistan, Hunza, Chitral and Dir.

The British had mapped most of India's northern frontier by 1893. They completed their cordon sanitaire two years later by affixing the Wakhan Corridor to Afghanistan, thus stretching the reluctant amir's domains to the Chinese frontier. (This arrangement held until 1981, when the Marxist Kabul regime formally ceded Wakhan to the Soviet Union.) By 1913 it was clear that there was no pass over which Russia could invade India, but the Bolshevik Revolution four years later — and Lenin's plan to take India through revolutionary subversion rather than invasion — rendered the question academic.

Though the Great Game proved in the end to be a comedy of hysteria and anticlimax, the journals published by the explorers of Central Asia remain an exciting record of exhilaration and drive, of deprivation and despair, of heroics and death. Interest stimulated by tourism and the popular histories of Peter Hopkirk and John Keay has recently brought back into print many of these books.

along the cliff-face on the south bank of the river. Passing through the former kingdoms of **Punial** and **Gupis,** with **Ishkoman** and **Yasin** up side valleys to the north, the road connects Gilgit town with all the tiny village oases of the upper Gilgit Valley which, upriver from Gakuch, is also known as the **Ghizar Valley.**

In late June or July, a polo match between Gilgit and Chitral is played at the Shandur Pass. At that time, there are a lot of public jeeps going up to the pass from both sides. During the rest of the year, however, public transport runs only as far as Teru, 225 kilometres (140 miles) from Gilgit and from Chitral, as far as Mastuj. Transport across the pass is hard to find.

Phundar, nine hours from Gilgit, is the recommended overnight stop *en route* to Chitral. The good PWD rest-house sits on a ridge overlooking on one side, the Ghizar River as it meanders along its flat, stony bed and, on the other, a steep slope into the deep blue of Phundar Lake. If not pressed for time, plan to spend two or three nights here. The trout fishing is excellent both in Phundar Lake and a little up a side valley at Handrap Lake. PTDC has built a new motel here and at Gupis.

The **Shandur Pass,** 3,734 metres (12,250 feet) above sea level, leads to Chitral (see page 218). The top is flat, open summer pastureland with two small lakes. The pass is blocked by snow from November to May.

North to China

The Karakoram Highway from Gilgit over the 258 kilometres (160 miles) to the Khunjerab Pass on the Chinese border follows the Hunza and Khunjerab rivers through barren gorges, past terraced oases and round the bases of the Rakaposhi, Distaghil and Ultar mountains, all three of which are over 7,300 metres (24,000 feet) high. It is an unforgettable six-hour drive, along which magnificent views emerge around every corner and the snouts of two glaciers press right down to the road.

Those planning to cross into China need a valid visa, which is obtainable at the embassy in Islamabad. China-bound travellers must clear the Pakistani border post at Sost by 11 am, while arrivals from China are processed until 4 pm. No private vehicles are allowed into China, but they can be taken as far as the border for sightseeing. The pass is closed in winter (see page 14).

Gilgit to Hunza

Two roads connect Gilgit with the KKH. If you have a small jeep, the shorter and more enjoyable route is across the longest suspension bridge in Northern Pakistan, which crosses the Hunza River near its confluence with the Gilgit

River. This road joins the KKH at Dainyor. The main road from Gilgit joins the KKH ten kilometres east of Gilgit on the south bank of the Gilgit River.

The KKH follows the east bank of the Hunza River, skirting halfway around Mount Rakaposhi and passing through a series of bleak gorges with sheer walls running up to towering mountains and down to the river rushing below. Wherever there is a patch of more or less flat land between the gorges, tiny settlements with terraced fields cling to the bases of the barren mountains.

The old jeep track, opened in 1958, follows the footpath that was once the only southern access to Hunza, running along the opposite side of the river. The first settlement of any consequence on the west side of the river is **Nomal,** 33 kilometres (21 miles) from Gilgit. From there the jeep track leads up to Naltar. (There is no bridge here; access is from Gilgit only.) A memorial to those who died building the KKH stands on the highway opposite Nomal.

Beyond the first long gorge is the large settlement of **Chalt**, also on the opposite side of the river, but connected to the KKH by a bridge. This is where the island plate ends and the Asian land mass begins (see page 227). A sign on the cliff reads, 'Here two continents collide.'

Chalt — with its near neighbour, **Chaprot**, and **Nilt**, nine kilometres (six miles) further on — was the scene of a rather smaller but better-documented collision in 1891 between British forces and the warriors of Hunza and Nagar. E F Knight, accompanying the British as a correspondent for *The Times*, described the action (for which three Victoria Crosses were awarded) as 'one of the most brilliant little campaigns in military history', and later wrote a stirring account of the battle in his book, *Where Three Empires Meet* (1893).

The British needed three weeks to defeat the local forces. They then crossed the Hunza River and occupied the palace of the *mir* (king) of Hunza in Baltit. The *mir* fled to his relations in Kashgar, and all resistance came to an end. The palace was ransacked in the search for 'the treasures of many a pillaged caravan and the results of many a raid', but little was found except some beautifully illustrated Korans and a secret chamber containing gunpowder and garnet bullets.

The KKH turns east at Chalt and hugs the Hunza River round the north side of **Rakaposhi**, at 7,788 metres (25,550 feet), the 27th highest mountain in the world. As you drive along, you catch intermittent glimpses of glaciers, precipices and gleaming white peaks and ridges surrounded by wide expanses of smooth snow. Two of the best views of Rakaposhi are two kilometres (about one mile) past the petrol pump at the turning to Chalt. Here you come

Taking the sun on the rooftops of Altit in Hunza

round a corner to find the great mass of Rakaposhi staring you down, and nine kilometres (six miles) further on, where a sign in English says 'Visitors please Rakaposhi on your right', put up by the restaurant on the left, an inviting place to take a break.

Beyond Chalt, the ex-kingdoms of Hunza and Nagar begin — Hunza on the north side of the Hunza River, and Nagar on the south. Once a united ancient kingdom, Nagar and Hunza were divided between warring brothers in the 15th century and have remained traditional enemies ever since. The conflict is exacerbated by religion, as the Hunzakuts are Ismailis, followers of the Aga Khan, and the people of Nagar are Shias, admirers of the Ayatollah Khomeini of Iran. The slopes of Hunza face south to the warming sun, while Nagar slopes north, often shivering in the shadow of Rakaposhi. Consequently (it is said), the Hunzakuts have a warm, open nature, while their neighbours across the river are known for their dour temperament.

The KKH runs through Nagar territory for about 20 kilometres (12 miles) before crossing over to Hunza at Nazirabad on another of the elegant Chinese bridges guarded by two rows of ornamental lions. About ten kilometres (six miles) from the bridge, the road turns a corner and the Hunza landscape opens up before you in dramatic contrast to the grim desolation of the earlier gorges.

Hunza

Called by Eric Shipton, 'the ultimate manifestation of mountain grandeur', Hunza, at 2,400 metres (8,000 feet), is indeed a fairytale land, 'rich, fecund and of an ethereal beauty'. The fields ripple in tiny terraces down the mountainside, as neatly arranged as fish scales, each supported by a high, mortarless stone wall. Everywhere, slender poplar trees cut strong vertical lines perpendicular to the horizontal terraces or stand out sharply against the glacier-scarred rock. The colours change with the seasons, the emerald green of spring deepening in summer and giving way to the golden yellow and orange of autumn. Above all, guarding the valley on all sides, stand Rakaposhi, Ultar and Distaghil.

The scene vanishes again as the road heads up the Hasanabad gorge to find a place to cross. Visible to the left (north) from the Hasanabad Bridge is the terminal moraine of Hasanabad Glacier, which ends a little way above the road and from which issues a stream. **Aliabad** straddles the KKH two kilometres (about one mile) further on, while **Karimabad**, the capital, sits on the mountainside about one kilometre (about half a mile) above Aliabad, accessible by two jeep roads. With its panoramic views and many hotels, Karimabad is the better place to stay. Walkers are happy here for days on end; non-walkers can relax and absorb the view.

History

The origin of the Hunza people is unclear. They look European (specifically Celtic), many with brown or russet hair and green or blue eyes. The Hunzakuts themselves tell a legend of three soldiers, from the army of Alexander the Great which passed through Pakistan in 325 BC, settling in the valley with their Persian wives and founding the first villages of Altit, Baltit and Ganesh: a pretty story, but unfounded. The old *mir* (king) of Hunza had an even better tale reported by E F Knight in *Where Three Empires Meet* (1893). He claimed to be descended from Alexander the Great's union with a fairy of the Hindu Kush, giving himself, as Knight says, 'certainly a very respectable pedigree'.

What is certain is that Altit, Baltit and Ganesh were the first three villages in Hunza, and were probably settled in the 11th century. Indeed, they were the only villages until the end of the 18th century, when improved irrigation techniques enabled the colony to expand.

Western researchers such as Karl Jettmar and Hermann Kreutzmann think the Hunzakuts are probably descended from the original mountain inhabitants. They speak Burushaski, an autochthonous language with no apparent link to any existing language family. Burushaski speakers probably once inhabited the entire Gilgit area as many of the place names are of Burushaski origin. Certainly the Tibetans in the seventh century AD refer to the whole area as Bruza and to the people as Burushos. As noted by Jetmar in *Bolar and Dardistan*, the Tibetans record that in 740 a king of Bruza married a Tibetan princess. The invading Shins, speaking Shina, drove the Burushaski-speakers into the Hunza and Yasin valleys in the 11th century. (See Gilgit for more history.)

Hunza has been ruled by the same family since the 11th century. From 1761 to 1937, they paid nominal tribute to Xinjiang, but in all essentials were independent. For centuries the Hunzakuts earned their livelihood by taxing the caravans along this branch of the silk route between Gilgit and Kashgar — and by well-organised brigandage. They were the terror of the people between Afghanistan and Yarkand, and made frequent raids across the Hindu Kush and Karakoram, even robbing the trade caravans as far away as Shahidula on the route from Leh to Yarkand across the Karakoram Pass. On one memorable occasion they captured a caravan of 50 laden camels and 500 laden ponies. Slave dealing was equally lucrative. All men, women and children taken in these raids were driven across the mountains and sold in Chinese Turkestan, or to the Kirghiz.

For centuries the tiny state was impregnable. When Kashmir sent a force to attack it in 1848, the Hunzakuts captured 200 of the Kashmiris and sold them as slaves.

Hunza was considered critical to the expansionist plans of both Russia and British India as it controlled the most important mountain passes linking Russia, India and China. John Biddolph, was the first Westerner to penetrate Hunza's southern defences in 1876, but was not allowed to explore beyond the capital at Baltit. In 1888 the Russians entering from the north, negotiated with the *mir* of Hunza, offering arms and training in return for a Russian post at Baltit. The British countered by sending Francis Younghusband to explore the mountain passes and by reopening their British Agency in Gilgit in 1889. They also negotiated with the *mir* of Hunza, offering a subsidy in return for safe passage for trade caravans between Gilgit and Kashgar, safe passage on the Leh–Yarkand route, and the breaking of relations with Russia. It did not take the *mir* long to calculate that the Russian deal was more advantageous, so he returned the English representative to Gilgit.

Therefore the British decided to invade Hunza, and in December 1891, a force led by Colonel Algernon Durand, advanced to Nilt. In a fierce battle lasting three weeks, the British, aided by a Nagar prince, defeated the combined forces of Nagar and Hunza. Durand was wounded by a bullet made of a garnet encased in lead. The *mir* fled to Xinjiang, and Baltit fort was ransacked in search of treasure. They found little, except for some beautifully decorated Korans and a secret room full of gunpowder, garnet bullets and a few Russian rifles.

The British installed the *mir*'s brother, Mohammad Nazim Khan (died 1938), as the new *mir* and ally, ensuring free passage to Kashgar. In 1895 the Russians and British met in the Pamirs and agreed that a strip of Afghanistan, the Wakhan corridor, should separate the two empires. There were many skirmishes along the Hunza–Chinese frontier until 1963 when Pakistan and China agreed on the present boundary about 40 kilometres west of that marked on the U502 map, with the result that Hunza lost to China its eastern grazing lands beyond Shimshal.

From 1897 to 1947 the British kept an assistant political agent in Hunza, but the *mir* remained in charge of his own government and administration. Following Pakistani independence, little changed until 1974 when the building of the Karakoram Highway began to open the area and Islamabad took over the political, legal and fiscal administration. To begin with *the mir's* son was elected to the Northern Areas Council, as he was respected by many of his ex-subjects for his lineage and wealth, but in 1994 he was voted out.

The Hunzakuts were animist until the 16th or 17th century when they became Shia Muslims. In the 1820s, the *mir* was converted to the Ismaili creed and brought most of his subjects with him to the new faith. The openness and friendliness of the Hunzakuts is in part the result of this, as Ismailis are freer in their outlook than other Muslems — as far back as 1904, for example, the then Aga Khan decreed that women should come out of seclusion and be educated.

The modern, green-roofed *jamat khanas* (community centres, not open to tourists) that dominate every village are the new Ismaili places of worship, introduced in 1922. The old carved mosques are falling into ruin or have already disappeared in most villages. Notices in every village announce the development projects of the Aga Khan, who takes a deep interest in Pakistan.

The great myth of Hunza's tranquillity, contentment and purity are perhaps the result of James Hilton's 1933 novel *Lost Horizon*, where everyone lived happily in Shangri'la. The miracle of the Hunzakuts' longevity, supposedly resulting from their largely vegetarian diet of cereals and fruit, was the invention of the Swiss dietician R Bircher who, in 1942, published *Hunza, Das Volk, das Kline Krankbert Keunt* (*Hunza — a People Untouched by Illness*). Bircher never visited the area. The myth got further play in articles in *Life Magazine* ('The Happy Land of Just Enough') and *National Geographic* in 1971 ('Every Day Is a Gift When You Are Over 100').

In fact, until the 1980s, life in Hunza was as hard as anywhere else in the Northern Areas, especially in springtime, when food stocks ran low. People looked older than their years, infant mortality was as high as 25 percent, about 7 percent of those who survived were cretins as a result of iodine deficiency and in-breeding, and — a final gloomy note — questions of succession were resolved by murder.

This much is true. Fruits and cereals have long been the staple diet. For centuries wheat, barley, buckwheat, millet, peas, beans and spinach have grown in Hunza. From late March to May the valley is covered in blossom from apricot, apple, peach, pear and plum trees; grape vines festoon the trees and terrace walls. Nothing is wasted: the apricot stone is used for fuel; the kernel is ground into flour, eaten as a nut (similar to an almond) or pounded for its oil, the pulp being used for fodder. This century has seen the arrival of

The Tibetan-styled Baltit Fort (Left) was occupied by the mir of Hunza until the 1950s A Hunzakut shepherd (right) guides his flock across almost barren scree.

maize, potatoes, cabbage, carrots, courgettes and tomatoes. Until the 1970s, the people ate only what they could produce, but now many men find paid jobs outside Hunza, causing agricultural production to drop, but providing the means to import nearly 60 percent of the Hunzakuts' dietary needs.

The Hunza women wear bright clothes: a long shirt over baggy trousers and an embroidered pillbox hat, over which they drape a light shawl. They do not cover their faces, but are embarrassed when foreigners attempt to photograph them.

Getting to Hunza

Several wagons and jeeps leave the Jamat Khana Bazaar in Gilgit daily for Karimabad (the best place to go in Hunza). Be sure to ask for Karimabad and not just Hunza. The vehicles make a second stop in Gilgit at the general wagon station, but it is better to catch them at their source where you can wait in the shade. NATCO buses on the KKH, heading for the Pakistan frontier post at Sost, will drop passengers at Aliabad or Ganesh, but this is not very satisfactory as most tourists will still want to get up to Karimabad. It is a steep, hot two-kilometre hike up from Ganesh or an expensive ride in a private jeep, whose drivers wait for the gullible at Ganesh monument. Local Suzukis ply up and down the KKH between Ganesh and Hasanabad (charging a few rupees). Pay as you get in to avoid a rip-off attempt at the end.

Sights

Baltit Fort, once the palace of the *mir* of Hunza, is perched on a hilltop at the entrance to Ultar Gorge, from where it overlooks the entire valley. It is about 600 years old and reflects Tibetan influence. The local people say that a princess of Baltistan ('Little Tibet') married a reigning *mir* and brought as part of her dowry some Balti masons, carpenters and craftsmen to build Baltit. It was inhabited until the 1950s, when the *mir* built a new granite house in Karimabad.

Baltit is a curious, rambling old place with 53 rooms scattered on three levels. It has recently been renovated by the Aga Khan Trust for Culture, and houses a museum, library and an excellent restaurant. Park in the polo ground and walk up. The hefty entrance fee goes towards its upkeep. It is open from 9 am to 1 pm and 2 to 5.30 pm.

The fort is sturdily built of stones reinforced with timber beams and plastered over with sun-dried mud. You approach the main door up a zigzag ramp and enter the ground floor into a dark 'hall' with guardrooms off it. On the same floor are guest-rooms, prisons, storerooms, kitchens and the mirs old apartments, he abandoned them because they were haunted by a witch. A wooden staircase leads up through a square hole to the floor above.

You emerge into a central courtyard, off which are the main reception rooms, where the *mir* held court. There is a throne-room, summer and winter living quarters, bedrooms, bathrooms, storerooms, guards' quarters and an arms depot. There is even a royal balcony, with a view over the kingdom. In the museum are photographs of the *mirs* and important visitors, coats of mail, weapons and the drums that sounded the alarm when the enemy attacked, warning the villagers to run into the fort for shelter. This was a feudalistic society: in return for his taxes, the *mir* provided protection in time of danger and distributed grain from his storerooms in times of need.

Another wooden ladder leads to the roof for a view straight across the valley to Rakaposhi. Nestled below are the adjoining villages of Baltit and Karimabad. The polo ground in Karimabad is now used as the school playground. The *mir*'s new palace is visible one kilometre (about half a mile) away to the south, and his family graveyard lies beyond. To the east, beyond the fields, village and fort of Altit, the Hunza Valley leads up to China. To the north is a sheer drop into Ultar Ravine, which leads up to Ultar Glacier.

For a spectacular view of the back of Baltit Fort, you can walk out along the irrigation channel that comes from **Ultar Glacier.** It is a steep, three-hour climb up the side of the glacier to the summer pastures and shepherds' hut on the slopes of Ultar Mountain. Follow the irrigation channel into the gorge, then keep to the left as you climb. (The 7,388-metre (24,240-foot) Ultar Mountain was first climbed in 1996, by the Japanese).

Altit Fort, a two-kilometre (about a mile) jeep ride from Karimabad, is perched on a rocky cliff with a sheer 300-metre (1,000-foot) plunge to the Hunza River. It has not yet been renovated. Like Baltit, it comprises a maze of small rooms on three levels. A curved passage from the door to the stairs leads past a storeroom with a sinister past. Ostensibly where wine was made, it also served as one of the entrances to the rabbit warren of storerooms and dungeons beneath the fort. The trapdoor in the floor (now blocked) leads to the cells below. The prisoners were kept in total darkness, and food was thrown down to them from time to time. It was also in this room that, three generations ago, the *mir* murdered his two brothers in a struggle for the throne. The wooden pillar beside the trapdoor has some evil-looking notches carved into it, but they represent only the tally of grain collected as revenue.

On the next floor are the royal apartments: the bedroom is to the west, the throne room to the east. Each has cantilevered ceilings, the beams of which are decorated with good-luck symbols. Beside the fireplace in the throne room is a post about one metre (three foot) high on which the lamp stood. Cupboards stand in two corners, and a door leads out to the lavatory and bath. The kitchen is between the bedroom and the throne room.

Stairs lead up to an open courtyard on the roof, with its dizzying view over the battlements to the river. The roof holds both 16th- and 20th-century buildings. Dominating all is the watch-tower, with carved windows and doors and dated Anno Hijrae 909 (AD 1503). To the right of the tower is a store for arms and ammunition, also with an old, carved door. To the left is a tiny, carved mosque. The passage beside the mosque leads to the 20th-century apartments of the raja, all strung along a carved verandah with a view up to Baltit Fort and Ultar Glacier. Close under the walls of the fort is the village of Altit, where women dry fruit and vegetables for the winter.

The **Pakistan Mineral Development Corporation** project in Aliabad is devoted to developing Hunza's mineral wealth. Precious and semiprecious stones are sold here. Some two kilometres (one mile) further on, a path leads off to the left toward some ruby mines.

Ganesh is the village enclosed in the S–bend of the KKH as it snakes down to cross the Hunza River on Ganesh Bridge, six kilometres (four miles) beyond Aliabad. It is one of the oldest villages in Hunza and clings firmly to its old traditions. The people here have remained Shia Muslims. Ganesh is guarded by an old watch-tower and fort, with a carved mosque standing at its side. The pool in front of the tower is where all the local boys once learned to swim. The test of swimming ability and bravery was to swim the Hunza River. Hunza's defence depended on initiations into manhood such as this.

The **Sacred Rock of Ganesh** is immediately beside the KKH, between the road and the river a few hundred metres (yards) east of Ganesh Bridge. The rock is covered with drawings and inscriptions in five different scripts: Kharoshthi, Brahmi, Gupta, Sogdian and Tibetan. There is a portrait of Gondophares, the Kushan king of Gandhara in the first century AD, labelled with his name and the date. Another inscription reads, 'Chandra sri Vikramaditya conquers', with a date corresponding to AD 419. Chandra sri Vikramaditya was Chandra Gupta II, the greatest of the Gupta emperors, who ruled over most of India in the early fifth century AD. Other names and dates appear in the many inscriptions.

Most of the drawings are of hunting scenes, with ibex figuring in almost every one: ibex being surrounded and shot at by horsemen, and men dancing round ibex. In remoter parts of Hunza, the people still perform ritual ibex dances at festival times. The local *bitan* (shaman) dons an ibex head-dress and falls into a trance, from the depths of which he extracts knowledge of the future.

Nagar

Nagar, the large kingdom across the river from Hunza, was possibly first settled by people from Baltistan who arrived over the mountains by walking along the Biafo and Hispar glaciers. It was settled again in about the 14th century by Hunzakuts who crossed the river. A man called Borosh from Hunza supposedly founded the first village of Boroshal, and married a Balti girl he found there. The legend says the girl and her grandmother were the sole survivors of a landslide that killed all the early Balti settlers.

The big fortified village of Nagar, the home of the rulers of Nagar (there is a list of kings from about 1500) was built in the late 15th century by Burushaski speakers from Gor, near Chilas. Early in the 20th century erosion undermined the village, which fell into the river; now only the ex-ruler's palace remains on top of the hill.

Nagar and Hunza were both converted from animism to Shia Islam in the 16th or 17th centuries. From about 1700 on, the two kingdoms were at war with one another, continually attacking each other and stealing women and children to sell as slaves. Everyone lived in fortified villages until the 19th century, when new immigrants arrived, first founding Askur Das and Shayar, and then, as the pressure of population increased, building new unfortified hamlets.

As Nagar has always had a better water supply, it is bigger than Hunza. The present population in the bowl of central Nagar is about 36,000, compared to 20,000 people in the bowl of central Hunza. (The population of the whole of Nagar from Chalt to Hispar is about 48,000; and that of the whole of Hunza, from the Maiun Valley to Khunjerab is about 32,000). The continuing conflict between the two kingdoms is exacerbated by religion, as the Hunzakuts are now Ismailis, followers of the Aga Khan, and the people Nagar are Shias. There is also a personality divide, which popular legend ascribes to the sun: the slopes of central Hunza face south to the warming sun, while Nagar slopes north, shivering in the shadow of Rakaposhi. Consequently, the legend suggests, the Hunzakuts have a warm, open nature, while their neighbours across the river are known for their dour temperament.

Getting to Nagar

Nagar is entered by the jeep road that leaves the KKH just beyond the Ganesh bridge across the Hunza River. The first five kilometres (three miles) of this road are dry and barren, then the road divides. One branch crosses the Hispar River on a bridge and climbs up into the fertile villages of central Nagar, where many kilometres of irrigation channels provide pleasant walks through fields and villages right up to the last village of **Hopar.** You can get here by public transport from Aliabad in Hunza, which leaves most days for Nagar, and occasionally continues to Hopar.

At Hopar is a small hotel on a ridge, from which there is a magnificent view back down the valley on one side and down on to **Hopar Glacier** (also known as Bualtar Glacier) on the other. This glacier drops 5,000 metres (16,500 feet) from its source on mount Diran, and ends at 2,270 metres (7,500 feet) above sea level, apparently making it the lowest glacier in the world between latitudes 40 north and 35 south. It's snout is certainly the lowest in the Karakoram–Himalaya ranges with Minapin and Pisan close seconds at 2,400 metres (7,900 feet). The glacier was surging forward in 1990, creaking and groaning as it ground forward at a reckless three metres (ten yards) a day, churned into huge ice pinnacles and yawning crevasses. (This is not a record: there is a glacier in Alaska that has surged more than 200 metres (660 feet) a day.)

You can cross Hopar Glacier to **Barpu Glacier** for a spectacular but easy trek up to summer pastures.

The other branch of the road from Hunza continues along the Hispar River through **Hora** (a single hut on the hillside), then past the gorge to the last village of **Hispar** at the northern end of the Hispar Glacier. Hispar, according to local legend, was first settled in about the 14th century by people from Baltistan, who came over the Hispar Pass, and down the Hispar Glacier. Interestingly, the people of Askole in Baltistan believe their ancestors came from Nagar at about the same time. But, whatever its origin, researchers do believe that Hispar, where the people speak Balti, hidden 25 kilometres (16 miles) up a difficult gorge, is one of the earliest Nagar villages.

'Across the Indus'

How beautiful it seems
That crowded, festering, insistent city,
Dirt, barren heat, the cruel drone of flies,
The sores paraded to indifferent eyes,
The ruined houses leaning to each other
Disgorging naked, unappealing children
Playing their games in self-created filth.
And rising, waiting, casting its heavy mantle,
The suffocating, obliterating dust
Swirling forever in the noisy lanes.
But I have crossed the river
Placing the deep and easy flow of green
Between that life and this.
Clear and toylike in the distance
Quiet, pure and captivating
Lies the city; gracefully the houses
jostle each other to the river's brink.
So the Indus mirrors
Those dirty shadows like a dream in crystal,
And the ugliness I saw and came away from
Along the placid water flows away

Shahid Hosain in J. Fairley, The Lion River, 1975

The KKH beyond Karimabad

The KKH is at its most spectacular between Ganesh and Gulmit. The road rides high on the eastern side of the river, twisting and turning round the barren foot of the Hispar Range, which boasts six peaks over 7,000 metres (23,000 feet). On the opposite bank, villages cling implausibly to the side of the 7,388-metre (24,240-foot) Ultar Mountain. Between the villages, grey scree slithers down to the river, looking in the distance like piles of fine cigarette ash. Above, the jagged teeth along the ridge hide the highest snow-covered peaks from view.

The KKH crosses back to the west bank at **Shishkot Bridge**, from which the view upstream of the serrated ridge of mountains above the river is one of the most photogenic prospects of the entire drive. From here to Tashkurgan in China the people speak Wakhi.

Gulmit, eight kilometres (five miles) past the bridge, is a fertile plateau 2,500 metres (8,200 feet) high, with irrigated fields on either side of the road. This is a good place to spend a night or two, marking the halfway point between Gilgit and the Khunjerab Pass. The small museum here belongs to the prince, Raja Bahadur Khan, and is full of interesting ethnic artefacts. And two of the hotels here belong to Mirzada Shah Khan, hero of the 1947 mutiny (see Gilgit history).

The rock and gravel-covered **Ghulkin Glacier** comes right down to the road about one kilometre (just over half a mile) past Gulmit. The road crosses the snout of the glacier at the very edge of the river, then climbs up on to the lateral moraine — a great, grey slag heap. About five kilometres (three miles) further on, you round a corner to find **Passu Glacier** straight ahead. It is shining white and deeply crevassed — just as you would expect a glacier to look. Above the glacier to the left is the jagged line of the Passu and Batura peaks, seven of which are over 7,500 metres (25,000 feet). On the opposite side of the river, which you can cross over a terrifying footbridge, the valley is hemmed in by a half-circle of saw-toothed summits, down the flanks of which slide grey alluvial fans.

Passu is a village of farmers and mountain guides 15 kilometres (nine miles) beyond Gulmit. This is the setting-off point for climbing expeditions up the Batura, Passu, Kuk and Lupgar groups of peaks, and for trekking trips up the Shimshal Valley and Batura Glacier. The Passu Inn, right beside the road, is the meeting place for mountaineers and guides.

The KKH passes through four more villages before reaching the immigration and customs post now at **Sost or Afiyatabad**, 35 kilometres

(22 miles) from Passu. Outgoing traffic must pass through Sost before 11 am. It is a four- or five-hour drive from here to Tashkurgan, and you must allow time for clearing Chinese customs and immigration two kilometres before Tashkurgan (moved down from Pirali). The time difference between China and Pakistan is three hours, so it will be around 7 or 8 pm Chinese time before you arrive in Tashkurgan. Incoming traffic is processed until 4 pm Pakistani time, 7 pm Chinese time (for more details, see pages 321-2).

From Sost to Tashkurgan

PTDC and NATCO run daily buses from Sost to Tashkurgan.

For the first 30 kilometres (19 miles) from Sost, the valley is narrow and barren, the cliff-face shattered into huge cubes and slabs that peel off and tumble down to the road, where they lie like forgotten building blocks belonging to giant children. The road leaves the Hunza for the Khunjerab River, and there is more of the same, with alluvial fans flowing down every gully, frequently blocking the way.

Khunjerab National Park begins 30 kilometres (19 miles) from Sost. The hills move back from the road, the valley opens out and the Khunjerab River dwindles to a tiny mountain stream with the odd tuft of grass, willow or birch along its banks.

The check-post at **Dih** consists of six lonely stone houses. The last 30 kilometres (19 miles) to the top of the pass are easier driving, as there is less mountain above and the slopes are gentler. The road follows the banks of the stream before winding up round 12 wide, well-engineered hairpin bends to the top.

The Khunjerab Pass, at 4,733 metres (15,528 feet), is reputedly the highest metalled border crossing in the world. A red sign announces 'China drive right', and a rival green sign says 'Pakistan drive left'. A monument declares that the highway was opened in 1982 and indulges in a bit of hyperbole by saying that the pass is 16,000 feet (4,875 metres). The Khunjerab is on a continental watershed. All water on the Pakistani side flows down to the Indian Ocean, while that on the Chinese side is swallowed by the Taklamakan Desert, the name of which means, 'if you go in, you don't come out'. It is 32 kilometres (20 miles) from the top of the pass to the abandoned Chinese border post at **Pirali**. The scenery is remarkably different on the two sides of the pass. The Pakistani side is a vertical world of desert gorges devoid of any sign of human life for the last 30 kilometres (19 miles), except for the road itself. The Chinese side is a wide, open and grassy high-altitude plateau with grazing herds of yaks, sheep and goats tended by Tajik herders. Children and dogs romp among round felt tents called *yurts*. The Tajiks are a smiling and friendly lot, and the women are as happy to be photographed as the men. Even the camels are altogether different animals. Pakistani drumedaries are tall, short-haired, one-humped beasts, while their Chinese cousins are squat, two-humped Bactrians with long hair down to their knees.

A valley in the Karakoram Mountains, Northern Pakistan.

Hotels, Restaurants, Shopping and Useful Addresses

All hotels in this section are listed in descending order of price .

Always try bargaining: ask for a special tourist discount or for a business or commercial rate, which should be anything from 10 to 50 percent off the quoted rates. Bargain especially hard in the cheaper hotels out of season — they will accept whatever they can get. The hoteliers will not offer you a discount unless you ask for one.

Finally, a hotel's quality depends on its manager and is therefore liable to change. Always ask around for recommendations from other businessmen and tourists. And please let me know of any great new discoveries, or changes in standard. I rely on you to keep this listing up-to-date.

KARACHI

Telephone: Pakistan international code is —92,
Karachi direct dialling code is 021

Hotels

International standard

International standard hotels (swimming pool, tennis courts and all facilities) are often fully booked, so it is wise to make advance reservations. All these hotels charge 25 percent taxes.

Sheraton, Club Road, tel 5681021, fax (92 21) 568 2875. Has the best service and food, making it worth the extra price. Good seafood, French and Italian restaurants. Famous for its all-you-can-eat brunch on Sunday for about US$10.

Pearl Continental, Dr Zia-ud-din Ahmed Road, tel 568 5021, fax (92 21) 568 1835. Has a golf course, good seafood and Chinese restaurants.

Avari Towers, Fatima Jinnah Road, tel 566 0100, fax (92 21) 568 0310. This is the tallest building in Pakistan with a good Japanese restaurant at the top, and the best hairdresser in town.

Marriott (once called Holiday Inn), 9 Abdullah Haroon Road, tel 568 0111, fax (92 21) 567 0111. Has a popular coffee shop and shopping arcade plus one of the best swimming pools.

Holiday Inn Crowne Plaza (previously known as the Taj Mahal), Shahrah-e-Faisal, tel 566 0611, fax (92 21) 568 3146.

Moderate

Beach Luxury, Maulvi Tamiz-ud-din Khan Road, tel 561 1031, fax (92 21) 561 1625. Has four restaurants including an excellent seafood barbecue in the garden on the waterfront.

Metropole, Club Road, tel 566 0145, fax (92 21) 568 4301. This is the oldest hotel in town and has a touch of colonial charm. It is centrally located, has been recently renovated and serves good food. It is the best value in this price range, though noisy.

Sarawan, Raja Ghazanfar Ali Road, Saddar Bazaar, fax (92 21) 568 0278. All facilities: good value, in the centre of town, but usually full.

Paradise, Abdullah Haroon Road, tel 568 0011, fax (92 21) 568 6829.

Sky Towers, Raja Ghazanfar Ali Road, tel 5675211.

Mehran, Shahrah-e-Faisal (Drigh Road), tel 566 0851, fax (92 21) 567 7019, large and adequate with most facilities.

Airport, on Star Gate Road, beside the airport, is run by PIA for in-transit passengers only. For overnight stops ask PIA for authorisation to stay in their hotel when you buy your ticket. You must then collect an entitlement slip from the PIA counter on arrival at Karachi — without it you will be refused at the hotel.

Less Expensive

The best value moderate and cheap hotels are in Saddar Bazaar between Abdullah Haroon Road and Daud Pota Road. Also in the narrow streets between Liaquat Road and Iraq Road. It's easy to walk from one to the other until you find a hotel to your liking. Try:

Gulf, Daud Pota Road, tel 566 1235-9, fax (92 21) 568 2388, over priced; **Sarah**, Parr Street, tel 567 7560-1, fax (92 21) 567 7540, poor value; **Jabees**, Abdullah Haroon Road, fax (92 21) 568 2354. Popular with foreigners, including Russian women on 'business' trips. **National City** tel 568 8982 and **Royal City** tel 568 0247, both on Sarmad Road; **Reliance** and **United** both on Daud Pota Road.

Inexpensive

The best of the really cheap lodgings are in and around Saddar Bazaar and between Liaquat Road and Iraq Road. They may not accept foreigners, but try:

Hotel Holiday, just off Daud Pota Road, tel 512081, fax 568 2388, is one of the best. **Al-Salatin**, tel 567 1093, **Ambassador, Chandni,** all on Daud Pota Road, are OK. Between Liaquat and Iraq Roads try **Al Sadaat** on Sarmad Road, and **Ocean**, tel 568 1922, **Al Dubai**, tel 568 5670 and **Al Haram,** all on nearby Sohrab Katrak Road.

Hostels

Amin House, 2 Maulvi Tamiz-ud-din Khan Road, tel 551491. This is the best hostel in town for men and women, with dorm beds, singles and double rooms with showers.

YMCA, Strachen Road, tel 568 6927. Temporary 30 day membership available, cheerless singles, doubles and family rooms.

YWCA, M A Jinnah Road, tel 733 2738. Women only, friendly, safe. Dinner and breakfast served.

Railway Retiring Rooms, Karachi City and Karachi Cantonment Stations. For passengers with AC and first class tickets (s/d Rs40/75).

Restaurants

Karachi now has hundreds of good restaurants, especially in the Clifton Shopping Centre and along Airport Road. Specialities are fresh fish, prawns, crab and lobster.

In the big hotels try the **Beach Luxury Sea Front Restaurant,** tel 561 1031, where delicious seafood is barbecued in the garden on the waterfront. Dinner only. The Italian food is good in the **Sheraton Hotel,** tel 568 1021, especially when there is a festival on, and the Chinese and Pakistani restaurants there are consistently good. The **Chandni**

Lounge, on the ninth floor of the Pearl Continental, tel 568 5021, gives a fine view while you eat a buffet lunch of international food and seafood. Residents also recommend the **Pearl's Thai restaurant.**

For a special treat, try the **Fujiyama Restaurant** on the rooftop of the Avari Towers, tel 566 0100, which serves good Japanese cuisine with a magnificent view — worth the expense. For good Japanese food that is cheaper, go to the **Miyako** on Zamzama Boulevard in Defence Housing Society, Phase V.

For Chinese try the **Beijing Palace** on Daud Pota Road, where the Mongolian hot pot is excellent, or go to the **ABC** on Zaibun Nisa Street, the oldest Chinese restaurant in town and still one of the best, or the **Hong Kong** on Abdullah Haroon Road. Karachi residents also recommend the **Summer Palace** and **Kim Mun,** in Clifton on Marine Drive. In P E C H S try the **Kowloon** and **Tung-Nan** on Allama Iqbal Road, and the **Nanking** and **Shanghai** on Tariq Road.

Those who like Korean food say the **Cafe Grand** near the Metropole Hotel is the best. Also near the Metropole, the **Village Garden Restaurant,** an open air barbecue, and **Shezan Ampi,** offering good chicken *karahi,* are both recommended. And the **Ponderosa** on Stadium Road, opposite the Aga Khan Hospital, has good South Indian food.

The fashionable young all meet in the **Copper Kettle**, on Zamzama Boulevard. In the same area near Bilawal House (the Bhutto residence), **Barbecue Tonite** with its choice of indoor or outdoor seating is also extremely popular for its excellent barbecue (especially quail). Another favourite is the **Pizza Hut**, on Khayaban-e-Roomi, where a large pizza for four costs about Rs 500. Cheaper pizzas are available in every shopping area.

Karachi residents also recommend the **Red Carpet** for barbecues and curries, and the **Seagull**, for barbecues and fish, both in the Seabreeze Centre in Clifton's Boat Basin, and the **Dolphin**, also in Clifton in Boat View Arcade on Khayaban-e-Saadi, for both Western and Pakistani food.

If you have a caste-iron stomach you can eat very cheaply at roadside stalls where you can satisfy your hunger for about US 50 cents. Recommended are the **stalls in Saddar Bazaar** between the Paradise Hotel and the passport office, or in the Nursery Area off Shahrah-e-Faisal (Drigh) Road, or along Tariq Road in PECHS, or further out beyond Tariq

Road in Bahadurabad. In these stalls you should try *golgupas* (small rice-flour puff balls crispy deep fried in oil, then filled with tamarind juice and pepper water), *aloo chole* (potato and chick-peas) and *dahi barha* (yoghurt and lentil dumplings). *Bun kebabs* (Pakistani hamburgers) are also good, as are the fruit juices, but be sure to have them squeezed in front of you so you can check they are not diluted.

Karachi is not complete without a visit to a huge family restaurant called **Bundu Khan** on M M Jinnah (Bundar) Road, near the Jinnah mausoleum — barbecue is the speciality here.

Entertainment

There is very little public entertainment for the foreign tourist anywhere in Pakistan. Karachi is unusual in that there is a **Disco** in the basement of **Shakey's Pizza** behind the Clifton Centre, diagonally opposite Agha's Supermarket across the roundabout. There are also **Pool rooms** all over the city that provide fun for Karachi's young men. The best you can offer your children are camel rides on the beach, or three funfairs with elderly equipment: **Funland** in Clifton, **City 2000** in the Nursery Area and **Sindbad** on Tariq Road.

Shopping

Good buys in Karachi are new Pakistani carpets and old tribal rugs (from Balochistan, Afghanistan and Iran), leather, furs, jewellery (antique and modern), cotton bedspreads, antique and modern brass and copper, and all sorts of other handicrafts. Most carpet shops are on Abdullah Haroon Road. Keep to the Sheraton arcade, hotel lobbies and shopping plazas for modern jewellery, furs and some leather, though the best leather handbags and wallets, in excellent modern designs are at **Jafferjee's** on Khayaban-e-Iqbal near Agha's supermarket. The best antique jewellery is in **Sarafa Bazaar**, north of Boulton Market. For the rest, try the **Saddar Bazaar** and especially **Zainab Market**. Two recommended handicraft shops in Zainab are Village Handicrafts and Crown Handicrafts. Zainab Market also sells very good and extremely cheap cotton shirts, ready-made *shalwar-kameez* and general export rejects.

Solo in the Shaheen Centre on Main Clifton Road is an excellent gift shop. **Cotton & Cotton**, tel 586 6978, behind the Clifton Centre, specialises in men's clothing, 100 percent cotton shirts, trousers, ties, suits and pyjamas.

For more expensive ladies' fashions, ask some fashionably dressed lady, or the public relations officer at the top hotels for the addresses of couturier designers, or try **Meheen** in Clifton near Agha supermarket. In the same arcade, **Generation** and **Unbeatable** sell cheaper off-the-peg ladies *shalwar-kameez*, while nearby **Selections** sells good furnishing fabrics that are cheap by Western standards. For hand-block printing on both cotton and silk, **Perahan**, behind Paradise Stores, Clifton, is the best. They also sell some ready-made clothes. **Florence** (was Cleo), a French designer, offers well-tailored ladies fashions suitable for wearing in both Pakistan and the West for around US$100 an outfit.

Useful Addresses

Ring directory enquiries, 117, if any of the following numbers have changed. They speak English and run a very efficient service.

Pakistan Tourism Development Corporation (PTDC) Karachi headquarters is at Metropole Hotel, Club Road.

For booking PTDC motels in Sindh, tel 567 8948, 567 8958.

PTDC Tourist Information Centre is half a block west of the Metropole on Club Road at Shafi Chambers beside KLM, tel 568 1293, 920 2971. Open 8 am to 6 pm, Monday to Friday. There is another PTDC at the **International Arrivals Lounge**, Karachi Airport.

Sindh Tourism Development Corporation, 114-115, C Block, Sea Breeze Plaza, Shahrah-e-Faisal, tel 778 2326, 778 2695, 778 2706, 778 8530. Open 9.30 am to 5 pm. Here you can book the STDC motels at Keenjar Lake, Haleji Lake, Sehwan Sharif, Larkana and Sukkur.

Sindh Wildlife Management Board, Strachen Road, tel 491 5610, for information on Kirthar National Park and other game and bird watching parks in Sindh.

Department of Archaeology, Karachi, tel 430638, 431387.

Post & Telecommunications

General Post Office (GPO) is on II Chundrigar Road near the City Railway Station.

Saddar Post Office is opposite St Andrew's Church.

Public Call Offices for overseas calls and faxes are in the Saddar area.

Banks

American Express, Shaheen Complex, Dr Ziauddin Ahmad Road, tel 263 0260 is always very crowded, open 9 am to 4 pm.

Bank of America, Citibank and the head office of **Habib Bank,** all on II Chundrigar Road, are open 9 am to 1 pm, Monday to Thursday, 9 am to noon, Friday and Saturday.

Passport Office, Shahrah-e-Iraq, Saddar Bazaar, tel 568 0360, 568 1135, and also 22 Block B Commercial Area, North Nazimabad, opposite the telephone exchange, tel 664 8571. Open for visa extension 9 am to 12 pm only.

Foreigners' Registration Office, tel 233 3737, is in the main **Police Station** on II Chundrigar Road.

Foreign Representatives

British Deputy High Commission, York Place, Runnymede Lane, Clifton, tel 587 2431.

USA Consulate, 8 Abdullah Haroon Road, tel 568 5170.

Cultural Centres

British Council, 20 Bleak House Road, tel 512036.

Pak-American Cultural Centre, 11 Fatima Jinnah Road, tel 513836.

Alliance Française, Block 8, Kehkashan, Clifton, tel 587 4302.

Goethe Institute, 256 Sarwar Shahid Road, tel 568 4811.

Hospital

Aga Khan Hospital, Stadium Road, tel 493 0051.

(following spread) Bathers in the tank at a Hindu temple at Ketas, in the Salt Range

Tour Agents

Bukhari Travel & Tourism Services, Karachi Sheraton Hotel, Club Road, tel 568 4205, 568 6962, 568 1433, fax (92 21) 568 2366, 568 4206.

Indus Guides, 202 C UNI Tower, II Chundrigar Road, tel 240 0265, fax (92 21) 241 0703, e-mail: indus@brain.net.pk.

Khamisani Sons, M A Jinnah Road, tel 242 7324, 242 5803, fax (92 21) 242 8006.

Rakaposhi Tours, Defence Housing Authority, 586 4848, 586 4949, fax (92 21) 587 0652, e-mail: rti@khi.fascom.com.

Roomi Travels, Hotel Mideast, Dr Daud Pota Road, tel 567 2821

Sitara Travels, 105 Trade Tower, 1st floor, Abdullah Haroon Road, tel 568 3887, 568 4024, fax (92 21) 568 9380, e-mail: sitaratr@khi.compol.com.

Travel Express, Mereweather Road, tel 511127, fax 514678.

Travel Walji's, 74-F, Block No 6, P E C H S, tel 454 0672, (fax 92 21) 454 0212, e-mail: travelw@paknet3.ptc.pk.

Zeb Travels, Hasrat Mohani Road, tel 241 1204, fax (92 21) 242 5181, e-mail: zeb@cyber.net.pk.

Transport

Air

Karachi's airport is 12 km east of the city centre and has two terminals, international and domestic. Most international airlines land in Karachi. About 50 airlines have offices in Karachi.

PIA and three private domestic airlines, Aero Asia, Shaheen and Bhoja, which are about 10% cheaper than PIA, run daily flights to the main cities in Pakistan. Night flights are cheaper still.

PIA, Strachen Road, tel 457 2011, fax (92 21) 457 0419. To reconfirm your flight call 111-786-786. PIA runs 70 flights a week to Lahore and Islamabad.

Aero Asia for domestic flights, opposite Holiday Inn on Shahrah-e-Faisal, tel 778 2851.

Shaheen Airlines, Avari Plaza, tel 513521.

Bhoja Air, tel 568 2337.

Train

Karachi has two main railway stations, Karachi City and Karachi Cantonment. The main lines run north to Sukkur, Multan, Lahore, Islamabad/Rawalpindi and Peshawar, with a branch line to Quetta. For sleepers and first class you need to book several weeks in advance at the City Station booking office.

Bus

There are government buses and many private bus companies, some air conditioned, that run services all over Pakistan. Ask at a good travel agent for up to date information and advice.

Taxi

Yellow cabs are everywhere and usually have meters that work. If the meter is not working, agree on the fare beforehand. Some taxi drivers are unwilling to pick up single women.

Hire cars

Most large hotels, travel agents and Avis offer cars with drivers for hire.

LAHORE

Telephone: direct dialling code for Lahore is 042

Hotels

International Standard

Lahore's better hotels are often fully booked, so it is wise to make advance reservations. These hotels charge 17.5% taxes.

Pearl Continental, Shahrah-e-Quaid-e-Azam (The Mall), tel 636 0210 fax (92 42) 636 2760, e-mail: pclhe@hotel.lhe.erum.com.pk. Recently opened new Atrium wing. All facilities and tennis courts.

Avari, Shahrah-e-Quaid-e-Azam (The Mall), tel 636 5366, fax (92 42) 636 2760. Good coffee shop, restaurant, swimming pool, gym and massage.

Holiday Inn, 25 Egerton Road, tel 631 0077, fax (92 42) 631 4515, e-mail: holiday@inn.brain.net.pk, is a recent addition with a rooftop barbecue.

Ambassador, 7 Davis Road, tel 631 6821, fax (92 42) 630 1868. Newly renovated.

Moderate

Faletti's, Egerton Road (behind the Avari), tel 636 3946, fax (92 42) 636 4819. This once-gracious old building with arcades and a garden, at the centre of town, is now run-down, but still my favourite hotel. It has more atmosphere and larger rooms than the big hotels. It is currently for sale.

Sun Fort, Liberty Market, Gulberg III, tel 576 3810-9, fax 575 4277. Recommended.

Regency Inn, 641 B Abid Majid Road, tel 666 4514-8, fax (92 42) 666 2239. A tastefully decorated 32-room hotel, good value, 500 metres outside the airport gate. Nearby **Serenity**, 50 B Nagi Road, tel 666 1238, 666 6584, fax (92 42) 666 6585, is poorer value.

Further into town on the canal, two small, clean and comfortable guesthouses, **Canal View Motel**, tel 575 9736, 571 0796, and **Executive Inn**, which has a small, quiet garden, tel 875633, 877522, fax 355431, are clean and friendly. In the same area, the small **Safari Motel**, on Anand Road, behind the old Services International building, tel 875381, 871857, is good value and very quiet though it has nightmarish decor.

Right in the centre, the **Indus**, 56 The Mall, tel 630 2856-8, is an old hotel offering great value — large rooms with bathtubs and friendly service. Extra beds available. The **Amer**, 46 Lower Mall, tel 711 5015–9, 722 9971–8, fax (92 42) 711 5013, is a large hotel with spacious hall and big, clean rooms in its new extension. The poky old rooms are cheaper.

Jello Tourist Village, 20 kilometres (12 miles) east from central Lahore, tel 352699, run by the Tourist Development Corporation of Punjab (TDCP), offers 16 double rooms, and allows camping. The park has a small zoo and **Suzo Park**, next door, offers a water playground with slides. Both are very crowded on Sundays.

Less expensive

The moderately cheap hotels near the city railway station and main bus station are very noisy and are not really safe.

The **Shan**, 46 McLeod Road, tel 723 8654-6, fax (92 42) 722 3952, is recommended, and the nearby **Orient**, 74 McLeod Road, tel 722 3906–8, has large rooms set around a courtyard where you can park. The rooms, with or without AC, are reached via a metal balcony so all doors can be supervised by the reception. Nearer Lakshmi Chowk, on Abbot Road the new **National**, tel 636 3011–3, fax (92 42) 636 3152, offers large clean rooms with TV, telephone, central AC and bathtubs. The hotel food is good but spicy, or you can eat outside cheaply at the Abbott Road food stalls. The nearby **Bakhtawar**, tel 631 6761, and cheaper **United** are also recommended.

The six-storey **Shah Taj**, on Nicholson Road, tel 636 7451, 627 9175, fax (92 42) 627 9174, has some deluxe rooms with central AC, and bathtubs.

The **Parkway**, in the same area, tel 636 5908–12, fax (92 42) 636 6029, which is built round a central courtyard, has a choice of rooms with or without AC. A better deal, slightly further from the station on McLeod Road, is the **Uganda**, tel 636 4393–4, offering cleaner rooms with attached bath, with or without AC.

The **Clifton** at Australia Chowk, tel 636 6740-3, has rooms set around a courtyard, some with AC and bath and is the best of the cheaper hotels. The nearby **Asia**, beside the Flying Coach office, tel 636 6449-50-52, has rooms with bath and AC. The cheapest I checked out was the **Shabistan**, tel 636 6193, 630 6423, which offered non-AC rooms.

Inexpensive

The really cheap hotels in Lahore, particularly those near the railway station, on Brandreth Road and along McLeod Road, are definitely not safe. Problems range from stolen travellers' cheques to planted drugs and blackmail. Cheap hotels that send touts to the bus and railway stations are to be avoided.

However, I can recommend:

Youth Hostel, 110–B/3 Firdous Market, Gulberg III, near Hussain Chowk, tel 878201. Temporary membership available. Always crowded with swimming pool (dry when I visited). Far from the centre, but bus 43 from the railway station and Mall takes you to the door. Camping allowed.

YMCA Hostel, near the GPO on the opposite side of The Mall, tel 735 4433. A run-down cement barracks full of long-term residents.

YWCA Hostel, Fatima Jinnah (Queen) Road, tel 630 4707. Has clean, four-bed and two-bed rooms, usually full. Lunch and dinner served. Camping is allowed in the shady garden. You can park in the compound for a small fee. It is five minutes walk from The Mall. Foreign men, accompanied by families, are allowed to stay.

Railway Retiring Rooms, Lahore City Station. For passengers with first class tickets.

Saint Hilda's Hostel, in the old deaconess' house in the grounds of the Anglican (Church of Pakistan) Cathedral of the Resurrection on The Mall, tel 732 5452. Built in the 1890s and set in a gracious garden, Saint Hilda's accepts guests with church or missionary connections. Morning prayers are held in the private chapel.

Restaurants

Restaurant food in Lahore is the most varied and imaginative in Pakistan, ranging from traditional Mughlai cuisine, through Continental to Chinese. Many of the best restaurants are in Gulberg, but quality, fashion and even the names of the restaurants fluctuate and change. In 1999 the following were popular:

Gulberg Restaurants

The Village, a Salt 'n Pepper enterprise on M M Alam Road, between Hussain Chowk and Mini Market, tel 875536, 874128, is laid out like a village: chefs in stalls prepare different local specialities, you walk around, watch the cooking and choose. It has wonderful atmosphere, is interesting and original, and costs about US$8-10 for all you can eat.

Nearby, three restaurants in Gulberg III, offer good Continental and Pakistani meals for US$6-8; **Menage**, tel 870411, 870442, has excellent service, the best non-alcoholic fruit cocktails in Pakistan, a pleasant atmosphere and some Thai dishes; **Tabaq**, tel 872136, 878240, whose speciality is *chergha* (steam-roasted chicken), and **Gulberg Kabana**, on Main Boulevard, tel 571 1737. Perhaps best of all in this area is **Kababeesh**, on Main Boulevard, tel 676018, because you can eat outside, in summer, in its large garden.

In the same area there are a number of Chinese restaurants, all pretty similar in quality, presentation and choice, and cheaper than the above; **Hsin Kuang**, tel 875655–6, which has an underground car park, and **Sichuan**, tel 879146, 571 1707, both in Gulberg II; **Xinhua**, tel 877994–5, **Tai Wah**, tel 873915, 878586, and **Hong Kong**, tel 870456, 874669, all in Gulberg III; and **Shanghai**, 62 Main Gulberg, tel 571 2683.

Still in Gulberg are various fast food outlets. The **Copper Kettle** on Main Boulevard, is where Lahore's fashionable young eat hamburgers, grilled sandwiches, cakes and ice cream with coffee. At **Salt 'n Pepper**, tel 870594, 874248, and **Burger Eleven**, tel 874982, both in Liberty Market; **MacBurger**, tel 875566, in Gulberg III, and **Gino** at Hafiz Centre, you can get kebabs, burgers, fried chicken, toasted chicken sandwiches and chips for about US$2 each.

There is even cheaper, though more risky eating, in **Gulberg's Mini Market** where burgers and chicken burgers from the **street stalls** cost less than US$1.

Polka Parlour is a popular, clean ice cream parlour on Main Boulevard, Gulberg, as is **Yummy** in Liberty Market, both safe places to eat charging around US$1.50–2.50 a serving.

Restaurants on The Mall
(Shahrah-e-Quaid-e-Azam)

In Central Lahore you can eat Continental and Pakistani food in the **Avari Hotel's** three restaurants, where the summer outside buffet is good value. **Pearl Continental** also cooks good barbecue dinners in the garden in summer, and **Saloos** in WAPDA House at Charing Cross, tel 636 7137, 636 7149, specialises in steaks (not Tuesday or Wednesday which are meatless days) and their *haleem* (boiled and ground lamb patties) is especially recommended, though service there is slow. Expect to pay about US$6–8 for each of these. Chinese food for about US$3.75 is available at **Kim Mun** on The Mall, and at **Shezan**, which also serves good Pakistani and Continental food. **Cathay**, 60 The Mall, opposite American Express, tel 302393, serves cheaper, pretty awful Chinese food. **Caspian**, 73 The Mall, tel 636 3588, 636 3420, has good Continental food, pizzas and coffee. **Gogo**, near the American Express office, sells take-away sandwiches, and the **Pak Tea House**, next to the YMCA, is worth visiting to spot Lahore's best-known poets and writers. Apparently the waiters ignore all but the famous.

Restaurants in Fortress Stadium

Shezen and **Salt 'n Pepper** also run popular branches at Fortress Stadium, and **Kings & Queens**, Peshawar Block, Fortress Stadium is popular for pizzas.

Cheaper Eating

Be sure to eat only food you have seen freshly cooked and served on clean, dry, uncracked plates. Never take anything with ice or water, and beware of ice cream and dairy products. Try:

Takatak (grilled chopped liver), so named from the chopping noise the cook makes as he cuts it up, and also the best grilled kebabs and chicken,

are the favourites at the **stalls** on **Abbott Road** where six kebabs cost about US$0.50. Even better value are the Afghani grilled kebabs and *tikkas* in **Block D, Model Town**.

In the **Mozang area**, at Qartaba Chowk try the *karahi gosht* (stir fried meat or chicken with tomatoes, vegetables and spices) at **Bhatti Tikka** restaurant; or stuff yourself with Bashir's fried fish at his **Dar-ul-Mahi** restaurant. You order these dishes by weight — 250 grams of fish or meat with *naan* and vegetables costs about US$1. The nearby **Benazir Kulfi** shop sells the best *kulfi* (ice cream hand-chilled in salt and mixed with vermicelli, milk and nuts).

Around the old city you can sample various local favourites: good kebabs are sold just inside Mochi Gate in the Lal Khoi (red well) area and you can finish off your meal there with *barfi* (a sort of fudge made by condensing milk) and *pateesa* (sweet yellow gram-flour cakes). The courageous who like pig's trotters might enjoy the Pakistani equivalent, *paae* and *sri* — sheep feet cooked to a sticky glue. The best are in Shahi Mohalla in the red-light area at **Fazal Din 'Phajja'**. Just inside Lahori gate the speciality is *nihari* (beef curry) which you eat with *naan* and salad for about US$1 a helping: the best is at **Pani Wala Talab**. You can finish your meal inside Lohari Gate with *kulfi* from

another branch of the **Benazir Kulfi** shop there. **Waris's Nihari Restaurant** in Paisa Akbar near Oriental College, is Lahore's most famous *nihari* restaurant and is always packed.

Among the other favourites you can buy from wheeled **street barrows** that move around, are grilled corn-on-the-cob for about Rs5 a cob, and fruit chaat, a mixture of fruit and yoghurt (it is spicy, not sweet), or *dahi bhalley* (gram-flour dumplings and yoghurt), or *daal chawal* (rice and lentils).

To finish your day in true Lahori style, buy a *paan* (stuffed betel leaf) from Mola Bakhsh *paan* shop opposite Saint Anthony's Church in Lawrence Road. The sweet ones are the best.

Shopping

Good buys in Lahore are new Pakistani carpets, *durries* (flat-weave cotton rugs that are cheap and cheerful), antique brass, silk and cotton cloth and blockprinted or embroidered table linen.

Lahore is celebrated for its **carpet-weaving**. New handmade carpets are for sale in the shops around Davis Road, Nicholson Road, along The Mall and in the hotel lobbies. Some antique Afghan carpets are also for sale. Carpet-weaving started on a large scale here after 1947, when Muslim carpet-weavers from old, established centres in Amritsar and Shahjahanpur moved over the border from India. There are now many large carpet factories using the finest wool and making carpets to order in any design or colour.

Ask at one of the hotel shops if you would like to see inside a carpet studio. It is quite an experience. The looms are in long rows inside a vast, shaded courtyard, each loom with its team of boys and a master. The masters sing out the colours and the eldest boys repeat them. Sometimes there are 150 masters and 500 boys at work at the same time, all concentrating furiously. When the carpet is cut down, it is sheared and then washed; up to eight men work rhythmically together scrubbing the carpet with stiff fibre brushes. Sometimes the carpet is treated chemically to tone down the bright colours, although this shortens its life considerably. Pakistani carpets are durable and attractive, and usually good value.

Old **brass** and **copper** ware is available around Charing Cross and from Faletti's Hotel arcade, where Aftab at **Eastern Carpets and Curios** displays the cards of various world celebrities. Ask him to take you to his showrooms in nearby Tegor Park — a real Aladdin's cave stuffed with treasures. Some good

At Kallar Kahar in the Salt Range

buys can be found in the brass bazaar in the old city, where prices are usually cheaper; most recommended is the tiny, two-floored shop called **Kashmiri Museum**. Here, though, the brass is often unpolished or still coated in tin, so it is difficult to see what you are getting. (Brass used for cooking must be coated or it will poison the food.)

Other handicrafts are in the shops along **The Mall** near **Charing Cross**. Especially recommended is the **Technical Services Association**, 65 The Mall, which sells shadow-work embroidery at reasonable prices. **Ichra Bazaar**, on Firozpur Road, has many good buys, including silk, cotton and printed cloth of all sorts, including ready–made clothing, **Shadman Bazaar** is also recommended for Chinese silk. The **Calico Printing** shop, near Firozpur Road, sells some particularly interesting hand-blockprinted cloth, bedspreads and tablecloths.

Anarkali Bazaar is a treasure-trove, selling virtually everything from handicrafts to transistor radios, tin saucepans to refrigerators. It is a maze of lanes and alleys stretching northwards from the Central Museum end of The Mall to the corner of the old city near Lahori Gate. Shopping is more fun here than in the shops along The Mall, and prices are lower. Bargain hard. This is a good place to look for costume jewellery, and cheap cotton clothes, especially in **Bano Bazaar**, as Anarkali's ladies-only bazaar is called.

For more up-market ladies ready–made fashions with stylish *shalwar-kameez* try **Art & Style** and the other nearby shops in **Liberty Market** and around **Fortress Stadium**.

Books

The best **bookshops** are all on The Mall: **Lion Art Press**, beside American Express, has the best selection of guidebooks, maps (not many) and coffee-table books on Pakistan. Enthusiasts may enjoy *Lahore, its History, Architectural Remains and Antiquities* (1892) by Sayed Muhammad Latif, photocopied by Lion Art Press in 1994, a book filled with information on Lahore's history and tombs.

Ferozson's, opposite across The Mall, and **Vanguard**, also on The Mall, are larger shops with more academic books, perhaps less useful to the casual tourist. The bookshops in the **Avari** and **Pearl Continental** hotels and **PTDC** in Faletti's also sell books on Pakistan. Avari is the best place for foreign newspapers and magazines.

Food

Supermarket, H Karim Bukhsh & Sons, 65 The Mall, has a selection of imported packaged goods and household essentials. Panorama, on The Mall, sells a complete range of goods.

Useful Addresses

PTDC Tourist Information Centre, Faletti's Hotel, Egerton Road, tel 630 6528, 636 3946–55. Open 8 am to 1 pm and 2 to 6 pm Monday to Saturday, closed 12 to 2 pm Friday, generally a most helpful, well-run office.

TDCP Tourist Development Corporation of Punjab, Information Centre, 4 A Lawrence Road, tel 636 0553, 636 9687, fax 636 9686. For Lahore city tours, good desert tours in winter and mountain tours in summer, and inter-city air-conditioned buses. Also book all TDCP motels here. There is a second TDCP information centre inside Delhi Gate in the Old City.

TDCP Headquarters, 74 Shadman-11, tel 757 6826-8, fax 758 9097.

Passport Office, 9 Fane Road, tel 732 5459. They will probably send you to Islamabad.

Foreigners' Registration is near the Lower Mall at 63 Kutcheri Road.

Director of Archaeology, Lahore Fort, tel 766 2645, 766 2657, fax (92 42) 766 5626.

Post & Telecommunications

The **GPO** (general post office) is on the Mall west of the High Court.

The **Central Telephone and Telegraph Office** is almost opposite at the beginning of McLeod Road.

Banks

American Express is on The Mall in Rafi Mansion near Charing Cross, open 9 am to 4 pm, Monday to Friday, 9 am to 1 pm Saturday, closed lunchtime and Sundays.

National Bank of Pakistan, Regal Chowk, The Mall, also changes travellers' cheques, other banks are suspicious of cheques as there is so much forgery and theft of cheques in Lahore. Be prepared to show your original travellers' cheques purchase receipt when changing cheques.

Citibank, Charing Cross is open during the lunch hour.

Bank of America, 2nd floor, LDA Plaza, Egerton Road, gives cash on Visa cards in the mornings only.

Money Changers are mostly located in Cooper Road near the Holiday Inn. Big hotels will also change money for guests.

Hospitals

Shaikh Zaid Hospital, tel 586 5731-6, on Canal Road, near the new campus of Punjab University.

Shaukat Khanum Memorial Hospital and Cancer Research Centre, Imran Khan's hospital is excellent.

Foreign Representatives

American Consulate, tel 636 5530, 50 Empress Road (Shahrah-e-Bin Badees).

Honorary British Consul Fakir Syed Aijazuddin, Syed Babar Ali Foundation Building, 308 Upper Mall, tel 575 3414-6.

Cultural Centres

Al-Hambra Arts Centre, beside the Avari Hotel on The Mall, is the principal cultural centre in Lahore with three theatres where music, drama and other shows are staged.

British Council, 65 Mozang Road, tel 636 2497-8, opens its excellent library to all, 9.30 am to 6.30 pm, Monday to Saturday.

American Center, tel 636 7591 is on Fatima Jinnah Road.

Goethe Institute is at 92 E–1 Gulberg III.

Alliance Française is at 20 E-2, Gulberg III.

Jinnah Library (or Quaid-e-Azam Library) in Jinnah Gardens (or Bagh-e-Jinnah), on the Mall (or Shahrah-e-Quaid-e-Azam) the biggest library in Pakistan, open 8 am to 8 pm. The imposing library building is the combined Lawrence and Montgomery halls built in 1862 and 1866 to commemorate the first two British governors of Punjab.

Churches

Cathedral Church of the Resurrection (Church of Pakistan — similar to Anglican) is on The Mall, Bishop's office: tel 723 3560, 724 3525, Vicar: 723 3561, Diocesan office: 722 6394, has English services on Sundays at 5.30 pm in winter and 6.30 pm in summer and at 8.15 am on first and third Sundays. Holy Communion on second and fourth Sundays.

The **Catholic (Sacred Heart) Cathedral** is in Lawrence Road, just off The Mall (see map on page 268).

St Andrews (Church of Pakistan) on Empress Road has services at the same times as the cathedral, but not at 8.15 am, tel office 636 6017, Vicar tel 575 8195.

There are some Irish priests at **St Columbans**, 194 A New Muslim Town.

Travel and Tour Agents

Indus Guides, 108A, C II, Gulberg III, tel 571 2159, fax (92 42) 571 2529, 627 8949, e-mail: indus@brain.net.pk, web site: www.brain.net.pk/~ indus/ welcome.htm. Run excellent jeep safaris to the deserts of Sindh and Balochistan. Also have offices in Karachi, Gilgit and Tashkent.

Muhammadi, 1 Cantonment Board Plaza, Tufail Road, tel 666 9159, fax (92 42) 572 6636.

Al Hayat, 19A Davis Road, tel 630 2909, fax (92 42) 541 5759.

Karavan, F26 Commercial, Phase I, LCCHS, tel 572 9380, fax (92 42) 572 9390.

Adventure 'n Culture, S-3 Nawab Building, 48 Shadwan Market, tel & fax (92 42) 757 9191.

Walji's Travel, 23 Empress Road (Shahrah-e-Bin Badees), tel 636 7845. The biggest travel company, very reliable.

Transport

Air

PIA Office in Transport House, Egerton Road, opposite Faletti's Hotel, tel 627 0599, 636 3685 (flight enquiries), 630 6411-7 (reservations). To reconfirm your flight call 111-786-786. Flights to all major cities in Pakistan, also direct to India, Far East, Middle East, Europe and USA.

Aero Asia, Shimla Tower, 5 Davis Road, tel 636 0994, 636 0741, runs daily flights to Karachi and Islamabad, cheaper than PIA.

Bhoja Air also runs daily flights to Karachi.

Air Canada, Air France, British Airways, Cathay Pacific, Emirate Airlines, Gulf Air, Indian Airlines, KLM, Lufthansa, Northwest Orient, Philippine Airlines, Singapore Airlines, Saudia Airlines, Swissair, Thai Airways and **Turkish Airlines** all have offices in Lahore: see the telephone directory or dial 117, directory enquiries for their addresses and telephone numbers.

Train

Railway reservations tel 630 3798 is at Lahore City Station. Pakistan Railways headquarters building (for a student or tourist discount) is on Empress Road (Shahrah-e-Bin Badees). For a sleeper, reserve weeks in advance.

Bus

New Khan Road Runners, depart from Asia Hotel on Brandreth Road, and from Shobra Hotel, Nicholson Road, tel 636 3755, 636 7330. Buses every 30 minutes to Rawalpindi, several buses daily to Karachi and other major cities.

Skyways buses tel 636 6260, 500 metres south of the railway station, run buses to all major cities.

Intercity buses, tel 636 7215, departs from Faletti's Hotel to Islamabad and Multan.

TDCP, tel 636 0553 (see above under TDCP Information Centre).

Carhire

Driving in Pakistan is difficult. It is easier to rent a car with driver. Apply to any of the travel and tour agents listed listed above, or try:

Din Tours beside Faletti's Hotel, tel 631 1130.

Voyager 62 A Block FCC, Gulberg IV, tel 575 7756-7.

Avis (self drive) at Walji's Travel and at the Avari Hotel.

ISLAMABAD

Telephone: direct dialling code for Islamabad is 051

Hotels

International Standard

Marriott (old name Holiday Inn), Aga Khan Road, F - 5/1, tel 826121, fax (92 51) 820648, 822174. International standard hotel

Holiday Inn (old name Islamabad Hotel), Municipal Road, G - 6/2, tel 827311, fax (92 51) 273273. Acceptable standard with all the usual facilities.

Best Western, 6 Islamabad Club Road, tel 921 8413, fax (92 51) 218421. Near Rawal Lake on the edge of Shakarparian Park between Islamabad and Rawalpindi.

Sheraton, tel 9225001 and **Avari**, tel 273172-4 have both opened new hotels.

Moderate

The **Civic** in the Blue Area, tel 213740–4, fax (92 51) 214450, has all facilities and being central is good value in this price range.
The **President**, tel 819206, 220995, nearby on Nazimuddin Road, behind the American Express, is similar quality. The **Royal**, further west on Jinnah Avenue, tel 223252–7, fax (92 51) 223258, gives discounts and is handy for the good restaurants nearby. The **Adventure Inn**, on Garden Avenue, in the heart of Shakarparian Park, tel 272536–7, fax (92 51) 212540, is remote unless you have your own transport, but is ideal for trekking and climbing groups as they allow camping on their lawn and have a locked store where you can leave your gear.

In a lower category the **Margala** on Kashmir Highway, in Shakarparian Park near the sports complex, tel 813345–9, fax (92 51) 274054, is very quiet but run–down and remote.

The **Shawnze** in Super Market, F–6, tel 211711–4, fax (92 51) 823519, is more central. The **Ambassador** in Aabpara Market, tel 824011–4, fax (92 51) 821320, is fair value with central AC and big bathtubs. The **Dreamland Motel**, tel 829072, fax (92 51) 829077, central AC, and

Lake View Motel, tel 821386, fax (92 51) 822394, (no view of the lake) are both on Club Road, in Shakarparian Park near Rawal Dam, halfway between Islamabad and Rawalpindi, on a bus line. They are quiet and make a good choice for bird-watchers, walkers and horse riders, but are rather remote.

Blue Sky, tel 275546, **Al Hujurat**, tel 828347 and **Simar**, tel 811134 are all good value, cheaper hotels in Satara Market, G-7.

Host Inn, tel 262645, 253544, fax 262645, and **Eden**, tel 260088–90, are both scruffy hotels on Kaghan Road near Ayub Super market in F-8.

Capital Inn in G–8 Markaz, tel 264680–3, fax 260980, is further out and **Dream Land** at Peshawar More, G–9/4, tel 858102, 252916, fax (92 51) 252915, is too remote to be convenient unless you have your own transport. Also remote, on the edge of Shakarparian Park is **Pak Tures Motel**, tel 824503, 813116.

Guesthouses

There are about 40 guesthouses scattered throughout Islamabad offering four to 12 rooms, usually with AC. On the whole they are good value and comfortable. Here are some suggested addresses in F–6, F–7 and F–8. They are often full, so it is a good idea to book in advance. Otherwise ask PTDC or your taxi driver for suggestions or just drive around looking for guesthouse signs.

Pearl House, 22 A College Road, north side of Jinnah Super Market, F–7/2, tel 822108, 278164, fax (92 51) 278165. Convenient, clean and good value.

Jacaranda, 17 College Road, north side of Jinnah Super Market F-7/2, tel & fax (92 51) 223183-4, 224484. Smart and up-market, recommended.

Lodgings, 41 A College Road, F–7/2, tel 827179, fax (92 51) 826146.

Decent Accommodators, 2, Street 15, F–7/2, tel 815275, 815468, fax (92 51) 815275.

Accommodators Two, 9, Street 36, F–7/1, tel 821428, fax (92 51) 817320. Clean with helpful management.

Best Accommodators, 6, Street 54, F–7/4, tel 212860, 821428, fax (92 51) 811358.

VIP Accommodators, House 18, Street 30, F-6/1, tel 823572, 815146, fax (92 51) 824151.

The nearby **Luxury Inn**, 2, Street 30, 7th Ave, F-6/1, tel 813218, 821204, fax (92 51) 823430, also offers family rooms and is smart, clean and recommended. Just round the corner in 28th Street, F-6/1 are three more side by side, **The House**, tel 278236, fax (9251) 214924; **The Home**, tel 823446, 816834, and **The Host**, tel 816834, 823446.

Decent Lodge, 261 A, Street 22, E–7, tel 825536, 823394, fax (92 51) 810411.

Shelton House, 11 Kaghan (School) Road, F–8/3, tel 856956, 856248.

Host, Block 3 A Market F–8, tel 823446, fax (92 51) 851902.

Camping ground

Situated in the woods on the edge of Shakarparian Park, an easy walk from Aabpara Market. There is a modest daily charge and parking fee for cars and wagons. For an extra charge you can rent a platform fitted with electricity supply. Kitchen, washroom and toilet facilities are provided. The camp is quiet and pleasant, good value in the dry season and a friendly meeting place, but beware of theft, carry all your valuables to the washroom with you, and leave your bag in the locked room if you go to town.

Youth Hostel The new youth hostel on Garden Road, G–6/4, near Aabpara, tel 826899, is for members (temporary membership available). It has four-bed rooms with cold shower and is full of Pakistani students in summer. Maximum stay three days. (Agha Afzal Hussain runs the head office in Islamabad, tel office 920 4798, home 920 4070.)

Restaurants

The best restaurants are mostly clustered in Jinnah Super Market and in the Blue Area, with a few notable outliers. But fashions and chefs change with the wind, so it is best to ask around for the current favourites.

In Super Market F-6

Romano Italian Restaurant, 9 Aga Khan Road, F-6/3, tel 822637 (near the Marriott Hotel) is run by Italians, is justifiably popular and is the smartest restaurant in town.

Luna Caprese, 34 School Road, F-6/3, tel 276603, is also recommended.

In Jinnah Super Market

Pappasalli's, tel 818287, on the north side of Jinnah,is a popular place in which to be seen. Small and intimate, it offers the best pizzas in town and a reasonable selection of the usual Italian favourites. Nearby, two Chinese restaurants, **Kim Mun**, tel 822331, and **Shifang**, tel 812903, are recommended, and high marks are given to **Kabul**, tel 273388, an Afghan restaurant a little further west on the same street which sells good cheap food. The fast food joints, **Mr**

Burger, **Mr Chips** and **Black Beard**, are popular with the young. In nearby Round Market in the centre of F–7/3, the Chinese **Xinhua**, tel 9217205, and its cheaper neighbour **Golden Dragon**, tel 827333, are both recommended. In Rana Market, in the centre of F–7/2, **China Town**, tel 810673, 810681, is the best Chinese restaurant, value for money, and serves excellent Szechuan food and Mongolian hotpot.

In the Blue Area

Near the Civic Hotel are three recommended restaurants, Chinese, Pakistani and Iranian: **Mei Hua**, tel 829898, **Usmania**, tel 811345, and **Omar Khayam**, tel 812847. Further west, opposite the huge Saudi Pak Tower, is a row of eight restaurants side by side, including **Pizzeria**, which also serves hamburgers, **Bolan** offering typical dishes from Balochistan — whole chickens and legs of lamb are roasted on a spit outside, **Jahangir**, barbecued kebabs on the street outside and other typical Pakistani dishes for about Rs70 (US$1.50) a meal, **McRonalds Burger King** and **Bar-B-Q** with the usual fast-food fare. **Athena** in the next block serves Greek food.

Zeno and **Sufi** in Melody Market are good for barbecues but for cheaper eating try the eastern side of **Melody Market**, near the British Council Library, where kebabs and chicken are grilled on the street.

And for a special treat go to the Chinese **Dynasty** restaurant or the Italian **Il Capriccio** both in the Marriott Hotel.

Out of Town

Daman-i-Koh, now run by PTDC, is the place to eat if you like a view over Islamabad, but the food is only fair. The barbecue outside is better than the buffet inside.

Laziza in Satellite Town Commercial Area, tel 840321, has a large family restaurant for very good Pakistani food especially *boti kebabs* — marinated beef and mutton cooked on a skewer.

Self-catered Picnics

Reasonably good brown bread is sold at the Afghan Bakery in Jinnah Super Market, F-7. Marmite, imported butter and cheeses, sardines, and tinned meats are sold at the supermarket in Kohsar Market F–6/3. **M and M's Deli**, in Kohsar Market next to London Books, sells frozen home cooking such as lasagne; also sugar free cakes and jam and health foods. Some supermarkets even sell frozen packets of American bacon. The **French Bakery** in Melody Market beside the Melody Cinema sells slices of 'pizza' and good brownies and banana bread. Cucumber and tomato can be peeled for a safe salad, but do not eat any lettuce unless you boil it first!

Shopping

Most shops in Islamabad are concentrated in designated shopping areas. The oldest shopping area is **Aabpara Market** on Khayaban-e-Suhrawardy, G–6/1, where you can buy household goods, fabrics, hardware, spices and food. **Melody Market**, in the centre of G–6, has souvenir, brass and carpet shops, and **Covered Market**, nearby in G–6/3, specialises in vegetables and groceries, and also has the best photography and haberdashery shops. **Super Market**, in the centre of F–6, and **Jinnah Super Market**, in the centre of F–7, concentrate on clothing, jewellery, handicrafts, leather goods and shoes. The **Blue Area** (so called because it was coloured blue on the original plan of Islamabad, to denote a commercial area), is developing fast and is a good place to look for carpets, brass and handicrafts. Many travel agencies, banks, courier services and import-export companies are located here.

The **Itvar Bazaar** (Sunday Market), G–6/4, near Aabpara, is Islamabad's most interesting market for tourists. Behind the main market, Afghan refugees lay out rows of carpets for sale, as well as jewellery, antiques and souvenirs. The food stalls are a wonderful source of cheap grills and snacks. The Itvar Bazaar is open only on Sunday.

The **Itvar Bazaar** (Sunday Market), The Afghan traders congregate in **Kohsar Market** on weekdays.

Handicraft Shops

On the NW corner of Super Market, F–6, **Threadlines Gallery**, a government-sponsored handicraft shop, sells some excellent pieces at reasonable prices. In the same arcade is **Maharaja**, among others, and don't miss **Anarkali** for embroidered slippers, and the general **Super Art Emporium** on the first floor. **Behbud Boutique**, nearby, has a good selection of table linen, traditional embroidery and tribal jewellery at reasonable prices, and the profits go to charity.

There are at least seven more handicraft shops in Jinnah Super Market, F–7, worth exploring, and try the shops in the Blue Area and Melody Market, G–6, as well. For **leather** goods, try **Flash Leather** for bags and jackets on the south side of Jinnah Super Market, and there is another good leather shop on the north side of Super Market, behind Watson Chemist.

Boutiques

The best clothes shops for ready-made *shalwar-kameez* are in the northeast end of **Jinnah Super Market** F–7. Try **Art & Style**, **Generation**, **Creation** and the others in the same area. **Adagio** in Super

Market, F-6, is a good place for 'Born to Shop' tee-shirts. **Erum** and **Behbud**, also in Super Market, F-7, sell a fair selection of ready-made shirts and trousers. **English Taylor** in Jinnah Super Market is a reasonable tailor.

Beauty Parlours

Daniella Liang's Hong Kong Beauty Parlour, 33 St 27, F–6/2, tel 824956, 822967, and **Effcee**, 45 School Road, F–7/1, tel 810135, 217686, are both good for hairstyling and waxing.

Spa indoor swimming pool, sauna and gym near Threadlines Gallery, is open to non-members for a small fee, tel 214923.

Bookshops

London Bookshop, in Kohsar Market F–6/2 is the best. **Vanguard** and **Book Fair**, in Jinnah Super Market F–7, **Lok Virsa**, in Super Market F–6, and **Old Bookshop**, in Melody Market G–6, are all well-stocked.

Carpets

The **Afghan Rug Shop** and **Kapkaz Carpets**, both in Bangash Plaza, between the Police Station and the Capri Petrol Station in Jinnah Super Market, F-7, and **Kundus**, also in Jinnah Super Market are recommended. **Pak Persian** and **Qureshi's Carpets**, in Melody Market, G–6, have good selections but are considered expensive. **Baluch Carpets,**

Lahore Carpet House, Shiraz Carpets, Nabeel Carpets and others in the Blue Area are all worth visiting.

Brass and Copper

Saad in the west end of the Blue Area in Fazal-ul-Haq Road, tel 251487, home tel 842813, specialises in brass fittings from ships, good quality silver plate and Christmas tree decorations, as well as the usual old and new orna- mental ware. Other shops are concen- trated in Melody Market, G-6, and the Blue Area.

Art Galleries

National Art Gallery, 77 Street 48, F-7/4.

Art Gallery, 61, St 5, F–8/3, tel 254341.

Studio Gandhara (Interiors), tel 281511.

Hunercada, 17, St 83, G–6/4, tel 275432, 278968.

Rohtas Gallery, 39, St 28, F–6/1.

Gallery Sadequain, St 50, F–7/4.

Useful Addresses

Ministry of Culture, Sports, Tourism and Youth Affairs for mountaineering and trekking per-mits. Attn: PRO (OP), Room No.1, Block 13-T/U, College Road, Jinnah Super Market, F-7, tel 920 3509, tel 920 2766, fax (92-51) 920 2347

Pakistan Tourism Development Corporation (PTDC) Head Office, House 170, Street 36, F-10/1, tel 294790, fax (92 51) 294540, e-mail: PTDC@tourism.gov.pk, or, tourism@isb.comsats.net.pk, web site: http://www.tourism.gov.pk.

Tourism Information Centres (TIC) are located opposite the **International Arrival lounge**, tel 928 0563 at the airport, and on **Aga Khan Road** (next to the Caltex petrol pump) on the southwest corner of Super Market, F-6, tel 921-2760, fax (92-51) 921 2760, open 9 am to 3 pm.

PTDC Motel bookings office, Block B-4, Bhitai Road, Jinnah Super Market, F-7, (Near Taj Mahal Restaurant), tel 111-555-999, 920 8948-9, fax (92 51) 921 8233

Passport Office, for visa extension, is somewhere near Peshawar More in G-8/1, tel 260773. Open in summer from 8 am to 2.30 pm, in winter 8.30 am to 3 pm. Or, Ministry of Interior, Block R, Visa Section, tel 9207290. (Application for visa extensions accepted from 9 am to 12 noon only).

Foreigner's Registration Office is in Ayub Super Market in the centre of F–8, beside the Senior Superintendent of Police's (SSP) office. The best time to go is 9 am to 1 pm.

Police Station, F–7 Markaz, tel 812393. Also in Melody Market, G-6, and Ayub Market, F-8.

Police Emergency numbers are 823333 and 810222.

Movers Freeline Movers, Khalid Plaza, Blue Area, tel 815254, fax (92 51) 825132, can inform on Import–Export Regulations.

Photo Shop. The best is in Covered Market, G–6/3.

Liquor Store, at the side entrance to Marriott Hotel, for permit holders only.

Post & Telecommunications

International Mailing Office, west end of Jinnah Super Market, F-7.

Telegraph and Telephone Office, behind Marriott Hotel, F–5, for overseas calls, cables, telex and fax, open 24 hours.

Customer Service Centres for overseas calls, cables, fax and telex are beside the International Mail Post Office in F-7 and in front of F–8 police station on the west side of F–8.

General Post Office, Post Office Road, Melody Market, G–6/2 (north end), accepts poste restante.

Banks

American Express, Ali Plaza, Blue Area, tel 821480, open 9 am to 4 pm, Monday to Friday and 9 am to 1 pm Saturday, cash travellers' cheques and foreign exchange and, for AmEx cardholders, will cash cheques up to

US$1,000 every 21 days providing the cheques are drawn from the same account that you use to pay your AmEx bill. You can also order your air tickets here, both domestic and international by phone and they deliver them to your house at no extra cost, tel 212425, 823713, manager's residence, tel 843217.

ANZ Grindlays Bank, Diplomatic Enclave, tel 815035, fax (92 51) 820316, open 9 am to 1 pm, Monday to Thursday, Friday and Saturday 9 am to 12 noon.

American Bank, tel 828801, near American Express in the Blue Area, will give you cash from your credit card for a 2% commission.

Money Changers, There are lots of authorised money-changers in town who give a couple of rupees more than the bank rate when changing cash without a receipt. They only accept new notes. I have used Asia Money Changers, shop 9, Block 46, West Jinnah Avenue, Blue Area (opposite petrol pump) tel 820744, 820844, and Riaz Money Changers, Usmania Hotel Building, Blue Area, near Civic Hotel, tel 220975, 215553.

Hospitals

The best hospitals are **PIMS** (Pakistan Institute of Medical Sciences), G–8/3, tel 859511–9, 859521–9, out-patients, 856348, and the new **Shifa**

International in H–8/4, off Peshawar Road, near Zero Point, tel 446801-3. Shifa has foreign-trained doctors and an excellent reputation, even for major operations. Accident emergencies are not accepted after 7 pm.

Dentist Dr Junaid Malik and Dr Samira Niazi, Street 24, F-6/2, tel 274300, and Dr Rehman, 90B Margalla Road, F–8/2, tel 280471 are all recommended.

Optician Syed Tanweer Ahmad, 8 Melody House, Civic Centre next to British Council, tel 206620, 828239.

Cultural Centres

Asian Study Group, 80 West Shahrah-e-Quaid-e-Azam, Malik Complex, Ist floor, almost opposite Saudi-Pak Tower, tel 815891, is open Monday to Friday, 3 to 5 pm and Tuesday and Thursday, 11 am to 1 pm. President, Mrs. Parveen Malik, tel 278027.

Lok Virsa — Institute of Folk and Traditional Heritage in Shakarparian Park, tel 812673–5, open 9 am to 1 pm and 2 to 5 pm, closed Monday and Friday, has an excellent collection of traditional handicrafts and a library of books and recordings.

Islasmabad Museum, tel 223826, House 41, Street 3, E-7. Open 9.30 am to 4.30 pm, closed Wednesday. Has a good archaeollogical display.

Museum of Natural Sciences, open 8.30 am to 1.30 pm and 2 to 3.15 pm, is in Shakarparian Park near Lok Virsa. Guided tours can be arranged by appointment.

American Center, tel 824051, in the Blue Area, has glossy American magazines and US Information Service propaganda.

British Council Library, Melody Market, tel 829041, 822505.

Alliance Française, House 15, street 18, F-7/2, tel 822176.

Islamabad Club, Murree Road near Rawal Lake, tel 216225.

Capital Development Authority (CDA) public relations office on Khayaban-e-Suhrawardy, tel 828301.

Himalayan Wildlife Project, 11, St 15, F-7/2, tel 220061, fax (92 51) 216116. Information centre and bookings for trips to the Bear Project on the Deosai Plateau.

Some Foreign Embassies

Check in the green pages at the beginning of the Islamabad telephone directory or with directory enquiries 117, as some numbers may have changed.

Afghanistan, 8, Street 90, G-6/3, tel 278213

Australia, Diplomatic Enclave, tel 279223, 824345

Austria, 13, Street 1, F–6/3, tel 279237-8

Britain see UK

Canada, Diplomatic Enclave, tel 279100

China, Diplomatic Enclave, tel 821114 (visa office), 824786

England, see UK

France, Diplomatic Enclave, tel 813433-5

Germany, Diplomatic Enclave, tel 829053

India, Diplomatic Enclave, tel 814371–5 (visa office), 272676

Iran, 222, Street 2, G–5/1, tel 822694–5, 276270

Italy, 54 Margalla Hills Road, F–6/3 tel 829030-1

Japan, Diplomatic Enclave, tel 279721, 279320

Nepal, 506, Street 84, G-6/4, tel 270642, 272754

Netherlands, PIA Building, 2nd Floor, Blue Area, tel 9214336-7

New Zealand, represented by the UK High Commission

Russia (and some ex-Soviet republics), Diplomatic Enclave, tel 274604

Spain, Street 6, G-5, Diplomatic Enclave, tel 827074

Switzerland, Street 6, Diplomatic Enclave, G-5/4, tel 279291

UK, Diplomatic Enclave, tel 822131

USA, Diplomatic Enclave, tel 826161

UNICEF, 58 & 62 Khayaban-e-Iqbal, F-7/2, tel 825135, 825142

UNDP, FAO, WHO, UN Building, G-5, tel 822070-9

UN High Commission for Refugees, 18 & 25, Street 8, F-7/3, tel 826003

UN Information Centre, 26, Street 88, G-6/3, tel 823465

ILO, 58 Khayaban-e-Iqbal, F-8/2, tel 854963, 852313

World Bank, 35-7, Street 1, F-6/3, tel 820280

Churches

There are four Christian churches in Islamabad with services in English: **Fatima Church** (Catholic), Kaghan Road, Street 55, F–8/4, tel 851535, has daily services at 6.30 am in winter and 7 am in summer. In addition there are services on Sunday at 9 am and at 6.30 pm. The **Protestant International Church**, University Road in the Diplomatic Enclave, tel 818188, has a Sunday service at 10 am. **St Thomas's** (Church of Pakistan, Diocese of Lahore), an ecumenical church on Hospital Road, G–7/2, office tel 276569, residence tel 270187, has two morning services in English on Sunday at 8 and 9.30 am in summer,

and 9 and 10.30 am in winter and another on Sunday evenings at 7 pm in summer and 6.30 pm in winter. **Apostolic Nunciate Chapel**, Embassy of the Holy See, Street 5, Diplomatic Enclave, near German Embassy, tel 9210490, 201491.

Tour Agents

Adventure Tours Pakistan, PO Box 1780, Islamabad, tel 252759, 260820, fax (92 51) 252145. e-mail: aminjan@infolink.net.pk, Website: www.atp.com/adventure. Run by Ashraf Aman from Hunza, the first Pakistani to climb K–2, this company is reliable and good value.

Adventure Travel, run by Malik, 15 Wali Centre 86, Blue Area, tel 212490, 212728, 212580.

Hindu Kush Trails, PO Box 2059, Islamabad or 37, Street 28, F–6/1, tel 821576, 821568, 277067, fax (92 51) 275031, 277067, e-mail: culture@trails.sdnpk.undp.org. Run by Maqsood ul-Mulk of the ex-royal family of Chitral who is very well-connected. Specialist in the Hindu Kush, trekking, mountain biking and jeep safaris.

Nazir Sabir Expeditions, PO Box 1442, Islamabad, tel 252580, 252553, 853672, fax (92 51) 250293. e-mail: nazir@isbb.comsats.net.pk, nazir@nse.sdnpk.undp.org. Nazir

Sabir of Hunza was the second Pakistani to climb K–2. He is an experienced and reliable mountaineer: specialises in mountaineering expeditions.

North Tiger Tours, PO Box 2356, Islamabad, tel 260467, 274944, fax (92 51) 263903, e-mail: osmond@infolink.net.pk. Run by Osmond Solomon who also manages the bear project on the Deosai..

Sitara Travel Consultants, 3rd floor, Waheed Plaza, 52 West Jinnah Ave, Blue Area, PO Box 1662, tel 813372-5, 274892-3, fax (92 51) 279651, 279676, e-mail: Sitarapk@isb.compol.com, web site: www.sitara.com. A well-established and reliable company with overseas offices in Canada and the US, that specialises in jeep safaris.

Silk route Explorers, 11A, Street 47, F-7/1, tel 273246, 271028, fax (92 51) 827912, e-mail: silk@paknet1.ptc.pk. Run by Anna Berghauser, the only foreign tour operator in Pakistan.

Trans Pakistan Adventure Services, PO Box 2103, or 8 Muzaffar Chambers, Fazal-ul-Haq Road, Blue Area, tel 274796, fax (92 51) 274838, 275404. Run by Haroon Pirzada, experienced mountaineer, reliable, efficient, imaginative trek and jeep safaris. Innovative trips to Balochistan.

Travel Walji's, PO Box 1088, Islamabad; 10 Khayaban-e-Shurawardy, Aabpara, tel 270757-58, fax (92 51) 270753, 828264, e-mail: walji@twlisb.sdnpk.undp.org. The biggest travel agent in Pakistan with offices in Lahore, Karachi, Peshawar, Gilgit, Hunza and Skardu, and international offices in Stanford, USA; Kronberg, Germany; Paris; Tokyo; Zurich and Kashgar, China. They have a very good reputation and reliable, experienced guides.

Transport

PIA, Fazal-ul-Haq Road, Blue Area, F–6/4, tel 815041, fax (92 51) 826354, flight reconfirmation, tel 111-786-786 or 816051. Accepts credit cards and travellers' cheques.

PIA Cargo Office, Blue Area, tel 815041, at airport tel 591071. The cargo manager, tel 825031.

Shaheen Air International, Buland Markaz, opposite American Express, Blue Area, 217530. Flights cost about 20 percent less than PIA.

Aero Asia, Block 12-D, SNC Centre, Blue Area, tel 823072, 219340. Ticket Office at Islamabad airport, tel 592314. Four flights a day to Karachi and cheaper than PIA.

Bhoja Air, Blue Area, tel 828123. Two flights daily via Lahore to Karachi.

Railway Booking and Information Office is at Melody Market, tel 9207474, 827474, open 9 am to 1 pm and 2 to 5 pm. The railway station is in Rawalpindi.

Mercedes bus and Toyota coasters: 25 seat, service to Lahore from City Linkers, F–8 Markaz, leave every hour.

For other destinations see buses from Rawalpindi.

RAWALPINDI

Telephone: Direct dialling code for Rawalpindi is 051

Hotels

International Standard

Pearl Continental, Mall Road, tel 566011, fax (92 51) 563927, is the best in town with a swimming pool and tennis courts. The **Shalimar** nearby, tel 562901, fax (92 51) 566061, offers all facilities but less style, cheaper.

Moderate

In Saddar Bazaar

Flashman's, PTDC, Mall Road, tel 581480–8, fax (92 51) 563294. The oldest hotel in town, in colonial-style bungalows, now sadly run-down with poor service and bad food, but still the best hotel for expeditions as the rooms are large and you can drive up to your door. A brand new alternative is the **Comfort Inn** on Kashmir Road, tel 516161–5, fax (92 51) 566697, which has central AC and most services.

In the next price range, **Kashmirwala's**, Mall Road, tel 583186–9, fax (92 51) 581554, is a large block hotel with no character but good food. **Paradise Inn** on Adamji Road, tel 581200, 568594–5, fax (92 51) 567048, with AC, and good value non-AC rooms. **Holiday**, tel 568068–70, fax (92 51) 583960, on Iftikhar Janjua Road, behind the Pearl Continental, a quiet hotel with good service and a powerful generator are both popular choices for expeditions.

Parkland International, Bank Road, tel 566080–3, is multi-storey and reasonable value for rooms with or without AC.

In Murree Road area

The big hotels along Murree Road and Liaquat Road near Liaquat Chowk tend to be noisy and overpriced. Here the **Akbar**, **Park**, **National City**, **Shangrila**, and **Potohar**, are all similar in price. Those just East of Committee Chowk are quieter and recommended - **Al Badar**, **Blue Sky**, **Rawal** and **United**. Noisier but cheaper, on Murree Road is the **Mushtaq**, tel 553998.

Less expensive

There are dozens in this price range, all with attached shower and toilet, plus a fan, in Saddar and Raja bazaars, and along Murree Road near Liaquat and Committee chowks. Saddar Bazaar is best because the street food on Kashmir Road is excellent.

In Saddar Bazaar

My favourite is the **New Kamran**, on Kashmir Road, tel 582040, with good value terraced rooms facing a courtyard. The old **Kamran**, just down the road, has one good inexpensive triple at the back. The **Khyaban**, tel 568822, across the road offers large, cleanish d/t/q for a reasonable price. I checked all the hotels in nearby Adamjee Road, and give top marks to the friendly **Al Falah**, tel 580799, with its large first floor restaurant overlooking the street. The **Venus**, tel 566501, further down Adamjee Road, is welcoming, popular and better value than any of its neighbours. The cheapest hotel near the railway station that accepts foreigners is the **Bolan**, tel 563416, a dirty rabbit-warren.

Railway retiring rooms, Rawalpindi City Station. For passengers with first class ticket only. Bring your own bedding.

In Raja Bazaar

The cheap hotels at Fowara Chowk in Raja Bazaar are cleaner, try **Al**

Falah, Al Maroof and **Evergreen**, behind the tonga stand. The nearby **Mashriq** on city Saddar Road is reasonable, and the wagons for Gilgit leave daily at 3 pm from the courtyard. **Seven Brothers** on Liaquat Road is charges slightly more.

In Murree Road

Rawalpindi Popular Inn, tel 531884 near Liaquat chowk is popular with backpackers, **Snow Ball Inn** further along College Road is clean. **Al-Hayat**, tel 557660, and **Faisal**, tel 73210, at Liaquat Chowk on Murree Road, are noisy but reasonable.

The **Asia**, tel 73362, **Queens** and **Al Farooq**, off Murree Road, near Committee Chowk, are quiet with big rooms.

Hostels

Youth Hostel, 25 Gulistan Colony, near Ayub Park. For members only, but too remote to be convenient. The new Youth Hostel in Islamabad is better but usually full. **YMCA**, 64 A Satellite Town, for women only. A bit run-down, but cheap and safe.

Restaurants

Aside from the restaurants in the principal hotels, most of the best-known restaurants are along The Mall or just off it. Most popular street eating is at **Jahangir's** tel 563352, on Kashmir Road for barbecued meat and *naan*. Opposite are cheaper versions of the same thing. You can finish off your meal with *kulfi* or sweets from **Rasheed Sweet House**, 50 metres (yards) along Kashmir Road towards the Kamran Hotel. **Burger Express** on Kashmir Road and **Pizza Kent** on The Mall are also popular.

Shopping

Sarafa Bazaar, in the old city is the place to go for old tribal jewellery. **Saddar Bazaar** in the Cantonment, is best for leather, carpets, cashmere shawls, furniture and tailors. The heart of the bazaar is along Kashmir Road and Massey Gate.

Shamas Din, in Massey Gate, sells boots, shoes, suitcases, saddles and poufs.

Carpets, brass and antiques are on Canning Road, behind Flashman's, and on The Mall in front. They are also in the lobby of the Pearl Continental Hotel.

Men's tailors and cashmere shawls are on Haider Road, but ladies' tailors are in Kamran Market, off Kashmir Road.

The best brass shop is **Shaukat Ali's**, in Satellite Town, 170 D Block (tel 842813), which has a large selection of quality, ready polished brass and copper. The shop is an unmarked private house. His son has a shop, **Saad**, in the Blue Area in Islamabad, near PIA, selling the best selection of brass and copper, including old fittings from ships (see Islamabad listing, page 283).

Bookshops

The **Book Centre** on Saddar Road, tel 565234, has some maps and guidebooks, **Ferozsons's**, 32 Saddar Road, tel 567901, **Capri Bookshop** on Haider Road and **Pak–American** on Kashmir Road (upstairs) have foreign magazines.

Useful Addresses

Pakistan Tourism Development Corporation (PTDC), tel 581480, is in Flashman's Hotel on The Mall. Open 9 am to 1 pm and 2 to 4 pm.

Pakistan Tours Ltd (PTL), Flashman's Hotel, The Mall. The best person to see is the manager, Saeed Anwar, tel 581489, 581480, ext 23.

Tourism Development Corporation of Punjab (TDCP) office is on The Mall at the corner of Kashmir Road, tel 564824, fax (92 51) 568421. They run daily buses to Murree and Lahore. And tours to the northern valleys in summer, and to the southern deserts in winter.

Foreigners' Registration Office, Rashid Minhas Road, Civil Lines, tel 590012, 585333. This is in the Civil Courts beside the Senior Superintendent of Police's (SSP) office, near Kuchehri (kuh-CHAIR-ree) Chowk. The best time is 9 am to 1 pm.

Passport Office, go to the Islamabad office near Peshawar More, for visa extensions

Post & Telecommunications

General Post Office, Kashmir Road, tel 565691. Open 8 am to 5 pm. Accepts poste restante.

Telegraph and Telephone Office, Kashmir Road, tel 565691, 567888, and another on The Mall. Open 24 hours.

Banks

American Express, tel 567827, 566001, Rahim Plaza, Murree Road. Open 9 am to 1 pm.

Citibank, Adamjee Road, tel 564905–6, **Habib Bank** on Haider Road and the **National Bank of Pakistan** on Bank Road, also change travellers' cheques.

Tour and Travel Agents

Himalaya Tours and Treks, PO Box 1769, or 112 Rahim Plaza, Murree Road (behind American Express), tel 515371, tel and fax 563014, fax (92 51) 584566, e-mail: himalia@isb.comsats.net.pk. Muhammad Ali Changazi, the owner is a Skardu man, specialising in Baltistan. He is knowledgeable, reliable and a skilled guide.

Jasmine Tours, PO Box 859, Rawalpindi, tel 586823, fax (92 51) 584566, e-mail: ali@porik.sdnpk.undp.org. Web: http://www.pakcyber.com/jtours. Run by Asghar Ali Porik, knowledgeable, reliable and interesting.

Pakistan Guides, PO Box 1692, 3rd floor, 62/2, Bank Road, tel 524808, fax (92 51) 539497, 524808, 567048, e-mail: guides@paknet2.ptc.pk. Knowledgeable and full of ideas, run by Kaiser Khan, a competent tour operator. Specialists in cultural tours, expeditions, treks, and jeep safaris. Also rents camping and kitchen gear.

Pakistan Tours Ltd (Government run) Flashman's Hotel, tel 563038, 565449, 581480 ext 23, fax (92 51) 513054, 565449, e-mail: ptl@isb.comsats.net.pk. It is best to see the manager, Saeed Anwar Khan, a prince from Nagar.

Transport

Air

PIA booking office is on The Mall, tel 568071, or for Northern Areas (round the side from the main office) tel 567011. Accepts credit cards and travellers' cheques

British Airways, Pearl Continental Hotel, tel 566791, 565413.

Railway Booking and Information Office is 300 metres south of the railway station in Saddar Bazaar, or in Islmabad at Melody Market, tel 9207474, 827474, open 9 am to 1 pm and 2 to 5 pm.

Bus

Both government and private buses leave from various stations in Saddar Bazaar, Committee Chowk, Liaquat Chowk and Pir Wadhai bus station. Services change frequently, so it is best to ask around for the best buses to your chosen destination.

For Gilgit try NATCO or Masherbrum Tours tel 863595, both leaving from Pir Wadhai, or Hameed Travel or Sargin Travel both leaving from near Fowara Chowk, Saddar Bazaar.

For Swat the most comfortable is the PTDC air conditioned coaster leaving from Flashman's Hotel. Ask around for others.

For Murree the TDCP coaches are the most comfortable, tel 564824, leaving from their office on the Mall. Minibuses leave from Station Road in Saddar Bazaar and from Faisabad.

For Lahore try TDCP, tel 564824, leaving from their office on the Mall. New Khan Road Runners leave from Committee Chowk, New Flying Coaches leave from near Liaquat Chowk. Skyways coaches leave from Faisabad, and Citylinkers from F-8 in Islamabad.

For Peshawar minibuses leave every hour from Committee Chowk.

For other destinations ask around.

MURREE

Telephone: Direct dialling code for Murree is 0593

Hotels

Hotel prices in Murree fluctuate according to demand; most are overpriced for what you get. The season is short, and the hotels are heavily booked in summer, but there are big discounts during the rest of the year.

By far the best (and most expensive) hotel in the Murree area is the **Pearl Continental** in Bhurban, eight kilometres (five miles) beyond Murree. New, in a magnificent site overlooking the wooded hills, it offers typical first class modern splendour with a swimming pool, squash and tennis courts and all facilities including airport pick-up. Tel (051) 427082, fax (92 51) 427081, 427092, special package deals sometimes available. The **Golf**, tel 410507, in Bhurban, a single-storey complex set around a lawn with willow trees beside the golf course, is an old colonial relic offering bedroom, sitting room and huge bath. It was run, until she died, by an English lady (Mrs Keesburn) who stayed on after Partition. Her old cook lives on and is celebrated for his roast chicken and caramel custard. Peak season rates range from Rs1000 upwards to whatever they can get (many thousands). In summer, when the garden is cluttered with tents, the place is best avoided, but in the off-season this is still one of my favourites. It is closed late October to early April.

In Murree proper, the more expensive hotels are **Cecil's**, the classic old PTDC hotel on Mount View (Imtiaz Shaheed) Road, tel 411131–4, 410247, 410257, or book through PTDC Islamabad, tel (051) 920 8948-9, or 111-555-999, fax (92 51) 921 8233. This colonial, stone two-storey building has large rooms, fireplaces and balconies. Take tea in the garden for a taste of colonial life. On the same road the **Lockwood**, tel 410112, **Brightlands**, tel 410270, and **Dilkusha**, tel 410005, are all older up-market hotels.

There are about 50 other hotels in Murree with no great distinguishing features, some with good views. They have flexi-rates and charge whatever they can get. **Kashmir Villa**, tel 410408, near Kashmir Point, has a fantastic view. **Treetop**, tel 410029, is well situated on Club Road, and the **Felton**, tel 410695-6, is just below it on Bank Road. The **Mehran**, **Al Sana**, tel 410449, **Lalazar**, tel 410153, and **Viewforth**, tel 411153, all on Viewforth (Abid Shaheed) Road with excellent views, and the **Ritz**, tel 410322, **Al-Hamra**, tel 410460, and others on the other side

of the GPO at the beginning of Mount View (Imtiaz Shaheed) Road are all in the middle price range. The **Breeze**, on the road to Pindi Point, tel 411088, is more expensive. On The Mall (Jinnah Road) the **Marhaba**, tel 410184, is characterless and its proprietor's flexi-prices are comparatively expensive (perhaps he thought I looked rich). The **Al-Saud** opposite, and the **Mall View**, tel 411111–4, and **Grand** further up are cheaper. Lower down at the entrance to Murree on Cart Road, the **Blue Pines**, tel 410235, **Chambers**, **Tanveer**, tel 410297, and **Gulberg**, tel 410301, are all adequate hotels in the middle range.

Murree is so crowded in summer that it is preferable to continue to Nathiagali for the night (see facing page).

There are **Youth Hostels** at Bhurban and Khanaspur, both of which are extremely popular and crowded in summer.

Useful Addresses

Tourism Development Corporation of Punjab (TDCP) information office, tel 411050 is on Cart Road, below the Blue Pines Hotel. There is another information centre on the Mall, tel 410730. Open 8.30 am to 5 pm.

General Post Office The GPO is on the Mall

Banks There are no banks in Murree that do foreign exchange.

Ask around in the bazaar for money changers and public call offices.

NATHIAGALI

The old colonial favourites in Nathiagali are the **Pines**, which offers charming rooms in an old single-storey building in the woods, and **Greens**, tel (05921) 352261-4, fax (92 5921) 268264, at the other end of the village, both charge half price in winter. **Summer Retreat**, tel 868200–1, and **Valley View**, tel 868202, are slightly cheaper, with a good views to the south. **Mukshpuri** tel 868287, is another cheaper possibility in nearby Dunga Gali. There are also about eight small local hotels including **Kamran**, **Skyways** and **Bismillah**, and some government rest houses (bookable in Peshawar), all very full in summer.

AYUBIA

PTDC run a motel hidden in the woods in the Ayubia National Park, book at PTDC Islamabad, tel (051) 920 8948-9, or 111-555-999, fax (92 51) 921 8233. The design of this motel is disappointing with little space to sit or eat outside.

PESHAWAR

Telephone: Direct dialling code for Peshawar is 091

Hotels

There is a choice of staying in Saddar Bazaar on the edge of the British-built cantonment, or south across the railway tracks in the old city. Saddar is slightly more expensive for what you get, but convenient for the Western-type restaurants in Saddar. The more adventurous get a better deal in the old town. All rooms have attached shower and toilet.

International Standard

Pearl Continental, Khyber Road, tel 276361–9, fax (92 91) 276465, 271095. Offers all facilities and a swimming pool.

Khan Klub, New Rampura Gate (Nevay Darwaza) Old City, PO Box 468, tel 214802, 256 7156, fax (92 91) 256 1156. Exciting new hotel in a painstakingly restored 200-year old Sikh *haveli* (family house). The most romantic and interesting place to stay.

Moderate

In Saddar Bazaar

Dean's, corner of Saddar Road and Islamia Road, tel 276483–4, 279781–2, or book at PTDC Islamabad, tel (051) 920 8948-9, or 111-555-999, fax (92 51) 921 8233. This old-colonial style hotel offers bungalows with verandas, a garden and some charm, but is now run-down. It is still my favourite hotel in Saddar.

Green's, Saddar Road, tel 273604, 276035, fax 276088. Overpriced but surprisingly popular with tourists. Its airless rooms are set around a central courtyard. They also offer cheap, claustrophobic cubicles with bunk beds.

Inexpensive

All the cheap hotels in Saddar are along Saddar Road or the parallel Sunehri Masjid (Mosque) Road.

The most popular is the **Tourist Inn**, tel 275632, in a shaded brick courtyard behind Jan's Bakery, opposite the central bus station. There are three double rooms and two walk-through dorms. Or, you can camp in the court and use the facilities. **Khani's**, tel 277512–3, down a lane beside Green's, has airless boxy cells with AC, or hot rooms with windows on the third floor, also dorm beds. The **Sindbad**, tel 275020, 275814, and **New Golden**, tel 276778, 279122, at the other end of Saddar Road, on opposite sides of the street near Belore Plaza, both have bigger rooms, some with windows.

On Sunehri Masjid Road, the **Paradise**, tel 273654, offers four floors of larger rooms, some with windows, the top floor is the cheapest. Full of visiting Pakistani officials and Afghans. The **Five Star**, next door, only showed me cheaper inside rooms. Buses for the old city leave from just outside. Further along, directly opposite the mosque, the **Mehran**, tel 272439, 276739, has good value bigger rooms with windows. The **Skyline**, next door, has similar prices.

In the Old City

Most hotels are in Shoiba Bazaar, nearby Khyber Bazaar, Cinema Road and Namak Mandi.

Moderate

Galaxie, tel 212172–5, fax (92 91) 218496, Khyber Bazaar, near Jail Bridge, has large rooms with AC and underground parking. The **Habib**, next door, tel 210517, 210116, 219316, has slightly cheaper AC rooms and some reasonably clean non-AC rooms too. The management is helpful and the place is popular with foreigners.

Inexpensive

The **Rose**, tel 210755–7, diagonally across Shoiba Chowk from Habib, is the best value and recommended. Set around a central court are big rooms with windows and fans. You can eat wonderful Afghani food in the street outside. The **Shan** across the road is cheaper, with not so clean rooms. The Kamran hotel has become a shopping complex selling carpets.

In nearby Cinema Road, the **Gulf**, **Relax Inn** and **Gohar Palace**, tel 219046, have good value small rooms with AC. **Salatin's**, the best Pathan restaurant, is nearby.

Cinema Road and Khyber Bazaar meet at Kabuli Gate, just inside which the truly adventurous can find the **National**, tel 212491, in Jangimala, a small side street along a canal off Qissa Khawani, with cheap, quiet doubles. Communal showers and toilets are downstairs and you can eat in the restaurants along the canal. This is the cheapest I visited, but there are at least 50 more in the city.

On the Grand Trunk Road

The new **Hidayat Hotel** north of the GT Road, tel 217839 is the best here. The hotels near the bus station along the G T Road are not recommended: **Three Star**, **Amin** and **Zabeel Palace**, are side by side, have cheapish non-AC doubles, and moderately priced AC rooms, but they are noisy and few foreigners stay

there. I was equally unimpressed by the **Alzar**, **Shangrila** and **Royal** hotels on the south side of the G T Road.

In University Town/Hyattabad

Several luxury air conditioned guesthouses cater to the international aid community here. **VIP House**, Old Bara Road, tel 842806, fax (92 91) 843392; **Decent Lodge**, 62 Syed Jamaluddin Road, tel 840221, fax (92 91) 840229; **S**helton House, 15 B Old Jamrud Road, tel 842087, fax (92 91) 842383. Ask around for others.

Alternative accommodation

Youth Hostel, 37, Block B–1, Phase 4, Hyattabad, about two kilometres (a mile) beyond University Town. To get there take the main (second) turning to Hyattabad, cross the railway and shortly afterwards turn left down a lane between some government offices. The newly-built hostel is just behind. It is comfortable but crowded and very remote. Maximum stay three nights. Camping here is safe.

Railway retiring rooms, Peshawar Cantonment Station for those with valid first class ticket.

Camping, at the Youth Hostel, or ask at the PTDC for suggestions.

Restaurants

The old city in Peshawar is famous for its street stalls especially in Shoiba Bazaar, outside the Rose Hotel, and in Namak Mandi for Afghan food. *Karai* — lamb quickly stir-fried with tomatoes and spices but no oil (on Tuesdays and Wednesdays, the meatless days, chicken is served instead of lamb). You buy the meat by weight, you need to calculate how much you need and make sure they give you good meaty pieces. The stalls also serve *tikka* and other dishes. The *tikka* kebab stalls along the GT Road and Kohat Road are also good value. If you have transport, try the fish stalls out on the road to Charsadda in Sardaryab, about 10 km away on the left of the road.

Salatin's, on Cinema Road, tel 210279, 213770, is one of the best, cheaper, indoor restaurants, famous for its Pathan atmosphere.

In **Saddar Bazaar** the street stalls around Fowara Chowk sell hot *naan* and fresh yoghurt. The **Hayat Café**, on Artab Road, sells toasted sandwiches and **Lala's Grill**, in Green's hotel, offers snacks and ice cream. Ask around for the latest favourite.

More expensive

Hong Kong, on The Mall, offers standard Chinese, and the **Pearl Continental** has two more Chinese restaurants, as well as Continental and Pakistani — the most expensive food in town — and wonderful barbecues. The **Khan Klub** in the old city offers good food in an elegant setting, and **Dean's**, **Green's** and **Galaxie** hotels all serve European and Pakistani food. There are several more restaurants on Jamrud Road on the way to University Town. **Usmania** and **Shiraz** are recommended, **Tikala** serves good Afghan food in a renovated Pushtun guesthouse (*hujra*). The **Azad Afghan** also serves generous portions of Afghan food, but is not so clean.

Shopping

Some of the best buys in Peshawar are the antique silver and tribal jewellery in the **Andarshar Bazaar** near the Mahabat Mosque. **Shinwari Plaza,** 70 metres beyond the Mahabat Mosque on the right, is a new plaza full of the best Afghan shops, happy hunting ground for jewellery and carpets, and all things Afghan. Copper, brass and Russian Gardner china is available at the end of Qissa Khawani, (see the Peshawar Bazaar Tour for directions). Also good value are the astrakhan hats, shawls and handprinted cloth in the **old bazaars** and silk and lace in **Saddar Bazaar.**

Peshawar is also famous for its **wooden furniture** with brass inlay work. If ordering furniture for export, try to find out if the wood is properly seasoned, otherwise it will crack, and the brass inlay will pop out. The best-known factories are: M Hyatt & Bros, who have a showroom opposite Jan's Bakery and a factory in the Jamrud Industrial Estate; Royal Furniture; Peshawar Woodworks; Khyber Wood Factory; Pak/Danish Industries and Pak/German Industries. You can arrange factory tours through PTDC.

Wax worked on cloth is another handicraft for which Peshawar is well-known, though not suited to every taste. You can find it in Saddar Bazaar and in the arcade of the Pearl Continental Hotel. The designs show a Chinese influence, especially the birds in brilliant colours and the dragons.

The **Afghan Metal Works,** behind the Pearl Continental Hotel on Pajjagi (Ashab Baba) Road, is open 8 am to 4 pm and welcomes visitors. You can watch the moulding, beating, engraving, tinning and polishing of the various copper and brass utensils for sale.

Smoked meat and sausages are available at Przyborowski's, in the Jamrud Industrial Estate, tel 812460, 812376, or at Abdullah Jan's shop on Artab Road. These sausages keep well for travelling and are not available elsewhere in Pakistan.

Useful Addresses

Tourist Information Centre, PTDC, at Dean's Hotel, tel 279781–3. Open 9 am to 1 pm and 2 to 4.30 pm. Friday 9 am to 1 pm only. Closed Sunday. Gentle, friendly, Mr Salahuddin has a mine of information at his fingertips.

Peshawar Museum, open 8.30 am to 12.30 pm and 2.30 to 5 pm in summer, 9 am to 4 pm in winter, closed Wednesday, tel 271310, 274452.

Banks and **GPO** are in Saddar Bazaar. Banks open: winter 9 am to 1 pm, Monday to Thursday, 9 am to 12 noon, Friday and Saturday; summer open and close one hour earlier. Change your money at **ANZ Grindlays** in Arbab Road, or ask around if there are any private authorised dealers who usually give the best rates.

Telephone, Telegraph and **Fax Office** is on The Mall, at the corner of Tariq Road. Open 24 hours.

PIA office on Artab Road, flight reconfirmation tel 279162-4; the Chitral PIA office is next door, same telephone, open 9 am to 1 pm and 2 to 5 pm, but you must reconfirm your Chitral flight before 3 pm.

Passport Office, Building 3473, Zaryab Colony, Jamrud Road, tel 240178, 42098.

Foreigner's Registration, Police Chowk No 2, Sahibzada Gul Road, tel 278165.

Permits for the Khyber Pass from the Political Agent, Stadium Road. Residents in Pakistan get their Khyber permits from the Home Secretary, Civil Secretariat, Police Road. The permits are free and delivered immediately. PTDC runs a daily tour to the Khyber — see page 184.

Permits for Darra from the Home Secretary, Civil Secretariat on Police Road. Obtain the day before; free.

British Council Library, tel 111 424 424, 42818-9, 17C Chinar Road, University Town has newspapers and magazines from the UK. Open noon to 6 pm.

Alliance Française, tel 274542, is off Artab Road in Saddar Bazaar.

American Center, tel 840321, is on Chinar Road in University Town where you can watch CNN and ABC news and read the US newspapers.

British High commission, 1A Michni Lane, tel 275565.

American Consulate, tel 279801, open 8 am to 4.30 pm, is at the corner of Khyber and Hospital roads.

Travel Agents

Sehrai Travels, Green's Hotel, Saddar Road, tel 272084-5, fax (92 91) 276088. Specialises in trips on the Khyber Steam train.

Travel Walji's, 12 Saddar Road, tel 274130, opposite Green's Hotel in Saddar Bazaar.

SWAT

Telephone: Direct dialling code for Swat is 0936

Hotels

Hotel prices vary according to demand. In the off season, from October to April, prices are cheaper and hard bargaining in the smaller hotels will make them cheaper still. I recommend avoiding Swat from June through August when it is very crowded.

Saidu Sharif

Moderate

Mingora is the old market town and business centre, Saidu Sharif the administrative centre, royal residence and Akhund's shrine. If you have your own transport and can afford it, Saidu Sharif is far quieter and pleasanter to stay in. Marghazar, ten kilometres (six miles) away at the end of the Saidu Valley is another option. Advance booking is essential in summer in the better hotels.

Swat Serena, Saidu Sharif, tel 711640, 710518, fax (92 936) 710402; or book through Serena, Karachi, tel (021) 5873789–91, fax (92 21) 5873812. An old colonial building with wide verandas shaded by huge *chinar* trees. Recommended for its great charm and excellent food. By far the best hotel in Swat.

PTDC Motel, tel 713774-5, fax (92 936) 711205, or book through Islamabad, tel (051) 920 8948-9, or 111-555-999, fax (92 51) 921 8233. New, near the Serena, charges standard PTDC rates. The Tourist Information Centre is at the PTDC Motel.

Royal Palace, Aqba Road, Saidu Sharif, tel 720239. The king's old winter palace with a view over the town. Three grades of rooms cheaper than PTDC. The smallest are excellent value, the middle grade, in the old house are the best value in Swat, permanently cool with high ceilings and enormous marble bathrooms. The expensive grade are huge and characterless. The lawns and shady garden are peaceful, but the public rooms and food are awful.

Green's Marghazar White Palace, Marghazar, tel 710848, 812008. This converted summer palace of the first Wali of Swat built in 1941, has a magnificent position at the end of the Saidu Valley, ten kilometres (six miles) south of Saidu Sharif. The ordinary doubles are large and well-furnished, the 4-bed family suite is good value, and the 4-bed royal suite with huge marble bathroom is fun. An ideal choice for walkers who wish to climb Mount Ilam, but remote and isolated with little public transport.

Mingora

Pameer, Grand Trunk Road, Mingora, tel 720201-5, fax (92 936) 720206. Prices moderate. A multi–storey, centrally air-conditioned block in the centre of the business area, convenient but noisy and lacks charm.

Shangrila, north of Mingora, beside the river Swat on the road up the valley, tel 81533-5, fax (92 936) 815336, or book in Islamabad, tel (051) 206301–3, fax (92 51) 206304, e-mail: resorts@isb.comsats.net.pk. is new and moderately priced, but rather remote for those without their own transport.

Swat Continental, on the road to Saidu Sharif, tel 711399, is new, clean and airy.

Some more new hotels a few kilometres north of Mingora on the road to Madyan look promising (they were still under construction at the time of research): **Fizagat**, **Rakaposhi**, and **Rock City** or **Citadel**, all offer views up the Swat Valley to Mount Falaksir.

Cheaper

There are about 30 middle-range and cheap hotels in Mingora along the Grand Trunk Road, New Road and around Green Chowk. The really cheap hotels are allergic to foreigners. The hotels with AC are expensive for what you get, and poor value compared with the Royal Palace in Saidu which is in a class by itself.

The most convenient hotels for those without transport, are clustered round the Pameer Hotel. All rooms in all grades have attached bathrooms and fans. The best value is the **Udyana**, set round a wide alley with more light and a view of the mountains. **Diamond**, tel 710321, with no view. **Erum**, tel 710961, set around an alley over music and video shops, has some good value rooms with and without hot water, a couple of deluxe rooms with view of the mountains and two super-deluxe with TV, a view and AC. **Al-Hamra**, tel 710966, offers small, dark rooms with AC above an alley. The seven hotels opposite the bus station are too noisy for comfort, but the **Zeeshan** is the best.

Of the cheap hotels along New Road, the **Rainbow**, tel 720573, looks the best deal, and round Green Chowk, the **Abasind**, tel 710961, set round a little court with potted plants is the best with cheap rather dirty doubles, and better, more expensive rooms with AC.

Further out the **De-Shahzad**, tel 812484, in a quiet area is set round a court with potted plants, and has dark rooms moderately priced with AC. On Airport Road near Ayub Bridge, the **Swat Riviera** has a choice of moderately priced doubles with AC.

There are some new hotels just out of Mingora on the main road north to Madyan and Kalam.

Shopping

Swat is famous for its woodcarving, embroidery, woollen shawls, gemstones and honey. The best shops are in Mingora, and along the main road up the valley.

Useful Addresses

Tourist Information Centre is in the new PTDC Motel. Helpful Mr Fazal Rahim gives information on hotels of all grades, and has good ideas on how to organise your sightseeing. Open in summer 9 am to 1 pm and 2 to 4.30 pm, tel 711205.

I can recommend Altaf Hussain of Falakser **rent a car** service at the Serena Hotel as a reliable driver-guide.

PTDC run daily bus services down to Rawalpindi and up-valley to Kalam.

PIA tel 711092, on Faizabad Road in Saidu Sharif, open daily 8 am to 4 pm. There are daily flights to Islamabad and Peshawar.

Banks in Bank Square, Mingora, can change travellers' cheques. Open in winter 9 am to 1 pm, Monday to Friday, 9 am to 12 noon, Saturday; in summer they open and close one hour earlier.

Post Offices, one is near Green Chowk in Mingora and another 500 metres beyond the Serena in Saidu. Open 8 am to 2 pm, closed Sunday.

Telephone Office, near the post office in Saidu, open 8 am to 9 pm, Friday 8 to 10 am and 3 to 5 pm.

Public Call Offices with fax near Chungi (or Sorab) Chowk in Mingora.

Central Hospital, before Serena in Saidu Sharif.

Malam Jabba

The newly opened resort here at 1,800 metres, has a chair lift to the top of the ridge, and offers skiing and ice-skating in winter.PTDC Hotel, tel (09 36) 755 588, or book through PTDC Islamabad, tel (051) 921 8235, 920 8948-9, or 111-555-999, fax (92-51 8233. This 50-room, ugly hotel was opened in 1998. having stood empty for years.

Miandam

At 1,800 metres, this is a good place to spend your first night in Swat in summer. There are 11 hotels, all moderate in price.

PTDC Motel, book through PTDC Islamabad, tel (051) 920 8948-9, or 111-555-999, fax (92 51) 921 8233, is well positioned, with a lovely garden and helpful staff. If all the rooms are full, you can take a spare bed outside and sleep under the trees in the garden.

None of the other hotels has the same charm: In descending price order, **Pameer**, book in Pameer Mingora, **Junaid**, **Wahid, Panorama, Green Peaks, Miandam Guest House, Miandam Palace**, **Karashma**, **Nizara**, and **Bright Star** are cheaper. All can be booked through PTDC. In the off-season, bargain for lower rates.

Camping is allowed and recommended.

Madyan

At 1,321 metres (4,335 feet), Madyan is too hot in summer for comfort, and is crowded with domestic tourists. It is the last Pushtu town and an excellent base for walking from September through May.

Madyan, tel 780032–4, fax (92 936) 780035, set high above the road and river in a quiet garden across the river from the town on the west bank, has three old-style, single-storey blocks with bedroom, dressing room and bath at moderate prices.

Caravans Guesthouse, on the west bank just beyond Madyan, is the cheapest deal, clean and friendly and run by Michael, a Danish Muslim, offering four inexpensive rooms below the road, right beside the river, or a charpoy on the veranda. Fida Muhammad's handicraft shop opposite is also good value.

On the east bank of the river in Madyan Bazaar, right on the main road, is the monstrous new four-storey **Zarin Palace**, with clean, pleasant doubles, and the older four-storey **River Palace**, which has cool balconies hanging over the river. The **Hunza Guest House** and **Gulf** are cheaper, and are off the main road near the river, and there are several more, cheaper still in the bazaar.

The best cheap deal on the west bank is **Muambar Khan's House Room Rental** on the left of the main road about 500 metres (yards) before the bridge. He has three rooms for rent, up the hill about ten minutes walk away with a view over the valley, and his brother, Noorul Amin can guide you on short overnight treks. **Ali Sher Khan**, in the first antique shop on the right as you enter Madyan from Mingora, also has rooms for rent.

Bahrain and Kalam

These villages are in the Kohistani area of Swat, and walking here is less safe. You are advised to take an armed guard if leaving the main road.

There are about 15 indifferent hotels in Bahrain, and a new **PTDC motel** under construction across the river at **Mankial** and another at **Barankali**.

Kalam is known as Little Punjab in summer as it is so popular and crowded with Punjabis from June through August. Over 40 greedy hotels, from moderate to grotty, line the road and river and perch on the bluff above the village. The more up-market ones are at the entrance to Kalam or up on the hill.

Foreigners give the best marks to the moderately priced **Walnut Heights**, a small six-room guesthouse two kilometres (a mile) above Kalam, reservations (021) 444785 or (042) 365 0001–5, fax (92 21) 437877. The rooms are large enough for extra beds, and good, simple food is served. It is difficult to choose between the rest. The **PTDC Motel**, book through PTDC Islamabad, tel (051) 920 8948-9, or 111-555-999, fax (92 51) 921 8233, has ruined a magnificent position on the bluff above Kalam, with ugly buildings. They offer safe camping in their enclosed compound. Higher up, the **Sangam**, is new and more secluded than PTDC, with a choice of doubles. The **Falaksir**, beside the PTDC is run-down. Two promising new hotels are under construction below the PTDC. **Panorama** and **Hilltop**, also on the bluff, are the best of the cheap hotels.

Along the main road as you enter Kalam, **Manano, Pameer, Marco Polo, Royal Regency** and **Khyber**, are the bigger hotels. Further in, **King's Valley, Punjab** and **Heaven Breeze**, are slightly cheaper.

Taj Mahal, Falk Naz, Lahore, Peshawar and many more in the main bazaar, are all in the cheap range.

Mehran, Summer Inn, De Agasso, Daryl, Khalid, and others are cheaper still. In these ranges it is best just to walk around and see what you can find.

Camping is free in the PTDC Motel garden. It is not recommended elsewhere, as the people in the area (Kohistanis) are hostile.

Shopping

Swat is celebrated for its wood carving, embroidery, woollen shawls, gemstones and honey. The best shops are in Mingora and along the main road up the valley.

CHITRAL

Telephone: Direct dialling code for Chitral is 0933

Hotels

Moderate

Hindu Kush Heights, a new hotel built by members of the Chitral royal family, on a magnificent site at Gankorini, three kilometres (two miles) north of the airport on the road to Garam Chashma, tel 413151-2, fax (92 933) 413153, or book in Islamabad tel 051 275484, fax (92 51) 275475. The best hotel in Chitral.

Pamir Riverside Inn, on the river beside the fort, tel 412525. Cool, quiet rooms on the banks of the Kunar River. Six rooms in double bungalows and ten more in a new two-storey block with balconies overlooking the river and Tirich Mir.

Mountain Inn, Ataliq Bazaar, tel 412581, 412781, 412800, fax (92 933) 412668, e-mail: mountain@inn.sdnpk.undp.org. Once the best in town with a pleasant, peaceful central garden, much used by expeditions.

PTDC Tourist Complex, tel 412683, fax (92 933) 412722, or book through PTDC Islamabad, tel (051) 920 8948-9, or 111-555-999, fax (92 51) 921 8233. Nicely furnished and clean. All the rooms have a fan and there is a small noisy garden in front beside the busy road.

Chitral Guest House, near the airport, new, tel 413077, 412461.

Inexpensive

Dreamland, Kublisht (New) Bazaar, tel 412806. Rooms dark and cramped but some upstairs rooms are airy with a view. A charpoy on the roof is a cheap alternative.

Tourist Lodge, Shahi Masjid Road, tel 412452. Poor value doubles but the restaurant affords a wonderful view of Tirich Mir.

Al Farooq, tel 412726, has clean d/t/q, is popular with foreigners and can arrange transport through Abdul Khyuum tel 412491.

Hindukush Towers, tel 412888, reasonably clean with view of Tirich Mir.

Summerland, tel 412337, offers cheap d/t.

Fairland, by Attaliq Bridge over the Chitral stream, tel 412768. Some good rooms hang over the stream and are cool. A charpoy on the veranda is good value.

Garden, on the Chitral stream, opposite the Mountain Inn. This tiny hotel with three dirt-floored rooms and a pit toilet, is the best value in town, the rooms face onto a pleasant, quiet garden. They might accept campers — I forgot to ask.

YZ, Government Cottage Road (Goldpur Road), tel 412690. Rooms set round a small central garden are fair value, **Pakistan**, Hospital Road, **Damdam** and **Chitral Luxury** are all basic and unappealing.

The **Saif**, Kublisht (New) Bazaar, offers very basic charpoys and good Afghan food, as does the **Shabnam** in Ataliq Bazaar.

Village Rest houses Ask at the PTDC and at the AKRSP offices on Hospital Road if there are any families that offer rooms for rent, along the lines of the European Bed and Breakfast. The idea is catching on in northern Pakistan too.

The **PTDC** are building new **motels** at **Birmoghlasht**, the old summer palace above Chitral town; in the Kalash valley of **Bumburet**, and at **Buni** and **Mastuj** on the road to Gilgit. For information and booking contact PTDC Islamabad, tel (051) 920 8948-9, or 111-555-999, fax (92 51) 921 8233

There are **Construction and Works (C&W) rest houses** in Chitral town, Garam Chashma, Buni, Reshun,

Mastuj, Shagram, Drosh, Birir and Bumburet; book through the Assistant Engineer in Chitral town, tel 412511, 412545.

Restaurants

For more expensive meals, **Hindu Kush Heights**, **PTDC** and the **Mountain Inn** are best.

For cheaper meals try one of the Afghan Restaurants. There are quite a few cheap restaurants in town. The one we tried on the corner of Government Cottage Road (PIA Chowk) reputedly has the best food.

The **Mujahir Hotel**, run by Afghan refugees is also recommended.

Useful Addresses

Tourist Information Centre is in the PTDC Tourist Complex, tel 412683. Ask at reception which is open most of the time.

Banks open in winter 9 am to 1 pm, Monday to Thursday, 9 am to 12 noon, Friday and Saturday. One hour earlier in summer. Foreign exchange only accepted from 11 am to 1 pm.

Moneychangers in New Bazaar change US, pounds sterling and German marks.

Post Office open 8 am to 2 pm, is on the road leading down to the fort.

Telephone and Telegraph Office open 9 am to 4 pm, closed Friday afternoons and Sunday.

PIA Booking Office is near the polo ground.

Police Station, open 8 am to 4 pm, is also on the road leading down to the fort.

Foreigners' Registration is at the Police Station and is compulsory for all visitors. Your hotel will help you with details.

Hospital is also on the road leading down to the fort.

Tour Agents

Hindu Kush Trails Trekking Agency, in the Mountain Inn, tel 412800, 412112 and 2370. Islamabad address: 37, Street 28 F-6/1, tel (051) 821576, 277067, fax (92 51) 275031, 277067, 215080, e-mail: culture@trails.sdnpk.undp.org. This agency is run by the ul-Mulk family, who once ruled Chitral; the princes themselves act as guides. They are well connected throughout the valley, well-organised, reliable, and happy to give expert advice.

Chitral Travel Bureau, tel 412461, fax 412516, e-mail: ctb@akrspcp.sdnpk.undp.org.

KAGHAN

Telephone: Direct dialling code for all the Kaghan Valley is 0985.

HOTELS

The Kaghan Valley is popular and crowded in summer so advanced booking is recommended, especially in the PTDC hotels.

Balakot

If possible do not stay in Balakot, go directly to Shogran or Naran. But if you have to stay here the best bet is the new **Pine Park**, tel 210544, which is across the river up the road to Naran with good views. Book through the Islamabad office at (051) 827885, 273246, fax (92 51) 827912.

Pine Park also have hotels in the Kaghan Valley at **Shogran** tel 410333, **Danna Meadows** tel 410114, **Khanian** tel 420111, **Kaghan village** tel 420053 and **Naran** tel 420010. All bookings are also accepted through Islamabad.

PTDC Motel, tel 210208, or book through PTDC Islamabad, tel (051) 920 8948-9, or 111-555-999, fax (92 51) 921 8233, is disappointing.

Other cheaper options are the **Hotel Gate Way**, tel 210591, across the river beside the bridge.

Taj Mahal, before the bridge, the upstairs rooms are the nicest, or the **Koh-i-Toor**, tel 210163 and **Balakot**, opposite each other before the bus station.

The **Youth Hostel** near the PTDC Motel was washed away by floods.

Throughout the Kaghan Valley there are Public Works Department and Forestry Department **rest houses**; the best are at Shogran and Sharan (see Shogran for booking).

Shogran

Shogran is 8 kilometres up a side road from Kawai. There are several new hotels here including the recommended **Pine Park** tel 410333, or book as for the Balakot Pine Park. The **Tourist** and **Hilltop**, have clean rooms and good views. Other options are the overpriced **Punjab Hazara**, and **Faisal**. The lovely **Forestry Department rest houses** are only for VIPs and very difficult to book. They are controlled by the Forestry Ministry in Peshawar and the Kaghan Valley Project Director in Abbottabad. The Abbottabad PTDC can help with bookings. A new **PTDC Motel** is under construction at **Paya Siri**, about five kilometres above Shogran on the top of the hill.

Camping is safe and recommended.

Naran

Pine Park, on the road up to lake Saif-ul-Muluk tel 420010, book as for the Pine Park in Balakot, is the best in town and offers fine views. **Springfield**, higher up the road towards the lake, has a good location and VIP rooms, book through the Springfield hotel in Abbottabad.

PTDC Motel, book in Balakot or in Islamabad, tel (051) 920 8948-9, or 111-555-999, fax (92 51) 921 8233. The oldest hotel in town on a magnificent site among the trees beside the river at the top end of town. PTDC also offer tents for a moderate charge. **Kunhar** and **Daricha Gul** are the better of the middle range hotels.

The other hotels in town charge whatever they can get, so always try bargaining. In the off-season they ask a fraction of the peak rates.

Dreamland, with Austrian chalet style decor, is reasonable value. **Mount view**, and **Balakot** are slightly cheaper. **Lalazar** is multi-storey and soulless.

The **Sarhad, Zamzam, Pakistan, Shalimar** and **Snow View** in the centre of town are cheaper, basic and are usually fully booked in summer. There are about 20 hotels in all, none of them cheap.

Camping is safe and recommended. Some small local hotels offer charpoys for Rs20–40.

Youth Hostel, three kilometres (two miles) before Naran on the right. The **PTDC** are also building new motels at **Kawai** and **Sojh**.

Restaurants

All the hotels have restaurants, or you can eat well and cheaply in the bazaar on mutton curry, lentils and fresh *naan* or *chapattis*. The best food is at the corner of the main street and the road up to Lake Saif-ul-Muluk.

Useful Addresses

Tourist Information Centres are in the PTDC motel in Balakot and the PTDC Tourist Complex, Naran, ask at reception which is open most of the time.

Fisheries Office in Naran is on the road up to Lake Saif-ul-Muluk.

Post Office and **Police Station** are almost opposite each other near the southern end of Naran.

KARAKORAM HIGHWAY

Besham

Besham is very crowded in summer, so book in advance.

PTDC, book through PTDC Islamabad, tel (051) 920 8948-9, or 111-555-999, fax (92 51) 921 8233, is on a lovely site beside the Indus a couple of kilometres (miles) before Besham. If you have your own camping equipment they may allow you to camp in the grounds.

In the bazaar, in the centre of the village, there are at least ten inexpensive local hotels of varying quality from middling to grotty, and more are under construction.

New Abasin and **Paris** cost a fraction more than the others. The **Prince, Falkser,** and **Taj Mahal,** offer two grades of rooms. The Al-**Safina, International,** and the **New Hazara** are cheaper. Of the really cheap open-air rope charpoy places at the Swat road junction, the **Swat** and **Karachi** are the most welcoming to foreigners.

There are many rest houses along the Karakoram Highway belonging to the various departments which you may be able to book.

Public Works Department (PWD) at Thakot, Pattan, Dobair, Kayal, Dassu, Shatial; book through the PWD, Dassu.

Public Works Department at Tangir, Darel, Thor, Niat, Jalipur, Chilas; book through PWD Headquarters, Gilgit.

Police and Government Departments at Dassu; book through the superintendent of police and the Deputy Commissioner in Dassu.

Communication and Works (C&W) rest houses; book with the Executive Engineer, Kohistan Division in Besham for rest houses at Besham, Alai, Pattan and Dassu.

The PTDC may be able to help you with some of these bookings, especially for rest houses at Dubair, Pattan and Kayal.

Useful Addresses

Tourist Information Centre is in the PTDC motel

Post Office and **Telephone Exchange** are on the KKH in the centre of Besham.

Police station is south of Besham village.

Hospital is down a side road near the Swat junction.

Barseen

PTDC run a four bedroom motel beside the Indus at Barseen, 14 kilometres (9 miles) north of Komila. Book through PTDC Islamabad, tel (051) 920 8948-9, or 111-555-999, fax (92 51) 921 8233,

Chilas

A group of moderate to expensive hotels cluster along the Karakoram Highway at the Chilas turn-off:

Chilas town is three kilometres (two miles) off the KKH, up the hill away from the Indus, out of sight of the road. Some hotels, a police post and petrol pump are right on the highway, beside the river.

Shangrila Midway House, book through Islamabad, tel (051) 206301–3, fax (92 51) 206304, e-mail: resorts@isb.comsats.net.pk. comparatively expensive, with all facilities. (There is a second **Shangrila motel** about 40 kilometres/25 miles nearer Gilgit at **Raikot Bridge**, and a new Shangrila motel will open in 2000 at **Fairy Meadows**, the base camp for Nanga Parbat, a one hour steep drive up a jeep road south of the KKH from Raikot Bridge.)

The **Chilas Inn, Panorama** and **Karakoram Inn**, all charge moderate prices. **Mountain Echo, Ibex Lodge** and **New Shimla** are cheaper hotels.

Up in the village, three kilometres (two miles) south of the KKH, the new **NAPWD rest house** is the best of all (book at NAPWD headquarters, Gilgit). There are also about six cheap hotels in the main bazaar. The **Valley View** is perhaps the best of the local hotels. **Khunjerab** used to have the best food. But unless you really have to, I suggest you do not stay in this hot hell-hole where the people are notoriously surly and unreliable.

Other Information

The **Post Office** is opposite the entrance to Chilas Fort, the **Police Post** is in the fort, and the government offices are out of town on the road to the Babusar Pass.

GILGIT

Telephone: Direct dialling code for Gilgit is 0572, the Gilgit telephone numbers are all being changed to five digits.

Hotels

Moderate

Gilgit Serena Hotel, Jutial, Gilgit, tel 55894, fax (92 572) 55900, or book through Serena Karachi, tel (021) 587 3789–91, fax (92 21) 5873812, is by far the best and most expensive hotel near Gilgit. About five kilometres (three miles) before Gilgit, it offers a view of Dobani (Domani) Peak and comparative luxury with video films and the best food in town, including an all-you-can-eat buffet. It runs a free shuttle Suzuki to town that is open to all — ask around for the latest timings.

Chinar Inn, run by **PTDC**, beside the Chinar Bagh, tel 2562, fax (92 572) 2650, or book through PTDC Islamabad, tel (051) 920 8948-9, or 111-555-999, fax (92 51) 921 8233, is the next best, and is popular with tour groups. It is comfortable, good value and convenient for town. You can camp in the walled garden and use the facilities for a small fee.

Mir's Lodge, Domyal Link Road, tel 2875. Big, efficient, new, but very hot with shadeless garden and no view.

Less expensive

Hunza Tourist House, Babar Road, opposite the jail, tel 3788, 2338, is the best deal. It has excellent management, a nice central garden, great food, bicycles for rent and is a good meeting place.

Hunza Inn, Chinar Bagh, tel 2814, 3814, dorm beds available, is popular with independent travellers and a great place to meet people. It has a peaceful, shady central garden, maps, trekking information, good food and dorm beds.

Riveria, River View Road, Chinar Bagh, tel 4184 belongs to the mir (prince) of Nagar. New with a nice, mature garden (cool in summer) beside the river. It serves good food.

Park, Airport Road, tel 2379, 3379, fax (92 572) 3796, is a three-storey monster in the centre of town. 50 rooms with a garden at the back, but no view, slow service, a noisy generator and is comparatively expensive.

Gilgit Alpine Motel, on the main road near the Serena Lodge, tel 2641, fax (92 572) 2525, is new but too far out of town.

JSR, Sodh Plaza, Airport Road, tel 2308, is near the PIA office and is noisy and over-priced as is its neighbour **Skyways**.

North Inn, tel 55118, 55545, on Shahrah-e-Quaid-e-Azam, near Khomer Chowk. Good management, nice garden, useful 'rumours book' and good food.

Gilgit Gateway, tel 55014, near Khomer Chowk, is slightly more expensive.

Younus, tel 2584, outside town beyond Jutial, seven kilometres from the bazaar, Aiming at tour groups, but too far out.

Tourist Hamlet, tel 2754, 2934, on Shahrah-e-Quaid-e-Azam, new, looks promising, with swimming-pool. Aiming at tour groups. Large garden with badminton court.

Marco Polo Huts shaded by lovely trees, out in the fields south of the airport runway. Looked rather dirty and remote.

Chinese Lodge on Kashrote Link Road, small garden, but too new to see what it will be like.

Rupal, a big new hotel under construction opposite the Tourist Cottage.

Mountain Movers Inn, tel 2967, on the other side of the river, at the west end of town, belongs to Mountain Movers travel agent. Jeeps, guides and camping equipment are available for hire and camping is allowed for clients.

Inexpensive

Mountain Refuge, on Chinar Garden Road, tel 2513, is the best of the cheaper hotels. Its owner, Ibrahim Baig, is an excellent manager, speaks German and is most interesting. Serves vegetarian food and runs another hotel in Sost. Highly recommended.

Medina, a small guesthouse by the NLI bazaar with a big garden where you can camp, is very popular and offers dorm beds and doubles, and serves a full menu and good vegetarian food. Rumoured to be moving elsewhere.

Golden Peak Inn, tel 3685, 3538, has moved with its manager, Latif Anwar, from Bank Road to Quaid-e-Azam Road, and reputedly still offers a good deal with doubles, triples, dorm beds and a campsite on Babar Road. It is popular with backpackers and a good relaxed meeting place.

Tourist Cottage, Jutial, tel 2376, offers doubles and dorm beds, is three kilometres (two miles) from the centre on the main road, and is still an old favourite with backpackers though now run–down and none too clean.

Hunza Inn, Park, Tourist Hamlet and **Chinese Lodge** mentioned earlier all offer cheap dorm beds.

Vershigoom Inn, Airport Road, tel 2991, with rooms round a central courtyard. It is one of the older hotels in town, now very drab and used mostly by Pathan traders.

New Lahore on Hospital Road, tel 3327, has small rooms patronised by locals. Nice shady garden.

Kashgar Inn and the **Indus** both in Cinema Bazaar, have noisy doubles and the seedy **Karakorum** has moved to Airport Road, and still offers a sleazy cheap deal.

Village Guesthouses

Ask at PTDC for a list of village guesthouses. Like the Bed and Breakfast idea in Europe, some families now keep a room for tourists. These are available in the villages of Ahmadabad, Aliabad, Altit, Borit, Ghulkin, Gulmit, Passu and Shimshal, but the idea is spreading. Charges are reasonable for a double room and half board.

NAPWD (Northern Areas Public Works Department) -run rest houses for government officials in Gilgit, Singal, Gakuch, Chatorkhand, Gupis, Yasin, Phundar, Teru, Nomal, Naltar, Chalt, Minapin, Karimabad and Nagar. Tourists can use them if they're not full. Book all rest houses through the Administrative Officer, NAPWD, Bank Road, tel 3375, 2515. He will give you a note for the rest house guardian (*chowkidar*). Take your own food and bedding. You can usually camp in the gardens. Some of the remoter rest houses are just two rooms with a roof, not a stick of

furniture, nor any cooking or toilet facilities. The best, like Phundar, are comparatively luxurious.

PTDC are building new motels at **Gupis** and **Phundar,** ask at the Chinar Inn if they are open yet.

Shopping

Gilgit is the only market town for hundreds of kilometres in every direction: the bazaar is packed with traders every day except Friday. Good buys include Chinese silk and porcelain, irregular seed pearls, cashmere sweaters, garnets and rubies.

Useful addresses

Tourist Information Centre, tel 2562, is in the Chinar Inn, PTDC hotel and at JSR Plaza, near the PIA office, tel c/o Sargian Travel 3939.

NAPWD (Northern Areas Public Works Department) head quarters is on Bank Road opposite the National Bank. See the chief engineer, tel 3375, to book any of the NAPWD rest houses in the Northern Areas.

Habib Bank and **Allied Bank** are beside the Post Office in Saddar Bazaar and **National Bank of Pakistan** is near the Deputy Commissioner's house off Bank Road. Open 9 am to 1 pm, Monday to Thursday and Saturday, 9 am to

12 noon on Friday. Sterling and US dollar travellers' cheques are accepted with identification. Merchants in the bazaar will change cash. **Alam Money Changer**, tel 2605, in JSR Plaza, is open 8 am to 8 pm, gives a better rate than the banks, and accepts most important currencies.

Post Office (GPO) in Saddar Bazaar is open 8 am to 2 pm, Monday to Thursday and Saturday, 8 am to noon on Friday. Go round the back to get your letters franked before posting and to collect your Poste restante.

Telephone and Telegraph Office is on Upper Hospital Road, past the hospital on the right. It is open 24 hours, seven days a week. You can direct dial international calls and send faxes to the rest of Pakistan but not internationally. There is a government Public Call Office (PCO) near Raja Bazaar, open 24 hours. Private PCOs charge more than government.

Hospitals: District Hospital and Women's Hospital occupy opposite sides of Hospital Road. Don't expect too much. There are several private doctors. The lady doctor, Parveen Ashrat, Huma Clinic, near the airstrip is recommended, but if you know what you want, you do not need a prescription to buy drugs at any of the pharmacies. Know your medicines, and read the labels — I was offered penicillamine as a substitute for penicillin.

Worldwide Fund for Nature, 543A Quaid-e-Azam Road sells a guide to the Khunjerab Park.

Khunjerab National Park Directorate, tel 55061, is in Jutial. Information centre.

Trekking Agencies

Mountain Movers, Airport Road, opposite the Park Hotel, tel 2967; or PO Box 985, Rawalpindi, tel and fax (92 51) 470519, fax (92 51) 470518 and 584566. Musarat Wali Khan, the owner, is a Gilgit man, treks himself and is knowledgeable, charming and reliable.

Adventure Center (Pvt) Ltd, PO Box 516, Gilgit, tel 2409, fax (92 572) 2409. Owner, Ikram Beg, runs the best bookshop in Gilgit, (GM Beg Son's Book Stall) and is an experienced guide. Small company, specialising in the Gilgit-Hunza area.

Himalaya Nature Tours, Chinar Bagh Link Road, or Silk Route Lodge, Gulmit, tel 2617, 2946, fax (92 51) 824245. Owned by Mirzada Shah Khan, an interesting prince from Upper Hunza and well-known guide of the 1950s, and his son, Asif Khan.

Adventure Travel has an office near the Serena Lodge, tel 2330-1, fax (92 572) 2525. Islamabad address 15 Wali Centre, 86 South Blue Area, tel (051) 212728, 212890, 214580, mobile (0351) 261063, fax (92 51) 214 580.

Pamir Tours, JSR Plaza, tel 3939, run by Ziaullah Baig who is full of useful information and will send faxes for you.

Trans Pakistan Adventure Services, Park Hotel (see Islamabad listing for Islamabad contact address).

Ashraf Aman who runs **Adventure Tours Pakistan**, tel Islamabad (92 51) 252759, fax (92 51) 252145 and **Nazir Sabir** of **Nazir Sabir Expeditions**, tel Islamabad (92 51) 252553, 853672, fax (92 51) 250293, 822401, are both Hunza men, so know the area well. They have both climbed K-2 and are extremely reliable, but much in demand for big expeditions.

Walji's Adventure Pakistan, Karakoram Tours and Sitara, all have local offices in Gilgit on Airport Road, but are best contacted in Islamabad, see Islamabad listing for addresses.

Finally, ask in your hotel for suggestions.

Jeep Hire

There is an official government rate for jeep hire differing for surfaced and unsurfaced roads plus a fixed overnight charge. The only surfaced road is the Karakoram Highway, so you need to compare prices and bargain for remote destinations. Jeeps are available from NATCO, PTDC, Mountain Movers, Adventure

Pakistan, Park Hotel, Hunza Inn, several other hotels and in the bazaar Ask around. Always note the name of your driver and registration number of the jeep. If you are offered a deal that is suspiciously cheap, beware — there is something fishy going on.

Bicycle Hire The Hunza Inn and the Hunza Tourist House rent out bikes, as do some of the shops along Airport Road and Jamat Khana Bazaar. Ask around.

Ordinary Petrol is available in Gilgit, Jaglot, Chitral, Chalt, Aliabad and Sost.

Camping gas Small gas stoves and canisters are sometimes available near the Aga Khan Polo Stadium; try also opposite the mosque and also near the dental clinic on the continuation of Pul Road.

HUNZA

Telephone: Direct dialling code for Hunza is 0572,

Hotels

The best place to stay is **Karimabad** which, at about 2,450 metres (8,000 feet), offers spectacular views over the valley, with Rakaposhi as the backdrop. The hotels are all in a row. Just walk along and choose one; there is usually no need to book, unless you are a group.

Expensive

Darbar Hunza, tel 4238, or book in Islamabad tel (051) 818537, 9212727, fax (92 51) 270608. Belongs to the mir (prince) of Hunza. 50 rooms, two restaurants, rooftop barbecue, coffee shop, conference rooms. Excellent views, large and unsightly, dominates the lower village. The mir also offers 18 VIP guest rooms in his palace.

Moderate

Hunza Baltit Inn, tel 47113, same good management and food as the Serena Hotel in Gilgit. Book as for Serena, Gilgit or in Karachi (021) 5873789-91, fax (92 21) 5873812. Small rooms.

Hilltop, tel 47010, 47060. Convenient and popular with tour groups, with hot water, good food, nice garden, great view and helpful management.

Tourist Park, tel 47045. Popular with tour groups with good food and nice garden but little view. Also offers a local house that sleeps six.

Mountain View, tel 47053. New and large with a good view from terrace but no garden. Popular with tour groups.

White Apricot Lodge in Altit village, new, up-market and promising.

Hunza View is a multi-storey barracks at the bottom end of Karimabad, which ruins the view for everyone else.

Inexpensive

Kisan Inn, tel 47041, beside the polo ground in **Altit village**, is the best deal with good food, wonderful atmosphere, vine–shaded arbour and excellent management full of information and ideas. Can arrange transport at most competitive prices.

Eagle's Nest set on a ridge at 3,000 metres (9,840 feet) **at Duikar** high above Hunza. Run by same family as Kisan Inn. The dawn view of Rakaposhi, and about ten other 7,000-metre (23,000-foot) peaks, is the stuff of dreams.

New Hunza Tourist, tel 47108, is quiet and well-positioned on the canal **in Karimabad**, communal meals make a good meeting place. Also has cheap dorm beds. Camping allowed.

New Golden Lodge has terrace with fantastic view, squat loos.

Hunza Lodge, tel 47061, has sunny doubles with good views.

Karim offers a dorm and choice of doubles. Sunny roof with a view. Also has a 6-bed local style room.

Rainbow, tel 47049, is gloomy and basic.

Garden Lodge, tel 47093, has garden and view, some dorm beds, good food. Camping allowed.

Hill View is more expensive.

Mountain Refuge at bottom end of village — deceptive — not the same management as in Gilgit and Sost.

New Hunza Inn, in lower Karimabad and the **Old Hunza Inn**, opposite, have sunny porches with good views and some dorm beds.

Hunza Guest House, tel 47022, good value, room centred round eating spaces. Recommended 6-bed local room. Camping allowed

NAPWD rest house, book in Gilgit.

Village Rest Houses. Ask around for a list of village guesthouses. Like the Bed and Breakfast idea in Europe, many families now keep a room for tourists. These are available in the villages of Ahmadabad, Aliabad, Altit, Borit, Ghulkin, Gulmit, Karimabad, Passu and Shimshal, and the idea is spreading fast. Most charge reasonable rates for a double room and half board, and some offer dorm mattresses. I visited the houses of Karim Baig and Wajid Ullah Baig in upper Karimabad. Both offer traditional rooms in family settings with stunning views. We stayed with the school master, Ahmad Karim, in Passu and recommend him highly.

Hotels in Central Hunza along the KKH

In **Aliabad** and **Garelt**, down on the KKH, are several new hotels, a welcome contrast if you have just come in from China, but poorer value than the hotels up in scenic Karimabad:

PTDC Hotel, Garelt, tel 47069, or book at PTDC in Islamabad tel (051) 920 8948-9, or 111-555-999, fax (92 51) 921 8233. Small garden, no good meeting place or view from rooms. PTDC also runs a camping ground in Aliabad with hot showers.

New Golden Peak View, just south of the PTDC motel, tel 47077, 47075, disappointing compared with the hotels in Karimabad.

Rakaposhi Inn, Aliabad, tel 45096. Comfortable, overpriced, no garden.

Domani View is scruffy but friendly.

The cheapos along the KKH in Aliabad are the **Prince**, **Shishper**, **Jubilee** and **Deluxe**, all with basic dorm beds. Camping allowed.

Village Rest Houses, Ali Ahmad in Aliabad offers two rooms for rent. Ask around for more names.

Useful addresses

National Bank on new Ganesh Road, Karimabad, open 9 am to 1.30 pm Monday to Saturday, accepts travellers' cheques and major currencies. There is another bank on the KKH in Aliabad. **Alam Money Changer** in Karimabad bazaar offers better rates, open 8 am to 8 pm. Some of the hotels in Karimabad will change dollars.

Post Offices are on the KKH in Aliabad and another on the main street in Karimabad, open 8.30 am to 4 pm Monday to Saturday, close at noon on Fridays.

Telephone Exchanges are on the KKH in Aliabad and near the Mountain View Hotel in Karimabad.

Trekking Agents: **Walji's Travel**, tel 47045, Tourist Park Hotel, **Concordia Expeditions**, tel 47010, Hill Top Hotel, Karimabad. **Nazir Sabir Expeditions**, Aliabad, tel (0572) 2661 - see Islamabad listing, (see page 287).

GOJAL (UPPER HUNZA)

Gulmit

Gulmit, the capital of Gojal, eight kilometres (five miles) past Shishkot Bridge, is a fertile plateau 2,500 metres (8,200 feet) high, with irrigated fields on either side of the road. This is a good place to spend a night or two, marking the halfway point between Gilgit and the Khunjerab Pass.

Hotels

It's more fun to stay up in Gulmit village, 500 metres (1,640 feet) above the KKH, with a sense of village life, but there are some new hotels on the highway.

In Gulmit Village

Marco Polo Inn, tel 46107. Owned by the prince, Raja Bahadur Khan, and built in his garden, has relaxed atmosphere, especially when the raja is there to relate anecdotes. Local style room in prince's house. Camping allowed.

Village Guesthouse, at the end of the polo ground, tel 46112. Owned by Mirzada Shah Khan of the Hunza royal family, a hero from the 1947 Gilgit Declaration of Independence and a well-known guide from the 1950s and 60s. Some cheaper rooms, one charming local-style room upstairs, good trekking information. Lovely garden. Camping allowed.

NAPWD rest house beside the polo ground. Run-down. Book in Gilgit.

Village Rest houses: Fazal Karim, Sadruddin, Raja Bahadur Khan, Rehemtullah Baig, Ghulamuddin, Didar Khan and Qurban Jan have rooms to rent, with half board. There are five more in Ghulkin village and one at Borit Lake. Ask around for more names.

On the KKH

Silk Route Lodge, tel 46118 or book in Gilgit (0572) 3956. Carpeted rooms with balconies. Same management as Village Guesthouse. Camping allowed.

Tourist Cottage, tel 46119. Building big new extension, with moderately priced doubles, or dorm beds in a traditional style room. Good atmosphere, helpful for trekking information. Big new dining room with great view.

An ugly new square block of a hotel just above the KKH looked deserted.

Useful addresses

The **Post Office**, and **Telephone Exchange** are both on the KKH.

The **government hospital** and **Aga Khan health centre** (intended for mothers and children) are in the village, and have some medicines.

Karakoram Explorers, Treks & Tour operators, in Ganesh Village, tel 47102, run by Mubarak Hussain. Islamabad office tel (051) 441258 fax (92 51) 442127.

Passu

Passu Inn, on the KKH, tel 46101, has a choice of doubles and a traditional family room that sleeps six. It is popular with hikers and is a good meeting place. The inn-keeper, Ghulam Muhammad, has a good map of Batura Glacier, and can arrange guides and porters.

Shishper View, on the KKH two kilometres (a mile) south of Passu, catches more sunshine and has comfortable doubles.

Batura Inn, on the KKH, 800 metres (half a mile) north of Passu, beside the old Chinese road-workers' camp, cheaper and popular with backpackers.

Passu Peak Inn 1.5 km (a mile) north of Passu, has spartan, cheap rooms.

NAPWD rest house, opposite the Passu Inn, book in Gilgit.

Village Rest houses Ahmad Karim, the school master, runs an excellent guesthouse in the village below the school. Quiet garden with spectacular view, good food. Dorm beds in family room and inexpensive doubles. Very popular, great meeting place. Rashid, next door, also has rooms for rent with meals. Three families in Shimshal also rent rooms. Ask around for more names.

Sost (or Sust) & Afiyatabad

The KKH passes through four more villages before reaching Sost, the last village in Pakistan on the KKH. **New Sost** (or **Afiyatabad**) is the new Pakistani immigration and customs post, at about 2,700 metres (8,860 feet), 2 kilometres north of old Sost, 35 kilometres (22 miles) north of Passu and 82 kilometres (51 miles) from the Chinese border. If crossing into China it is best to spend the night here. Some companies run rafting trips from Sost down to Karimabad (two to three days).

Getting to and from Sost

To Gilgit: NATCO (Northern Areas Transport Company) runs inexpensive daily buses to and from Gilgit in the early morning. Other companies run minibuses costing slightly more. For onward travel to China see below.

To China: NATCO and PTDC run daily buses from Sost to Tashkurgan, for about US$25 one way.

Crossing the border

The Khunjerab Pass is open (weather permitting) from 1 May to 31 October for tours and to 15 November for individual travellers. The border post at Sost is open until 11 am for outgoing traffic to China. It is four to five hours' drive from here to Tashkurgan, and you must allow time for passing the Chinese customs and immigration two kilo- metres (a mile) before Tashkurgan (moved down from Pirali). The time difference between China and Pakistan is three hours, so it will be around 7 or 8 pm, Chinese time, before you arrive in Tashkurgan. Incoming traffic is processed until 4 pm Pakistani time, 7 pm Chinese time.

The border post is a big walled compound which, when completed, will contain **customs** and **immigration, telephone exchange, post office** and **bank**. Ask around among other travellers for the best place to change money. Most dealers are open 9 am to 4.30 pm. Until the border post is finished, the bank, post office and telephone exchange remain in old Sost, two km to the south.

Entering Pakistan

It is easier if you have a valid visa. The nearest Pakistan Consulate is in Beijing. In theory you can receive a 30 day landing permit or transit visa at the frontier if the immigration officer is satisfied that you are a genuine tourist (except if you come from Algeria, Bangladesh, Bhutan, India, Israel, Nigeria, Palestine, Philippines, Serbia, Somalia, Sri Lanka, Tanzania, Uganda or Yemen). You will be asked for proof of onward travel out of Pakistan and sufficient foreign exchange.

In practice, the immigration officer on duty may try to make things difficult. If you are a genuine tourist from a western country, remain persistent and polite, eventually you will be let in. If you plan to stay longer than the time specified by the immigration officer, you must go to Islamabad to obtain a visa.

Leaving Pakistan

Chinese visas are not available at Sost. The nearest Chinese Consulate is in Islamabad. You must have a valid Chinese visa to enter China.

Make sure you obtain an exit stamp in your passport from the Pakistani Emigration officer. The Chinese officials will check this at several checkposts before you reach Tashkurgan, and will send you back if you do not have one.

You are not allowed to take private vehicles into China unless arranged in advance. At the moment (1998) you are allowed to cycle into China at the discretion of the Pakistani officials, but you may be forced to put your bicycle on a bus.

It may take several hours for your whole bus to clear customs and emigration.

Hotels

The KKH is lined with new hotels mostly hurriedly built with little planning and few facilities. The hotels are in two clusters in old and new Sost separated by a barren two-kilometre stretch of road below a crumbling cliff. The more expensive hotels are in the northern cluster, New Sost or Afiyatabad, near the new customs post. Ranging from cheap to moderate, most hotels are overpriced for what you get. There is no need to book (unless you are a group). The bus drops you beside the custom's post, and it is a long hot walk back from there to the southern group of hotels.

Northern group of Sost Hotels - New Sost (Afiystabad)

PTDC (Pakistan Tourism Development Corporation) has opened a new hotel opposite the new customs and immigration post. Book through PTDC Islamabad, tel (051) 921 8235, 920 8948-9, or 111-555-999, fax (92 51) 921 8233, or through PTDC Gilgit, tel (052) 2562, fax (0572) 2650. Comfortable looking with attractive walled garden.

Sky Bridge, (popular with tour groups, good food) and **North Star** both larger, up–market hotels.

Asia Star, **Al Mahmood** and **Four Brothers** offer clean rooms.

Everest, **Badakshan**, **Fairyland**, **Park** and **GMJ** are basic with squat loos and little appeal.

More hotels are under construction.

Sothern group of Sost Hotels - "old Sost"

Mountain Refuge, tel 46219, is the best and most popular deal in town with a choice of clean doubles and dorm beds. Serves a full menu and good vegetarian food. Dinner is served at 8 pm round a large communal table. A recommended place to meet people and exchange information. Good rumours books and helpful management. Free shuttle service to New Sost.

Tourist Lodge, tel 46210, at the north end of the southern settlement has overpriced doubles, and dorm beds.

Khunjerab View, tel 46213, at the south end of the southern settlement, below the old village, has expensive, dark carpeted doubles, and a cold, dirty dorm.

Hunza Dreamland, tel 46212, two kilometres (a mile) south down the KKH, offers doubles and a sad dorm. Magnificent view but difficult for those without their own transport.

New Mountain Refuge, off the KKH and up the road to the old village.

Al Zaman and **Karawan**, are both badly managed and overpriced with seedy, unappetising dorms.

Al Karam, **Pameer**, **Pak-China** and **Shaheen** cheap, bare and cold.

Sost Information

There is a small Health Centre up the road to the old village of Sost near the *jamat khana* (the Ismaili prayer hall and community centre).

SKARDU

Telephone: Direct dialling code for Skardu is 0575

Skardu, the capital of Baltistan, has a population of about 15,000 and stands at an altitude of 2,340 metres (7,680 feet). It serves as the starting-point for some of the most scenic and adventurous trekking in the world.

Hotels

Shangrila Tourist Resort, Kachura Lake, tel 2970; book Islamabad tel (051) 206301–3, fax (92 51) 206304, e-mail: resorts@isb.comsats.net.pk. Lovely lakeside setting planted with fruit trees. 96 bungalow-style rooms, swimming pool, boats and horses. Comparatively luxurious but isolated and expensive.

K2, PTDC (Pakistan Tourism Development Corporation) Motel, tel 2946, fax 3322 or book at PTDC in Islamabad tel (051) 921 8235, 920 8948-9, or 111-555-999, fax (92 51) 921 8233. By far the best place to stay. Great central garden with a view over the Indus, a 15–minute walk from the main bazaar. Most expeditions stay here, so it is a good place to exchange stories, get information and find trekking mates. This is also the best place to camp.

Concordia, near the K2 and similar price.

Sehr, near the K2 with a view over the Indus. New, slightly cheaper, and has comfortable doubles.

Hunza Tourist House, in an ordinary house with a small pleasant garden near K2 Motel, same management as the excellent HTH in Gilgit. Good value.

Karakoram Yurt and Yak Serai, Link Road, tel 2856, or book through Karakoram Tours, Islamabad, tel (051) 829120. Closed for renovation. Round canvas yurts (nomads' tents) with attached bathrooms on a peaceful side road. Spacious but rather empty and isolated. Camping allowed.

Pioneer, near airport, tel 2646, rather run-down.

Indus, College Road, tel 2771, 2608. Small rooms, only four with a view, no garden, but good food and helpful management. You can camp on the roof for a small fee.

Al Amin, College Road, tel 2789. Two rooms have views south across the nullah to the mountains but the other rooms are claustrophobic with windows onto corridor.

Sadpara Inn, College Road, tel 2951. Flexirates — inexpensive. Big bathrooms with sit-down loos. Dining room with nice view.

Hunza Inn, College Road, tel 2570. The best value of the cheaper hotels. This is an older hotel with rooms set around a small garden with resident cow and friendly mice. Popular with backpackers and useful meeting place with a good, cheap restaurant.

Baltistan Tourist Cottage (old name Kashmir Inn), Yadgar Chowk, tel

2707, offers inexpensive doubles and cheap dorm mattresses with cold water and an outside loo. Muhammad Abbas Kazmi, the owner is friendly and informative.

Karakoram Inn, Yadgar Chowk, tel 2449, 2122. Multi-storey, 30 rooms with windows looking into central well — noisy and sleazy. The food tastes okay but we were poisoned.

NAPWD Baltoro Rest House, Satellite Town. Very isolated, but good value if you can get a permit to stay there.

NAPWD (Northern Areas Public Works Department) also has rest houses at Shigar, Khaplu and Machlu; book through the chief engineers for Skardu District, tel (0575) 2788; for Ghanche District, tel (0575) 2406, 2433 or through NAPWD headquarters, Gilgit, tel (0572) 2416.

Camping is allowed, ask at the PTDC Tourist Information, in K2 motel for details. Himalayan Treks and Tours have a pleasant camping ground in a secluded walled garden by a stream, office beside Indus Hotel.

Village Rest Houses Ask PTDC if any families offer rooms for rent.

Useful Addresses

PTDC Tourist Information Centre is in the K2 Motel, tel 2946. Your best source of information is other travellers, and a good place to meet them is on the lawns of the K2 Motel overlooking the Indus.

Habib Bank and **National Bank of Pakistan** are in the bazaar, open 9 am to 1 pm, Monday to Thursday, 9 am to 12 noon, Friday and Saturday. Sterling and US dollar travellers' cheques are accepted with good identification.

Post Office is near the football ground, open 9 am to 2 pm.

Telephone and Telegraph Office, near the aqueduct, is open 7 am to 11 pm seven days a week. You can make international calls and send cables.

Hospital is at the east end of town. There is a doctor on duty for emergencies, but do not expect too much. It is better to try to find a foreign expedition doctor and beg help. You can buy drugs in pharmacies without a prescription, but read the labels and be sure you know what you are doing.

NAPWD offices are up on Link Road. Contact the chief engineers for Skardu District, tel (0575) 2788, and Ghanche District, tel (0575) 2406, 2433, for rest house bookings.

Ordinary petrol is available in Skardu and Khaplu only.

Second–hand equipment and clothing Janjungpa's shop at Alam Dar Chowk (see below).

Recycling tin cans Janjungpa also buys your old cans and used equipment.

Trekking Agencies

Himalayan Treks and Tours, PO Box 621, College Road, next to Indus Hotel, tel 2528. Mohammad Ali Changazi, the owner, is a Skardu man, knowledgeable, reliable and a skilled guide. He has a pleasant campsite on Airport Road in a secluded walled garden by a stream. His Rawalpindi address is 112 Rahim Plaza, Murree Road, PO Box 1769, tel (051) 515371, fax (92 51) 563014 or 584566, E-mail: himalia@isb.com.sats.net.pk

Karakoram Chogolisa Travels and **Janjungpa Climbing School**, PO Box 602, Alam Dar Chowk, Link Road, tel 3478, fax (92 575) 2876. Ali Mohammad Janjungpa, a reliable guide from Khane village, also sells sleeping bags and mats, tents, gas stoves and high altitude clothing at his shop at Alam Dar Chowk. Also has offices in the Ghanche Hotel in Khaplu and in the Holiday Hotel, Rawalpindi, tel (051) 568070, 517416, fax (92 51) 583960, attn Karakoram Chogolisa Travels.

Karakoram Tours, Karakoram Yurt and Yak Serai, Link Road, tel 0575 2856, cable YURT SKARDU. Raja Alamdar, from the Khaplu royal family, knows the area intimately, is reliable and extremely helpful. See Islamabad listing for Islamabad address.

Baltistan Tours, Link Road, Satellite Town, PO Box 604, tel 2626, 2108, fax (92 575) 2108. Islamabad office tel (051) 270338, fax (92 51) 278620. Mohammed Iqbal organises the Karakoram Experience tours, pricey but knows his stuff. He is invaluable as a source of imported canned and bottled camping gas. e-mail: btadvent@karakorm.sdnpk.undp.org.

Siachen Travels & Tours, PO Box 622, Hussaini Chowk, New Bazaar, tel 2844, 2608. The owner, Rosi Ali of Hushe, is a famous mountain guide, reliable and charming. Islamabad address, PO Box 2014, tel (051) 264213, fax (92 51) 260469.

Concordia Trekking Services, PO Box 626, office tel 3440, home tel 2829, the owner Abbas Kazmi speaks good English and knows some interesting history of Baltistan.

Mountain Travels Pakistan, PO Box 621, Satellite Town, tel 2750. Islamabad office, same as Siachen Travels & Tours. Ghulam Abbas, the owner is another of Baltistan's well-known guides.

Nazir Sabir Expeditions, Skardu office on Airport Road, tel 3346. Nazir Sabir from Hunza is Pakistan's most famous guide. See Islamabad listing.

Adventure Travel Walji's, Prince Market, College Road, tel 3468. This is the branch office of Pakistan's biggest tour company.

Ask at your hotel for other ideas and guides.

Urdu Glossary

Urdu is a mixture of Persian, Arabic and various local languages. The spoken language is similar to Hindi, but it is written in the Perso–Arabic script.

1	ek	13	tera
1.5	dehr	14	chawda
2	doh	15	pandra
2.5	dhai	20	bees
3	teen	25	pachees
4	char	30	tees
5	paanch	40	chalees
6	chhe	50	pachaas
7	saath	100	ek saw
8	aath	2,000	doh hazaar
9	naw	100,000	ek
10	dus	1 million	dus lakh
11	gyara	10 million	ek crore
12	bara		

(Beware of similar-sounding 25 and 50.)

greeting (Peace be with you)	Salaam alay kum.
reply (With you also be peace)	Waalay kum as salaam.
How are you?	Aapka (or Tumhara) kya hal heyh?
I am well.	Theekh heyh or Theek thak.
What is your name?	Aapka (or Tumhara) naam kya heyh?
Do you speak English?	Kya aap angrezi boltay heyn?
I am English/American/French.	Meyn angrez/amrikan/fransisi hun.
Which way to Lahore?	Lahore kiss taraf heyh?
How much is this/that	Yeyh/Voh kitnay ka heyh
What is this/that	Yeyh/Voh kya heyh
thank you	shukria
good bye	khoodha haafiz
yes	ji haan, haanji or haan
no	naheen (na'en)
okay/good	achhaa
When?	kub?
three o'clock	teen bajay

morning	subha
evening	shaam
go/going	jao/jaana
near	nazdeek
far	dur
food	khana
to eat food	khana khana
to drink	peena
meat	gosht
beef	gai ka gosht
goat meat	bakri ka gosht
chicken	murghi
fish	machii/machhlii
egg	anda
vegetable	subzi
potato	aalu
spinach	palak
lentils	daal
rice	chavel
bread	roti, naan, chapati,
baked bread	double roti
yoghurt	dahi
water	pani
tea	chai
salt	namak
sugar	cheeni
home/house	ghar/makaan
bed	palang, charpai
blanket	kambal
pillow	takya
sheet	chader
fan	pankha
candle	mombutti
hot	garam
cold	thanda (m)/thandi (f)
small	chhota (m)/chhoti (f)
big	burha (m)/burhi (f)
clean	saaf
expensive	mehenga

Recommended Reading

History, Politics and Culture

Ahmed, Akbar S, *Pakistan Society — Islam, Ethnicity and Leadership in South Asia* (Karachi: OUP, 1986) An attempt to explain the complexities of Pakistan society by Pakistan's leading anthropologist.

Ahmed, Akbar S, *Pukhtun Economy and Society* (London: Routledge, 1980) Anthropological view of Pathan society in the NWFP.

Aijazuddin, F S, *Historical Images of Pakistan* (Lahore: Ferozsons, 1992) Beautiful coffee-table book of old prints with articulate text.

Allen, C, ed., *Plain Tales from the Raj* (London: Deutsch, 1975) Compiled from BBC interviews with people who lived in British India — most enjoyable.

Barr, P, *The Memsahibs* (London: 1976; Delhi: Allied, 1978) Describes the life of British women in Victorian India.

Basham, A L, *The Wonder that was India* (New York: Grove, 1954; London: Sidgwick & Jackson, 1967; New York: Taplinger, 1968) Excellent book for the general public on the prehistory, history, art, religion, language and politics of the subcontinent.

Bunting, E-J, *Sindhi Tombs and Textiles — the Persistence of Pattern* (Albuquerque: Maxwell Museum of Anthropology, 1980) Good monograph on patterns on stone, wood and cloth.

Caroe, O, *The Pathans* (London: Macmillan, 1958; reprinted Karachi: OUP, 1975) Scholarly but readable history.

Collins, L, and Lapierre, D, *Freedom at Midnight* (London: Pan, 1977) Racy, accurate and easy to read account of the partition of India and Gandhi's assassination.

Duncan, E, *Breaking the Curfew – A Political Journey Through Pakistan* (London: Michael Joseph, 1989) Penetrating insight into what makes Pakistan tick.

Feldman, H, *From Crisis to Crisis – Pakistan 1962–1969* (London: Oxford University Press, 1972) Describes the Ayub Khan years.

Gascoigne, A B, *The Great Moghuls* (London: Cape, 1971) Beautifully illustrated coffee-table book.

Hopkirk, P, *The Great Game* (London: Murray, 1990) Britain versus Russia — the struggle for Central Asia from 1810 to 1900. Gripping reading.

Jamal, Mahmood, *The Penguin Book of Modern Urdu Poetry* (Harmondsworth: Penguin, 1986) Good selection of modern Urdu poetry.

Keay, J, *When Men and Mountains Meet* (London: Murray, 1977) Readable stories of the exploration of the Karakorams and western Himalaya between 1820 and 1875.

Keay, J, *The Gilgit Game* (London: Murray, 1979) Continuation of the above between 1865 and 1895.

Khan, F A, *Architecture and Art Treasures in Pakistan* (Karachi: Elite, 1969) An articulate study of Pakistan's major archaeological sites by one of Pakistan's foremost archaeologists.

Knight, E F, *Where Three Empires Meet* (London: Longmans, 1893; reprinted Karachi: Indus, 1973) *The Times* correspondent travels in Ladakh and Kashmir, including a colonial account of the British invasion of Gilgit and Hunza in 1891.

Lamb, C, *Waiting for Allah* (London: Viking, 1991) Tell it how it is — an honest but pessimistic account of corruption and power-play in Pakistani politics during Benazir Bhutto's first term as Prime Minister, written by a journalist who was asked to leave.

Lorimer, D L R, *Folk Tales of Hunza* (reprint Lahore: Allied) Shows the pre-Islamic beliefs of the Hunza people.

Loude, J-Y, & Lievre V, *Kalash Solstice* A detailed study of the culture, beliefs and ceremonies of the Kalash people of Chitral.

MacKenzie (trans.), *Poems from the Divan of Khushal Khan Khattak* (London: Allen & Unwin, 1965) Translation of the work of the Pushtu poet.

Maraini, F, *Where Four Worlds Meet* (London: Hamilton, 1964) Beautifully written account of the first ascent of Mt. Saraghrar in Chitral, including an interesting discussion of the Kalash people.

Marshall, Sir J H, *A Guide to Taxila* (Delhi: 1936; reprint Karachi: Sani Communications) Extremely detailed guide with good plans and maps.

Miller, K, *Continents in Collision* (London: Philip, 1982) Royal Geographical Society scientific expedition to the Karakoram.

Mittmann, K, & Z Ihsan, *Culture Shock! Pakistan* (London: Kuperard, 1991) Some good tips on life and customs in Pakistan, irritatingly patronising in parts, excellent on how to conduct business affairs.

Morris, J, *Pax Britannica, Heaven's Command* and *Farewell the Trumpets* (trilogy) (London: Faber & Faber, 1968, 1973 and 1978) Beautifully written history of the British Empire.

Mumtaz, K K, *Architecture in Pakistan* (Singapore: Concept Media, 1985) Excellent, well-illustrated and readable history of architecture from the Indus Civilisation to the present.

Munir, Mohammad, *From Jinnah to Zia* (Pakistan: Vikas) Informative analysis by a former Chief Justice.

Robertson, G S, *Chitral, the Story of a Minor Siege* (1898; reprint 1977) Account of the 1895 siege of British forces in Chitral Fort by local forces contending for the throne of Chitral, by the surgeon–general who fought in the action.

Schofield, V. *Every Rock, Every Hill: A Plain Tale of the North-West Frontier and Afghanistan* A modern analysis of NWFP culture and history with many interviews and quotes from the original sources.

Shah, Nasra, *Pakistani Women – A Socio-economic and Demographic Profile* (Islamabad: Pakistan Institute of Development Economics, 1986) Major collection of demographic essays on the status of women in Pakistan.

Sorley, H T, *Shah Abdul Latif of Bhit* (London: Oxford University Press, 1940) Classic introduction to the Sufi saint and leading poet of Sindh.
Spear, P, *A History of India II* (Harmondsworth: Penguin, 1965) Concise readable history from the Mighal period to 1960.

Stein, Sir A, *On Alexander's Track to the Indus* (London: Macmillan, 1929; reprint Karachi: Indus Publications, 1975) An account of Stein's research in Swat in the 1920s.

Tandon, P, *Punjabi Century*, 1857–1947 (Berkeley: University of California Press, 1968) Fascinating family biography set in the last century of British rule.

Thapar, R, *A History of India I* (Harmondsworth: Penguin, 1966) Clear historical narrative covering the period from 600 BC to AD 1500.

Wheeler, Sir M, *Civilisations of the Indus Valley and Beyond* (London: Thames & Hudson, 1966) Well-illustrated prehistory and early history of the subcontinent.

Wolpert, S, *Jinnah of Pakistan* (New York: Oxford University Press, 1984) Authoritative biography of the enigmatic lawyer who founded Pakistan.

Wolpert, S, *Zulfi of Pakistan: His Life and Times* (New York: Oxford University Press, 1993) The ultimate biography of Z A Bhutto.

Woodruff, P, *The Men who Ruled India* (London: Cape, 1954) The British involvement in India and the men who worked there.

Younghusband, G J and F E, *The Relief of Chitral* (English Book House Reprint, 1980) Another contemporary account of the relief of Chitral in 1895 by two brothers who fought in the action.

Younghusband, G.J, *Heart of a Continent* (London: 1896; reprint Murray, 1986) Personal account of a British agent who travelled across China and all round northern Pakistan and India collecting information.

Fiction in English
Fraser, G M, *Flashman* (London: Pan) Hilarious, irreverent, sexy account of the 1857 Indian Mutiny. Historically accurate; a terrific read.

Fraser, G M, *Flashman in the Great Game* (London: Pan, 1976) Flashman carouses through the First Afghan War, and survives; another terrific read.

Fraser, G M, *Flashman and the Mountain of Light* (many reprints) Flashman roars through the Sikh Wars.

Kaye, M M, *Far Pavilions* (New York: St Martin's, 1978) First half mushy romance, second half well researched account of the Guides fighting in the Second Afghan War.

Kipling, R, *Kim* (London: Macmillan, 1899) Classic novel of the Great Game. A street-wise orphan is trained as a spy in the late 19th century.
Lambrick, H T, *The Terrorist* (London: Benn, 1972) Sindhi rebellion, explains the power of the *Pirs* (religious leaders); excellent read.

Moggach, D, *Hot Water Man* (London: Cape, 1982; Harmondsworth: Penguin 1983) Interesting and funny about expatriates and local people in Karachi.

Rushdie, S, *Midnight's Children* (London: Cape, 1981; Pan, 1982) Extraordinary, imaginative account of Partition. Booker prize-winner.

Rushdie, S, *Shame* (London: Cape, 1983; Pan, 1984) Hilarious novel on modern Pakistan, spiteful in places; excellent read, not to be taken too seriously.

Scott, P, *The Raj Quartet* (London: Heinemann, 1952; Panther, 1973) Life in India before Partition.

Scott, P, *Staying On* (London: Heinemann, 1977; Longman, 1985) The life of a British couple who stayed on after Partition. Set in India, but could just as easily be Pakistan.

Sinclair, G, *Khyber Caravans.* Light, amusing; also describes the Quetta earthquake in 1935.

Singh, Kushwant, *Last Train to Pakistan* (New York: Grove, 1961) Describes the horrors of Hindu–Muslim slaughter at Partition.

Sidhwa, B, *The Crow Eaters* (London: Cape, 1980) Parsi family in Lahore; very amusing, good insight.

Sidhwa, B, *The Bride* (London: Cape, 1983) Starts with the horrors of Partition, ends less convincingly in Kohistan; a good read.

Travel and Adventure
Amin, Willetts and Hancock, *Journey through Pakistan* (London: Bodley Head, 1982) Coffee-table book with beautiful photographs, light text, none too accurate.

Barry, J, *K2: Savage Mountain, Savage Summer* (Oxford Illustrated Press, 1987) Harrowing account of the disastrous summer of 1986 when 13 people died on K–2.

Buhl, H, *Nanga Parbat Pilgrimage* (London: reprint Hodder & Stoughton, 1981) Classic autobiography of the climber who first conquered Nanga Parbat, solo without oxygen in 1953.

Churchill, Winston, *My Early Life* (London: Butterworth, 1930; Fontana, 1959) Exuberant tales of life as a young officer in the North-West Frontier in the 1890s.

Clark, J, *Hunza — Lost Kingdom of the Himalayas* (reprint, Karachi: Indus Publications) One of the earlier Western families to visit Hunza.

Fairley, J, *The Lion River* (London: Allen Lane, 1975) Good account of the Indus river from source to mouth.

Herrligkoffer, K M, *Nanga Parbat – the Killer Mountain* (New York: Knopf, 1954) Describes the tragedies of Nanga Parbat and the first successful ascent.

Jamie, K, *The Golden Peak: Travels in Northern Pakistan* An English female poet travels fresh-eyed through the north — beautiful images and some insights into women's lives.

King, J S, *Karakoram Highway — the high road to China* (Victoria: Lonely Planet, revised 1993) Excellent survival kit on how to budget travel but short on details of what you see when you arrive.

King, J S, & D. St Vincent, *Pakistan, a travel survival kit* (Victoria: Lonely Planet, 1993) Good on how to travel cheaply but gives little historical background or detail of sites.

Mathewson, S, *The Tigers of Baluchistan* (London: Barker, 1976) A Western woman's account of five years living among the Bugti tribesmen of Baluchistan.

Moorhouse, G, *To the Frontier* (New York: Holt, Rinehart & Winston, 1985) A journey round Pakistan with descriptions of people and places.

Murphy, D, *Where the Indus is Young* (London: Murray, 1977) Diary of an eccentric Irishwoman who spent a winter walking in Baltistan with her six year old daughter.

Murphy, D, *Full Tilt* (London: Murray, 1965) Bicycling from Ireland to India via Pakistan's Northern Areas.